The Metrowerks
CodeWarrior
Professional

**Streamline
Mac Application
Development**

Book

Dan Parks Sydow

VENTANA

The Metrowerks CodeWarrior Professional Book, Macintosh Edition
Copyright © 1998 by Dan Parks Sydow

Library of Congress Cataloging-in-Publication Data

Sydow, Dan Parks.
   Metrowerks CodeWarrior professional edition book / Dan Parks Sydow.—
     Macintosh ed.
   p. cm.
   Includes index.
   ISBN 1-56604-733-1
   1. Macintosh (Computer)—Programming. 2. CodeWarrior. I. Title:
    CodeWarrior Developer's Guide.
QA76.8.M3S95827 1997
005.26'8—DC21   97-26433
                                     CIP

First Edition 9 8 7 6 5 4 3 2 1

Printed in the United States of America

Ventana Communications Group
P.O. Box 13964
Research Triangle Park, NC 27709-3964
919.544.9404
FAX 919.544.9472
http://www.vmedia.com

Ventana Communications Group is a division of International Thomson Publishing.

About the Author

Since graduating from the Milwaukee School of Engineering with a degree in computer engineering, Dan Parks Sydow has worked on software in areas as diverse as the control of nuclear reactors for defense purposes, and for the display of heart images for medical purposes. Currently a free-lance writer, he is the author of over a dozen books—several of which have recently gone into second edition. Audiences for the author's books range from the programming neophyte (*Mac Programming for Dummies*) to the skilled programmer (*Programming the PowerPC* and *More Mac Programming Techniques*). The author's most recent work is a Java programming tutorial—*Jumping to Java: Fast Track for C and C++ Programmers*.

Acknowledgments

First and foremost I'd like to thank the many fine people at Ventana who put so much effort into this book:

Neweleen Trebnik, Acquisitions Editor, for kicking things off.

Rachel Anderson, Project Editor, for keeping things rolling along.

Paul Cory, Development Editor, for helpful suggestions and comments too numerous to mention.

Kristin Miller, Desktop Publisher, for a page layout effort that resulted in such a polished looking book.

Ginny Phelps, CD-ROM Specialist, for getting this book's Companion CD-ROM in order.

Ellen Strader, freelance Copy Editor, for adding much-needed clarity to my writing!

As happens every time I work with Metrowerks, a number of people associated with this maker of the best Macintosh Integrated Development Environment came to my aid. Among those at Metrowerks who answered questions, provided input, or contributed to making this book's Companion CD-ROM happen: Greg Galanos, President and Chief Technology Officer; Dave Mark, VP Discover/Academic Products; Jim Trudeau, CodeWarrior Documentation; Ron Liechty, Online Representative and Technical Writer; Greg Dow, PowerPlant; Eric Scouten, PowerPlant Constructor; Joshua Golub, ZoneRanger; Steve Nicolai, Profiler; and Greg Combs, CD Burnmeister.

Finally, thanks to Carole McClendon, Waterside Productions, for making this book happen.

—D. P. S.

Dedication

To Nadine...

Dan

Contents

SECTION II

Developing an Application With CodeWarrior & PowerPlant

Introduction

Welcome to Macintosh application development using Metrowerks CodeWarrior! You've made several good choices in choosing to program for the Mac using CodeWarrior and this book. With over 28 million Macs sold to date and millions more about to be sold this year, you're targeting a huge base of potential users. And by choosing Metrowerks CodeWarrior as your development tool, you've selected what is far and away the best and most popular Macintosh programming environment. Finally, by using this book as your reference, you'll be making your programming endeavors easier—and smoothing the transition to Rhapsody, should you decide to port your application to that operating system at some time.

While reading the pages of this book, you'll learn much about writing programs that run on Macintosh, Power Macintosh, and Macintosh clone computers. If you aren't familiar with CodeWarrior, this book sees to it that you quickly get up to speed in the use of this full-featured programming environment. You'll also get an overview of PowerPlant, the Metrowerks application framework that is part of the CodeWarrior software package. Once you're comfortable with CodeWarrior and PowerPlant, it's on to the details of writing a full-scale, feature-packed Macintosh application.

If you've already purchased CodeWarrior, you'll be able to use the examples supplied on this book's Companion CD-ROM—as well as create your own projects from scratch. If you don't already own a version of CodeWarrior, you aren't out of luck—the Companion CD-ROM also contains a special limited version CodeWarrior. This enclosed copy of CodeWarrior doesn't do everything the full-featured version does, but it does allow you to open, view, edit, modify, and compile all the included source code files. It also includes the PowerPlant application framework, discussed at length in this book.

Who Should Use This Book

This book is for anyone who has programming experience and falls into one or more of the following categories:

- You want to understand the methodology of writing non-trivial applications that run on the Macintosh platform.
- You want to get the most out of the Metrowerks CodeWarrior integrated development environment (IDE).
- You want to master the Metrowerks PowerPlant application framework to speed up application development.
- You want to write code that compiles to an application that runs on the Mac OS now, and with minimal modification will compile to an application that will run under Rhapsody in the future.

What's Inside

In this book, you'll find in-depth discussions on using the Metrowerks CodeWarrior Integrated Development Environment (IDE) and the Metrowerks PowerPlant application framework to develop full-blown, feature-filled Macintosh applications. Here's a summary of what you'll find in each chapter:

Chapter 1, "Overview"

Why should you write programs for the Macintosh operating system? And why should you use the Metrowerks CodeWarrior IDE and the Metrowerks PowerPlant application framework to develop such applications? This chapter answers these questions. You'll also find an introduction to what the Metrowerks CodeWarrior's IDE consists of, with an emphasis on PowerPlant.

Chapter 2, "Using the CodeWarrior IDE"

CodeWarrior is more than just a compiler—it's a software package composed of a source code editor, several compilers, linkers, a debugger, and a project manager used to manage all these development tools. In this chapter, you get an introduction to using the main components of the CodeWarrior IDE.

Chapter 3, "Introduction to Application Frameworks"

PowerPlant is a large, powerful application framework. To the novice, getting started with PowerPlant programming can be intimidating. If you've never worked with a framework, don't jump right into PowerPlant. Instead, read this chapter to learn what an application framework is and how it's used to simplify the programming process.

Chapter 4, "PowerPlant Basics"

This chapter introduces PowerPlant—the Metrowerks application framework that takes much of the drudgery out of programming. An application framework is code that handles the tasks common to all programs—such as working with menus. By using the Metrowerks-written code that is the PowerPlant framework, you can concentrate your programming efforts on the fun stuff—such as graphic effects, animation, and sound playing. In this chapter, you'll also get an introduction to Constructor, the resource editor Metrowerks developed to work in conjunction with PowerPlant.

Chapter 5, "Introduction to the Example Application"

Throughout this book, you'll encounter short source code snippets that demonstrate the code used to implement discussed topics. More importantly, you'll also find MediaCenter—a complete, non-trivial project developed and enhanced from chapter to chapter. By the time you complete this book, you'll have developed an application that creates, opens, prints, and saves text files; opens and prints picture files; and opens and plays both sound files and QuickTime movies. While this project of course won't exactly match the project you'll want to create, it will demonstrate the implementation of almost all the book's topics in the context of a complete application.

Chapter 6, "Setting Up the Project"

Any Mac application developed using the CodeWarrior IDE starts out as a project. In this chapter, you learn about the MediaCenter project—the project that represents the origins of this book's MediaCenter example program.

Chapter 7, "Menus"

In an application created using PowerPlant, a menu and its items exist as resources—just as they do for applications developed without PowerPlant. What is different is the way a PowerPlant program communicates with these resources. Here you see how to create menu resources and how to get your PowerPlant project to acknowledge and respond to these resources.

Chapter 8, "Panes & Views"

In this chapter, you learn all about panes—the self-contained drawing areas that hold all the text and graphics found in the windows of programs created from projects that use the PowerPlant framework. Here you see how a pane makes graphics-handling easy and how using panes allows you to easily add program features (such as allowing the user to click on a drawing area and drag it around a window) that would take a far greater programming effort using traditional programming practices. This chapter also discusses views—a special type of pane that can hold other panes within it.

Chapter 9, "Controls"

Along with menus, controls enable a user to interact with a program. In this chapter, you'll see how to add controls such as buttons, check boxes, and scroll bars to your application. You also learn how to enable a control to send out a message to which other elements of your program can hear and respond.

Chapter 10, "Windows & Dialogs"

Windows are introduced early in the book and are used throughout. This chapter summarizes the information covered and then provides the details of several window-handling techniques not discussed earlier. Here, you also find out how to implement a close relative of the window—the dialog box.

Chapter 11, "Debugging & Testing the Application"

CodeWarrior is a powerful, feature-filled programming environment, and you and I are skilled programmers. So there's little likelihood that our programs execute in a less-than-perfect fashion, or manage memory poorly, right? True enough, but just to play it safe, this chapter discusses the use of the Metrowerks debugger, Profiler (the Metrowerks code-timing tool), and ZoneRanger (the Metrowerks memory-watching utility).

Chapter 12, "Files & Input/Output"

Much of the PowerPlant application framework is devoted to assisting you in putting together your program's user interface. But PowerPlant also helps with some of the important "behind the scenes" chores such as file-handling and printing. In this chapter, you learn how PowerPlant helps provide your application with file-handling capabilities—the next chapter covers printing. You'll learn how to give your program the power to create a new file, save data to a new or existing file, and open an existing file.

Chapter 13, "Printing"

Like Chapter 12, this chapter is devoted to demonstrating how PowerPlant helps with parts of your program that aren't interface-related. Here you learn all about printing. In this chapter, you see how to give your program the ability to print the contents of a window. And, of course, you read how to actually implement page printing for the example program.

Appendix A, "About the Companion CD-ROM"

The Companion CD-ROM includes a feature-limited version of the Metrowerks CodeWarrior integrated development environment, as well as projects and source code for all of this book's examples. Read this appendix for tips on getting CodeWarrior and the examples to your hard drive.

Appendix B, "Moving From C to C++"

To aid in the development of a Macintosh application, the PowerPlant application framework is used throughout this book. PowerPlant is a set of C++ source code and header files. If you know C, but don't know C++ (or know C++ but need to brush up on the language), read this lengthy appendix to get up to speed in C++ programming on the Macintosh.

Appendix C, "Glossary"

For definitions of the terminology appearing in this book, refer to this glossary.

Appendix D, "Moving to Rhapsody"

Moving your Mac OS program to Apple's new Rhapsody OS is a straightforward process using CodeWarrior Latitude. This appendix lays out the general technique for porting to Rhapsody.

Appendix E, "Porting Considerations"

If the time comes to port your program to Windows 95/NT or to write a Windows 95/NT program from scratch, you'll be happy to find that you can do so from the comfort of your Macintosh and the CodeWarrior IDE.

Appendix F, "Web Sites of Interest"

Here you'll find a the URLs for a few Web sites of interest to Macintosh programmers.

About the Companion CD-ROM

The CD-ROM that accompanies this book contains a Lite version of the CodeWarrior IDE. This Lite, or limited, version of CodeWarrior can be used to perform most of the tasks you'd normally perform when developing an application, including viewing, editing, compiling, and debugging source code files. CodeWarrior Lite, however, only allows you to perform these chores on the example projects included on the Companion CD-ROM. Fortunately (and quite intentionally) the examples on the Companion CD-ROM correlate to all the examples presented in this book. When you're ready to create a new project of your own, you'll want to order the full-featured version of CodeWarrior. The Companion CD-ROM in the back of this book contains a file with specific ordering information.

This book includes numerous snippets that provide you with the code that turns discussed theories into reality. Many of these snippets have been integrated into small projects that appear on the Companion CD-ROM. The book also includes one full-scale program that evolves from chapter to chapter. The Companion CD-ROM has several projects that hold the code for the various intermediate versions and one final version of this program. You can examine, edit, and compile the code in these projects using the included CodeWarrior Lite compiler. If you already own the full-featured version of CodeWarrior, you can of course use that version to work with the example projects.

TIP   *CodeWarrior Lite won't let you create new projects or rename or add new source code files to an existing project—but it will let you edit or add source code to an existing source code file in an existing project. This means that you can experiment with any of the projects by altering the existing source code and then compiling the new code.*

The Companion CD-ROM includes the files that make up the Metrowerks PowerPlant application framework. PowerPlant significantly reduces the amount of effort you'll expend writing code for a Macintosh application. This book describes in detail and makes extensive use of PowerPlant. Metrowerks Constructor is a graphic interface-building tool used in conjunction with PowerPlant. The full-featured version of Constructor appears on this book's Companion CD-ROM.

The Companion CD-ROM also comes with a couple of Metrowerks programming tools that are beneficial as you near completion of your application. Metrowerks ZoneRanger is a utility that tracks how your program makes use of memory. ZoneRanger lets you see how any program dynamically allocates memory. Metrowerks Profiler is code-profiling code that allows you to run your program and then view a detailed report of the amount of processing time spent in any or all of the program's routines. Armed with this information, you can determine where to devote your programming energies in order to speed up and fine-tune your application. The versions of ZoneRanger and Profiler included on the Companion CD-ROM are full-featured versions.

What You Should Already Know

To get the most from this book, you should already know the C++ language. You should also have at least a basic knowledge of the Macintosh Toolbox, and how to use it to write a simple C program. While knowledge of the PowerPlant application framework or application frameworks in general is helpful, no such knowledge is assumed.

If you don't know C++, you should know how to program in C and be prepared to do a little supplemental reading to at least get a feel for the basics of C++. Appendix B, "Moving From C to C++," exists for just such readers. That appendix is devoted to easing the transition from C to C++ and may be the only reading C programmers need.

If you've never developed a program with the aid of an application framework, then Chapter 3, "Introduction to Application Frameworks," is for you. That chapter provides an introduction to application frameworks.

What You Need to Get Started

To program with PowerPlant you'll need version 12 (CW12) or higher of CodeWarrior (CodeWarrior Professional 1 or higher qualifies as well) or CodeWarrior Lite IDE, the PowerPlant application framework, a PowerPlant book, PowerPlant example source code, and a Macintosh (or Power Macintosh or Mac clone) computer. In this book and software package, Ventana and Metrowerks have thoughtfully seen to it that you have all but the last of the above-mentioned items. Knowing that, there's nothing stopping you from getting started *right now*!

Getting Started With the CodeWarrior Environment

Overview

This book assumes you want to develop an application that runs on the Mac OS. It also assumes you want to use the Metrowerks CodeWarrior programming environment to accomplish that task. Further, this book expects you to use the CodeWarrior application framework PowerPlant to assist you in this endeavor. In this chapter you'll learn exactly why these three decisions are the soundest ones you can make!

In this chapter, you will read about all of the following: the huge installed base of Macintosh machines awaiting your new application; Apple's commitment to the Mac OS; the ease with which a Mac OS program can be ported to the new Rhapsody operating system—the number one Mac programming environment in the world; and PowerPlant—a set of already written source code files that slash your development time. If all this doesn't convince you to program for the Mac OS using Metrowerks CodeWarrior and the PowerPlant application framework, nothing will!

Why Develop for the Mac OS?

This section could be subtitled "Why Not Wait For Rhapsody?" There's a lot of talk about Rhapsody, the code name for Apple's NeXT-based operating system that's currently being developed. As of this writing Rhapsody is not complete— it isn't scheduled to be finished until mid- to late-1998. With a new operating system on the not-too-distant horizon, some programmers may wonder if it might not be better to hold off Macintosh application development for a while. On the surface this concern seems legitimate. However, if you read on you'll see why the impending release of Rhapsody isn't a reason to delay Mac software development.

Rhapsody: Now & Later

The *marketing* of a technology often precedes the technology itself—often by several months or even years. Such is the case with Rhapsody, which has a scheduled release date of mid- to late-1998, a date that could of course slip. Regardless of whether Rhapsody is released on time or late, there will be an acceptance lag-time. That is, Rhapsody will not immediately appear on all Macintosh machines. Don't expect to see a large installed base of Rhapsody users until the start of 1999—or later. You can program for Rhapsody today, but you won't have customers lining up for your product tomorrow!

Mac OS: Now & Later

Just released as of this writing is Mac OS 8—the most radically improved version of the Macintosh operating system since System 7 replaced System 6. Figure 1-1 shows the new grayscale appearance and multithreading capabilities that allow multiple operations to be performed simultaneously (such as copying files and emptying the trash). A few of the numerous new features that have been added to the Mac operating system are an improved system installer for easier custom installs, an Appearance manager and Desktop Pictures for more advanced desktop customization, and a faster, improved help system.

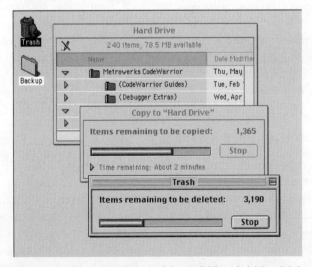

Figure 1-1: The grayscale look of the multithreaded Mac OS 8.

The release of Mac OS 8 means 1997 is the year of radical improvement in the Mac OS. The years 1998 and 1999 will also see new strides. Apple has promised that numerous minor upgrades of OS releases will be released in the next two years, but more importantly they've announced that a significant upgrade will also occur in each of the those two years. In mid-1998 a version of the Mac OS code-named Allegro will appear, and mid-1999 will mark the arrival of a version code-named Sonata.

The release of the vastly improved Mac OS 8, along with promises of Allegro and Sonata and an Apple announcement that the Mac OS will be continually improved for years to come, demonstrates that Apple's Macintosh commitment goes well beyond Rhapsody. Mac OS is, and will be, an operating system separate from Rhapsody. Apple's commitment to maintain complete support for the 28 million Macintoshes that have been sold to date is sound business. After all, an installed base that huge isn't something to be ignored; Apple isn't ignoring it, and developers of new programs shouldn't either.

Mac OS Applications & Rhapsody

As you await Rhapsody, develop your Macintosh application so that it runs on the Mac OS. If you're concerned about the arrival of Rhapsody cutting your product's shelf life by making it obsolete, don't be. Programs that run on today's version of the Macintosh operating system will also run on Macs that have Rhapsody as their operating system. That's because the Rhapsody OS will have a dual nature that allows it to act as both the current Mac OS and the newer, more modern Rhapsody OS.

The lowest level of the Rhapsody OS will be the core operating services that provide for low-level tasks such as file management, memory management, and peripheral device communication. On top of this operating system core, and making use of these core services, will be other software that is conceptually divided into two areas that Apple has dubbed the Yellow Box and the Blue Box.

The Yellow Box is a rich set of object-oriented frameworks that facilitates programmers in the building of Rhapsody applications. The Yellow Box can be likened to the Macintosh Toolbox—the routines that enable programmers targeting the Mac OS to write programs that make full use of Mac OS features such as windows, menus, and resources. A programmer who wants to write a Rhapsody application will use the Yellow Box application programming interface (API).

The Blue Box is a process that runs on top of the core operating system. The Blue Box implements the current Macintosh operating system and is essentially like having the Mac operating system (such as Mac OS 8) built into

Rhapsody. Note that the Blue Box won't be software that emulates the Mac OS—it will *be* the Mac OS. The Blue Box runs in its own protected area of memory and makes use of Toolbox routines stored in ROM chips—just as a pre-Rhapsody machine running, say Mac OS 8, does.

A Mac user who has Rhapsody will face a monitor that displays the look and feel of the Yellow Box. Whatever modifications and enhancements Apple puts in its new Rhapsody OS will be present for the user to enjoy. If such a user wants to run an older Mac program or a newer one that was developed for the Mac OS rather than Rhapsody, he or she will open a separate window that holds the Mac OS desktop. In other words, this user will seem to be running an operating system within an operating system. From within this Mac OS window, the user can run any Mac OS program—including the one you develop with the help of this book—and view and work with the application in the same manner as a user working on a Macintosh running the Mac OS rather than Rhapsody.

The division of Rhapsody into a Yellow Box and a Blue Box is of great benefit to Mac programmers. It means that a developer can write a program designed to run on today's Power Macs running the Mac OS, and that same application—without porting or recompiling—will be able to run on tomorrow's Power Macs running Rhapsody.

Porting Mac OS Applications to Rhapsody

The Rhapsody Blue Box allows an application developed with the Mac OS as the target operating system to run on a Macintosh using Rhapsody as its operating system. So it might seem unproductive for a developer to expend any effort porting an application so that it runs in the Yellow Box of Rhapsody rather than in the Blue Box. For many applications, that may very well be true. Other applications, though, will benefit from this port.

Porting a Mac OS application to a Rhapsody application won't result in an application that is radically different. Instead, the application will retain the same features set it originally had, but will now be able to run in the Rhapsody Yellow Box rather than in the Rhapsody Blue Box. One advantage to this application is that the ported version will now immediately benefit from Rhapsody technologies such as running in protected mode—it won't be possible for a bug in the program to affect memory outside of the program's own address space. This means that while the ported program may fail, it won't be able to crash the user's machine. Another advantage is that some Rhapsody users are bound to prefer the more modern Rhapsody OS over the Mac OS and may prefer to work in the Yellow Box whenever possible. The biggest advantage of porting to Rhapsody, however, is that the converted program will be ready to incorporate any of the advanced features found in the Yellow Box but not in the Blue Box.

After porting a Mac OS to Rhapsody, a programmer can use the Yellow Box API to begin to incorporate Yellow Box features into the new version of your program. Porting an application means generating a new set of source code, and any calls that are native to the Yellow Box can be added into this new code.

Why Use CodeWarrior?

To develop an application you need a compiler. Ideally you'll want your compiler to be a part of an integrated development environment (IDE)—a software package that includes a source code editor, compiler, linker, debugger, and other programming tools, all controlled from a single application. CodeWarrior, by Metrowerks, Inc., is just such an IDE.

A Summary of CodeWarrior Advantages

While CodeWarrior isn't the only IDE for developing Mac applications, it is the one you'll want to program with. Consider these arguments in favor of making CodeWarrior your IDE of choice:

- CodeWarrior is the best-selling suite of Macintosh development tools.
- Control of the Metrowerks editor, compiler, linker, and debugger is handled from a single, well-designed, easy-to-use application—the CodeWarrior IDE.
- The CodeWarrior IDE uses plug-in compilers so that you can choose to program in C++, C, Java, or Object Pascal—all from the same programming environment.
- Metrowerks provides superior technical support to all CodeWarrior owners.
- The large installed base of CodeWarrior owners means support is also available from other programmers (if you have Web access, check out the sys.mac.programmer.codewarrior newsgroup).

CodeWarrior Does Windows

CodeWarrior has another advantage—one that requires a little extra explanation. While CodeWarrior isn't a cross-platform tool—it can't take one set of source code and build applications that run on different platforms without special libraries or other third-party tools—it is the best development tool for Mac programmers who also have an interest in Windows.

The CodeWarrior IDE for Macintosh allows you to specify a target—an operating system on which the generated program will run. Among those targets are the Mac OS, Windows 95, and Windows NT. With CodeWarrior, a programmer who knows how to write Windows programs but prefers to work on a Mac, can do so.

CodeWarrior offers another way of supporting Windows programmers—especially programmers who primarily "do Windows." The CodeWarrior Professional package provides two almost identical CodeWarrior IDEs—one that runs on Macintosh computers (which I'll be using in this book) and another that runs on Windows machines. So while CodeWarrior for Macintosh allows a developer who is primarily a Macintosh programmer to create Windows programs from a Mac, CodeWarrior for Windows allows a developer who is primarily a Windows programmer to work from a Windows machine.

A Rhapsody-Hosted CodeWarrior

Metrowerks offers a Macintosh IDE and a Windows IDE that are almost identical both in feature set and in look and feel. That's a plus for programmers who work on both types of machines—they don't have to devote time to learning the details of using different programming environments for their two different platforms. Metrowerks is committed to doing the same for Rhapsody. When Rhapsody arrives, so will CodeWarrior. Metrowerks has CodeWarrior for Rhapsody in the works. The CodeWarrior IDE that runs on Rhapsody will bear similar features and a similar look as the Mac OS-hosted and Windows-hosted CodeWarrior IDEs. If you upgrade your operating system to Rhapsody, you'll be able to continue working in an almost identical programming environment.

CodeWarrior & Porting to Rhapsody

Earlier in this chapter, you read that it makes sense to write a Mac OS program now and port it to run on Rhapsody later. If you're considering that route, then Metrowerks offers you one more very big reason for using their products—CodeWarrior Latitude.

CodeWarrior Latitude includes a porting library that allows a Mac OS application to be ported to UNIX-based operating systems. Rhapsody is an evolution of NeXT's Mach-based OpenStep operating system. Mach is itself a version of UNIX. The Rhapsody OS will be one of several target platforms that CodeWarrior Latitude supports (as of this writing, the CodeWarrior Latitude product is in development release).

A developer who has built a program with the Mac OS as its target can use CodeWarrior Latitude to port that program to Rhapsody. CodeWarrior Latitude will be responsible for changing the Mac OS application's calls to the Mac Toolbox to calls to the Rhapsody Yellow Box API. Thus by linking a Mac OS to the CodeWarrior Latitude libraries, a programmer generates a new version of an application—one that runs native on a Rhapsody machine.

Why Use PowerPlant?

You can develop a program by using CodeWarrior as you would any other programming environment: write source code to one or more files, compile that source code, and link the resulting object code to build a stand-alone application. You *can* develop a program that way, but there's a much better way—a way that involves a change to the first step in the development process. Instead of relying on only your own source code, you can mix your own code with a huge body of source code that's already been written by others. PowerPlant is just such a body of code, and it is a part of the software package that makes up the CodeWarrior IDE. The PowerPlant code was planned and written to handle many of the tasks common to most programs, eliminating much of the work normally involved in writing an application.

PowerPlant & Application Development

PowerPlant is an application framework; this is source code that exists to handle the tasks that are basic to most programs that run on a specific platform. For the Mac OS, those tasks are the display and workings of a user interface and the handling of events. For instance, PowerPlant holds the code that handles the display, updating, moving, and zooming of windows. PowerPlant also holds the event loop that Mac programmers are used to writing themselves. With these somewhat mundane tasks taken care of for you, you're free to devote your programming energies to writing code that adds the pizzazz that will make your program unique.

To use PowerPlant, you add to a project some or all of the many C++ source code files that make up the PowerPlant application framework. You then add some of your own source code to the project. Your own source code will make use of the many C++ classes that the PowerPlant code defines.

Macintosh applications rely on resources—sometimes a great number of resources. Metrowerks had this in mind when they created PowerPlant Constructor. Constructor is a visual resource editor, much as Apple's ResEdit and Mathemaesthetics' Resorcerer are. Constructor, however, was developed specifically for projects that use PowerPlant. You use Constructor to visually edit windows, menus, menu bars—just as you've done in the past with ResEdit or Resorcerer. Constructor, however, also has built-in editors for visually editing PowerPlant-specific elements such as views (PowerPlant's way of displaying and organizing text and graphics in windows).

In short, PowerPlant and PowerPlant Constructor allow you to write a full-featured Mac application in a much shorter period of time than would be possible if you started from scratch. I'll take advantage of this fact by discussing and using these program development aids throughout this book.

PowerPlant & Porting to Rhapsody

Like any other CodeWarrior project that you target to the Mac OS, a project that uses PowerPlant will result in a program that can run on a Macintosh running a version of the Mac OS or within the Blue Box of a Macintosh running Rhapsody. Projects that rely on PowerPlant code can also be ported to Rhapsody using CodeWarrior Latitude.

Introduction to Metrowerks CodeWarrior

Throughout this book you'll be working with Metrowerks CodeWarrior. Whether you've purchased Metrowerks CodeWarrior Professional or are using this book's Companion CD-ROM Metrowerks CodeWarrior Lite, you'll want to have a good handle on what's included in the CodeWarrior programming environment and on how you use CodeWarrior to develop a program. This section takes a look at the key components of CodeWarrior and offers a sneak peak at how a program is developed. Chapter 2 elaborates on the basics of application development.

This book's Companion CD-ROM holds a Lite, or trimmed-down, version of the CodeWarrior IDE. While this Lite version doesn't include everything provided in the full-featured CodeWarrior Professional version, it does provide you with more than enough to start programming. As you peruse the CD-ROM folders, you'll find a number of applications, utilities, and support files. In this section I'll provide a brief overview of some of the more important folders and files. Note that because the CodeWarrior Professional package is a superset of CodeWarrior Lite, everything discussed here is also present on the CodeWarrior Professional CD-ROM.

Metrowerks CodeWarrior Folder

Installing CodeWarrior on a hard drive places thousands of files in several folders within one main folder titled Metrowerks. Within the Metrowerks folder is a folder named Metrowerks CodeWarrior, which contains the majority of what is thought of as CodeWarrior. Figure 1-2 shows the contents of this folder (the contents of your Metrowerks CodeWarrior folder may vary somewhat depending on the version of CodeWarrior you own).

Figure 1-2: The contents of the Metrowerks CodeWarrior folder.

The Metrowerks CodeWarrior folder holds the CodeWarrior IDE application, which you launch each time you start a programming session. From this one application, you create a project to group all the files related to a single program, create and edit source code files, compile and debug source code, and build the final stand-alone, double-clickable application you set out to develop.

Many of the other folders and files in the Metrowerks CodeWarrior folder are important. However, they're of importance to the CodeWarrior IDE rather than to you. That's because you won't have to work directly with these files—the CodeWarrior IDE application will. For instance, within the Compilers folder in the CodeWarrior Plugins folder (refer to Figure 1-2) are a host of compilers, including a C/C++ compiler and a Java compiler. The compiler that the CodeWarrior IDE uses to compile your source code is based on the extension you give to a source code file. If the extension is *.cp* or *.cpp*, the CodeWarrior IDE will automatically select a C/C++ compiler. If it's *.java*, the CodeWarrior IDE will instead choose the MW Java compiler.

Metrowerks PowerPlant Folder

Within the main Metrowerks folder is a folder named Metrowerks PowerPlant. Within this folder is an alias to the PowerPlant folder. Double-clicking on this alias opens the PowerPlant folder that resides in the MacOS Support folder in the Metrowerks CodeWarrior folder (refer back to Figure 1-2).

The Metrowerks PowerPlant folder also holds PowerPlant Constructor, the application that allows you to edit resources graphically. As you'll see later in this book, one of Constructor's primary purposes is to assist you in the layout of the contents of the windows your application will create.

Other Metrowerks Tools Folder

Within the main Metrowerks folder is a folder titled Other Metrowerks Tools. Here you'll find two programming utilities: Metrowerks Profiler and Metrowerks ZoneRanger. Both of these tools are discussed in Chapter 10, "Windows & Dialogs," of this book.

When you launch ZoneRanger, it monitors the memory usage of all other running programs. After you've built a working version of your own program, you'll launch your program and then launch ZoneRanger. As you put your program through its paces, ZoneRanger will respond by showing you the amount of memory your program is using at any given time, along with information about what's loaded in the memory that your program is using.

Profiler is both a set of code libraries and an application. You add one of the libraries to a project and then add a few calls to Profiler functions to your own source code. When you build your program, the result is an application that keeps track of how much time is spent executing each of its routines. After giving your program a test run and then quitting, Profiler generates an output file that holds an analysis of how and where your program spends its time. You view the output file with the Profiler application.

CodeWarrior Projects & Application Development _____

An application that is developed using CodeWarrior begins its life as a CodeWarrior project. A project serves as the means to organize the files that eventually generate a single application.

The Project Window _____

The project is a file that, when opened, displays a window that lists all of the source code files, resource files, and libraries that collectively hold the code that builds the application. Figure 1-3 shows this project window for a project file named *PlayMovie.μ*—a project that holds the code for a program that displays a QuickTime movie in a window.

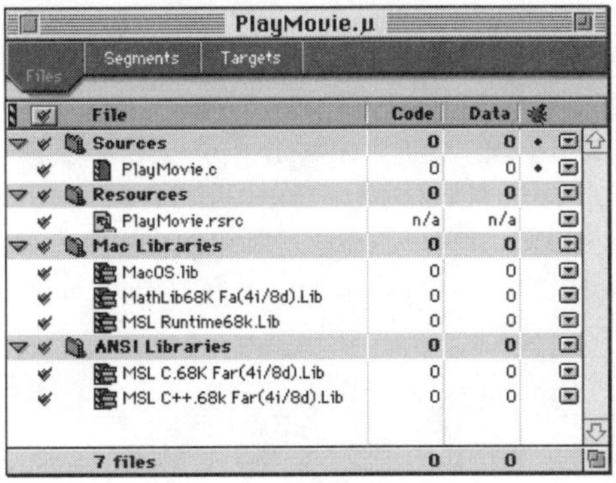

Figure 1-3: The project window of the PlayMovie.μ project.

As shown in Figure 1-3, the *PlayMovie.μ* project consists of a single C language source code file, a single resource file, and five libraries.

Typically, a project's source code file or files will be of most interest to you—that's where the code you write is stored. The PlayMovie application that is generated from the *PlayMovie.μ* project is a simple one, so it has very little source code—the *PlayMovie.c* file consists of only about thirty lines of code. The *PlayMovie.rsrc* resource file holds a single resource—a 'WIND' that serves to specify the look of a window that will display a QuickTime movie. The libraries are of much less interest. Libraries hold supporting code that is linked to your compiled source code. Not only do you not need to know the contents of libraries, you don't even need to know where they're physically located on a disk. That's because the proper libraries for any project are automatically added by CodeWarrior when the project is created.

TIP

This section serves as a very brief overview of CodeWarrior. Chapter 2, "Using the CodeWarrior IDE," provides more details about CodeWarrior projects in general and about the PlayMovie.μ project in particular. If you're new to CodeWarrior, and you're the type of person who likes to jump into things rather than pour over a user manual, make sure to read Chapter 2, "Using the CodeWarrior IDE." If you want all the details on CodeWarrior projects, refer to the definitive guide to working with the CodeWarrior IDE—the "IDE User's Guide (Mac)" electronic document that is a part of the CodeWarrior Professional package.

Altering Project Settings

You can alter many of the settings of a project from the project settings dialog box that displays when you open a project and then choose Project Settings from the Edit menu. Clicking on an item in the Target Settings Panels list on the left side of this dialog box displays a panel of settings on the right side of the same dialog box. Figure 1-4 shows the 68K Target panels for the *PlayMovie.μ* project. Here you see that this panel provides you with the means of specifying certain features of the project target (the application that gets built), including the application's name and memory partition size.

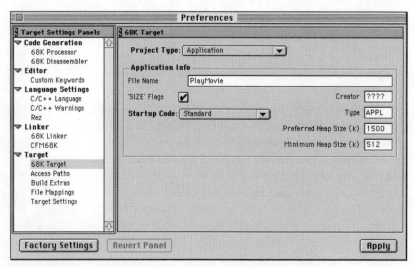

Figure 1-4: The project settings window for the PlayMovie.μ project.

Working With a Project

Most of the action you perform on a project is initiated from the Project menu of the CodeWarrior IDE. From this menu you add or remove source code files and resource files, compile one or more source code files, run the debugger, build and test run an application, and more. Figure 1-5 shows the items in the Project menu.

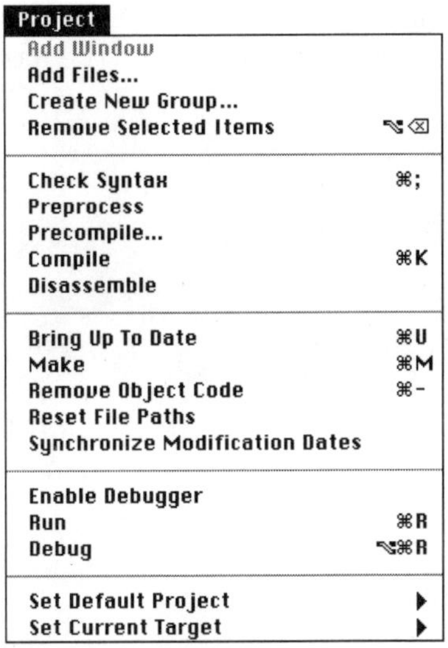

Project	
Add Window	
Add Files...	
Create New Group...	
Remove Selected Items	⌥⌫
Check Syntax	⌘;
Preprocess	
Precompile...	
Compile	⌘K
Disassemble	
Bring Up To Date	⌘U
Make	⌘M
Remove Object Code	⌘-
Reset File Paths	
Synchronize Modification Dates	
Enable Debugger	
Run	⌘R
Debug	⌥⌘R
Set Default Project	▶
Set Current Target	▶

Figure 1-5: The Project menu of the CodeWarrior IDE.

The CodeWarrior IDE includes more menus than just the Project menu, of course (for instance, there's a Search menu from which you can perform myriad search functions). But the Project menu is the menu which you'll use the most.

Moving On

Apple has vowed to support the Mac OS for years to come—and the release of the radically improved Mac OS 8 supports that claim. For that reason alone, now is the time to develop applications for the Mac OS. But there are a couple other reasons as well. First, sales of 28 million Macs over the last decade means there is a huge installed base ready for new applications. Second, Apple's forthcoming Rhapsody operating system will support both new applications written specifically for Rhapsody as well as existing applications that were written for the Mac OS.

Using an IDE greatly speeds application development. Metrowerks CodeWarrior Professional is the choice of the majority of Mac programmers. This book's Companion CD-ROM holds a Lite version of this program. Chapter 2, "Using the CodeWarrior IDE," will show you how you can use CodeWarrior to create a project that consists of your own code and then turn that code into an application. Chapter 3, "Introduction to Application Frameworks," will provide a simple example of how you can use this IDE to create a project that consists of some of your own code and a lot of PowerPlant code, and merge these two sets of code into an application. The rest of this book provides you with the details of how to use PowerPlant to write more sophisticated programs.

Using the CodeWarrior IDE

The CodeWarrior IDE (integrated development environment) refers to both a set of programming tools and a single application. The CodeWarrior IDE tools include a multitude of compilers and linkers (to allow you to program in languages such as C, C++, Java, and Pascal), a source code editor, and a source-level debugger. The CodeWarrior IDE application allows you to organize files and control all of the IDE tools from a single vantage point. In this chapter you'll look at just how a programmer makes use of the CodeWarrior IDE.

An application developed using the CodeWarrior IDE starts as a set of files (including source code, resource, and library files). To conveniently organize and update these files, you create a CodeWarrior project file that uses a single window to display information about each application-related file. In this chapter, you'll examine the creation of a project that holds the files used to create a simple QuickTime movie-playing program.

While this book uses the CodeWarrior PowerPlant application framework to reduce the time spent developing an application, the example project developed in this chapter doesn't. However, it does exhibit concepts that apply to such projects.

Setting Up a Project

In this section I'll walk through the process of setting up a project that will be used to generate, or build, a Macintosh application.

Because this chapter is about working with projects, not about the details of how to write Macintosh code, I'll use a very simple example to make sure the emphasis is on working with projects rather than on explaining source code listings. The remainder of this book is devoted to the details of writing code.

Creating a New Project

To begin the development of a new program you start with a new CodeWarrior project. As you carry out that task, CodeWarrior lets you choose both a project stationery (which helps specify the contents of the project) and a name for the new project.

Selecting Project Stationery

You create a new project by, intuitively enough, choosing New Project from the File menu. That displays the New Project dialog box shown in Figure 2-1.

Figure 2-1: Project stationery is selected for a project from the New Project dialog box.

The New Project dialog box holds a list of several *project stationeries*. These designate which libraries are to be included in the new project. Different types of projects require different libraries; using project stationery lets you include the necessary libraries with a few quick clicks of the mouse.

TIP

Stationeries are stored in the Project Stationery folder in the Metrowerks folder. The stationeries that are in Project Stationery folder are subject to the version of CodeWarrior you use and to the items you elect to install during the install of CodeWarrior. If you develop a project that holds a specific set of files and libraries that you feel will be of use in future projects, you can create your own project stationery from the set. Refer to the electronic document "IDE User Guide" that is included with the purchase of CodeWarrior Professional.

The choice of project stationery is based on a few factors. First is the target, or platform (such as the Mac OS or Windows 95) in which the application will be built. Another factor is the language in which the project will be programmed. If the application is targeting the Mac OS, then another factor is whether the application will use calls to the Macintosh Toolbox (as any "real" Mac program does) or will instead rely solely on ANSI code (as do programs that use a console window). Another issue in selecting a project stationery is whether PowerPlant will be used in the project.

Since you've had only a cursory look at PowerPlant at this point, I'll save the use of PowerPlant stationery for the next chapter. Here I'll use project stationery to set up a project using C or C++ to create an application that runs on the Mac OS, but doesn't use PowerPlant application framework code. As you'll see in the next chapter, the general concepts described here apply to projects that use PowerPlant as well.

For a project that is to generate a Macintosh 68K application, choose a 68K project stationery. If the project is to instead generate a Macintosh PowerPC-only program, choose a PPC project stationery. For the development of a fat binary application (one that runs on a 68K Mac using the 680x0 instruction set and on a Power Mac using the PowerPC instruction set), choose either a 68K or PPC project stationary and then modify the resulting project a little later. (I save the particulars of setting up a fat application for Chapter 3, "Introduction to Application Frameworks.") For simplicity, this example will create a project that results in a 68K application (one that runs on both a 68K Mac and a Power Mac, though on the Power Mac it won't take advantage of faster PowerPC-native code).

Referring back to Figure 2-1, you see that I'm selecting the Basic Toolbox 68k project stationery under the C/C++ listing. This implies that my project will use either C or C++ code, will make use of Toolbox functions, and won't rely on PowerPlant.

Before dismissing the New Project dialog box, make sure the Create Folder checkbox is checked, so that CodeWarrior will create a new folder in which to store the new project. Now click on the project stationery of choice and then click on the OK button.

Naming the New Project

After dismissing the New Project dialog box, a standard Save File dialog appears. In it, type the name for the new project. It's common practice to end a CodeWarrior project name with an extension of µ (the character resulting from typing Option-m). The example program I'm creating will be named PlayMovie, so in Figure 2-2 you see I'm giving the project the descriptive name of *PlayMovie.µ*.

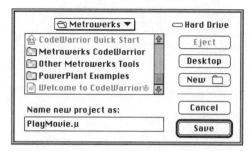

Figure 2-2: Providing a name for a new CodeWarrior project.

A completed *PlayMovie.µ* project can be found in this chapter's folder in the book examples folder on the Companion CD-ROM. Also included is the QuickTime movie that the PlayMovie application loads into memory and plays.

Though you checked the Create Folder checkbox in the New Project dialog box, a new project folder hasn't been created yet. It will be when you click the Save button in the current dialog box. Before clicking that button, use the pop-up menu at the top of the dialog box to bring up the name of the folder in which you'll save the new project folder. Now click the Save button to tell CodeWarrior to create a new project like the one shown in Figure 2-3.

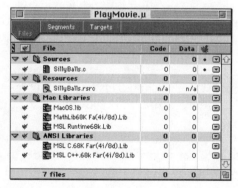

Figure 2-3: The project window for the PlayMovie.µ CodeWarrior project.

TIP

Your project window may display a toolbar of icons just below the window's title bar. If you don't make much use of toolbars, you can hide this one by choosing Hide Window Toolbar from the Toolbar hierarchical menu item in the Window menu—as I've done for PlayMovie.µ.

The Project Window

The newly opened project window lists all of the files that, when compiled and linked, generate one application. This one window provides a wealth of information—as shown in Figure 2-4 and summarized next:

■ **Category Tabs.** Use the three Category Tabs (Files, Segments, or Targets) to change the view of a project window. To view the files in a project, click on the Files tab. A feature new to CodeWarrior Professional is a programmer-defined link order. To view, and optionally change, the order in which a project's files are linked, click on the Segments tab. To view the different targets (platforms) that a project can build applications for, click on the Targets tab.

■ **Groups.** For organization purposes the files in a project are placed into groups. A project can have as few or as many groups as makes sense for the project. Move files from one group to another by dragging and dropping. Add new groups by dragging a file below the last group. Edit the group's name by double-clicking on it.

Figure 2-4 shows that the *PlayMovie.µ* project consists of four groups: Sources, Resources, Mac Libraries, and ANSI Libraries.

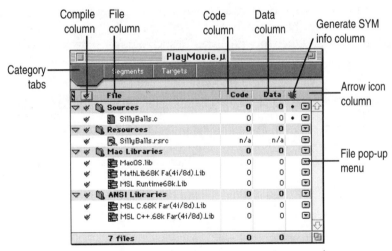

Figure 2-4: The various elements of a project window.

■ **Compile column.** Changes to an edited file affect an application only after the altered file is recompiled and a new version of the application is built. CodeWarrior uses the Compile column to provide an indication of which files have been edited (or touched) since the last compilation. A checkmark appearing to the left of a file name means that the file has been edited.

- **File column.** The File column of the project window lists the names of the groups and files that are a part of the project.

- **Code column.** The Code column shows the size of the executable compiled, or object, code for each file in the project. The Code column number for a group is the object code size for all files in the group. A Code column number is expressed in bytes for a file and kilobytes for a group.

- **Data column.** The Data column shows the size of the nonexecutable data for each file in a project and for the group as a whole. In short, the data size is the amount of memory occupied by variables. The values in this column are expressed in the same manner as they are for the Code column.

- **Generate SYM info column.** A file with an extension of .SYM is used by the CodeWarrior debugger. A project has a single .SYM file that holds symbols such as routine names and variable names. The Generate SYM info column can be used to prevent any source code file from having its symbols included in the project's .SYM file. The default condition places a mark in the Generate SYM info column for each source code file, which means the information from each of these files is a part of the project's SYM file. To exclude a file's information, click on its marker.

- **Arrow icon column.** The arrow icon at the far right of any row in the project window is used to display a pop-up menu. For a group, this menu lists the files in the group. For a file, this menu lists the header files that the file includes. Open any file listed in such a pop-up by selecting its name.

Adding a Resource File to a Project

In developing your own program, you'll be replacing the *SillyBalls.c* and *SillyBalls.rsrc* files that CodeWarrior by default adds to a project created using either of the Basic Toolbox project stationeries. Here you'll create a new, empty resource file and use it to replace the *SillyBalls.rsrc* file. This is a straightforward process:

1. Launch your resource editor of choice (such as ResEdit or Resorcerer).
2. Create a new, empty resource file.
3. Save the new resource file.
4. Return to the CodeWarrior IDE.
5. Click on the name of the group that you want the resource file to end up in (typically the one named Resources).
6. Choose Add Files from the Project menu.

7. Double-click on the name of the resource file in the top list of the dialog box that displays.

8. Click the Done button to dismiss the dialog box and add the selected file to the project.

9. Remove the original resource file (the CodeWarrior placeholder file) from the project by clicking on the file name in the project window and holding the mouse button down. On the pop-up menu that displays, choose Remove Selected Items.

Figure 2-5 shows that a new resource file has been added to the *PlayMovie.μ* project, and the old resource file is selected and about to be removed.

TIP *While files can be placed in any group (you could even place all of a project's files in a single group), I've found that it's easier to manage your projects if you organize your files into sub-groups that each have a meaningful name, such as Resources.*

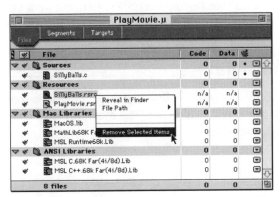

Figure 2-5: Removing a file from a project window.

TIP *I set up a project before creating resources or writing source code. Here I created and added an empty resource file to the project. Later I opened the resource file and added the resources necessary for the project. Another approach would be to add all the resources at the time the resource file is created.*

Adding a Source Code File to a Project

The *SillyBalls.c* source code file that CodeWarrior adds to a new project serves only as a placeholder to remind you of where you'll want to add your own source code file or files. To create a new source code file and use it in place of the *SillyBalls.c* file, follow these steps:

1. Create a new, empty source code file in the CodeWarrior IDE by choosing New from the File menu.

2. Save and name the empty file by choosing Save from the File menu. In the Save File dialog box, type a name for the file, including the appropriate extension (*.c* for a C project, *.cp* or *.cpp* for a C++ project). Now dismiss the dialog box by clicking the Save button.

3. Add the new source code file to the project by first clicking on the name of the project window group to which the file is to belong, and then choosing Add Window from the Project menu.

4. Remove the original source code file from the project in the same way the original resource file was removed—click on the file name in the project window, hold down the mouse button to bring up a pop-up menu, and then choose Remove Selected Items from this menu.

Developing the Application

At this point the *PlayMovie.µ* project is all set up: it contains a source code file, a resource file, and the appropriate libraries. The easy part is finished—now the source code and resources need to be added!

Project Resources

If you use ResEdit to create your project's resource file, you can double-click on the resource file name in the project window to open the file. If ResEdit isn't running at the time you do that, CodeWarrior will automatically launch it and then open the resource file. If you use Resorcerer to create a project's resource file, return to the desktop and double-click on the resource file icon to open the file.

With the resource file open, create any resources your project needs (you should already be familiar with the tasks of creating and editing resources). The *PlayMovie.µ* project requires only a single resource—a 'WIND' that will create a window that displays a QuickTime movie. Figure 2-6 shows the contents of the *PlayMovie.rsrc* file.

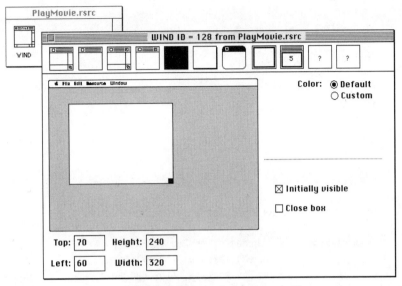

Figure 2-6: The one resource in the PlayMovie.rsrc resource file.

Project Source Code

Open a project source code file by double-clicking on the source code file name in the project window. Then type away, choosing Save from the File menu often to save your work.

The *PlayMovie.µ* holds a single source code file that consists of only about forty lines of code. Here, in its entirety, is the listing of *PlayMovie.c*:

```
#include <Movies.h>

void    InitializeToolbox( void );

#define   WIND_Fireworks          128
#define   fireworks_Movie_Name    "\pFireworks"


void  main( void )
{
    OSErr       theError;
    long        theResult;
    Str255      theMovieName = fireworks_Movie_Name;
    FSSpec      theFSSpec;
    short       theMovieRefNum;
    Movie       theMovie;
    short       theMovieResID = 0;
```

```
   Boolean    theChanged;
   WindowPtr  theWindow;

   InitializeToolbox();

   theError = Gestalt( gestaltQuickTime, &theResult );
   if ( theError != noErr )
      ExitToShell();

   EnterMovies();

   FSMakeFSSpec( 0, OL, theMovieName, &theFSSpec );

   OpenMovieFile( &theFSSpec, &theMovieRefNum, fsRdPerm );

   NewMovieFromFile( &theMovie, theMovieRefNum,
                     &theMovieResID, theMovieName,
                     newMovieActive, &theChanged );

   CloseMovieFile( theMovieRefNum );

   theWindow = GetNewWindow( WIND_Fireworks, nil, (WindowPtr)-1);

   SetMovieGWorld( theMovie, (CGrafPtr)theWindow, nil );

   StartMovie( theMovie );

   do
      MoviesTask( theMovie, 0 );
   while ( IsMovieDone( theMovie ) == false );
}


void  InitializeToolbox( void )
{
   InitGraf( &qd.thePort );
   InitFonts();
   InitWindows();
   InitMenus();
   TEInit();
   InitDialogs( OL );
   FlushEvents( everyEvent, 0 );
   InitCursor();
}
```

While the focus of this book isn't to teach the basics of Macintosh programming, a short walk through of this first example listing is appropriate. While the *PlayMovie.µ* project doesn't rely on PowerPlant code, it does nonetheless include code you'll find in PowerPlant projects.

Including Universal Header Files

The universal header files is the name of the set of Apple-supplied header files that include function prototypes for the Toolbox functions. CodeWarrior projects automatically include the most commonly required of these universal header files, such as *Windows.h* (almost all projects will include calls to the Toolbox functions **GetNewWindow()** or **NewWindow()** to display windows). This means that your projects won't need to explicitly include many (or any) of these header files. One header file not automatically a part of all projects is *Movies.h*. Playing QuickTime movies isn't a task common to most programs, so if your own project plays movies, it is responsible for bringing in the code from this header file. *PlayMovie.c* does that in this line:

```
#include <Movies.h>
```

Prototyping Application-defined Functions

CodeWarrior requires that a function prototype be supplied early in a source code file for each application-defined function that appears in that file. *PlayMovie.c* includes just one application-defined function—**InitializeToolbox()**. Here's that function's prototype:

```
void    InitializeToolbox( void );
```

Defining Constants

General programming practice dictates that source code minimize the use of hard-coded numbers—the scattering of numbers throughout a listing makes changes difficult. As you see in Chapter 4, "Introduction to the Example Project," PowerPlant has its own convention for naming constants. While the *PlayMovie.µ* project doesn't use PowerPlant, I've gone ahead and followed the PowerPlant guidelines here. A constant that represents the ID of a resource begins with the four characters of the resource type, is followed by an underscore, and finishes with a word that's descriptive of the constant's purpose. This word begins with an uppercase character. The 'WIND' resource with an ID of 128 creates a window that will display a QuickTime movie of fireworks, so the constant definition looks like this:

```
#define    WIND_Fireworks        128
```

Application-defined constants that aren't resource-related start with a lowercase character. Subsequent words in the constant name should be preceded by an underscore and should begin with an uppercase character. For the constant that defines the Pascal-style string that serves as the filename of the QuickTime movie to be played, the following is appropriate:

```
#define   fireworks_Movie_Name   "\pFireworks"
```

Declaring Local Variables

Another PowerPlant convention is that the name of an application-defined local variable should begin with the word "the." Subsequent words in the variable name should begin with an uppercase character. All of the variables local to **main()** in *PlayMovie.c* follow that convention:

```
OSErr      theError;
long       theResult;
Str255     theMovieName = fireworks_Movie_Name;
FSSpec     theFSSpec;
short      theMovieRefNum;
Movie      theMovie;
short      theMovieResID = 0;
Boolean    theChanged;
WindowPtr  theWindow;
```

Initializing the Toolbox

Macintosh programs must initialize the Macintosh Toolbox. *PlayMovie.c* defines a routine named **InitializeToolbox()** to do just that:

```
void  InitializeToolbox( void )
{
    InitGraf( &qd.thePort );
    InitFonts();
    InitWindows();
    InitMenus();
    TEInit();
    InitDialogs( OL );
    FlushEvents( everyEvent, 0 );
    InitCursor();
}
```

Toolbox initialization must be performed near the start of **main()**—so that's where the call to **InitializeToolbox()** appears in *PlayMovie.c*.

Playing a QuickTime Movie

Before an application attempts to play a QuickTime movie, it should verify that the user's machine has the QuickTime extension installed in the Extensions folder of the System Folder. That task is accomplished using the following few lines of code. If QuickTime isn't present, the program simply aborts. A more full-featured application would display an alert that informs the user as to why the program can't continue.

```
theError = Gestalt( gestaltQuickTime, &theResult );
if ( theError != noErr )
   ExitToShell();
```

The Movie Toolbox is the part of the Macintosh Toolbox devoted to QuickTime-related functions. Initialize the Movie Toolbox before working with it. The call to **EnterMovies()** accomplishes that. Next, you need a record that describes the directory location of the movie file that is to be played. A call to the Toolbox function **FSMakeFSSpec()** handles that. The task of opening the movie file and reading the movie data into memory is performed by the Movie Toolbox function **OpenMovieFile()**. Once the data is read to memory, you can safely close the file by calling the Movie Toolbox routine **CloseMovieFile()**:

```
FSMakeFSSpec( 0, 0L, theMovieName, &theFSSpec );

OpenMovieFile( &theFSSpec, &theMovieRefNum, fsRdPerm );

NewMovieFromFile( &theMovie, theMovieRefNum,
                  &theMovieResID, theMovieName,
                  newMovieActive, &theChanged );

CloseMovieFile( theMovieRefNum );
```

With the movie in memory, it's almost time to begin playback. First, however, you need to open a window in which to display the movie. A call to the Toolbox routine **GetNewWindow()** loads 'WIND' resource ID 128 data into memory and displays that window. A call to the Movie Toolbox routine **SetMovieGWorld()** associates the QuickTime movie data pointed to by variable **theMovie** with the window data pointed to by variable theWindow:

```
theWindow = GetNewWindow( rFireworksWindow, nil, (WindowPtr)-1);

SetMovieGWorld( theMovie, (CGrafPtr)theWindow, nil );
```

Finally, it's time to play the movie. The Movie Toolbox routine **StartMovie()** readies the movie for playback by activating it and by setting its playback rate. The actual playing of the movie takes place within a **do-while** loop. Each call to the Movie Toolbox routine **MoviesTask()** services the movie. That is, it plays a part of the movie. **MoviesTask()** should be called until the movie has completed playing. Just when a movie has completed is determined by calling the Movie Toolbox routine **IsMovieDone(),** which returns a value of true when movie playback is complete.

```
StartMovie( theMovie );

do
   MoviesTask( theMovie, 0 );
while ( IsMovieDone( theMovie ) == false );
```

Compiling & Running the Project's Code

CodeWarrior allows you to compile any or all of the source code files in a project. To compile one file, click on its name in the project window and then choose Compile from the Project menu. To compile more than one file, hold the Command key down while clicking on the names of the files to compile and then choose Compile from the Project menu. To compile all of a project's touched files (all of the files that have been edited since the last compilation), choose Make from the Project menu.

Compiling Source Code

If the compiler encounters any problematic code during compilation, CodeWarrior will display the Errors & Warnings window. The top pane displays a list of errors. Clicking on one of these errors causes the bottom pane to display the source code of the file in which the error is present. The bottom pane will automatically scroll to, and display, the area surrounding the offending line of code. In this bottom pane CodeWarrior will also highlight and point to the line containing the error. This line will generally follow the one actually holding the error. In Figure 2-7 you see that CodeWarrior has marked the call to the Toolbox function **InitCursor()**. Looking up one line you notice that I inadvertently omitted the semicolon that should end the call to the Toolbox initialization function **FlushEvents()**.

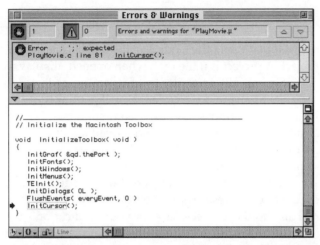

Figure 2-7: The Errors & Warnings window as it appears after a compilation error.

You can correct source code errors in the bottom pane of the Errors & Warnings window. Changes you make in this pane will be reflected in the actual source code file.

Building & Running the Application

If compilation was successful, you won't face the Errors & Warnings window. If that's the case, it's time to build an application and give it a test run. To do that choose Run from the Project menu. This results in the compilation of any touched files, the building of a stand-alone application, and the launching of that application. If all goes smoothly, your program will be up and running. To return to the CodeWarrior IDE, just quit your program.

With the *PlayMovie.µ* project open, choosing Run from the Project menu results in building and launching the PlayMovie program. This application first displays a window centered on the monitor and then plays a movie in this window. The QuickTime movie runs for only a few seconds, and consists of a 4th of July fireworks display. Note that in order for the PlayMovie application to find and play the movie, the movie file must be named "Fireworks," and it must be in the same folder as the PlayMovie application.

Moving On

An application developed using the CodeWarrior IDE begins its life as a CodeWarrior project. A project is a file that, when opened, displays a project window. This window lists all of the files (such as source code, resource, and library files) that collectively hold the code that will get linked into a single application. This project window serves as a "command post" of sorts—from here files can be added to, removed from, and moved about in a project, and source code files can be created, edited, compiled, debugged, and, finally, turned into a stand-alone application.

You develop a Macintosh application by creating a CodeWarrior project and then adding source code and resource files to the project. CodeWarrior supplies the libraries that hold code necessary for your application's use of the Toolbox, but you must of course add the source code and resources that become the program itself. Or do you? In this chapter you followed the development of a program named PlayMovie. The *PlayMovie.μ* project held a source code file that consisted of only a few dozen lines of code. In the remainder of this book you'll read about, and participate in, the development of a much more complex application. And while this upcoming program results from a project that consists of *thousands* of lines of code, you'll be responsible for supplying only a very small fraction of that code. The PowerPlant application framework makes this possible; we'll examine PowerPlant and how to utilize it in the next chapter.

3

Introduction to Application Frameworks

PowerPlant is a large, powerful application framework consisting of dozens of C++ classes that collectively define hundreds of member functions. All this code is housed in dozens of source code files and header files. Regardless of how skilled you are at programming, if you've never worked with an application framework, the idea of developing a program that relies on one may seem daunting. If you've never worked with a framework, don't jump right into PowerPlant. Instead, read this chapter to learn just what an application framework is and how you program with one. Even if you are familiar with an application framework (such as MacApp or the THINK Class Library), you may still benefit from this chapter—all frameworks are not set up the same.

In this chapter you'll work with a *very* small application framework. The SimpleWorks framework consists of just a few dozen lines of code housed in only a couple of files. The projects you create using this trivial framework won't result in applications that are ready for prime time. The projects will, however, demonstrate the fundamentals of programming with an application framework. The lessons learned here apply directly to the projects you'll create with the more complex and powerful PowerPlant application framework.

About Application Frameworks

An application framework is source code—usually a *lot* of source code—that was written by skilled programmers very familiar with the platform for which the framework was designed. PowerPlant, for instance, is a large body of code written by a team of programmers and engineers at Metrowerks for use with the Mac OS.

The code that makes up an application framework is used in conjunction with your own code to create a program. You write a little of your own source code, add it to a project, and then add the prewritten application framework source code to the same project. When you build an application from the project, the result is an executable that combines your code and the framework code.

The focus of the code of an application framework is the display of a program's interface and the handling of the program's flow of control. That is, the framework is devoted to displaying element, such as windows and the buttons within them, and to the handling of user actions, such as mouse button clicks and the pressing of keyboard keys. Very little of a framework's code is devoted to what can be thought of as a program's content. This isn't, however, a shortcoming of application frameworks. A program's content is in many cases unique to that program and in all cases unpredictable to the framework. A framework can anticipate that most programs will open windows and handle events, but it can't predict the particular purpose of a program or how a programmer wishes to implement the particular behavior of his or her program.

The advantages of a powerful application framework are immediately obvious. With little or no work, you already have a complete application shell ready to be filled with your own content. In addition, because many programmers have worked on or with the framework, its code is likely to be extremely reliable.

Using an application framework in your development of a program has several benefits. An application framework:

■ Makes for the easy implementation of a program's interface—its look and feel.

■ Assists in the handling of a program's events—the actions that drive a program, such as mouse clicks or keystrokes.

■ Helps avoid reinventing the wheel—the struggle to determine how to implement a solution for a particular task when the code solving that problem already exists.

■ Provides a skeleton program that, while devoid of any unique functionality, allows programmers to devote their energies to the unique content of a program.

SimpleWorks: an Example Application Framework

Metrowerks created PowerPlant, an application framework that consists of *dozens* of classes and *thousands* of lines of code. I've created SimpleWorks, an application framework that consists of a *single* class and less than *forty* lines of code. Before you jump to the conclusion that one of us must have done something terribly wrong, consider the purpose of each framework. PowerPlant helps you write full-featured Mac applications. PowerPlant handles everything from menus and windows to scroll bars and the playing of QuickTime movies. SimpleWorks does nothing more than display a single window and respond to a click of the mouse button. Quite obviously, SimpleWorks isn't useful for writing a real Mac application. So what good is it? Taking up less than one printed page, SimpleWorks is easy on the eyes. It also provides you with a refresher on the C++ concepts of derived classes and inheritance. Finally, and most importantly, it demonstrates at a simplistic level how PowerPlant works.

The FApplication Class

Frameworks have a naming convention that lets programmers perusing source code quickly know when they've encountered a class defined by the framework. PowerPlant, for instance, begins each of its classes with an uppercase letter "L." For my SimpleWorks framework I've opted to begin a SimpleWorks-defined class with an uppercase letter "F" (for "framework"). The SimpleWorks framework consists of only a single class, but if I decide to turn the framework into a more useful one, I'll have my class naming convention established. The sole SimpleWorks class is named **FApplication**. Here's its definition:

```
class  FApplication {
   public:
      virtual void  Run();
      virtual void  HandleMouseDown();
};
```

A good framework exists to unburden the programmer of some of the drudgery of writing the basic code common to most applications. The **FApplication** class does this by defining a **Run()** member function that holds an event loop and a **HandleMouseDown()** member function that responds to a mouse button click. An application that uses the SimpleWorks framework won't need to implement its own event loop or define a mouse button handling routine. Instead, it will rely on the **Run()** and **HandleMouseDown()** functions that are already defined in the **FApplication** class.

The FApplication Member Functions

When invoked, the first of the two **FApplication** member functions, **Run()**, does the following:

■ Creates a window based on a 'WIND' resource with an ID of 128.

■ Displays the new window.

■ Makes the new window's port active so that subsequent drawing takes place in this window.

■ Enters an event loop that watches and responds to mouse clicks or key presses.

As a Macintosh programmer, you should be very familiar with the code used to implement the preceding steps. The window-related tasks are taken care of by the **GetNewWindow()**, **ShowWindow()**, and **SetPort()** Toolbox functions. The 'WIND' resource used by **GetNewWindow()** is in a resource file that is a part of the SimpleWorks framework. The event loop is a **while** loop, the heart of which is a call to the Toolbox function that obtains information about the most recent event—**WaitNextEvent()**. Here's the listing of the **Run()** member function:

```
void  FApplication::Run()
{
    WindowPtr     theWindow;
    EventRecord   theEvent;
    Boolean       theProgramDone = false;

    theWindow = GetNewWindow( 128, nil, (WindowPtr)-1L );
    ShowWindow( theWindow );
    SetPort( theWindow );

    while ( theProgramDone == false ) {
        WaitNextEvent( everyEvent, &theEvent, 15L, nil );

        switch ( theEvent.what )
        {
            case mouseDown:
                HandleMouseDown();
                break;

            case keyDown:
                theProgramDone = true;
                break;
        }
    }
}
```

The **Run()** event loop begins by calling **WaitNextEvent()**, which returns event information in the **EventRecord** variable **theEvent**. The **switch** statement then compares the value held in the **what** field to two Apple-defined constants, **mouseDown** and **keyDown**. If the event that just occurred is a press of a key, the event loop sets the **Boolean** variable **theProgramDone** to **true** to terminate the event loop (and thus indicate that the program is done). If the event was instead a click of the mouse button, then the event loop invokes **HandleMouseDown()**, the second **FApplication** class member function.

The **HandleMouseDown()** function—the code of which follows—draws two lines of text to the window that was opened in the **Run()** function:

```
void  FApplication::HandleMouseDown()
{
   MoveTo( 20, 30 );
   DrawString( "\pThe framework controls what happens" );
   MoveTo( 20, 45 );
   DrawString( "\pwhen the mouse button is pressed!" );
}
```

You've now seen that the SimpleWorks framework helps you create a program that handles only **mouseDown** and **keyDown** events. And, it forces such a program to handle events of these types by drawing text in a window or quitting. Obviously, this framework needs work if it is to be truly of use to a programmer! Keep in mind that the purpose of SimpleWorks is to demonstrate the principle behind how a framework functions and how a programmer uses one. You won't be using SimpleWorks for your Macintosh programming—you'll be using PowerPlant!

Using the FApplication Class

A program that uses SimpleWorks could create an **FApplication** class object and then have that object invoke the **FApplication Run()** member function to jumpstart the program's event loop. After that, the application need do nothing. From this point on the framework code is executing. The event loop in the **Run()** function cycles until a mouse button click or a key press occurs. If a key press takes place, the event loop, and thus **Run()** and the program, ends. If a mouse button click occurs, **Run()** invokes **HandleMouseDown()** to draw text to the program's window. Figure 3-1 illustrates this.

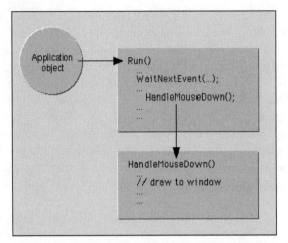

Figure 3-1: An application object invokes Run(), which in turn invokes HandleMouseDown().

The following version of **main()** represents the *entire* listing for a program that uses SimpleWorks.

```
void main( void )
{
    InitializeToolbox();

    FApplication  theApp;
    theApp.Run();
}


void InitializeToolbox( void )
{
    InitGraf( &qd.thePort );
    InitFonts();
    InitWindows();
    InitMenus();
    TEInit();
    InitDialogs( 0L );
}
```

The application-defined **InitializeToolbox()** routine holds the tried-and-true code that performs the necessary Toolbox initializations. After calling **InitializeToolbox()**, **main()** declares an **FApplication** variable to create an **FApplication** object and then invokes that object's **Run()** member function. That's all there is to it. Once **Run()** is called, the framework takes over to open and display a window, enter the event loop, and respond to a user's key press or mouse button click.

Declaring a class variable (rather than a class pointer) automatically creates an object. A member function of the object can then be invoked using the dot, or member access, operator (.). **Run()** could also be executed by declaring an **FApplication** pointer, using the new operator to create a new **FApplication** object, and then calling **Run()** by using the pointer operator (->):

```
FApplication  *theApp;

theApp = new FApplication;
theApp->Run();
```

If this approach isn't intuitive, you should brush up on your C++. Everything you need to know is in this book's C++ reference, Appendix B. Refer to the "Objects" section of that appendix for background information.

TIP *I've opted to use the first method—declaring a class variable rather than a class pointer—because this is the technique Metrowerks uses in its PowerPlant example projects. Chapter 4, "PowerPlant Basics," describes the PowerPlant **LApplication** class, which is analogous to (and far more powerful than) my SimpleWorks **FApplication** class. There you see a **main()** function very similar to the one presented here.*

Using an FApplication-derived Class

An application that uses SimpleWorks *could* create an **FApplication** object that would then invoke the **FApplication** member functions—but there's a better way to make use of the framework. An application can define a class *derived* from the **FApplication** class. This derived class will of course inherit the member functions of the **FApplication** class and will also have the luxury of adding new member functions that take care of tasks specific to the particular application being developed. Figure 3-2 illustrates this concept.

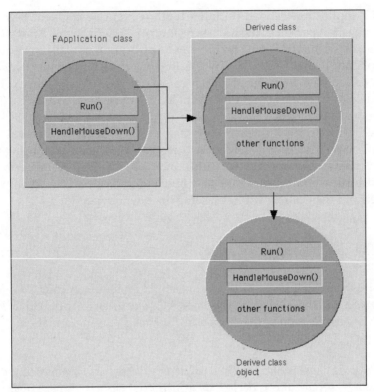

Figure 3-2: A project that uses SimpleWorks defines an FApplication-derived class and then creates a single instance of that class.

The definition of a class named **CMyApp** that is derived from the **FApplication** class would look like this:

```
class  CMyApp : public FApplication {
    public:
        // my member functions
};
```

The implementation of **main()** would be similar to the previous example. Only the type of the object would change—from FApplication to **CMyApp**:

```
void main( void )

{
    InitializeToolbox();

    CMyApp  theApp;
    theApp.Run();
}
```

Just as a framework defines a naming convention for its class (a SimpleWorks class begins with an uppercase letter "F" and a PowerPlant class begins with an uppercase letter "L"), you'll want to define a naming convention for your own classes. As you can see from the **CMyApp** class, I've elected to start my application-defined class names with an uppercase letter "C" (for "Class").

File Organization of the SimpleWorks Framework

The code that makes up an application framework is usually distributed across several files. And, if a framework includes resources—as Macintosh frameworks do—those resources will reside in one or more resource files. SimpleWorks is a very small application framework, so it's organized into only three files, as shown in Figure 3-3.

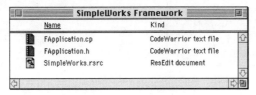

Figure 3-3: The files that hold the code that makes up the SimpleWorks application framework.

Code Organization

Typically a framework has a header file and a source code file for each class defined by the framework. The header file holds the declaration of a class and the source code file holds the definition, or implementation, of each of the member functions of a class. Each file bears the same name as the framework class declared or defined within it, with the appropriate extension added (.h or .cp).

The SimpleWorks framework consists of only one class—the **FApplication** class—so the SimpleWorks code is held in just two files. The class declaration is in a file named *FApplication.h* and the class member functions are implemented in a file named *FApplication.cp*. Figure 3-4 shows the content of the *FApplication.h* header file and a part of the content of the *FApplication.cp* source code file.

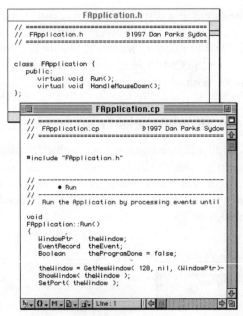

Figure 3-4: The one header file and source code file of SimpleWorks.

Resource Organization

Application frameworks that exist to aid the development of Macintosh programs include resources. These are stored in one or more resource files. A framework resource file can have any name, but typically has an extension of *.rsrc*. The SimpleWorks framework has a single 'WIND' resource stored in a resource file named *SimpleWorks.rsrc*. Figure 3-5 shows the contents of this file. The 'WIND' resource has an ID of 128 and defines the window that's opened by the **FApplication Run()** member function.

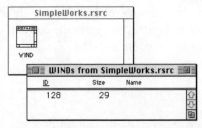

Figure 3-5: The one resource file that is a part of SimpleWorks.

SimpleWorks Example Project

You've seen all of the SimpleWorks code and all of the code necessary to create an application that uses SimpleWorks. You've also seen how the SimpleWorks code is organized into files. Here I'll show how these files are included in a CodeWarrior project that's based on SimpleWorks.

The *Generic.μ* project is very simple and does nothing more than make use of the code in the SimpleWorks framework without adding any functionality of its own (hence its name). Running the Generic program results in the display of the window that's created in the **Run()** member function of the **FApplication** class.

Creating the CodeWarrior Project

The SimpleWorks framework is code that's added to a project. To create a project that will include SimpleWorks code, choose New Project from the File menu and choose a standard Macintosh project stationery such as the Basic Toolbox 68K stationery. As described in Chapter 2, "Using the CodeWarrior IDE," you then replace the default source code and resource files with your own files.

You can create the *Generic.μ* project from scratch to get a feel for the process of creating a project that relies on application framework code, or you can simply work with the completed *Generic.μ* project that appears in this chapter's folder in the book examples folder on the Companion CD-ROM.

The *Generic.μ* project doesn't use any of its own resources, so it only requires the addition of a single file—the *CGenericApp.cp* source code file. Make this addition by doing the following:

1. Add a new, empty file to the project.

2. Type the code that's shown on the following pages.

3. Create one more new, empty file and save it as the *CGenericApp.h* header file.

4. Type the **CGenericApp** class definition (the listing is shown ahead) in this file. Note that the compiler will include the code from the *CGenericApp.h* header file in the *CGenericApp.cp* file, so the header file doesn't have to be added to the project.

In order for the compiler to be aware of application framework code, some or all of the source code and resource framework files need to be added to any project that uses the framework. SimpleWorks consists of only one source code file and one resource file, so adding the SimpleWorks files is easy. Figure 3-6 shows the files that are a part of the *Generic.μ* project.

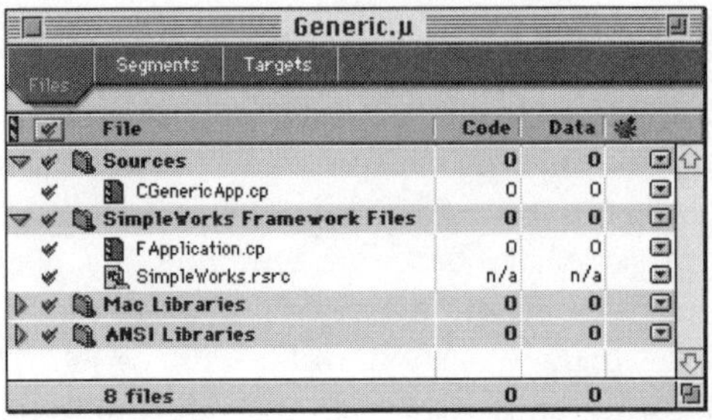

Figure 3-6: The project window of the Generic.μ project.

TIP *You can change the name of a group of files in the project window by double-clicking on the group name and typing a new name. That's what I did to rename the Resources group to SimpleWorks Framework Files.*

The Application-defined Code

A project uses framework code, but it must also include code of its own. The *Generic.μ* project includes a single, application-defined class named **CGenericApp**. As mentioned, projects that use SimpleWorks define a class derived from the **FApplication** class and then create an object of that class type. To show off SimpleWorks with the least amount of code, and still follow this **FApplication**-derived class convention, the *Generic.μ* project defines such a class but adds no new member functions to it. If in the future I want to improve the Generic program, I have the project set up to ease that task. The **CGenericApp** class definition appears in a header file named *CGenericApp.h*. The code from that file is shown in its entirety below. To make the **FApplication** class known to the compiler, you must include the *FApplication.h* header file.

```
#include "FApplication.h"

class  CGenericApp : public FApplication {

};
```

TIP *Later in this chapter you'll see* Improved.μ, *a project that demonstrates how to add a member function to the* **FApplication**-*derived class. That example also shows how to override a class member function to change the behavior of the framework.*

The source code for the Generic program creates a **CGenericApp** object and then calls that object's **Run()** member function to start the program running. The *CGenericApp.cp* source code listing is shown next:

```
#include "CGenericApp.h"

void InitializeToolbox( void );


void main( void )
{
   InitializeToolbox();

   CGenericApp   theApp;
   theApp.Run();
}


void InitializeToolbox( void )
{
   InitGraf( &qd.thePort );
   InitFonts();
   InitWindows();
   InitMenus();
   TEInit();
   InitDialogs( 0L );
}
```

Compiling & Running the Example

Choose Run from the Project menu to compile the *Generic.µ* project's code and test-drive the resulting application. You'll see an empty window. A click of the mouse button displays two lines of text in the window, as shown in Figure 3-7. To end the program press any key.

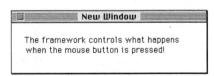

Figure 3-7: The window that results from running the Generic program and clicking the mouse button.

Overriding Framework Class Member Functions _____

The member functions of the classes of an application framework take care of many basic program interface requirements. But these member functions aren't intended to meet every need of an application. The tasks that are unique to a program can't be anticipated by the framework, and need to be handled by the program either through the use of classes that the application defines "from scratch" or by classes derived from application framework classes. When a program derives a class from an application framework class, it may add functionality to the derived class by adding new member functions. It may also alter the functionality of an inherited member function. When that's necessary, the inherited function can be overridden (refer to the "Overriding Member Functions" section in Appendix B if you need information about how to override a member function in C++).

Overriding an FApplication Member Function

SimpleWorks is a learning tool—not an example of a real-world application framework. This is evident in the code that makes up the **FApplication** member function **HandleMouseDown()**. This routine is called in response to a click of the mouse button. As implemented in the **FApplication** class, **HandleMouseDown()** draws a couple of lines of text to the active window. The intent is to provide you with immediate feedback when the routine executes. Having a couple of lines of text drawn to a window may not be your idea of the way a mouse button click should always be handled, of course. You can overcome this dilemma by overriding the **HandleMouseDown()** routine.

 FApplication declares its two member functions using the **virtual** keyword. That means that any class derived from **FApplication** can override either of these routines. To create a new version of **HandleMouseDown()**, an **FApplication**-derived class redeclares the routine in its class declaration. Here I'm creating a class named **CMyApp** that does this:

```
class  CMyApp : public FApplication {
   public:
      void  HandleMouseDown();
};
```

 Redeclaring the member function is the first of two steps necessary to override the routine. The second step is to reimplement the function to actually write a new version of the routine. I've done that in the next snippet. This new version of **HandleMouseDown()** again writes text to the active window. But now the text has changed a bit (to tell you that now the application is handling the mouse button click rather than the framework) and the text inverts to white on black and back a few times.

```
void  CMyApp::HandleMouseDown()
{
   Rect    theRect;
   long    theLong;
   short   theCount;

   SetRect( &theRect, 10, 10, 255, 55 );

   for ( theCount = 0; theCount < 5; theCount++ ) {
      MoveTo( 20, 30 );
      DrawString( "\pThe program controls what happens" );
      MoveTo( 20, 45 );
      DrawString( "\pwhen the mouse button is pressed!" );

      InvertRect( &theRect );
      Delay( 20, &theLong );
      InvertRect( &theRect );
      Delay( 20, &theLong );
   }
}
```

Another SimpleWorks Example Project

The Improved example program is an improvement (surprise!) over the previous Generic example. The *Improved.µ* project uses the SimpleWorks application framework to provide an example of overriding a member function that's been inherited from an application-framework base class. Instead of relying on how the framework handles a mouse button click, the Improved program defines the action that is to take place.

The *Improved.µ* project appears in this chapter's folder in the book examples folder on the Companion CD-ROM.

Creating the CodeWarrior Project

To create the *Improved.µ* project, follow the process used to create this chapter's other SimpleWorks example. Refer to Figure 3-8 to see what the project window for the *Improved.µ* project should look like. Here are the steps:

1. Create a new project using a basic Macintosh project stationery and name it *Improved.µ*.

2. Create a new, empty file and save it as *CImprovedApp.cp*.

3. Type the Improved source code in the new *CImprovedApp.cp* file.

4. Replace the default source code file and resource file with the *CImprovedApp.cp* file.

5. Add the *FApplication.cp* and *SimpleWorks.rsrc* files to the project.

6. Create a new, empty file and save it as *CImprovedApp.h*.

7. Type the header file code in the new *CImprovedApp.h* file.

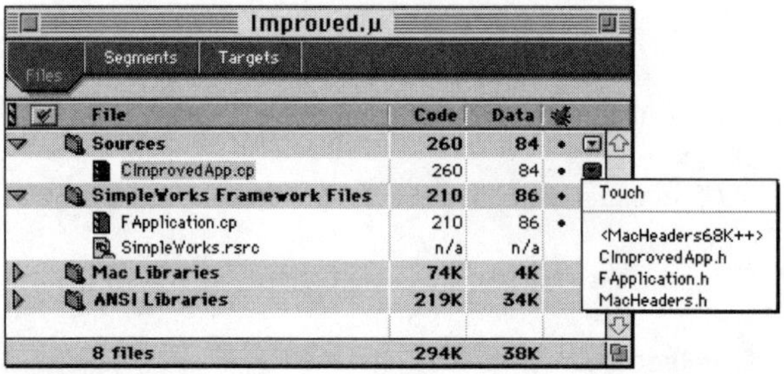

Figure 3-8: The project window of the Improved.μ project.

TIP

Figure 3-8 shows the project window after compilation. It also shows the pop-up menu that appears when the arrow button for the CImprovedApp.cp *file is clicked. This menu is useful for quickly opening a header file included in a source code file.*

The Application-defined Code

The code that makes up the *Improved.μ* project is set up much the same as the *Generic.μ* project code is—define a class that's derived from the **FApplication** class, create an object of this derived class type, and start the program by invoking the object's **Run()** member function. There is one important change in the derived class, however. Instead of being an empty class that relies on only inherited functions, the **CImprovedApp** class defines a function named **HandleMouseDown()**. Here's the contents of the *CImprovedApp.h* header file:

```
#include "FApplication.h"

class CImprovedApp : public FApplication {
    public:
        void HandleMouseDown();
};
```

Because the **CImprovedApp** class inherits a function named **HandleMouseDown()**, the **CImprovedApp** version of this similarly named routine is said to override, or take precedence over, the inherited version.

When a **CImprovedApp** object invokes **HandleMouseDown()**, it will be the version defined in the **CImprovedApp** class that executes.

A few pages back, in the "Overriding Framework Class Member Functions" section, you saw a specific example of how a class derived from **FApplication** could override the **HandleMouseDown()** function. The Improved example overrides this routine in the same manner:

```
void  CImprovedApp::HandleMouseDown()
{
   Rect    theRect;
   long    theLong;
   short   theCount;

   SetRect( &theRect, 10, 10, 255, 55 );

   for ( theCount = 0; theCount < 5; theCount++ ) {
      MoveTo( 20, 30 );
      DrawString( "\pThe program controls what happens" );
      MoveTo( 20, 45 );
      DrawString( "\pwhen the mouse button is pressed!" );

      InvertRect( &theRect );
      Delay( 20, &theLong );
      InvertRect( &theRect );
      Delay( 20, &theLong );
   }
}
```

The source code for the Improved program creates a **CImprovedApp** object and then calls that object's **Run()** member function to start the program running. The *CImprovedApp.cp* source code listing is shown next:

```
#include "CImprovedApp.h"
void InitializeToolbox( void );

void main( void )
{
   InitializeToolbox();

   CImprovedApp  theApp;
   theApp.Run();
}
void InitializeToolbox( void )
{
```

```
    InitGraf( &qd.thePort );
    InitFonts();
    InitWindows();
    InitMenus();
    TEInit();
    InitDialogs( OL );
}
```

Compiling & Running the Example

Choose Run from the Project menu to compile the *Improved.μ* project's code and run the Improved program. When Improved launches, it opens an empty window. A click of the mouse button displays two lines of text in the window, and then the text inverts five times. Figure 3-9 catches the flashing text as it inverts to white text on a black background. Pressing any key terminates the program.

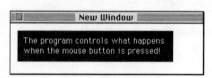

Figure 3-9: The window that results from running the Improved program and clicking the mouse button.

Moving On

An application framework consists of a number of classes used in conjunction with your own code. From this code you build an application that is a combination of both framework code and your own code. The advantage of basing a project on an application framework should be quite apparent—much of a program's coding has been done for you!

The SimpleWorks application framework presented in this chapter is extremely small and of very limited use. Its purpose, however, isn't to serve as a powerful programming utility. Instead, SimpleWorks demonstrates basic application framework concepts that you'll find in Metrowerks' larger and infinitely more powerful PowerPlant framework.

One of the concepts that SimpleWorks shares with PowerPlant is the definition of an application class used to embody the application itself. SimpleWorks defines an **FApplication** class. PowerPlant defines an **LApplication** class. A project that uses either SimpleWorks or PowerPlant creates a single application object used to start the program running and serve as the home of the program's event loop.

Another concept common to SimpleWorks and PowerPlant is the practice of declaring many class member functions virtual so that an application can override them. Overriding member functions is a common practice in projects that use PowerPlant. In a framework, one member function may invoke another member function. You saw an example of this in the **FApplication** class of the SimpleWorks framework. In this class the **Run()** member function handles a mouse button click by invoking the **HandleMouseDown()** member function. For a program to handle a mouse button click in a manner appropriate for the application, the application will override the **HandleMouseDown()** function in order to reimplement the routine such that it provides the needed functionality.

Enough lead-in to PowerPlant—it's time to get started with the real thing! In Chapter 4, "PowerPlant Basics," you're introduced to some of the specifics of PowerPlant, such as its naming conventions. You'll also see a lot more of the one PowerPlant class that you were introduced to here—the **LApplication** class. And, to complete the transition from this chapter's application framework theory to the remainder of this book's PowerPlant framework specifics, Chapter 4 provides a walkthrough of a small, simple PowerPlant-based project.

PowerPlant Basics

If you've never worked with PowerPlant, don't skip this chapter. What you learn here applies to all PowerPlant-based projects—from a trivial example program to a full-blown, commercial-grade application.

Using PowerPlant is simple. You incorporate some or all of the header files and source code into your CodeWarrior project. You then access this large body of existing code through the much smaller amount of application-defined code that you write. The result: a full-featured application developed in a fraction of the time it would take you to write and debug all the code from scratch.

Of course, it helps to understand how PowerPlant does things, just like it's a great help to understand how the information in an encyclopedia is organized. So we'll go over PowerPlant's naming convention. Learning how PowerPlant names classes, files, data types, and so forth will be of great benefit as you explore deeper and deeper into the framework in Chapters 7 through Chapter 13.

You'll also get an overview of two of the most important and powerful of PowerPlant's dozens of C++ classes: the **LApplication** class and the **LWindow** class. What you will learn about these two classes will give you further understanding of the basics of PowerPlant and will apply to everything else you read in this book.

Once the basics are covered, we'll look at a pair of sample projects. There's no better way to understand how something works than to take it apart and see what makes it tick. You can't do that with PowerPlant literally, of course, but you can do the next best thing. You can create a new PowerPlant-based CodeWarrior project (a project that makes use of the classes in some or all of the files that make up PowerPlant), and then examine the code and resources that are in that project. Over half of this chapter is dedicated to just this type of study.

Finally, we'll take up another topic fundamental to programming for the Mac OS: using the Metrowerks PowerPlant Constructor resource editor to create and edit PowerPlant-specific resources. These resources are a part of every PowerPlant based project.

PowerPlant Conventions

Source code that is a part of the PowerPlant application framework follows a naming convention. By always providing classes, data members, member functions, and so forth with names that follow a well-defined set of rules, Metrowerks makes it easier to learn how to use PowerPlant. This naming convention also makes it easy for a programmer looking over a source code listing to quickly identify which code is PowerPlant-defined and which is application-defined.

Classes

A PowerPlant-defined class always has a name that begins with either an *L*, *U*, or *St*. These prefixes stand for library, utility, and stack-based, respectively. A class that is application-defined (that you define) should begin with *C* to indicate that it is a class, but not a part of the PowerPlant framework.

PowerPlant Classes

The majority of the PowerPlant classes that you'll encounter are library classes; for example, the **LApplication**, **LDocApplication**, and **LCommander** classes. A library class usually has a dependency on one or more other library classes. For instance, the **LButton** class (which is used to create a button) is derived from the **LView** class (which is a class that supports drawing).

A class that starts with *U*, such as **UMarchingAnts**, is a PowerPlant utility class. These classes are used less often than library classes and don't have dependencies on any other class.

TIP | *And yes, there really is a PowerPlant class named **UMarchingAnts**! It's used to place a moving border around a selected item, such as when the selection tool is used in a drawing program.*

StHandleLocker is an example of a stack-based class. In this case, the class constructor is responsible for all the setup work, and the class destructor takes care of all the cleanup work. This is beneficial when saving the current condition of something that is important. For instance, the **StColorPenState** class is used to save, and later restore, the current state of the graphics pen. That is, it saves descriptive information about drawing (such as line thickness, starting location, color, and so forth). Even if any of these traits become altered, the saved state can be restored at any time.

Application-Defined Classes

Your PowerPlant-based project will define classes of its own. Often your classes will be derived from PowerPlant classes. You shouldn't begin the name of your class with an *L, U,* or *St* in order to keep the distinction between your application-defined classes and PowerPlant-defined classes. PowerPlant has its own naming convention, but it can't impose one on your source code. However, Metrowerks suggests that your own application-defined class names begin with a *C* (for class). For instance, a project that defines a class derived from the PowerPlant class **LApplication** might name the class **CMyApp**, and define it like so:

```
class   CMyApp : public LApplication {

   // member functions

   // data members
}
```

Files

PowerPlant is organized into a number of header files and source files. A header file usually declares a single class, and a source file usually defines all the methods of a single class. This means that in general there is a pair of files associated with each PowerPlant class. If a header file does declare only a single class, then the pair of files associated with the class has the class name with the appropriate file extension added. For instance, the **LWindow** class (a class that a project uses to easily create feature-rich window objects) is declared in a file named *LWindow.h*. The **LWindow** member functions are defined in a file named *LWindow.cp*.

Some header files, such as, many of the utility classes, declare more than one class. In such instances PowerPlant groups a number of logically related class declarations in one header file and groups all of the corresponding member functions in a single source file. Since more than one class exists in a file, the convention of giving a file the name of the class within it can't be followed. Instead, the file will bear the name of either the most important class in the file or a name indicative of the nature of the classes in the file. For instance, the previously mentioned **UMarchingAnts** class is declared in a file named *UDrawingUtils.h*.

The files that make up PowerPlant are organized into folders, all of which are held in a folder named *PowerPlant*. Provided the name of your root Metrowerks folder is *Metrowerks*, the PowerPlant folder is found at the following path:

    Metrowerks: Metrowerks CodeWarrior: MacOS Support: PowerPlant

The names of the folders that hold the PowerPlant files hint at the category of classes defined by the files in the folder. For instance, PowerPlant classes that have to do with Apple Events are in a folder named *AppleEvent Classes*, and PowerPlant classes used to create objects that can be drawn to are in a folder named *Pane Classes* (in PowerPlant a pane is an object that can display drawing).

TIP | *If you own a full-featured version of CodeWarrior (such as CodeWarrior Professional), you'll find the PowerPlant files in the PowerPlant folder. If you are relying on the Companion CD-ROM for your CodeWarrior programming, you won't find the individual PowerPlant files on the Companion CD-ROM. Instead, you'll find a library that holds the compiled code for all of the PowerPlant files. When used in a CodeWarrior project, this library works just as well as the individual PowerPlant source code files.*

Data Types

PowerPlant defines some data types for its own use. These types are based on existing data types, and are provided as a means of adding clarity to code listings and to aid Metrowerks, should redefining any of the types become necessary.

PowerPlant-Defined Integral Data Types

PowerPlant defines several data types based on the standard C data types **char**, **short**, and **long**. The PowerPlant-defined types more clearly indicate the bit size of each type. For instance, the PowerPlant-defined **Int8** type is simply based on the C **char** data type:

```
typedef  signed char   Int8;
```

To reserve a single byte of storage for a variable named **theByte**, a C or C++ program might make this declaration:

```
char    theByte;
```

PowerPlant code, however, would declare **theByte** as follows:

```
Int8    theByte;
```

PowerPlant defines its own data types for a second reason—to aid in porting code to other platforms. The size of standard C++ data types such as **int** and **long** may vary from one platform to the next. By using its own data types, PowerPlant makes the changing of data type definitions easy.

Code within PowerPlant-defined classes will use the PowerPlant-defined data type **Int8**, as well as the other PowerPlant-defined types shown in Table 4-1. Your own source code that is a part of a PowerPlant-based project can use standard C types such as **char**, but for consistency it's best that you too use the PowerPlant-defined types.

PowerPlant integral type	C type
Int8	char
Int16	short
Int32	long
Uint8	unsigned char
Uint16	unsigned short
Uint32	unsigned long
Uchar	unsigned char
Char16	Uint16

Table 4-1: PowerPlant integral data types.

PowerPlant-Defined Integral Synonym Data Types

PowerPlant also defines some data types that are based on its own integral data types. These data types, shown in Table 4-2, simply serve as synonyms for some of the PowerPlant-defined types listed in Table 4-1. For instance, the **ResIDT** type is simply a redefinition of the **Int16** type:

```
typedef  Int16    ResIDT;
```

PowerPlant defines multiple types based on a single type purely as a convenience. That is, these types help supply additional meaning to some PowerPlant code. The **ResIDT** type, for instance, is used when defining a constant that represents a resource ID. Here's an example:

```
const  ResIDT  WIND_Fireworks = 128;
```

The preceding line of code defines a constant that will be used elsewhere to represent 'WIND' resource ID 128. Seeing **ResIDT** in the preceding definition makes it clearer that the constant **WIND_Fireworks** is a resource-related constant. While not quite as clear in meaning, this definition could have been written as:

```
const  Int16  WIND_Fireworks = 128;
```

Throughout the remainder of this book you'll encounter several of the data types listed in both Tables 4-1 and 4-2.

PowerPlant synonym type	PowerPlant integral type
CommandT	Int32
MessageT	Int32
ResIDT	Int16
PanelDT	Int32
ClassIDT	Int32
DataIDT	Int32

Table 4-2: PowerPlant integral synonym data types.

Variables & Function Parameters

PowerPlant variables—including function parameters—follow a simple naming convention. The general rule is that a variable name starts with a lowercase character, and each word within the name begins with an uppercase character. The lowercase prefix of a name varies, depending on the variable type.

Class Data Members

A data member declared in a PowerPlant class begins with an *m*. For instance, the **LWindow** class declares the **mBackColor** data member as a means of allowing a window to set and keep track of its background color. A static data member—a data member whose value is shared by all objects of a class (as opposed to a "normal" data member, of which each object has a private copy)—begins with an *s*. An example is **sClickCount**, which is defined in the

LPane class (in short, a pane is an object that serves as a drawing area that can respond to a mouse click).

Local variables declared within a PowerPlant class member function have no particular lowercase prefix. Instead, the first word simply appears in lowercase. An example of a variable that is local to a member function is **currPort**, which is used to hold the current graphics port.

Function Parameters

A PowerPlant class member function parameter begins with either *in*, *out*, or *io*. A parameter that serves to provide input to a function begins with *in*, for input. A parameter that will end up returning a value to the calling routine begins with *out*, for output. A parameter that brings a value to the called function and returns a value to the calling routine begins with *io*, for input/output.

The **LApplication** class **ObeyCommand()** member function, which is used to respond to a menu selection by the user, provides an example of input and input/output parameters:

```
Boolean LApplication::ObeyCommand( CommandT  inCommand,
                                   void      *ioParam)
{
   // function body
}
```

The **LApplication** class **FindCommandStatus()** member function, which is used to determine current features of a menu item, such as whether it is enabled, offers an example of a routine that has input and output parameters:

```
void LApplication::FindCommandStatus(
                    CommandT  inCommand,
                    Boolean   &outEnabled,
                    Boolean   &outUsesMark,
                    Char16    &outMark,
                    Str255    outName)
{
   // function body
}
```

Application-Defined Local Variables

Metrowerks recommends that local variables in your own code in a PowerPlant-based project begin with the prefix *the*. So a function that declares a variable that serves to hold the returned result of an operation might be named **theResult**, and a variable that is to hold a **Boolean** value that signifies whether some value has changed could be named **theChanged**.

TIP | *While the* PlayMovie.µ *project introduced in Chapter 2 wasn't a PowerPlant-based project, it did introduce you to PowerPlant's local variable naming convention. Peek back at that chapter to see the variable declarations in the **main()** function of the* PlayMovie.c *listing.*

Constants

Your PowerPlant-based projects should define constants using the **const** keyword. Each should also include an underscore, and use uppercase for the start of a word within the name.

Resource-Related Constants

A constant that will be used to represent a resource ID should begin with the four characters of the resource type. An underscore comes next, followed by a word descriptive of the purpose of the constant. This word should begin with an uppercase character. In the Chapter 2 example project, *PlayMovie.µ*, you saw the following definition used to represent a 'WIND' resource with an ID of 128:

```
#define   WIND_Fireworks        128
```

That's good—but you can go one better by using the C++ keyword **const**. Defining a constant using **const** rather than **#define** means you also supply a data type in the definition, which can be of help to the compiler. Now that you know about PowerPlant's data type naming convention, you can go ahead and write the above constant definition as follows:

```
const  ResIDT  WIND_Fireworks  128
```

Other Constants

Application-defined constants that aren't resource-related should start with a lowercase character. Each word following the first should be preceded by an underscore and begin with an uppercase character. Using this convention, a constant that represents the value 1000 might look like this:

```
const  Int16  one_Millennium  1000;
```

PowerPlant Classes

PowerPlant consists of dozens of classes and hundreds of member functions. You'll encounter many of these classes and functions in this book. However, there are only a couple of classes that you need to be familiar with in order to get started with PowerPlant. The **LApplication** and **LWindow** classes described on the next pages are used in every application that is PowerPlant-based. Later in this chapter you will see a simple PowerPlant-based project that uses both these classes.

The LApplication Class

All PowerPlant classes are not of equal importance. One standout is the **LApplication** class, which every PowerPlant-based project will use. This class contains about three dozen member functions—several of them are shown in the partial listing of the **LApplication** class declaration that follows:

```
class  LApplication :  public LCommander,
                       public LEventDispatcher,
                       public LModelObject {
public:
                  LApplication();
  virtual        ~LApplication();
  . . .
  . . .
  virtual void    Run();
  virtual void    ProcessNextEvent();
  virtual void    ShowAboutBox();

  virtual Boolean ObeyCommand(
                       CommandT  inCommand,
                       void      *ioParam);

  virtual void    FindCommandStatus(
                       CommandT  inCommand,
                       Boolean   &outEnabled,
                       Boolean   &outUsesMark,
                       Char16    &outMark,
                       Str255    outName);
  . . .
  . . .
};
```

The **LApplication** class is derived from three other PowerPlant classes: **LCommander**, **LEventDispatcher**, and **LModelObject**. You'll hear more about these classes throughout this book.

For brevity, the preceding listing of **LApplication** shows only a few of the member functions of this class. The **ProcessNextEvent()** function hints that the **LApplication** class is responsible for event handling. The **ObeyCommand()** and **FindCommandStatus()** functions suggest that **LApplication** also takes care of menu choices (a menu item is a command in PowerPlant terminology). If these observances lead you to believe that the **LApplication** class serves as the hub of a program, you're correct. A project that uses PowerPlant always declares a class derived from **LApplication**, and then creates a single instance, or object, of this class type. In a sense, this one object acts as the application itself.

Creating an LApplication-Derived Class

Each PowerPlant-based CodeWarrior project needs to declare a class that uses **LApplication** as its base class. As mentioned earlier in this chapter, Metrowerks recommends that your own classes begin with C. Here's the look of such an application-defined class:

```
class    CMyApp : public LApplication {
public:
    // Constructor
    // Destructor

    // Override some inherited LApplication member functions

protected:
    // Other member functions
};
```

From this definition you can see that the class derived from **LApplication** contains declarations for a constructor, destructor, any **LApplication** member functions that the derived class reimplements (overrides), and any additional member functions necessary to implement the functionality not found in the member functions inherited from the **LApplication** base class.

TIP

For a broader overview of how an application framework might include an application class and how a project might use that class, refer to Chapter 3, "Introduction to Application Frameworks." While that chapter doesn't center on PowerPlant, it does discuss this topic and provide a simple CodeWarrior example project that demonstrates it.

The Application Object

The application-defined class derived from **LApplication** is used to create a single object. Declaring a variable of this class type takes care of that. For the application-defined **CMyApp** class just shown, that declaration looks like this:

```
CMyApp    theApp;
```

After declaring what's referred to as the application object, the program invokes the object's **Run()** member function. Refer back to the partial listing of the **LApplication** class (which serves as the **CMyApp** base class) to see that **Run()** is declared in **LApplication**.

```
theApp.Run();
```

The **Run()** member function displays the program's menu bar on the screen and then enters a loop that executes until the user terminates the program.

The body of the loop in **Run()** calls another **LApplication** member function—**ProcessNextEvent()**. This routine calls the Toolbox routine **WaitNextEvent()**—as the event loop of any program does. After receiving event information from **WaitNextEvent()**, **ProcessNextEvent()** passes it to another member function—**DispatchEvent()**.

The declaration for **DispatchEvent()** won't be found in the **LApplication** class definition. That's because **LApplication** inherits this function from the **LEventDispatcher** class (refer back to the partial listing of **LApplication** to see which classes serve as base classes for **LApplication**). **DispatchEvent()** examines the event type and then invokes the PowerPlant function appropriate for handling the particular event. The following shows a part of **DispatchEvent()**. If you're curious, refer to the *LEventDispatcher.cp* PowerPlant source file to see the full implementation:

```
void
LEventDispatcher::DispatchEvent(
        const EventRecord &inMacEvent )
{
   switch ( inMacEvent.what )
   {
     case mouseDown:
        AdjustCursor( inMacEvent );
        EventMouseDown( inMacEvent );
        break;

     case mouseUp:
        EventMouseUp( inMacEvent );
        break;

     case keyDown:
```

```
            EventKeyDown( inMacEvent );
            break;
      ...

      ...
      case kHighLevelEvent:
            EventHighLevel( inMacEvent );
            break;

      default:
            UseIdleTime( inMacEvent );
            break;
   }
}
```

TIP
*As just demonstrated, a PowerPlant member function definition uses the conven-
tion of listing the function return type on its own line and each function parameter
on its own line.*

The LWindow Class

The **LWindow** class is also a very important class. Every PowerPlant-based
project must use the **LApplication** class, and almost every such project uses
the **LWindow** class. Any PowerPlant-based project that generates a program
displaying one or more windows must use the **LWindow** class. Again, like
LApplication, **LWindow** consists of numerous member functions. This partial
listing of the class declaration shows several:

```
class   LWindow : public LView,
            public LCommander,
            public LModelObject {
public:
   ...
   ...
                     LWindow( LStream   *inStream);
   virtual          ~LWindow();

   static LWindow*  CreateWindow(
                        ResIDT        inWindowID,
                        LCommander *inSuperCommander);
   ...
   ...
   virtual void    Select();
   virtual void    Show();
```

```
    virtual void      Activate();
    virtual void      Deactivate();
    virtual void      Enable();

    virtual void      Suspend();
    virtual void      Resume();
    ...
    ...
    virtual Boolean   ObeyCommand(
                            CommandT  inCommand,
                            void      *ioParam);

    virtual void      FindCommandStatus(
                            CommandT  inCommand,
                            Boolean   &outEnabled,
                            Boolean   &outUsesMark,
                            Char16    &outMark,
                            Str255    outName);
    ...
    ...
};
```

The **LWindow** class is derived from three other PowerPlant classes: **LView**, **LCommander**, and **LModelObject**. You'll encounter each of these classes later in this book.

In a PowerPlant-based project window, objects of the **LWindow** class (or a class derived from **LWindow**) essentially replace the **WindowPtr** variables you've grown accustomed to working with. The **LWindow** class holds dozens of member functions—a few of which were listed previously. These functions replace the Macintosh Toolbox Window Manager routines. That means instead of creating a new window and then passing a **WindowPtr** to the Toolbox routine **Show()**, you'll create a new window object and invoke that object's **Show()** member function. While the name of an **LWindow** member function may not exactly coincide with the name of the Toolbox routine that performs a similar task, the member function name will give a good indication of which routine it replaces.

You'll probably note that the **LWindow** class declares two functions with names identical to functions declared in the previously discussed **LApplication** class: **ObeyCommand()** and **FindCommandStatus()**. In PowerPlant, the handling of a menu item selection by the program's user may become the responsibility of different objects at different times. Which object handles a menu item selection is subject to the following chain of command. While the chain of command is fully described in Chapter 7, "Menus," the concept is important enough—and interesting enough—to warrant a very brief example here.

Consider NumberGenerator, a hypothetical, very simple random number generator program created from a PowerPlant-based project. This program allows only one window to be open at any time. In that window a random number displays upon the user's command. NumberGenerator has a New item in the File menu. The program could be designed such that choosing New produces two different effects. If no window is currently open, a new, empty window opens. If, however, a window is already open, a new random number generates and displays. In the first instance it would be the application object (the object of the **LApplication**-derived class) that is responsible for executing its version of **ObeyCommand()** to handle New. In the second instance it would be the window object (the object of the **LWindow** class or **LWindow**-derived class) that has the honor of executing its own version of **ObeyCommand()**.

A Simple PowerPlant Example Project

The best way to get an idea of how to use PowerPlant is to take a good look at a simple PowerPlant-based project. In this section you will see how to create such a project. You will also see what application-defined source code and resources are in the project. Because the intent is to examine the basics of using PowerPlant, the example project will be a small one. Even so, it will generate a program that opens and draws text to any number of windows, each of which can be dragged about the screen and closed at any time. Figure 4-1 shows a few such windows.

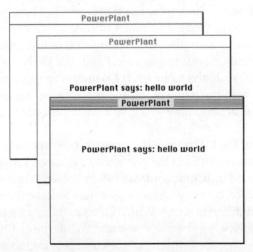

Figure 4-1: The example project builds a program that displays a number of identical windows.

The example program displays three menus in its menu bar: Apple, File, and Edit. The Apple menu is implemented in the standard way: it displays an About item and all of the items in the user's Apple Menu Items folder. The File and Edit menus are pictured in Figure 4-2. When you run the program (which, along with the completed project, appear on the Companion CD-ROM), you'll notice that many of the items in these two menus are dim and remain so for the duration of the program's execution. These items are common to most programs, so PowerPlant automatically includes them in PowerPlant-based projects. If the program you're developing won't need some of these items, you can easily remove them.

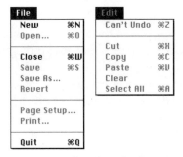

Figure 4-2: The File and Edit menus from the example project's program.

A little later in this chapter I'll show the application-defined code for this project. It might help you to understand the power of PowerPlant if I point out something now, while you're trying out the example program. The application-defined code doesn't specify how a mouse button click should be handled. That is, there's no code to handle a click that activates a window or drags a window. There's no code to display an alert when the About item is selected from the Apple menu, or to open whatever item the user chooses from this menu. There's also no code to implement the handling of the Quit item from the File menu. All of these tasks are handled by PowerPlant-defined code.

The PowerPlant Project

A PowerPlant project is simply a CodeWarrior project that has several PowerPlant source code files and a few PowerPlant resource files added to it.

TIP
> *If you're working with CodeWarrior Lite from the Companion CD-ROM, PowerPlant is installed on your hard drive. If you're working with a full-featured version of CodeWarrior such as CodeWarrior Professional instead, make sure PowerPlant is installed on your hard drive—it may not have installed by default. To check, choose New Project from the Project menu and look in the New Project dialog box for PowerPlant stationery—there should be a number of such stationeries listed. You can peek ahead to Figure 4-3 to see what I'm referring to. If you don't have PowerPlant installed, run the CodeWarrior installer and opt to install PowerPlant.*

Creating the Project

When creating a new project, CodeWarrior places the appropriate libraries in the project. CodeWarrior also adds one or more files that set up the project so that it can immediately be turned into a simple application. Choosing one of the Basic Toolbox project stationeries, for instance, results in a project that includes a *SillyBalls.c* source file and a *SillyBalls.rsrc* resource file. Choosing Run from the Project menu builds the SillyBalls application—a program that displays a window, and then draws randomly placed and randomly colored balls in the window until the user clicks the mouse button.

Creating a PowerPlant-based project follows a similar pattern. You begin by choosing New Project from the File menu to bring up the New Project dialog box. Here you'll find a number of PowerPlant-related project stationeries listed. In Figure 4-3 the stationery for creating a PowerPlant-based project that results in a fat application is being selected. If you want your application to be able to run on both 68K-based Macs and PowerPC-based Macs, and you want the application to take advantage of the fast PowerPC instruction set when running on a PowerPC-based Mac, this is the route you'll take.

Figure 4-3: Selecting project stationery to create a PowerPlant-based project.

To tell CodeWarrior to place all of the project-related files in a new folder, leave the Create Folder checkbox checked. Then click the OK button to dismiss the New Project dialog box and to bring on the standard Save As dialog box. Type a project name. Give the file name the .μ (Option-m) extension to make it clear that the file is a CodeWarrior project; then click the Save button. Figure 4-4 shows the project window that results from using the Basic PowerPlant FAT stationery and then provides a name of *FirstPowerPlant.μ* (for, obviously enough, this book's first PowerPlant example).

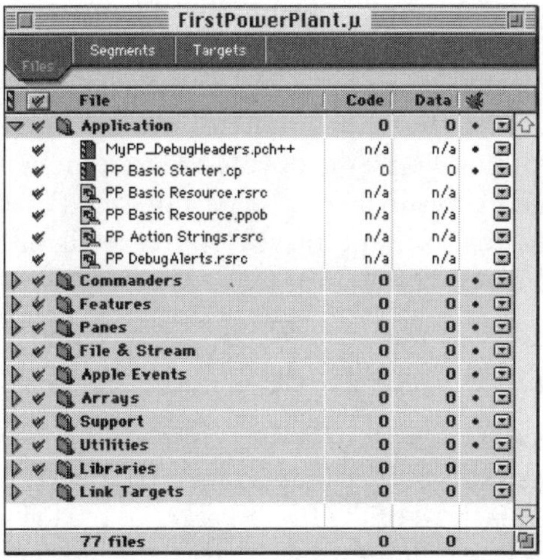

Figure 4-4: The project window for a PowerPlant-based project.

The Project Window

Figure 4-4 shows that a PowerPlant-based project consists of many more files than a project that doesn't rely on the application framework. CodeWarrior by default adds many of the PowerPlant source files to a new PowerPlant-based project. These files hold code common to many applications. If you're developing what will be a small application, though, the code from some of these files may not be needed. In such a case you can remove some files from the project. Before doing so, be aware of two facts. First, there are file interdependencies— removing one file may remove code that another file counts on. If that happens you'll get an error at compilation, and will have to determine which file or files to return to the project. Second, even with the large number of PowerPlant files that are included in a default PowerPlant-based project, the resulting executable can be as small as 200K in size. If your small project may later become a larger one, it might make sense to keep all of the default PowerPlant files in the project so that the project is all set up for future expansion.

The project that CodeWarrior creates from any of the PowerPlant project stationeries includes a file named *PP Basic Starter.cp* (refer back to Figure 4-4). Inclusion of this file makes it possible to test the project without writing any of your own code. To do that, simply choose Run from the Project menu. Then wait a moment while all of the seventy-plus project files are compiled and linked. After that, the application will launch. The program that runs will be the one discussed at the start of this section—the simple example that opens any number of windows, each one displaying the text "PowerPlant says: hello world."

The *PP Basic Starter.cp* file holds the minimal amount of code necessary to create a PowerPlant-based program. You'll of course add more code of your own to create a program that does much more than simply open windows. The imperative word in that last sentence is "add." There's no need to replace the code Metrowerks has supplied. Instead, you'll use it as a foundation. With that in mind, the remainder of this chapter is devoted to examining this starter code—including the starter resources that are also part of each PowerPlant-based project. Understanding this code and these resources will take you a long way to understanding PowerPlant.

The Application-Defined Source Code

PowerPlant consists of thousands of lines of source code—a number of which are present in the seventy or so source files that CodeWarrior adds to PowerPlant-based projects. In fact, all of the files in eight of the ten groups in a PowerPlant-based project are PowerPlant source files (the Application and Libraries groups are the exceptions). To make use of this PowerPlant code, you need to write a little of your own code. Metrowerks supplies a good example of how to do this in the *PP Basic Starter.cp* and *PP Basic Starter.h* files that get added to each PowerPlant-based project. The following pages discuss the code found in these two files.

The LApplication-Derived Class

Every PowerPlant-based project must declare an **LApplication**-derived class. The *PP Basic Starter.h* header file declares **CPPStarterApp** as such a class:

```
class  CPPStarterApp : public LApplication {
public:
                    CPPStarterApp();
    virtual         ~CPPStarterApp();

    virtual Boolean  ObeyCommand(CommandT inCommand,
                                 void*     ioParam);
```

```
    virtual void        FindCommandStatus(CommandT inCommand,
                                          Boolean  &outEnabled,
                                          Boolean  &outUsesMark,
                                          Char16   &outMark,
                                          Str255   outName);
protected:

    virtual void        StartUp();
};
```

The **CPPStarterApp** class declares a constructor and destructor function. The constructor implementation consists of a single line of code—a call to a **RegisterAllPPClasses()**. This function is a utility routine that isn't a part of any PowerPlant class, so it can be invoked from anywhere in your code. Here's the definition for the **CPPStarterApp** constructor:

```
CPPStarterApp::CPPStarterApp()
{
    RegisterAllPPClasses();
}
```

Some PowerPlant-defined classes use a special PowerPlant resource type known as a 'PPob' resource. Such a class needs to be registered. That is, PowerPlant needs information regarding which 'PPob' resource should be associated with which classes. The **RegisterAllPPClasses()** handles this task for all of the PowerPlant classes that rely on 'PPob' resources. Don't concern yourself with just what a 'PPob' resource is at this point—you'll encounter this resource type later in this chapter, and throughout the rest of this book.

The **CPPStarterApp** class declares a destructor that is empty. This empty function is defined as a convenience. If you're basing your own project's **LApplication**-derived class on the **CPPStarterApp** class, and your application object needs to perform some type of "clean up" work when the program terminates, you have a function ready to handle that chore.

The three remaining member functions in the **CPPStarterApp** class are all routines inherited from **LApplication**. The **CPPStarterApp** overrides each so that it can reimplement them to fit the needs of the program.

ObeyCommand() is a routine that is automatically invoked when the user makes a menu selection. **ObeyCommand()** receives the selected menu item in the form of the **inCommand** parameter, and then uses a **switch** statement to take the action appropriate for the menu item selected.

```
Boolean
CPPStarterApp::ObeyCommand(
    CommandT    inCommand,
    void        *ioParam)
```

```
{
    Boolean    cmdHandled = true;

    switch (inCommand) {

        case cmd_New:
            LWindow    *theWindow;
            theWindow = LWindow::CreateWindow(window_Sample, this);
            theWindow->Show();
            break;

        default:
            cmdHandled = LApplication::ObeyCommand(inCommand, ioParam);
            break;
    }

    return cmdHandled;
}
```

The **FindCommandStatus()** function is another menu-related routine. Under certain circumstances an application may find it necessary to change the status of a menu item. For instance, if no windows are open, a program should disable the Close item in the File menu. **FindCommandStatus()** determines this type of menu item status and is where suitable action (such as disabling an item) is taken. Like **ObeyCommand()**, **FindCommandStatus()** is automatically called by PowerPlant code. In the example project the **CPPStarterApp** class overrides the routine in order to reimplement it, but nowhere in the application-defined code is the routine ever invoked. Instead, PowerPlant code invokes this function repeatedly so that the application's menus and menu items are constantly updated:

```
void
CPPStarterApp::FindCommandStatus(
    CommandT    inCommand,
    Boolean     &outEnabled,
    Boolean     &outUsesMark,
    Char16      &outMark,
    Str255      outName)
{
    switch (inCommand) {

        case cmd_New:
            outEnabled = true;
            break;
```

```
        default:
            LApplication::FindCommandStatus(inCommand,
                            outEnabled, outUsesMark,
                            outMark, outName);
            break;
    }
}
```

ObeyCommand() and **FindCommandStatus()** are important routines that every PowerPlant-based project will want to override. For this reason both routines are described in great detail in Chapter 7, "Menus."

The last member function declared in the **CPPStaterApp** class is **StartUp()**. Once again, this is a routine that is automatically invoked by PowerPlant. If the **LApplication**-derived class overrides this routine, it will be this application-defined version that automatically gets invoked upon application launch. Here's how the **CPPStarterApp** class defines **StartUp()**:

```
void
CPPStarterApp::StartUp()
{
    ObeyCommand(cmd_New, nil);
}
```

You just read that **ObeyCommand()** is a function that PowerPlant is responsible for invoking—it does so when a menu item selection is made. Here you see that **ObeyCommand()** can also be explicitly called by application-defined code. That approach makes sense when you want to achieve the same effect as if a menu item were selected by the user. If you look back at the implementation of **ObeyCommand()**, you'll see that **CPPStarterApp** defines it such that a menu choice of **cmd_New** results in a new window being created and displayed. By invoking **ObeyCommand()** with a parameter of **cmd_New** at application startup, the program causes a new window to open—a feature found in many applications.

TIP *Constants used in the switch of **ObeyCommand()** can be PowerPlant-defined (as is the case for **cmd_New**) or application-defined. In Chapter 7, "Menus," you'll read about these constants, and also about the specifics of the window-creation code that appears under the **cmd_New** label of the switch in **ObeyCommand()**.*

The main() Function

Like any C++ program, one that originates as a PowerPlant-based project must include a **main()** function. Here's how the example project defines its brief **main()** routine:

```
void main(void)
{
    SetDebugThrow_(debugAction_Alert);
    SetDebugSignal_(debugAction_Alert);

    InitializeHeap(3);

    UQDGlobals::InitializeToolbox(&qd);

    new LGrowZone(20000);

    CPPStarterApp    theApp;
    theApp.Run();
}
```

In C++ parlance, the occurrence of a serious error *throws an error*, while the occurrence of what might be an unusual event *raises a signal*. PowerPlant provides a means for your program to catch and respond to such problematic situations. The first two lines of **main()** are calls to the PowerPlant macros **SetDebugThrow_()** and **SetDebugSignal_()**. Inclusion of calls to these macros lets application-defined code use other PowerPlant debugging macros. These macros are discussed in Chapter 11, "Debugging & Testing the Application."

The Mac OS reserves a partition of memory for each application that is launched. The PowerPlant utility function **InitializeHeap()** sees to it that your program gets the memory it needs. The parameter to **InitializeHeap()** specifies the number of master pointer blocks that are to be dedicated to the application. CodeWarrior supplies a value of 3 here, which will be adequate for most programs.

InitializeToolbox() is a member function in the PowerPlant utility class **UQDGlobals**. True to its name, this routine invokes a number of functions that initialize the Mac Toolbox. To invoke a utility routine that is a "normal" function, you simply call it. The **RegisterAllPPClasses()** routine invoked in the **CPPStarterApp** constructor routine is an example. To invoke a routine that is a member function of a utility class, you need to specify the class name. The preceding call to **InitializeToolbox()** is an example. Note that with utility functions you needn't first create an object and then execute the function via that object.

The PowerPlant class **LGrowZone** creates an object that can deliver extra memory to an application, should an unusual situation demand it. When creating the new object, the size of a small memory reserve is specified. In this example, a reserve of 20K is being set aside. Your program will most likely never use this reserve, so this value should suffice.

Earlier in this chapter you read that a PowerPlant-based project declares an **LApplication**-derived class, creates an instance of that class, and then invokes that object's **Run()** member function to start the program running. That's exactly how **main()** ends. Declaring the **CPPStarterApp** variable, **theApp** creates the application object. Invoking **Run()** from this object starts the program running:

```
CPPStarterApp    theApp;

theApp.Run();
```

When the user terminates the program by choosing Quit, **Run()** will end—and so, too will **main()** and the program.

PowerPlant Resources

When you create a PowerPlant-based project, CodeWarrior adds four resource files to it: *PP Basic Resource.rsrc*, *PP Basic Resource.ppob*, *PP Action Strings.rsrc*, and *PP DebugAlerts.rsrc*. These files hold resources that are used by most programs. Since Metrowerks couldn't possibly anticipate every resource every program will use, these four files obviously don't include all the resources your program will need. As you see in this section, these files do, however, greatly reduce the effort you'll need to expend to get your project's resources in place.

Basic Resources

The *PP Basic Resource.rsrc* file holds a few of the basic resources common to most applications that are created from a PowerPlant-based project. Figure 4-5 shows the five resource types in this file, as well as a look at one of the 'ALRT' resources.

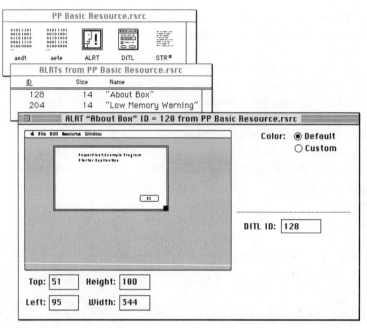

Figure 4-5: The PP Basic Resource.rsrc file, as opened in ResEdit.

As a Mac programmer, you're familiar with the 'ALRT', 'DITL', and 'STR#' resource types. You may not have worked with the resources of type 'aedt' or 'aete'. The following list briefly describes the resources found in the *PP Basic Resource.rsrc* file:

■ **ALRT**—An application developed from a PowerPlant-based project will display an alert, defined as 'ALRT' 128, in response to the user's selection of the About item in the Apple menu. Such an application will also automatically display an alert, 'ALRT' 204, when a low memory condition occurs.

■ **DITL**—The text that appears in the About and low memory alerts is defined in these two 'DITL' resources. You'll want to edit the text in 'DITL' 128 so that 'ALRT' 128 tells the user the name of your program (rather than displaying the text "PowerPlant Example Program Starter Application," as it does by default).

■ **STR#**—The one string list resource holds three strings that are used by PowerPlant. You should replace the text of the first string with your program's name. PowerPlant code that is a part of your program will look to this resource to occasionally display your program's name in informative alerts. Leave the other two strings unchanged.

- **aedt**—This resource type stands for Apple Event Description Table. It is defined by PowerPlant for the purpose of supporting Apple events. PowerPlant uses these resources internally, so leave them unchanged.

- **aete**—This resource type stands for Apple Event Terminology Extension. It specifies the language of the people that your program targets. By default this resource is set to English.

Action String Resources

The *PP Action Strings.rsrc* file holds the resources that support Undo and Redo items in the Edit menu. This file holds four string list resources (type 'STR#') that each hold a number of strings. These strings are used by PowerPlant to fill in the menu item name for the Undo item in the Edit menu. This menu item name changes in response to certain conditions in a program, so it requires special treatment.

Debug Alert String Resources

The *PP DebugAlerts.rsrc* file holds the resources for displaying error messages when debugging this project. When you test run your (hopefully) completed program, an error could occur. If it does, an informative alert will appear. The alert and the text in it are defined in the *PP DebugAlerts.rsrc* file.

PPob Resources

The *PP Basic Resource.ppob* file holds the basic user-interface resources common to most applications. Here the menu bar, menus, and menu items are defined. Unlike the other three resource files that CodeWarrior places in a PowerPlant-based project, the *PP Basic Resource.ppob* file is not a ResEdit file. Instead, it was created using PowerPlant Constructor. This Metrowerks resource editor is used to create and edit common resource types such as 'MBAR' and 'MENU'. More importantly, it is used to create resources of a type unique to PowerPlant—the 'PPob'. To understand the 'PPob' resource, you must understand Constructor. You'll learn about the *PP Basic Resource.ppob* file in the next section.

Constructor

A PowerPlant-based project includes resources—just like a project that doesn't rely on PowerPlant code. So everything you already know about resources still applies. However, PowerPlant code makes use of a few resource types that Metrowerks has designed. In particular, PowerPlant relies on 'PPob' resources to define windows and their contents and 'Mcmd' resources to define menus and menu items. While you can use your favorite resource editor (such as ResEdit or Resorcerer) to create and edit many of your project's resources (such as those of type 'DLOG', 'DITL', 'PICT', and so forth), you'll use Metrowerks PowerPlant Constructor resource editor to create and edit PowerPlant-specific resources such as the 'PPob'.

The default project that opens in response to choosing a PowerPlant project stationery includes a file named *PP Basic Resource.ppob*. A file extension of *.ppob* is the Metrowerks naming convention for a resource file created by the PowerPlant Constructor resource editor. You can open a *.ppob* file (and first launch Constructor if it's not already running) by double-clicking on the file's icon on the desktop or on the file's name in the CodeWarrior project window. Figure 4-6 shows the window that appears when *PP Basic Resource.ppob* is opened with Constructor.

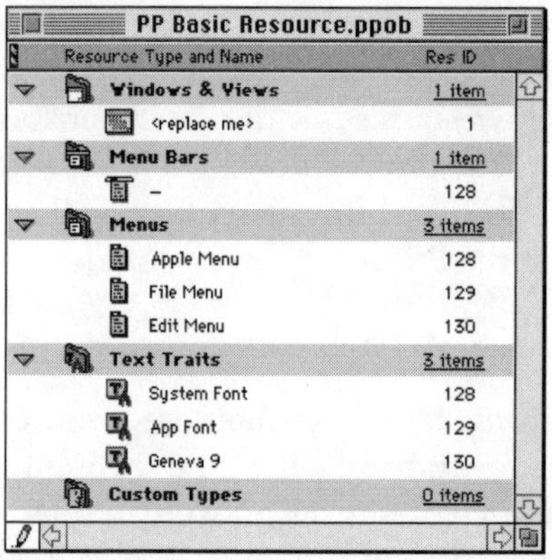

Figure 4-6: The PP Basic Resource.ppob file, as opened in Constructor.

Creating a new resource in Constructor is simple. First, click on the heading of the resource type you want to create. Then choose New resourceType Resource from the Edit menu. The name of this menu item is context-sensitive, so resourceType will be replaced with the type of resource you're adding. For instance, if you click on the Menus heading, this menu item will say New Menu Resource. Before you go adding new resources, you'll of course want to know a little something about the types of resources Constructor supports. Information on each resource type appears throughout this book—beginning with an overview right now.

The 'Mcmd' Resource

Metrowerks has developed the 'Mcmd' (for "menu command") resource as
PowerPlant's means of keeping track of menu items. A single 'Mcmd' resource
specifies all of the items in one menu. Constructor keeps 'Mcmd' information
under the Menu heading. As shown in Figure 4-6, the *PP Basic Resource.ppob*
file holds three such resources—they're named Apple Menu, File Menu, and
Edit Menu.

Examining a Menu

Double-clicking on a name under the Menus heading opens a window that
displays a menu in much the same way as ResEdit displays a 'MENU' resource. Figure 4-7 shows how Constructor displays the File Menu.

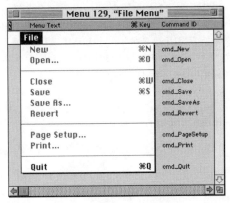

Figure 4-7: The File Menu, as displayed in Constructor.

The left side of the window in Figure 4-7 shows how a menu will look. The
right side displays a column titled Command ID. Each menu item in a menu
has a command ID, or command number. It is by this number that application-
defined code refers to a menu item. This number, which can often be represented by a PowerPlant-defined constant such as **cmd_New**, is used in your
source code so that your program can respond to this menu item selection.
You'll see a detailed example of this in Chapter 7, "Menus."

You can use a resource editor other than Constructor to examine a .ppob
file. If you open the *PP Basic Resource.ppob* file using ResEdit, you'll find that
among the resources in this file are resources of type 'MENU' and 'Mcmd'.
What Constructor calls a menu is actually a single 'MENU' resource and a
single 'Mcmd' resource. The 'MENU' resource is the same type you're familiar
with from past Mac programming experience. The 'Mcmd' resource is a

Metrowerks-defined type created specifically for use with PowerPlant. An 'Mcmd' resource holds all of the command IDs (command numbers) of the items in one menu. To pair an 'Mcmd' resource with a 'MENU' resource, each has the same ID. Again, all the details are provided in Chapter 7, "Menus."

TIP *If you do open* PP Basic Resource.ppob *from ResEdit, you'll be able to open a 'Mcmd' resource—but don't be surprised when what you view doesn't appear very meaningful. ResEdit doesn't have an 'Mcmd' editor, so it will display such a resource in its hex editor.*

Editing a Menu

To edit a menu in Constructor, first open it by double-clicking on its name under the Menu heading in Constructor's main window. To edit an existing menu item, double-click on the name of the item. In Figure 4-8 the New menu item has been double-clicked. The result is the display of a *property inspector* window. In PowerPlant, a property inspector is used to specify the characteristics, or properties, of something. In the case of a menu item, the property inspector window is used to specify such characteristics as the menu item's name and whether the item is enabled. It is also this window that allows you to edit the menu item's command number.

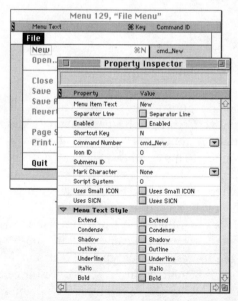

Figure 4-8: The property inspector window for the New item in the File Menu, as displayed in Constructor.

When you edit a menu in Constructor, you may actually be editing two resources: a 'MENU' and an 'Mcmd.' For example, if you were to change the name and command number of a menu item, the name change would be reflected in a 'MENU' resource and the command number change would show up in a 'Mcmd.' Chapter 7, "Menus," provides more details on menu editing.

The 'PPob' Resource

Metrowerks defines a 'PPob' (for "PowerPlant object") resource as one that holds information about one type of window. Besides defining the "normal" characteristics of a window (such as the window's size and screen placement), a 'PPob' resource defines some or all of the contents of a window (such as pictures, text, and buttons). Figure 4-6 shows that the *PP Basic Resource.ppob* file holds a single 'PPob' resource—it's named <replace me>.

Examining a 'PPob'

Double-clicking on the <replace me> name under the Windows and Views heading opens a window with a gray background. This gray area represents the desktop, and on the gray area is a representation of what the new window will look like. Here you can edit the characteristics of the window you're creating, and the changes will be reflected on this pseudo-desktop. Figure 4-9 shows how Constructor displays this window.

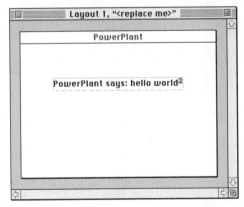

Figure 4-9: The 'PPob' resource, as displayed in Constructor.

Constructor displays what appears to be simply a window, but is in fact both a 'WIND' resource and a 'PPob' resource. The 'WIND' resource is the same type with which you are familiar. The 'PPob' resource is the Metrowerks-defined type that holds information about the contents of the window. In PowerPlant, the contents of a window are organized into a hierarchy of self-contained drawing areas, each one being either a pane or a view.

A view can contain other drawing areas (either other panes or views), whereas a pane cannot. The entire window content area is defined to be a view so it can contain other drawing areas. The 'PPob' resource found in the *PP Basic Resource.ppob* file and pictured in Figure 4-9 consists of the view that is the window itself and a single pane. Constructor has provided a dashed frame around the pane. There are numerous types of panes—the one in this window is a caption pane that is used to display a small amount of text. Because the text area is a pane, no other drawing area can be nested inside it. Chapter 8, "Panes & Views," clarifies and elaborates on the concept of how drawing areas are organized in windows.

Editing a 'PPob'

To edit a 'PPob' in Constructor, begin by double-clicking on its name under the Windows and Views heading in Constructor's main window. To edit an existing pane or view, double-click on it. A property inspector displays that allows you to edit the characteristics of the pane or view. Figure 4-10 shows a part of the large property inspector for the window view of the one 'PPob' resource in the *PP Basic Resource.ppob* file.

Figure 4-10: The Property Inspector window for the window view in the 'PPob' resource, as displayed in Constructor.

PowerPlant consists of different view and pane types, so Constructor provides different property inspectors for this variety of drawing areas. Clicking on the caption pane in the 'PPob' resource brings up the property inspector shown in Figure 4-11.

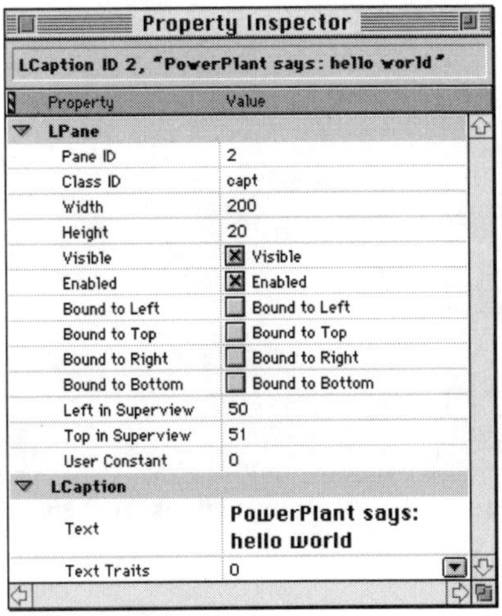

Figure 4-11: The Property Inspector window for the caption pane in the 'PPob', as displayed in Constructor.

Just as the editing of a menu in Constructor may affect two resources (a 'MENU' and an 'Mcmd'), the editing of an item in the Windows and Views category may affect two resources (a 'WIND' and a 'PPob'). For instance, changing the values of the Top, Left, Width, or Height fields in the window view property inspector would alter the 'WIND' resource. Editing the text of the caption pane would affect the 'PPob' resource. Chapter 8, "Panes & Views," provides additional information on the editing of 'PPob' resources.

The 'MBAR' Resource

Constructor allows for the editing of menus, so as a convenience Constructor also provides a means of editing your program's menu bar. Constructor has no special resource type for a menu bar—the standard 'MBAR' resource is used. This means you could use ResEdit to create a menu bar. However, Constructor's 'MBAR' editor is at least as good as ResEdit's, so you have little reason to leave the Constructor environment to handle this chore.

Editing an existing menu bar starts by double-clicking on the item under the Menu Bar's heading in Constructor's main window. A window then displays a menu bar that holds the menus currently defined in Constructor. Figure 4-12 shows this window for the one menu bar found in the *PP Basic Resource.ppob* file.

Figure 4-12: The Property Inspector window for the Apple menu in the 'MBAR' resource, as displayed in Constructor.

Clicking once on a menu name in the menu bar highlights the name and allows you to enter a new name. If you double-click on a menu name instead, a property inspector window for that menu appears. Figure 4-12 shows the property inspector for the Apple menu.

The 'Txtr' Resource

Metrowerks has devised a powerful way for your PowerPlant-based projects to easily assign a multitude of text traits to any text in your program. The 'Txtr' (for "text traits") resource lets you specify and package together a variety of text characteristics. You can then use this 'Txtr' resource in conjunction with any text in order for all of the traits to be applied to that text.

Under the Text Traits heading in the main window of Constructor are three 'Txtr' resources—they're named System Font, App Font, and Geneva 9. Double-clicking on one displays a property inspector for that resource. Figure 4-13 shows the property inspector for the 'Txtr' resource named Geneva 9.

Figure 4-13: The property inspector window for the Geneva 9 'Txtr' resource, as displayed in Constructor.

You'll learn more about the 'Txtr' resource in Chapter 8, "Panes & Views." Until then you can glance back at Figure 4-11 to see an example of its use. That figure shows the property inspector for the caption pane of the *PP Basic Resource.ppob* file's one 'PPob' resource. The last field in this property inspector allows you to enter a 'Txtr' resource ID that specifies how the caption text will appear when drawn in the window.

Moving On

PowerPlant is a set of source code and header files that is used in conjunction with your own code to speed up the time spent creating an application. To use PowerPlant, you create a new CodeWarrior project that is based on one of the PowerPlant project stationeries. Along with the many PowerPlant files that CodeWarrior adds to this project is a single source code file named *PP Basic Starter.cp*. This file (and the associated header file *PP Basic Starter.h*) holds application-defined code (as opposed to PowerPlant-defined code).

The **LApplication** and **LWindow** classes may be the most important of the dozens of classes that make up PowerPlant. Every PowerPlant-based program will define a class derived from the **LApplication** class and then create a single instance of this class. This object serves to start the application. Any PowerPlant-based program that uses windows will make use of the **LWindow** class. The dozens of member functions of the **LWindow** class mean that **LWindow** objects automatically include all the properties common to windows.

The small amount of application-defined code in the *PP Basics Starter.cp* file makes use of some of the thousands of lines of PowerPlant-defined code from the project's PowerPlant files. To get a simple 'skeleton' program that displays windows but does little else, all you need do is choose Run from the Project menu. Of course, you'll want to develop a program that does more than display a few windows. To achieve that goal you should edit and add to the application-defined code in the *PP Basics Starter.cp* file. And just what code should you change, and what code should you add? For those answers, read on—much of the rest of this book is devoted to the study of these questions!

Before delving into PowerPlant code, the next chapter introduces MediaCenter—a program that you'll be seeing much of in the remainder of this book. Chapter 5 presents the first version of this program's CodeWarrior project. As the book progresses, we'll be adding resources and code to the project until the project is completed in Chapter 13.

Introduction to the Example Application

Chapter 2 discussed a simple CodeWarrior project named *PlayMovie.μ*. Chapter 4 covered a PowerPlant-based project named *FirstPowerPlant.μ*. This project-a-chapter pace is about to change. The remainder of this book, up to and including Chapter 13, "Printing," is dedicated to the creation of a single project—one named *MediaCenter.μ*. From the *MediaCenter.μ* project comes a multimedia Macintosh application named, of course, MediaCenter. Chapter 6, "Setting Up the Project," introduces the project, and each subsequent chapter builds on the same project. As we introduce new topics, we'll present new versions of the same project.

Before jumping right into the project, it's best to get an understanding of what the final version of the MediaCenter application looks and acts like. Then, as each new topic is covered you'll be better able to visualize in advance how the topic will be implemented. For instance, knowing up front how many menus the MediaCenter program has, what items are in those menus, and what happens when a user selects a menu item, will be of benefit when the topic of menus is covered in Chapter 7, "Menus."

In this chapter you'll see the final version of the MediaCenter program. In the next chapter you'll learn how the MediaCenter.μ project is set up.

The Example Application

The MediaCenter program is a stand-alone multimedia Macintosh application that runs on either 68K-based or PowerPC-based Macintosh computers. MediaCenter serves as a text editor that can be used to create new text files or open existing ones. You can use MediaCenter to open a picture file and display the picture in its own window. Once displayed, a picture can be dragged about the window. You can also use the program for playing QuickTime movies. Figure 5-1 shows MediaCenter running with a file of each of these types open. MediaCenter can open any number and any combination of these three file types—the limiting factor is only the amount of free memory on the user's machine. Finally, MediaCenter can play sound files.

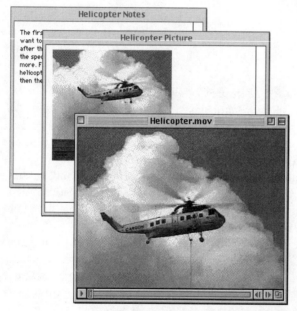

Figure 5-1: The MediaCenter program can work with a variety of file types.

Menus

MediaCenter displays six menus in its menu bar: Apple, File, Edit, Movie, Picture, and Sound. Apple programming conventions dictate that all Mac applications include an Apple, File, and Edit menu (see Figure 5-2). Figure 5-3 shows the remaining MediaCenter menus. The File and Edit menus support text; the three remaining menus (Movie, Picture, and Sound) support the other three media types that MediaCenter works with.

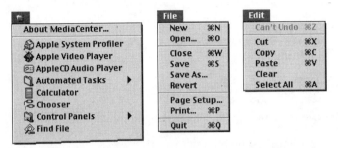

Figure 5-2: The Apple, File, and Edit menus as displayed in MediaCenter.

Figure 5-3: The Movie, Picture, and Sound menus of MediaCenter.

A brief summary of each MediaCenter menu follows. As you look over these descriptions, keep in mind that PowerPlant code will be responsible for the handling of most of the menu items in the Apple, File, and Edit menus. For you that represents a huge savings in programming effort, allowing you to focus on the implementation of the items in the remaining three menus.

Apple Menu

The Apple menu's first item displays an alert that provides information about the MediaCenter program. Following the gray line in this menu is a listing of all the items in the user's Apple Menu Items folder.

File Menu

With the exception of the Quit command, all of the File menu items pertain to text files. MediaCenter allows the user to open any number of text files. You can create a new, empty text file (by choosing New or typing Command-N) or open any existing text file (Open or Command-O).

You can, of course, close any open text file (Close or Command-W). An attempt to close an open text file that has been edited results in the alert shown in Figure 5-4. You can save the changes in an open, edited text file (Save or Command-S). If a new text file has been created and text added to it, you can name and save that file (Save As). Figure 5-5 shows the standard Save File dialog box that allows a text file to be named. If a saved text file is then edited, you can return the file's contents to the most recently saved version (Revert).

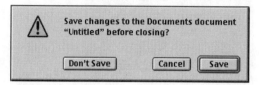

Figure 5-4: MediaCenter warns you if you try to close an edited window.

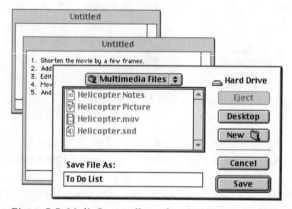

Figure 5-5: MediaCenter allows the text in a window to be saved to a text file.

MediaCenter supports the printing of text files. A Page Setup dialog box similar to the one shown in Figure 5-6 supplies page information such as paper size and print scaling. The actual printing of a text file (Print or Command-P) is done from a Print dialog box like the one shown in Figure 5-7. As with any Mac program, the exact look of both the Page Setup and Print dialog boxes are dependent on the model of printer used.

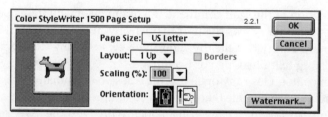

Figure 5-6: MediaCenter supports the standard Page Setup menu item and dialog box.

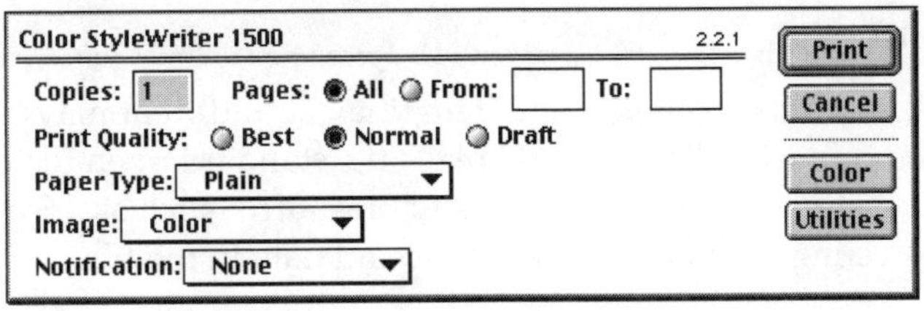

Figure 5-7: MediaCenter lets you print any text file via the standard Print dialog box.

Edit Menu

With a text file open, the Edit menu becomes enabled. You can manually select text or select it from the Edit menu (Select All). Once text is selected, it can be cut, copied, or cleared (Cut, Copy, Clear). Cut or copied text is placed on the clipboard, so you can paste it into any MediaCenter text window (Paste).

Movie Menu

The Movie menu allows you to open any QuickTime movie from the standard Open file dialog box (Open Movie). A movie is displayed in its own window, complete with a movie controller (refer to Figure 5-1). You can play an open movie using the controller or from the Movie menu (Play Movie).

Picture Menu

The Picture menu consists of a single menu item (Open Picture) that opens a picture file. The program displays the standard open file dialog box to allow you to select a file of type 'PICT.' The program then opens a new window larger than the picture and displays the picture within that window. Rather than simply "stamp" the picture into the window, MediaCenter treats the picture as an object. This means that any time the window is active, you can click on the picture and drag and drop it anywhere in the window.

TIP *Allowing the picture to be moved about in the window may not seem like a particularly useful feature in this program. Should you decide to enhance the MediaCenter program, however, you might be glad that this feature is already a part of the program. If you modify the program to allow a window to hold more than one picture, then the user could rearrange pictures—and even overlap them—to form a montage. Including this feature in MediaCenter does serve another, even more important purpose, however—it serves as a good example of the power of* panes, *which are self-contained drawing areas. Panes will be discussed in detail in Chapter 8, "Panes & Views."*

Sound Menu

The Sound menu holds a single menu item (Play Sound) that plays the sound stored in a sound file. MediaCenter displays the standard open file dialog box to allow you to select a file that holds a 'snd ' resource (such as a System 7 Sound file). Selecting such a file plays the sound data in the file.

Control Window

You control the features of MediaCenter from the previously discussed menus. You'll handle some of the most commonly used features, though, from a small control window that is always present, as shown in Figure 5-8.

Figure 5-8: MediaCenter includes a small control window with buttons that carry out several commands.

The control window, aptly titled Control, holds four picture buttons, each used to open a different type of file. From left-to-right in Figure 5-8 these buttons are: open a text file, open a QuickTime movie, open a picture file, and play a sound (playing a sound from a file being the closest analogy to opening a sound file).

MediaCenter & PowerPlant Programming

As the designer of an application, you have some freedom as to the interface your program will present to the user. I've set up MediaCenter in such a way that it's a combination of menus, windows, and buttons that demonstrate the many features that PowerPlant helps to implement. Those features, and the chapters in which those features are described and detailed, include:

■ **Commands**. The program's menu bar, six menus, and numerous menu items provide several examples of how PowerPlant makes it easy for a program to handle commands. A command is PowerPlant's term for the action that results from a menu item selection. Chapter 7, "Menus," covers the creation of the menu bar and menus and the handling of commands.

- ■ **Panes and Views**. The picture window's entire content area is a view. Within this view is a pane that displays a picture. In PowerPlant, a view and a pane are both types of drawing areas. Chapter 8, "Panes & Views," details both views and panes.

- ■ **Controls**. The picture buttons in MediaCenter's control window demonstrate controls. In PowerPlant, check boxes, radio buttons, picture buttons, and push buttons are all considered controls. You'll find controls discussed in Chapter 9, "Controls."

- ■ **Windows and Dialogs**. MediaCenter works with three types of windows: one to display text, one to display and play a QuickTime movie, and one to hold a movable picture. MediaCenter doesn't use any dialog boxes—but that's not a significant absence. In PowerPlant, there is almost no distinction between a window and a dialog box. Chapter 10, "Windows & Dialogs," covers the creation and display of windows and dialog boxes.

- ■ **File Input and Output.** MediaCenter receives data from several file types: text, movie, picture, and sound. It can also output some data by saving it to a new text file. File input and output is described in Chapter 12, "Files & Input/Output."

- ■ **Printing.** You can print any text or graphics file—whether created by MediaCenter or simply opened by MediaCenter—by choosing Print from the File menu. Chapter 13, "Printing," details exactly how printing is implemented—for both text and graphics files.

Moving On

The MediaCenter program is a Macintosh application designed to run on any Macintosh that has System 7.1 or later (including Mac OS 8) as its operating system. MediaCenter can open a variety of file types, including text, picture, movie, and sound.

After reading this chapter, you have a good idea of what MediaCenter looks like and how its interface works. What you've viewed here is the final version of this application. Before creating a project capable of building such an application, you need a much deeper understanding of PowerPlant. You'll start building that understanding in the next chapter by creating a *MediaCenter.µ* project that, when compiled, serves as little more than a text editor. Subsequent chapters take this project and add resources and code to it. Each chapter ends with a more sophisticated version of the *MediaCenter.µ* project, and thus a more advanced version of the MediaCenter program.

Developing an Application With CodeWarrior & PowerPlant

Setting Up the Project

Project setup is vitally important when working with PowerPlant. When
you first set up a PowerPlant-based project, you select a project stationery to
be the basis of the new project. This stationery determines what PowerPlant
source code and resources are added to your project; choosing the wrong
stationery can leave you with a lot of extra code to write, while choosing the
right stationery will save you untold hours of typing, compiling, debugging,
and general frustration.

Using MediaCenter as an example, we'll go over how to choose the proper
project stationery. We'll then discuss the files of application-defined code that
PowerPlant automatically adds to new projects based on stationery. We'll
examine the contents of the most important of these files and discuss what
they do and their value to you.

Finally, we'll return to the PowerPlant Constructor resource editor introduced in Chapter 4, "PowerPlant Basics." Constructor is useful in planning
out new projects; CodeWarrior recognizes this by adding Constructor resource
files to most new stationery-based projects. We'll cover what you need to
know about this powerful tool before jumping into the nitty-gritty of
PowerPlant programming.

Creating the New Project

As seen in Chapter 5, "introduction to the Example Project," the MediaCenter
program is document-centric—it's a program that makes extensive use of documents. In that respect MediaCenter is typical of most Macintosh programs.

You'll want to follow the steps taken in this section to set up a PowerPlant-based project to be used to develop your own document-centric application. Then you'll follow the techniques presented in the remainder of this book to add all the features unique to your new program.

▼ **Project Stationeries & Application Types**

Many Mac applications are document-based, but not all are. Some programs, especially single-purpose utilities, don't need to offer features common to document-centric applications (such as page setup and printing). A program that uses the console window rather than Mac windows (such as a simple port of a DOS program) is another example. Network-based applications, may also not need all of the features of a document-centric program.

CodeWarrior offers a range of project stationeries that correspond to different application types. When setting up a new project, you'll choose the stationery that most closely matches the type of program your project is to generate.

- A project that generates a document-centric application should be based on one of the Basic Toolbox stationeries (for a project that doesn't use PowerPlant) or one of the Doc PowerPlant stationeries.
- A project for an application that doesn't rely heavily on documents should be based on one of the Basic Toolbox stationeries (for a project that doesn't use PowerPlant) or one of the Doc PowerPlant stationeries.
- A project that will build a program that uses the console window should be based on one of the ANSI C Console or ANSI C++ Console stationeries (again, for a non-PowerPlant project) or one of the Basic PowerPlant_MSL stationeries (MSL, by the way, stands for Metrowerks Standard Libraries).
- A project for a network application should use one of the Basic Toolbox stationeries (non-PowerPlant) or one of the Network PowerPlant stationeries.

Selecting the Project Stationery

In Chapter 4, "PowerPlant Basics," you used the Basic PowerPlant FAT stationery to set up this book's first PowerPlant-based project. A second PowerPlant stationery is named Doc PowerPlant FAT. A project resulting from choosing this project stationery includes many of the same files found in a project that results from using the Basic PowerPlant FAT stationery. Such a project, however, also includes extra PowerPlant files that support handling many of the tasks common to document-centric applications.

To create the project, begin by choosing New Project from the File menu. Then double-click on the Doc PowerPlant FAT project stationery in the stationery list of the New Project dialog box. Finally, type the name of the project (*MediaCenter.μ*) in the standard save file dialog box and click on the Save button. The resulting project is shown in Figure 6-1.

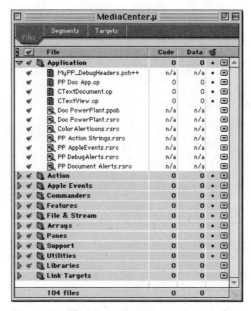

Figure 6-1: The MediaCenter.μ *project window.*

Building an Application

An application can be immediately built from any CodeWarrior project that's based on project stationery. It's a good idea to compile a new project's files and build an application after you've selected project stationery, named the project, and saved it. This will verify that all of the project files are present and that all of the Metrowerks-added code works.

Without adding any additional files or application-defined code, a new Doc PowerPlant FAT project generates an application that serves as a simple text editor. Figure 6-2 shows that the default program displays a window that's ready for text entry. The figure also shows that the File menu has most of its items enabled.

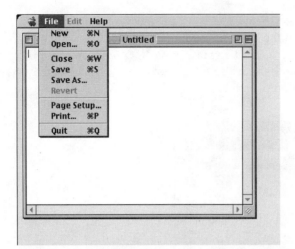

Figure 6-2: Running the application that's built from the default project.

It's to your benefit to run this chapter's version of the MediaCenter program—a copy of it can be found on the Companion CD-ROM in the Chapter 06 folder. Open several windows, move and resize them, type in some or all of them, and print one or two as well. As you do these things, keep in mind that this version of the application was created without my adding or editing a single line of code to the project that CodeWarrior created.

The Project Files

Figure 6-1 shows that the *MediaCenter.μ* project holds many of the same groups and files found in the *FirstPowerPlant.μ* project that was introduced in Chapter 4, "PowerPlant Basics" (refer back to Figure 4-4). Figure 6-1 also shows, however, that *MediaCenter.μ* contains extra, document-related files. The application-defined code that you write will reference the code and resources in these Metrowerks-supplied files. While you don't need to understand the details of all the code or all of the resources in these files, a brief examination of a few of the more important files will be helpful.

Doc PowerPlant.ppob

CodeWarrior adds a Constructor resource file named *Doc PowerPlant.ppob* to a project created from the Doc PowerPlant FAT project stationery. This file defines many of the same resources that appear in *PP Basic Resource.ppob*—the Constructor resource file that is a part of a project created from the Basic PowerPlant FAT stationery (compare Figure 6-3 to Figure 4-6 in Chapter 4).

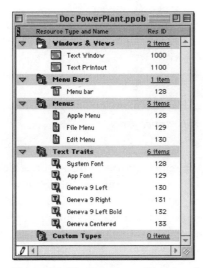

Figure 6-3: The Doc PowerPlant.ppob *file as viewed in Constructor.*

The *Doc PowerPlant.ppob* file also holds some resources not present in the *PP Basic Resource.ppob* file. The resource of most interest may be the one on which new text windows are based. In a PowerPlant-based project, you use Constructor to create a 'PPob' resource that holds a window's characteristics and contents. PowerPlant source code uses the information in the 'PPob' resource when your application opens a window. When a MediaCenter user chooses New from the File menu, a window based on 'PPob' resource 1000 is created and displayed. To see how this resource is set up, double-click on Text Window under the Windows & Views heading. A window opens like the one pictured in Figure 6-4. Here you see that this 'PPob' resource contains two panes, or drawing areas, that are numbered 1 and 2.

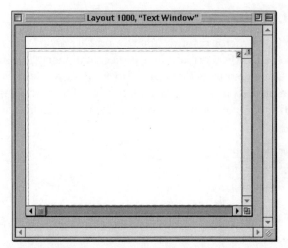

Figure 6-4: The Text Window 'PPob' resource holds two panes.

Double-clicking on pane 1 opens the pane's property inspector, which is shown in Figure 6-5. This pane is an object of the PowerPlant **LScroller** class, which is derived from the **LView** class, which itself is derived from the **LPane** class (Chapter 8, "Panes & Views," explores the topics of panes and views). The property inspector lists many scroller attributes that can be controlled from within Constructor.

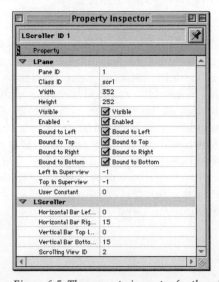

Figure 6-5: The property inspector for the window's scroller.

TIP *How a pane is added to a window is described in the "Working With Constructor" section that appears ahead. There is an example that includes the addition of a scroller pane.*

Double-clicking on pane 2 in the Text Window opens the property inspector for the second pane (Figure 6-6 shows part of it). This pane is an object of the PowerPlant **LTextEdit** class, which is derived from three classes, including the **LView** class (and thus the **LPane** class). The property inspector lists the attributes for an area that is to be used to hold editable text.

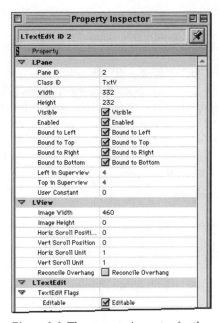

Figure 6-6: The property inspector for the window's text area.

When the MediaCenter program opens a new window that's based on the 'PPob' resource named Text Window, a new window object (of the **LWindow** class, or a class derived from it) will be created. That object in turn creates a scroller object (of the **LScroller** class) and an **LTextEdit** object. Setting up a window's scroll bar and text edit area in Constructor is all the work that is necessary to add scroll bars to a window and to make that window support text editing. The project's application-defined source code won't have to support the display or functioning of the bar or the handling of text editing.

CTextDocument.cp

Using Constructor to add an editable text area to a 'PPob' resource is almost all you need to do to set up a window that allows text entry and supports the Edit menu commands of Copy, Cut, Paste, Clear, and Select All. As you'll see in Chapter 7, "Menus," your source code must then include just a few lines of supporting code. First, you should declare a constant with the value of the window 'PPob' resource. Next, declare an **LWindow** pointer and create an **LWindow** object by calling the **LWindow** member function **CreateWindow()**. This **LWindow** object is a new window based on the 'PPob' resource. Here's how that code looks:

```
const ResIDT  textWindow  = 1000;

LWindow  *theWindow;

theWindow = LWindow::CreateWindow(textWindow, this);
```

If a program's text windows are also to support File menu items such as Save and Print, then extra programming effort becomes necessary. CodeWarrior assists you here by adding a couple of files to a project created from the Doc PowerPlant FAT stationery: *CTextDocument.cp* and *CTextView.cp*. Each of these files also has a header file associated with it. From the *CTextDocument.h* header file comes the declaration of the **CTextDocument** class:

```
class CTextDocument : public LSingleDoc {
public:
   CTextDocument( LCommander *inSuper, FSSpec *inFileSpec );

   virtual Boolean  IsModified();

   virtual void     DoAESave( FSSpec &inFileSpec, OSType inFileType );
   virtual void     DoSave();
   virtual void     DoRevert();
   virtual void     DoPrint();

protected:
   CTextView *      mTextView;

   void             NameNewDoc();
   void             OpenFile( FSSpec &inFileSpec );
   void             SetPrintFrameSize(void);
};
```

Your project can create a generic, empty window by creating an object of the PowerPlant **LWindow** class, or it can create a document window by creating an object of the PowerPlant **LDocument** class or its derived class **LSingleDoc**. None of these classes include member functions that automatically handle saving and printing (because how those tasks are handled varies with the type of content of each window). So it's more likely that your project will declare its own class— one derived from one of the existing PowerPlant window/document classes. That's what's being done in the *MediaCenter.µ* project. The **CTextDocument** class isn't a PowerPlant class—it's an application-defined class that's derived from the PowerPlant class **LSingleDoc**. CodeWarrior included this class in the *CTextDocument.h* and *CTextDocument.cp* files that it places in each new project that's based on the Doc PowerPlant FAT stationery. You could—and may very well—end up writing a similar class for one of your own PowerPlant-based projects. If you do, don't start from scratch. Copy the **CTextDocument** class declaration from *CTextDocument.h* and the implementation of its member functions from *CTextDocument.cp*.

CTextView.cp

Because the application-defined **CTextDocument** class is designed as the basis for text windows, it includes a data member that is a text view object (refer to the **CTextDocument** declaration that was just presented). The **CTextView** class is an application-defined class derived from the PowerPlant **LTextEdit** class. You'll find its declaration in the *CTextView.h* file and its member function implementations in the *CTextView.cp* file. Here's the class declaration:

```
class CTextView : public LTextEdit {
public:
    enum { class_ID = 'TxtV' };

    static CTextView *  CreateTextViewStream( LStream *inStream );
                        CTextView( LStream *inStream );

    virtual void        UserChangedText();

    virtual void        SavePlace( LStream *outPlace );
    virtual void        RestorePlace( LStream *inPlace );

    Boolean             IsDirty() const {
                            return mIsDirty;
                        };
```

```
    void               SetDirty( Boolean inDirty ) {
                          mIsDirty = inDirty;
                       };

protected:
   Boolean             mIsDirty;
};
```

PP Doc App.cp

In Chapter 4, "PowerPlant Basics," you saw that a project based on Basic PowerPlant FAT stationery includes a CodeWarrior-added file named *PP Basic Starter.cp*. That file holds the **main()** function, as well as definitions of the member functions of the class derived from **LApplication**. The *PP Doc App.cp* file is the Doc PowerPlant FAT stationery's analogy to this file. Its **main()** routine is almost identical to that defined in *PP Basic Starter.cp*. Most PowerPlant-based projects do have a **main()** function that differs little from this template:

```
void
main( void )
{
    SetDebugThrow_( debugAction_Alert );
    SetDebugSignal_( debugAction_Alert );

    InitializeHeap( 4 );

    UQDGlobals::InitializeToolbox( &qd );

    new LGrowZone( 20000 );

    CPPDocApp  theApp;
    theApp.Run();
}
```

For a Doc PowerPlant FAT project, CodeWarrior calls the **LApplication**-derived class **CPPDocApp**. Its declaration looks like this:

```
class CPPDocApp : public LDocApplication {
public:
            CPPDocApp();
    virtual  ~CPPDocApp();

protected:
    virtual void        StartUp();
    virtual void        OpenDocument( FSSpec *inMacFSSpec );
```

```
    virtual LModelObject *  MakeNewDocument();
    virtual void            ChooseDocument();
    virtual void            PrintDocument( FSSpec *inMacFSSpec );
};
```

Where a Basic PowerPlant FAT project includes code defining an application class that's derived from the PowerPlant **LApplication** class, a Doc PowerPlant FAT project includes code defining an application class that's derived from the PowerPlant **LDocApplication** class. The **LDocApplication** class is derived from **LApplication**, so it provides objects of this class with all the functionality of **LApplication** objects. Additionally, **LDocApplication** includes member functions that support documents, such as page setup and printing functions.

Working With Constructor

Almost all PowerPlant-based projects include a Constructor resource file. The MediaCenter project is no exception. You'll be working with Constructor in several chapters, so you need to understand its use before you delve into more advanced topics. Chapter 4, "PowerPlant Basics," provided an introduction to Constructor, but made no mention as to how panes and views are added to a window. Constructor not only simplifies the process of creating these interface elements, it aids in the understanding of the relationship between panes, views, and windows. A window maintains a hierarchy of views and panes; keeping track of that hierarchy is an important part of designing and developing an application.

When creating a new PowerPlant project, CodeWarrior always provides a starter Constructor file that holds several resources that are common to most applications. CodeWarrior knows just what it's doing, but you may not. Here I'll create a duplicate of one of those resources so that you can see how Constructor is typically used. I've chosen to create a window like the Text Window shown in Figures 6-3 through 6-6 for a couple of reasons. First, one of your primary uses of Constructor will be to design your application's windows. Second, by looking at a window in Constructor, you'll be able to see the class hierarchy within it.

Adding a New Resource

You'll add a new resource to an open Constructor file by first clicking on the appropriate resource heading in the main Constructor window. Then choose New resourceType Resource from the Edit menu. This is a context-sensitive menu item, so "resourceType" will be replaced by the type of resource being created.

Figure 6-7 shows a new window resource being added to a Constructor file. (I first opened the *Doc PowerPlant.ppob* file from the *MediaCenter.μ* project by double-clicking on its name in the *MediaCenter.μ* project window.) Constructor refers to a window or view as a Layout resource, so, as shown in Figure 6-7, that word appears in the Edit menu item.

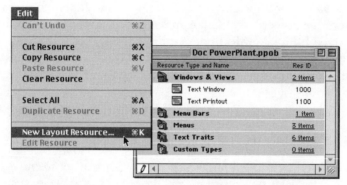

Figure 6-7: Adding a new resource to a Constructor resource file.

Choosing New Layout Resource results in the display of the Create New Resource dialog box pictured in Figure 6-8. Here you can provide a name and ID for the new resource. While a name may help in organizing resources, it is unimportant from a programming standpoint. The ID, however, is vital. As shown in the window-creation snippet earlier in this chapter, the ID is used in source code when a new window object is created.

Figure 6-8: Providing a name and ID for the new resource.

Editing the New Resource

To edit a resource, double-click on its name in Constructor's main window. As shown in Figure 6-9, what results is an empty window appearing on a desktop background.

Figure 6-9: Editing a resource begins when that resource is opened.

Add new panes to a window by first choosing Catalog from the Window menu. That results in the display of the Catalog window. By clicking on the various tabs that appear along the top of this window, you can see all of the many types of panes of which PowerPlant is aware. Figure 6-10 shows that the **LScroller** class is listed under the Views tab. To add a scroller to a window, click on **LScroller** in the Catalog window, drag it to the window to which you'll add the item, and release the mouse button—as is shown in Figure 6-10.

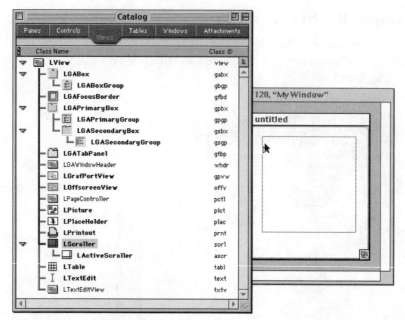

Figure 6-10: Dragging a new LScroller from the Catalog window to a Layout resource.

Releasing the mouse button places a new scroller in the window—as shown in Figure 6-11. To edit the scroller's properties, double-click on it to bring up the item's property inspector.

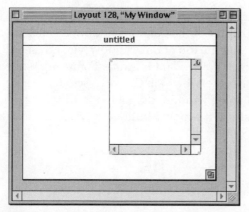

Figure 6-11: The window with the new LScroller added to it.

In Chapter 8, "Panes & Views," you'll learn more about the properties of a scroller, including how to adjust the size of a scroller to match that of the window in which it appears. Scroll bars don't have to frame a window, however—they can appear anywhere in a window. That makes sense if, for instance, a window is to display more than one large picture. Each picture could appear in its own scroll area, and the user could view different portions of the picture via the scroll bars. This topic is also covered in Chapter 8.

Adding a text area to a window is as easy as adding a scroller to it. A text area is also a pane, so the Catalog window is used again. The **LTextEdit** class appears listed under the Views tab, just a little below the **LScroller** class (refer back to Figure 6-10). Clicking on the **LTextEdit** class name and dragging to the window will add a new text area to the window. If the text area is to be surrounded by the scroller, it should be dropped within the scroller. That places it in the proper place in the window's view hierarchy—as discussed next.

The View Hierarchy

The entire content area of a window is a view—a drawing area that can have other drawing areas nested within it. If your program will use windows that display a variety of items, such as scroll bars, text areas, pictures, and controls, this hierarchy can become complex. Constructor provides an aid to your visualization of a window's view hierarchy. To get a graphical representation of a hierarchy, make a window active by clicking on it. (If the window isn't open, first double-click on its name under the Windows & Views heading in Constructor's main window.) Then choose Show Object Hierarchy from the Layout menu. A hierarchy window appears.

After adding the scroller to the new window, the view hierarchy looks like the one pictured in Figure 6-12. Note that **LScroller** appears indented under **LWindow**, implying that **LScroller** is in **LWindow** (the scroller is in the window). After adding the text area next, the view hierarchy looks like that shown in Figure 6-13. Here **LTextEdit** is indented under **LScroller**, signifying that **LTextEdit** appears within **LScroller** (and consequently, within **LWindow** as well).

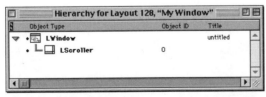

Figure 6-12: The view hierarchy for a window with one pane in it.

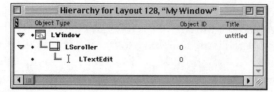

Figure 6-13: The view hierarchy for a window with two panes in it.

You'll encounter the view hierarchy throughout this book—especially in Chapter 8, where panes and views are discussed at length.

Moving On

When you create a new project, you base it on project stationery. The type of application you'll be developing determines which project stationery you'll use. Basic PowerPlant FAT and Doc PowerPlant FAT are two of the most common—but there are others from which to choose. This book's example program, MediaCenter, is built from a PowerPlant-based project that is created from Doc PowerPlant FAT stationery.

MediaCenter is a complete application, but it is ripe for expansion. If you're interested in multimedia programming (and as a Mac programmer you *must* be!), the Companion CD-ROM supplies you with a project that serves as an excellent foundation on which to base your own application. However, don't do that just yet. Read the remainder of this book so that you have a full grasp of how all the features of MediaCenter are implemented via PowerPlant code. Revealing the details of PowerPlant programming begins in the next chapter.

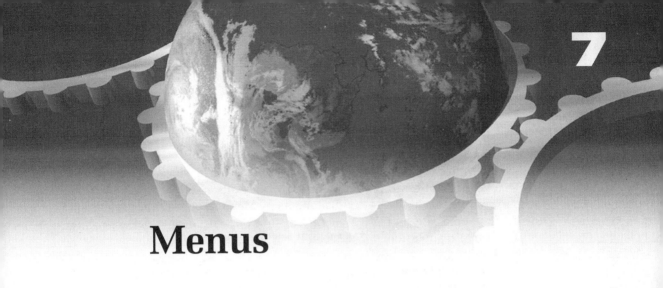

Menus

The effective handling of menus is one of PowerPlant's strongest features. In Chapter 5, "Introduction to the Example Project," you saw that the generic application that gets built from the Doc PowerPlant project stationery implements several important menu items, including the items found in the File and Edit menus of most Macintosh applications. PowerPlant code doesn't stop at the handling of standard menu items such as New, Open, Copy, Cut, and Paste, however. It includes a system that makes it relatively easy to integrate the handling of your own application-defined menu items with the core, or standard, menu items that have built-in support.

Constructor plays a pivotal role in adding menus to your application as well. While PowerPlant code helps with menu handling, Constructor takes care of the creation of the menu-related resources that make up those menus.

In this chapter, we'll add new menus and menu items to the MediaCenter project. First, we'll use Constructor to create the necessary resources. Then, we'll use PowerPlant to get the MediaCenter program to respond to the selection of these menu items.

Menus & Constructor

In Chapter 3, "Introduction to Application Frameworks," you read that PowerPlant-based CodeWarrior projects include standard Macintosh menu-related resources of type 'MBAR' and 'MENU,' as well as resources of the PowerPlant-specific 'Mcmd' type. Here we reveal the details of using Constructor to create and edit these resources.

Menu Bar & Menu Resources

In Constructor, an 'MBAR' resource is referred to as a Menu Bar, and a 'MENU' resource—in conjunction with an 'Mcmd' resource—is called a Menu. When a PowerPlant-based project is created, CodeWarrior supplies the project with a *.ppob* file that holds a Menu Bar and a few Menu resources. The Menus define the Apple, File, and Edit menus—the three standard menus that appear in all Macintosh applications. The Menu Bar is set up to hold these three menus.

In all cases, the PowerPlant-supplied Menu Bar will have an ID of 128, and the three menus will have IDs of 128, 129, and 130, respectively. Figure 7-1 shows that this is the case for the *Doc PowerPlant.ppob* resource file that's a part of the *MediaCenter.µ* project. At application startup, the PowerPlant code responsible for setting up your program's menu bar looks for resources with these particular IDs.

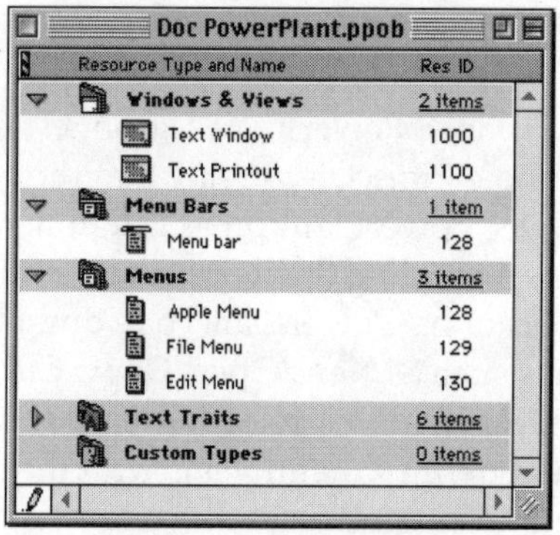

Figure 7-1: A PowerPlant-based project includes menu-related resources for the standard menus.

Menu Items & Command Constants

Projects that *don't* make use of PowerPlant implement menu handling by defining a constant for each 'MENU' resource ID, and a constant for each menu item in each menu. When a user makes a menu selection, the program's event loop then uses nested **switch** statements to first determine which menu was involved, and then to determine which item was selected. If menu items are repositioned under this system, either within the same menu or to a different menu, then changes must be made to the constant definitions in the source code, the source code must be recompiled, and the program rebuilt.

Projects that *do* make use of PowerPlant define one unique constant for each menu item. There is no need to define constants for the 'MENU' resources. A menu item constant in the source code must match a menu item command number that's associated with a menu item in a Menu in the project's Constructor resource file. Defining a source code constant for a menu item command number is a one-time task. As you enhance your program, you may end up rearranging menu items in your menu resources. Regardless of any such rearranging, your source code stays untouched. The responsibility of deciphering a constant to determine in which menu and wherein that menu an item is located is PowerPlant's—not yours.

Collectively, all of the command numbers for a single menu comprise one 'Mcmd' resource. Like 'MBAR' and 'MENU' resources, Constructor hides the details of 'Mcmd' resources from you. While you will work with command numbers, you won't encounter the 'Mcmd' resource type in Constructor. You simply deal with Menu Bars and Menus.

Command Numbers & Standard Menu Items

Command numbers for standard menu items that are defined for all Mac programs are displayed in Constructor as PowerPlant-defined constants. Figure 7-2 shows this for the Menu used to define the Edit menu.

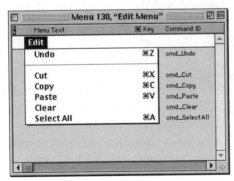

Figure 7-2: The command numbers for the items in the standard menus are represented as PowerPlant-defined constants.

Your source code won't have to define constants for menu items that have command numbers defined by PowerPlant constants.

For a standard menu item, the command number will already have been supplied, because the standard menus and all their items have been supplied by CodeWarrior. It is possible to change the command number of a standard menu item by clicking on the pop-up menu located in the Command Number field and then choosing a different command number constant from the pop-up menu that appears. Figure 7-3 shows this pop-up menu.

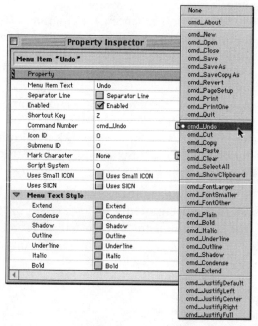

Figure 7-3: Constructor displays the PowerPlant-defined command number constants.

There's no reason to change the command number of a standard menu item. If you do, your application will have a menu item that won't act as expected when the user chooses it. However, you may want to use a PowerPlant-supplied constant for one of your own application-defined menu items. For instance, assigning a command number of **cmd_New** to a menu item means that a selection of that menu item results in the appearance of a new, empty text editor window. While this act is normally reserved for the New menu item in the File menu, there's nothing stopping you from including a New Text Window menu item in any one of your application-defined menus.

Command Numbers & Application-Defined Menu Items
When you create an application-defined menu item (an item defined specifically for your application, as opposed to a standard item such as New or Copy that PowerPlant automatically handles), you assign that item a command

number. Double-click on the menu item to display its property inspector window, click on the Command Number field, and type the number. Figure 7-4 shows a command number being entered for the Open Movie menu item in MediaCenter's Movie menu. Figure 7-5 shows the command numbers for each of the program's application-defined menu items.

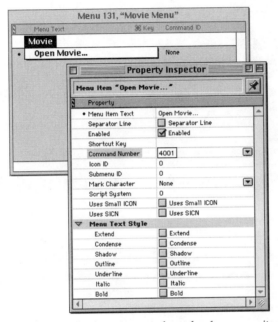

Figure 7-4: Entering a command number for a menu item.

To coordinate a menu item's command number defined in a resource with source code that is to reference the menu item, you must define a constant in the code. For instance, the MediaCenter program's three application-defined menus have a total of four menu items. Figure 7-5 shows that the four items have command numbers of 4001, 4002, 5001, and 2222. Here's the four constant definitions that will appear in the source code:

```
const  CommandT  cmd_OpenMovie    =  4001;
const  CommandT  cmd_PlayMovie    =  4002;
const  CommandT  cmd_OpenPicture  =  5001;
const  CommandT  cmd_PlaySound    =  2222;
```

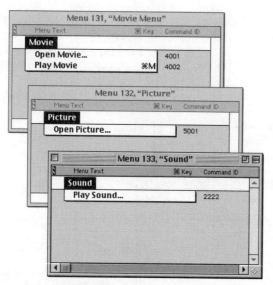

Figure 7-5: Each menu item has a command number (a command ID) associated with it.

Adding a New Menu Resource

The CodeWarrior-supplied Constructor resource file provides you with the Apple, File, and Edit menus—you provide application-specific menus. Do this from the Menu Bar resource so that this resource is aware of the newly added menus.

To add a new menu, begin by opening the resource file from Constructor. The *MediaCenter.µ* project uses the *Doc PowerPlant.ppob* file, so that's the file I open. Next, double-click on the menu bar listed under the Menu Bar heading in the main window of Constructor. The menu bar editor opens and displays the menu bar.

When a new menu is added, it's added to the right of the currently selected menu. Click on the name of the Edit menu to designate that the new menu become the rightmost menu. Then choose New Menu from the Edit menu of Constructor. As shown in Figure 7-6, a new untitled menu appears to the right of the Edit menu.

You can supply a name for the new menu by simply typing one or by opening the menu's property inspector and entering it in the Menu Title field. Double-click on the new menu's name (untitled) to open the menu's property inspector.

Constructor will have assigned the new menu an ID—that's shown in Figure 7-6. This number isn't of significance to you and can be left as is. After examining the various fields, close the menu property inspector and the menu bar editor.

Figure 7-6: The property inspector for a newly added menu.

Adding Menu Items & Command Numbers

You can add menu items to a menu from within the menu bar editor or by opening the menu with the menu editor. Here I'll use the menu editor. If the menu bar editor is open, close it now. Then double-click on the name of the new menu under the Menus heading in Constructor's main window. The new menu opens in its own menu editor window.

TIP *Looking under the Menus heading in Constructor's main window, you'll note that the name of the newly added menu appears. The name that appears here in the main window of Constructor is for your reference only—it doesn't have to match the name of the menu as it appears in the menu bar. To change the name, click on it in the main window and type in a new name (such as "Movie Menu").*

To add a menu item, choose New Menu Item from the Edit menu, and then type a name for the item. In Figure 7-7, I've given the menu item the name Open Movie. To see more information about the new item, double-click on it to open its property inspector. From the property inspector you can supply the item with a command number—just click on the Command Number field, and then type the number. Remember, PowerPlant reserves command numbers in the range of -999 to 999 for its own use, so use command numbers in the range of 1000 to 65535 for your application-defined items. In Figure 7-7, you see that I've arbitrarily given the Open Movie item a command number of 4001. Keep in mind that as long as the number falls within the range described above, the particular number you choose isn't important.

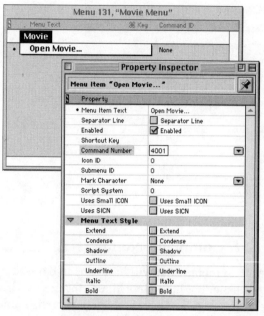

Figure 7-7: The property inspector for a newly added menu item.

Managing Menus With Source Code

While resources define menus, the source code handles the heavy lifting: managing the display of menus, highlighting selected menu items, and carrying out the correct action when an item is selected. PowerPlant code takes care of menu display and item highlighting, as well as actions for the predefined menu items.

So, what's left for you to do? Well, you have to implement the tasks your application-defined menu items are to perform and disable in appropriate menu items. To do this, you need to understand one vital concept: the chain of command, and two important functions: **ObeyCommand()** and **FindCommandStatus()**.

The Chain of Command

When a user of an application built from a PowerPlant-based project makes a menu selection, the handling of the menu selection (or *command*, in PowerPlant parlance) starts with application-defined code in the application object (the object created from the **LApplication**-derived class, such as the

CPPDocApp class in MediaCenter). The application object first checks to see if the selected menu item is one that the application handles (such as Open Movie in MediaCenter), or if it is one that PowerPlant code handles (such as Quit in MediaCenter). If the command is one that PowerPlant is responsible for, the command is passed on to PowerPlant code. This, in short, is the idea of chain of command—an important PowerPlant programming concept.

Commands & Targets

To handle a menu selection or command, the command must be directed at a *target*. The target is the object that the menu item is to act upon. For instance, if Cut is selected from the Edit menu, then whatever object holds the current selection is the target. If a picture is selected, the picture object is the target on which the Cut command is to act. If text is highlighted in an editable text area, then the text area object is instead the target for the Cut command.

When a PowerPlant-based program runs, it may have any number of objects in existence. An object that is capable of responding to commands (menu item selections) is referred to as a *commander*. When a command is issued (when a menu selection is made), only those objects that are commanders are eligible to handle the command. And of those commander objects, only one will in fact handle the command. How the program determines which object should respond to the command is based on a command hierarchy and the program's chain of command at the time the menu selection was made.

PowerPlant defines a ranking system, or *command hierarchy*, that specifies which types of objects are considered higher than other types. At the top of the chain is always the application object. Window objects lie below the application object, and window-content elements lie lower still. The commander object that gets first dibs at a command is always the target, or active, object. Unless the target is the application object, the target object has an object above it in the command hierarchy. The purpose of the command hierarchy is this: if the target object is unable to handle a command, it passes the command to the object that is next up in the command hierarchy. This command passing continues until an object that is able to handle the command is reached. This path through the command hierarchy is called the *chain of command*.

Chain of Command Example

As a simple example of the chain of command, consider a program that has two open windows. One window is empty; the other window consists of a picture embedded in a scroll area. Figure 7-8 shows how this program might look.

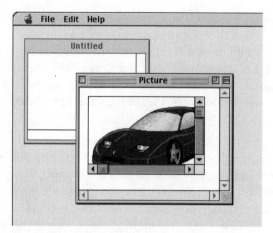

Figure 7-8: A program that displays two windows, one with a scrolling picture.

At the time the screen shot was taken for Figure 7-8, the program had five commander objects: the application, two windows, the scroll area, and the picture. Figure 7-9 provides a look at the command hierarchy for the program. Looking at Figure 7-8, you see that the window with the picture in it is active, so it is the left side of the command hierarchy in Figure 7-9 that is the current chain of command. If the user has clicked on the picture within the scroll area, then it is the picture that is active, and thus the picture object is the target. Any menu selection that is made at this point will send a command to the picture object. If the picture object isn't able to handle the command, then the command will be passed to the scroll object. If the scroll object can't handle the command, then the command rises to the window object. Finally, if the command doesn't apply to the window object, the command moves to the top of the chain—to the application object.

If the program supports basic edit operations on the picture in the scroll area, then a selection of Cut from the Edit menu serves as an example of a command that the picture object could handle. In this case the target is able to service the command, and the command would not be passed up the chain of command.

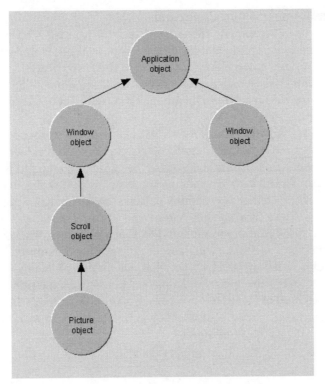

Figure 7-9: The command hierarchy for the application shown in Figure 7-8.

An example of a command that would make its way all the way up the chain of command would be Quit, from the File menu. Application-defined code that supports the display of the picture wouldn't include code to handle a Quit command—a picture doesn't "quit." Similarly, a scroll area doesn't quit, and neither does a window. The Quit command only makes sense when applied to the application—so this command would "bubble up" from the picture object target all the way to the application object. The PowerPlant **LApplication** class (from which the application class is derived) includes code to handle a Quit command, so the program would terminate properly.

MediaCenter & the Chain of Command

At this stage in its development, the launching of the MediaCenter program results in the opening of a single text editing window. So after starting up, MediaCenter consists of two objects: an object of the **LApplication**-derived class **CPPDocApp** class (which represents the application itself), and an object of the **LSingleDoc**-derived **CTextDocument** class (which represents a text-editing window).

You know that the window object will be the target—a newly opened window is always active (and with nothing else to make active, there's no way to inactivate the one text editing window!). The chain of command is shown on the left side of Figure 7-10. If a menu selection occurs, it will generate a command that is directed at the window object. If the command applies to the window (such as Close from the File menu), the window object will handle it. If the command doesn't apply to the window (such as New from the File menu), then the window object will pass it to the application object.

If the user closes the one window, the chain of command changes. Now, only one object exists—the application object. As shown on the right side of Figure 7-10, the chain of command now consists of nothing more than the application object. Any menu item selection generates a command directed at the new target—the application object.

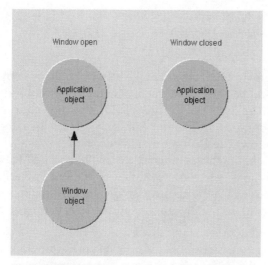

Figure 7-10: The chain of command for MediaCenter when a window is opened, then closed.

TIP

What if a menu item doesn't apply to any object? In that case, such a menu item should be disabled. PowerPlant takes care of this for the standard menus. For instance, if no text edit windows are open, then the Close item in the File menu will be dim. If a text edit window is open, but no text is selected, then the Copy item in the Edit menu will be dim. Your application-defined source code is responsible for disabling application-defined menus when appropriate. You'll see an example of this later in this book when the Open Movie and Play Movie items in the Movie menu are implemented. Then, when no QuickTime movie is open and active, the Play Movie item will be disabled.

Commander Objects & the LCommander Class

You've worked with the application object and window objects, so you're familiar with the **LApplication** and **LWindow** classes. Here are partial declarations for those two classes:

```
class    LApplication : public   LCommander,
                        public   LEventDispatcher,
                        public   LModelObject {
...
}

class    LWindow      : public   LView,
                        public   LCommander,
                        public   LModelObject {
...
}
```

As you can see from the above declarations, PowerPlant relies on multiple inheritance—a PowerPlant class can be derived from more than one class. Note that among the classes **LApplication** and **LWindow** are derived from is the **LCommander** class. An object capable of handling a command is called a commander. Commander objects are all derived from the PowerPlant **LCommander** class. The member functions of this class are important because they are responsible for keeping track of the chain of command and for directing commands to the correct object in the chain.

If you peruse the class declarations in the PowerPlant header files, you'll find that many of the classes are derived from **LCommander**. An instance of each such class can thus be a commander—a target object.

ObeyCommand()

Chapter 3, "Introduction to Application Frameworks," introduced
ObeyCommand()—a member function that appears in both the **LApplication**
class and the **LWindow** class. **ObeyCommand()** is also defined in other
PowerPlant classes, including the just-introduced **LCommander** class. You've
read that a target commander object will attempt to handle a command. If it
can't, it passes the command up the chain of command. The **ObeyCommand()**
function is the mechanism for the handling and passing of a command.

A PowerPlant class that includes an **ObeyCommand()** function will know
how to handle some, but not all, commands. Consider the **LWindow** version
of **ObeyCommand()**:

```
Boolean
LWindow::ObeyCommand(
    CommandT  inCommand,
    void      *ioParam)
{
    Boolean  cmdHandled = true;

    switch (inCommand) {

        case cmd_Close:
            AttemptClose();
            break;

        default:
            cmdHandled = LCommander::ObeyCommand(inCommand, ioParam);
            break;
    }

    return cmdHandled;
}
```

When a menu selection affects a window that is an **LWindow** object, that
object's **ObeyCommand()** routine automatically executes. Looking at the above
snippet, you should be able to deduce that an **LWindow** object knows how to
close itself. If the menu selection was Close from the File menu, a **cmd_Close**
command is generated and sent to the active window object's **ObeyCommand()**
routine. There the **LWindow** member function **AttemptClose()** is invoked to
close the window.

The **cmd_Close** command is the only command an **LWindow** object understands. Any other command that reaches an **LWindow** object will be sent up the chain of command. The specifics of what lies above the window in the chain of command are left to the **LCommander** class. If the **LWindow** version of **ObeyCommand()** doesn't understand a command, it invokes the **LCommander** version of this **ObeyCommand()**—which you can see under the **default** label in the above snippet.

ObeyCommand() & Command Passing

Every PowerPlant class that is derived from the **LCommander** class overrides **ObeyCommand()**. It implements its own version of the function, and that version includes a default section that invokes the **LCommander** **ObeyCommand()**—as you saw above in the **LWindow** version of this routine. Your application-defined class that is derived from **LCommander** (or from a class that itself is derived from **LCommander**) will do the same. You've already encountered such a scenario in Chapter 3, "Introduction to Application Frameworks".

The Chapter 3 example was a project that resulted from using Basic PowerPlant stationery. It included a **CPPStarterApp** class that was derived from the **LApplication** class. From the above discussion you would expect both the PowerPlant-defined **LApplication** class (which is derived from **LCommander**) and the application-defined **CPPStarterApp** class (which is derived from **LApplication**) to declare and define **ObeyCommand()**. That is indeed the case.

The **CPPStarterApp** version of **ObeyCommand()** handles a **cmd_New** command by opening a new window. That's the only command an object of this class handles, so any other command is passed on to the **LApplication** version of **ObeyCommand()**:

```
Boolean
CPPStarterApp::ObeyCommand(
    CommandT    inCommand,
    void        *ioParam)
{
    Boolean    cmdHandled = true;

    switch (inCommand) {

        case cmd_New:
            LWindow    *theWindow;
            theWindow = LWindow::CreateWindow(window_Sample, this);
            theWindow->Show();
            break;
```

```
        default:
            cmdHandled = LApplication::ObeyCommand(inCommand, ioParam);
            break;
    }

    return cmdHandled;
}
```

One of the primary purposes of the **LApplication** version of **ObeyCommand()** is to handle a synthetic command—a command that originates from a menu that is built at runtime. The contents of the Apple menu provide the most obvious example of such commands. With the exception of the About menu item, Apple menu items aren't listed in a resource. Instead, they're determined and inserted in the menu when a program launches. This implementation is necessary because the contents of this menu vary from machine to machine—they're dependent on the contents of the user's Apple Menu Items folder in the System Folder.

After checking for a synthetic menu command, the **LApplication** version of **ObeyCommand()** checks to see if the command is either **cmd_About** or **cmd_Quit**. If the command wasn't a selection of About from the Apple menu or Quit from the File menu, the command is passed to the **LCommander** version of **ObeyCommand()**:

```
Boolean
LApplication::ObeyCommand(
    CommandT   inCommand,
    void       *ioParam)
{
    Boolean  cmdHandled = true;

    ResIDT  theMenuID;
    Int16   theMenuItem;
    if (IsSyntheticCommand(inCommand, theMenuID,
                        theMenuItem)) {

        if (theMenuID == MENU_Apple) {
            Str255   appleItem;
            ::GetMenuItemText(GetMenuHandle(theMenuID),
                            theMenuItem, appleItem);
            ::OpenDeskAcc(appleItem);

        } else {
            cmdHandled = LCommander::ObeyCommand(inCommand, ioParam);
        }
```

```
    } else {

      switch (inCommand) {

        case cmd_About:
          ShowAboutBox();
          break;

        case cmd_Quit:
          SendAEQuit();
          break;

        default:
          cmdHandled = LCommander::ObeyCommand (inCommand, ioParam);
          break;
      }
    }

  return cmdHandled;
}
```

When **ObeyCommand()** of a PowerPlant class can't handle a command, it passes the command to **LCommander**. You saw this for the **LWindow** and **LApplication** versions of **ObeyCommand()**. When **ObeyCommand()** of an application-defined class that's derived from a PowerPlant class can't handle a command, it passes the command to the base class. You saw this when the **CPPStarterApp** class **ObeyCommand()** invoked the **LApplication** class version of this routine.

ObeyCommand() & the CPPDocApp Class

The **CPPDocApp** class that is declared in the *PP Doc App.h* file that CodeWarrior includes in a project based on Doc PowerPlant project stationery doesn't declare an **ObeyCommand()** member function. Instead, that class relies on the **LDocApplication** base class version that it inherits:

```
Boolean
LDocApplication::ObeyCommand(
  CommandT   inCommand,
  void       *ioParam)
{
  Boolean  cmdHandled = true;

  switch (inCommand) {
```

```
case cmd_New:
   SendAECreateDocument();

case cmd_Open:
   ChooseDocument();
   break;

case cmd_PageSetup:
   SetupPage();
   break;

default:
   cmdHandled = LApplication::ObeyCommand(inCommand, ioParam);
   break;
}
```

When you run MediaCenter, you see that the approach of using the inherited version of **ObeyCommand()** works fine for a program that only makes use of the standard Apple, File, and Edit menus. The **LDocApplication ObeyCommand()** handles New, Open, and Page Setup selections from the File menu, and invokes its **LApplication** base class version of **ObeyCommand()** to take care of other menu items. MediaCenter is destined to do much more than the generic Doc PowerPlant application, so its **CPPDocApp** class needs to override **ObeyCommand()**. I'll do that next.

Declaring ObeyCommand() in a Class
Adding **ObeyCommand()** to the **CPPDocApp** class begins with the declaration of **ObeyCommand()** in the **CPPDocApp** declaration:

```
class CPPDocApp : public LDocApplication {
public:
                        CPPDocApp();
   virtual              ~CPPDocApp();

   // Override LDocApplication version of ObeyCommand() by
   // declaring it here in the header file and then
   // implementing it in the source code file
   virtual Boolean      ObeyCommand(CommandT inCommand,
                                    void* ioParam);
```

```
protected:
    virtual void            StartUp();
    virtual void            OpenDocument(
                                    FSSpec *inMacFSSpec );
    virtual LModelObject *  MakeNewDocument();
    virtual void            ChooseDocument();
    virtual void            PrintDocument(
                                    FSSpec *inMacFSSpec );
};
```

The P01 MediaCenter folder in the Chapter 07 folder on the Companion CD-ROM holds the version of the MediaCenter project that includes **ObeyCommand()** as a member function of the **CPPDocApp** class.

The prototype for **ObeyCommand()** is always the same. The function is declared **virtual** so that it can be overridden by other classes. The return type is **Boolean** so that the routine can let the caller know whether or not it handled the command that was passed. The first **ObeyCommand()** parameter holds the menu command to be handled. The second is a pointer to additional command-specific information. In many cases additional information isn't needed, and **ObeyCommand** ignores this parameter.

Implementing ObeyCommand()

After declaring **ObeyCommand()** in the class declaration, a definition of the function needs to be written. The implementation always follows the same format, so you'd be wise to copy an existing version of the function and start with that. The following snippet is from the **CPPStarterApp** class that is a part of the Chapter 3 example—the project created from Basic PowerPlant project stationery.

```
Boolean
CPPStarterApp::ObeyCommand(
    CommandT   inCommand,
    void       *ioParam)
{
    Boolean   cmdHandled = true;

    switch (inCommand) {

        case cmd_New:
            LWindow  *theWindow;
            theWindow = LWindow::CreateWindow(window_Sample, this);
            theWindow->Show();
            break;
```

```
        default:
            cmdHandled = LApplication::ObeyCommand(inCommand, ioParam);
            break;
    }

    return cmdHandled;
}
```

I'll begin the editing of the routine by changing the class name from **CPPStarterApp** to **CPPDocApp**. The return type and parameters can be left as is:

```
Boolean
CPPDocApp::ObeyCommand(
    CommandT  inCommand,
    void      *ioParam)
```

Within **ObeyCommand()**, the local variable **cmdHandled** specifies whether or not the command has been handled—its code can be left unchanged. What does need to be edited is the code within the **switch** statement.

The **switch** statement is used to compare the selected menu item (stored in parameter **inCommand**) to the **case** constants. MediaCenter doesn't need to handle the New item from the File menu (the **LDocApplication ObeyCommand()** takes care of that), so I'll cut that code. Commands that aren't handled in this routine should be passed to the base class, which for **CPPDocApp** is the **LDocApplication**. So I'll change **LApplication** to **LDocApplication** under the **default** label to reflect this:

```
switch (inCommand) {

    default:
        cmdHandled = LDocApplication::ObeyCommand( inCommand, ioParam);
        break;
}
```

The **switch** statement needs to include a **case** section for each application-defined menu item. In the "Menus and Constructor" section of this chapter, I used Constructor to add the Movie menu and Open Movie menu item in the *Doc PowerPlant.ppob* resource file. MediaCenter will eventually have more application-defined menu items, but for now this is the only one. Before adding code to the **switch**, I'll define an appropriately named constant that serves to hold the command number of the Open Movie menu item. I gave this menu item a command number 4001, so the constant definition that I place after the **#include** directives and before **main()** in *PP Doc App.cp* looks like this:

```
const  CommandT  cmd_OpenMovie  =  4001;
```

From Chapter 3 you know that **CommandT** is a PowerPlant-defined synonym for the **Int32** data type, and that **Int32** itself is a PowerPlant-defined data type that is the size of the C data type **long**. From this same chapter you'll also recall that an application-defined constant should start with a lowercase character. The second word in the constant name should begin with an upper-case letter and be preceded by an underscore.

Now, back to the **switch** statement in **ObeyCommand()**. To complete the changes to this routine, I'll use **cmd_OpenMovie** as a **case** label and add the code that takes care of an Open Movie menu item selection:

```
case cmd_OpenMovie:
   ::SysBeep(1);
   break;
```

I've opted to handle an Open Movie selection by doing nothing more than playing the system sound on the user's Macintosh. That's hardly what I'm after—but it will do for now. I can test my resource additions and changes to the **CPPDocApp** class by building a new version of MediaCenter, running it, and choosing Open Movie from the Movie menu. If my Mac's speakers emit the system sound, I know my changes up to this point have worked.

The next snippet shows how **ObeyCommand()** looks after all the changes. You'll find this function in the *PP Doc App.cp* file in the P01 MediaCenter folder in the Chapter 07 folder on the Companion CD-ROM.

```
Boolean
CPPDocApp::ObeyCommand(
   CommandT   inCommand,
   void       *ioParam)
{
   Boolean   cmdHandled = true;

   switch (inCommand) {

      case cmd_OpenMovie:
         ::SysBeep(1);
         break;

      default:
         cmdHandled = LDocApplication::ObeyCommand( inCommand, ioParam);
         break;
   }
   return cmdHandled;
}
```

Testing the New Code

As mentioned, I can test MediaCenter by building a new version of the application and trying out Open Movie from the Movie menu. When I do this, however, I find that my testing efforts are stymied by the fact that the Movie menu is disabled. Why that's the case, and how this problem can be remedied, are covered in the next section.

FindCommandStatus()

As a Mac program runs, menu items often change state—the changing conditions in the program affect the status of certain menu items. For instance, if no windows are open, some of the items in the File and Edit menus should be disabled (such as Close in the File menu). Keeping track of which menu items should be enabled or disabled, and when, can be a complicated affair. PowerPlant helps in this respect by doing much of the menu item state tracking for you. To take advantage of this PowerPlant feature, you need to implement a **FindCommandStatus()** member function in your project's application class.

Just as **ObeyCommand()** is found in several PowerPlant classes, so to is **FindCommandStatus()**. If a class can handle menu selections, then it should include a version of **FindCommandStatus()** to ensure that the application properly updates menus and menu items. This chapter's discussion of **ObeyCommand()** led off with a look at the **LWindow** version of that routine. Here let's look at the **LWindow** version of **FindCommandStatus()**:

```
void
LWindow::FindCommandStatus(
    CommandT  inCommand,
    Boolean   &outEnabled,
    Boolean   &outUsesMark,
    Char16    &outMark,
    Str255    outName)
{
    switch (inCommand) {

        case cmd_Close:
            outEnabled = HasAttribute(windAttr_CloseBox);
            break;
```

```
      default:
        LCommander::FindCommandStatus(inCommand,
                        outEnabled, outUsesMark,
                        outMark, outName);
        break;
  }
}
```

In response to an event, PowerPlant code checks an application's menus and menu items to see if any updating is necessary. The code that determines whether a particular menu or menu item needs updating is found in a **FindCommandStatus()** routine. In the above snippet you see that the **LWindow** version of **FindCommandStatus()** holds information about the Close item in the File menu. The parameter **outEnabled** is a Boolean that gets assigned a value of true if the Close item is to be enabled and false if it is to be disabled. Because **outEnabled** enters **FindCommandStatus()** as a pointer, it's value is returned to the caller (a PowerPlant routine) that will perform the actual update of the item. In this instance **outEnabled** is assigned a value based on the value returned by the **LWindow** member function **HasAttribute()**. The details of **HasAttribute()** aren't important—suffice it to say that it is used to check on window-related attributes, such as whether any windows are currently open.

A class is only responsible for updating menu items that are handled by the class. Only commands that are handled by a class are the responsibility of the class. The **cmd_Close** command is the only command an **LWindow** object handles (you can refer back to the listing of **ObeyCommand()** for **LWindow** to see that this is the case), so it is the only command that needs to appear in **FindCommandStatus()**. Unhandled menu updates are passed from **LWindow** to **LCommander**—just as unhandled commands are.

Declaring FindCommandStatus() in a Class

The **CPPDocApp** class declared in the generic Doc PowerPlant project doesn't include a **FindCommandStatus()** member function—it relies on the **LDocApplication** version of **FindCommandStatus()** to take care of its menus. Once application-defined menus are added to the project, though, a version of **FindCommandStatus()** needs to be added. This is necessary both to initially enable newly added menus as well as to keep menu items in these menus properly updated.

Adding **FindCommandStatus()** to the **CPPDocApp** class begins with the declaration of the routine in the **CPPDocApp** declaration. Note that this latest version of **CPPDocApp** now includes both **ObeyCommand()** and **FindCommandStatus()**:

```
class CPPDocApp : public LDocApplication {
public:
                        CPPDocApp();
    virtual             ~CPPDocApp();

    virtual Boolean     ObeyCommand(CommandT inCommand,
                                    void* ioParam);


    // Override LDocApplication version of
    // FindCommandStatus() by declaring it here
    // in the header file and then implementing
    // it in the source code file
    virtual void        FindCommandStatus(
                            CommandT inCommand,
                            Boolean  &outEnabled,
                            Boolean  &outUsesMark,
                            Char16   &outMark,
                            Str255   outName);


protected:
    virtual void          StartUp();
    virtual void          OpenDocument( FSSpec *inMacFSSpec );
    virtual LModelObject * MakeNewDocument();
    virtual void          ChooseDocument();
    virtual void          PrintDocument( FSSpec *inMacFSSpec );
};
```

TIP

*The P02 MediaCenter folder in the Chapter 07 folder on the Companion CD-ROM holds the version of the MediaCenter project that includes both **ObeyCommand()** and **FindCommandStatus()** as member functions of the **CPPDocApp** class.*

The prototype for **FindCommandStatus()** is declared to be virtual, consists of no return value, and has five parameters. The **inCommand** parameter holds the current command. When the routine has executed, **outEnabled** will hold a **Boolean** value that tells the caller whether the menu item should be enabled

or disabled. The **outUsesMark** and **outMark** parameters tell the caller
whether the menu item should have a mark (such as a checkmark) placed
beside it, and if so, what the mark should be. The last parameter, **outName**,
tells the caller what the menu item name should be—if the item name hasn't
changed, then this parameter isn't important.

Implementing FindCommandStatus()

As I did for **ObeyCommand()**, I start out a new version of
FindCommandStatus() by copying an existing version. The following snippet
is from the **CPPStarterApp** class found in the Chapter 3 example:

```
void
CPPStarterApp::FindCommandStatus(
    CommandT    inCommand,
    Boolean     &outEnabled,
    Boolean     &outUsesMark,
    Char16      &outMark,
    Str255      outName)
{

    switch (inCommand) {

        case cmd_New:
            outEnabled = true;
            break;

        default:
            LApplication::FindCommandStatus(inCommand,
                                    outEnabled, outUsesMark,
                                    outMark, outName);

            break;
    }
}
```

I'll begin altering the routine by changing the class name from **CPPStarterApp**
to **CPPDocApp**. The return type of void and all the parameters remain:

```
void
CPPDocApp::FindCommandStatus(
    CommandT    inCommand,
    Boolean     &outEnabled,
    Boolean     &outUsesMark,
    Char16      &outMark,
    Str255      outName)
```

The switch statement is used to compare the selected menu item to the case labels. As in **ObeyCommand()**, the **cmd_New** code can be removed—the **LDocApplication** version of **FindCommandStatus()** takes care of updating the New item in the File menu. And again like **ObeyCommand()**, unhandled commands are passed on to the **LDocApplication** version of **FindCommandStatus()**—so I'll change the default code to make this happen:

```
switch (inCommand) {

    default:
        LDocApplication::FindCommandStatus(inCommand,
                                  outEnabled, outUsesMark,
                                  outMark, outName);
        break;
}
```

At this point MediaCenter has only one application-defined menu item—the Open Movie item in the Movie menu. I'll finish the changes to the routine by adding a **case** section that updates this menu item:

```
case cmd_OpenMovie:
    outEnabled = true;
    break;
```

By setting **outEnabled** to true I'm writing the **CPPDocApp** version of **FindCommandStatus()** such that it always enables the Open Movie menu item. For some menu items you'll want to include logic that enables the item under one condition and disables it under another. The following code fragment provides a clue as to how the Open Movie menu item could be enabled and disabled depending on how many QuickTime movies are already open.

```
case cmd_OpenMovie:
    // add check here to see if maximum number of movie
    // windows are now open
    // if maximum open, disable Open Movie item:
    outEnabled = false;
    // else enable Open Movie item:
    outEnabled = true;
    break;
```

The next snippet shows how **FindCommandStatus()** looks after editing. You'll find this routine in the PP Doc App.cp file in the P02 MediaCenter folder, in the Chapter 07 folder on the Companion CD-ROM:

```
void
CPPDocApp::FindCommandStatus(
    CommandT    inCommand,
    Boolean     &outEnabled,
```

```
   Boolean      &outUsesMark,
   Char16       &outMark,
   Str255       outName)
{

   switch (inCommand) {

      case cmd_OpenMovie:
         outEnabled = true;
         break;

      default:
         LDocApplication::FindCommandStatus(inCommand,
                              outEnabled, outUsesMark,
                              outMark, outName);

         break;
   }
}
```

Testing the New Code

With both **ObeyCommand()** and **FindCommandStatus()** as a part of the
CPPDocApp class, MediaCenter now supports the Open Movie menu item in
the Movie menu. You'll be able to verify this after building an application from
the project in the P02 MediaCenter folder.

Menus & the Example Project

Knowing how Constructor is used to create and edit menu-related resources
and how PowerPlant displays menus and handles menu selections via the
FindCommandStatus() and **ObeyCommand()** functions is enough to implement all of the menus that MediaCenter will use. By the close of this chapter,
the *MediaCenter.µ* project will have advanced to a stage where it will generate a
program that has six enabled menus. The proper implementation of each item,
such as having the Open Movie item display a standard open file dialog box
that is used to actually open and display a QuickTime movie, is reserved for
later chapters.

The P03 folder in the Chapter 07 folder on the Companion CD-ROM holds
this chapter's final version of MediaCenter—the version that is developed on
the following pages.

Project Resources

Only one of the CodeWarrior-supplied resources needs to be changed—the 'DITL' resource that defines the text that appears in the About box when the user chooses About from the File menu. All of the rest of the resource editing involves creating new menus and menu items.

Editing the About 'DITL'

The About menu item in the Apple menu is automatically handled by PowerPlant code. In response to a user choosing this item, PowerPlant posts an alert. This alert is defined by an 'ALRT' resource with an ID of 128 and a 'DITL' resource with an ID of 128. You'll find both resources in the *Doc PowerPlant.rsrc* file that CodeWarrior included in the default Document PowerPlant project.

Besides an OK button, the CodeWarrior-supplied 'DITL' includes a static text item with the words "PowerPlant Starter App for Documents." You should edit this text to reflect the name of your program. You can also add other text items and pictures to the 'DITL' if desired. In Figure 7-11 you see that I've simply edited the one text item.

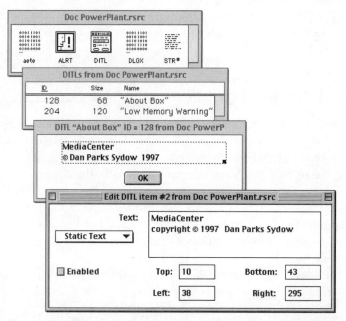

Figure 7-11: Changing the text that gets displayed in the About alert.

After editing the 'DITL' resource, save and close the *Doc PowerPlant.rsrc* file. You can test your changes by rebuilding the *MediaCenter.μ* project, running the resulting application, and choosing About from the Apple menu.

Editing the Apple Menu

By default, a program created from a PowerPlant-based project displays the words "About This App..." as the first menu item in the Apple menu. You'll want to change the text of this menu item to something more specific to the application being created.

All of the *MediaCenter.μ* project's menu resources are in the *Doc PowerPlant.ppob* file. If you don't have that file open at this time, double-click on the file name in the *MediaCenter.μ* project window to launch Constructor and open this file.

Double-click on the Apple menu under the Menus heading in the main window of Constructor to open the menu editor. Click on the first menu item and highlight its text. In place of "About This App..." type "About MediaCenter...". Then close the menu editor window by clicking on its close box.

Adding Menus to the Menu Bar

In this chapter's "Adding a New Menu Resource" section, you added a new menu named Movie to the menu bar resource. Here you add the remaining two menus that MediaCenter requires. To begin, double-click on the menu bar that's listed under the Menu Bar heading in the main window of Constructor. That displays the menu bar in Constructor's menu bar editor. Now follow these steps for each menu to be added:

1. Click on the name of the menu on the far-right of the menu bar.

2. Choose New Menu from the Edit menu to add a new, untitled menu to the menu bar.

3. Type the appropriate name for the new menu.

Figure 7-12 shows the menu bar resource after the Picture and Sound menus have been added. You can click on any menu to see the items that are currently defined for that menu.

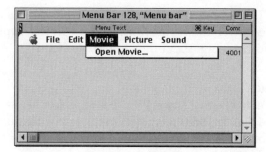

Figure 7-12: The MediaCenter menu bar with three application-defined menus.

Completing the Movie Menu

In this chapter's "Adding Menu Items and Command Numbers" section, you added the Open Movie item to the Movie menu and then gave it a command number of 4001. Repeat that process here to add the second and final item and constant to the Movie menu:

1. Double-click on the name of the Movie menu under the Menus heading in the main constructor window to open the menu in the menu editor.

2. Choose New Menu Item from the Edit menu.

3. Type "Play Movie" as the name of the new menu item.

4. Double-click on the new menu item to open its property inspector.

5. Click on the Command Number field and type a command number.

Figure 7-13 shows that I chose 4002 as the command number of the Play Movie item. Any number in the range of 1000 to 65535 would suffice, provided the number is unique from any other command number I've assigned to an application-defined menu item. At this point MediaCenter only has one other such menu item—the Open Movie item in this same menu. So the only number in the valid range that shouldn't be used is 4001.

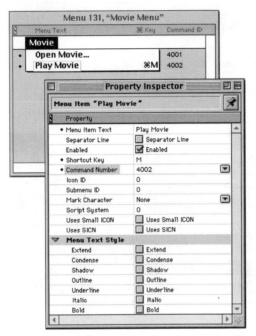

Figure 7-13: Assigning a command number to the Play Movie menu item.

Completing the Picture Menu

The Picture menu exits, but it doesn't have the Open Picture item in it. Add that item now, following the steps presented in the "Completing the Movie Menu" section that you just read. I've given this menu item a command number of 5001. You'll want to do the same if you want your project to match mine.

Completing the Sound Menu

Finish the Sound menu by adding its one menu item—the Play Sound item. Open the Sound menu, choose New Menu Item from the Edit menu, and type the menu item name. Then double-click on the new menu item to open its property inspector. Enter a command number for the item. Just to demonstrate that you don't need to implement any particular numbering scheme for menu items, I gave the Play Sound item a randomly selected command number of 2222.

At this point the editing of the menu resources are complete. Figure 7-14 shows the three menus that have been added to the *Doc PowerPlant.ppob* file. Any remaining work that needs to be done in this chapter will involve source code—so you can close the *Doc PowerPlant.ppob* file and quit Constructor.

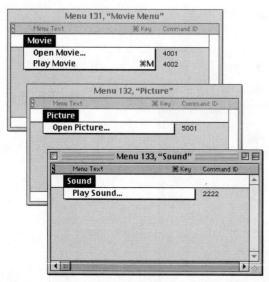

Figure 7-14: The three application-defined menus, as shown in Constructor.

Project Source Code

Adding new menus and menu items is the first of two menu-related tasks. Now the project's source code has to be modified so that the new menus are displayed and handled appropriately.

Adding Command Number Constants

Each application-defined menu item has a command number. Those command numbers now need to be defined in the source code. Earlier you saw how I did that for the Open Movie menu item—an item that I assigned a command number of 4001:

```
const  CommandT  cmd_OpenMovie   =  4001;
```

The MediaCenter project now has four application-defined menu items. Here are the four constant definitions that need to be added near the top of the *PP Doc App.cp* file:

```
const  CommandT  cmd_OpenMovie    =  4001;
const  CommandT  cmd_PlayMovie    =  4002;
const  CommandT  cmd_OpenPicture  =  5001;
const  CommandT  cmd_PlaySound    =  2222;
```

Modifying ObeyCommand()

Earlier I declared the **ObeyCommand()** function in the **CPPDocApp** class declaration in the *PP Doc App.h* file and then implemented it in the *PP Doc App.cp* file. In that earlier implementation the function was written such that the program would handle the Open Movie menu item from the Movie menu. Now I'll add to the implementation so that the program also handles selections of any of the newly added items.

Each application-defined menu item needs its own **case** label and section added to the **switch** in **ObeyCommand()**. For the handling of an Open Movie menu selection, I simply played the system sound one time. For now I'll handle each menu selection, that way. Here's how this chapter's final version of **ObeyCommand()** looks. Note that the four **case** labels are the four application-defined command number constants.

```
Boolean
CPPDocApp::ObeyCommand(
    CommandT  inCommand,
    void      *ioParam)
{
    Boolean  cmdHandled = true;

    switch (inCommand) {

        case cmd_OpenMovie:
            ::SysBeep(1);
            break;

        case cmd_PlayMovie:
            ::SysBeep(1);
            break;

        case cmd_OpenPicture:
            ::SysBeep(1);
            break;

        case cmd_PlaySound:
            ::SysBeep(1);
            break;

        default:
            cmdHandled = LDocApplication::ObeyCommand( inCommand, ioParam);
            break;
    }
    return cmdHandled;
}
```

In subsequent chapters, I'll modify **ObeyCommand()** so that the four application-defined menu items each perform the task that's expected of them.

Modifying FindCommandStatus()

The **FindCommandStatus()** function is the second member function that I added to the **CPPDocApp** class. Earlier in this chapter, I wrote the function such that it would enable the Movie menu. Here I'll modify this routine so that the program also enables the Picture and Sound menus.

Each application-defined menu item needs its own **case** label and section that holds the code that tells the program how to display the item. I've elected to enable each menu item. As you look over the code, note that again the four application-defined command number constants are used as the **case** labels:

```
void
CPPDocApp::FindCommandStatus(
    CommandT    inCommand,
    Boolean     &outEnabled,
    Boolean     &outUsesMark,
    Char16      &outMark,
    Str255      outName)
{

    switch (inCommand) {

        case cmd_OpenMovie:
            outEnabled = true;
            break;

        case cmd_PlayMovie:
            outEnabled = true;
            break;

        case cmd_OpenPicture:
            outEnabled = true;
            break;

        case cmd_PlaySound:
            outEnabled = true;
            break;
```

```
    default:
        LDocApplication::FindCommandStatus(inCommand,
                                outEnabled, outUsesMark,
                                outMark, outName);
        break;
    }
}
```

After testing the MediaCenter program, you may want to return to the **FindCommandStatus()** function and make one change. If you assign **outEnabled** a value of **false** under the **cmd_PlayMovie case**, then this item will be disabled. If a movie isn't open (and at this point the Open Movie menu item is incapable of opening a movie), then having this item enabled doesn't make sense. Later you'll see how **FindCommandStatus()** can be modified so that the opening and closing of a movie will toggle the value of **outEnabled** in order to keep the state of the Play Movie menu item correct.

Running the Program

After making the suggested changes to the project, choose Run from the Project menu to compile the new code, build a new version of the MediaCenter program, and run that application. Test all the new menu items to make sure each responds to a selection by playing the sound to which you currently have your system sound set.

When you're finished trying out the program, return to the *MediaCenter.µ* project and open the *PP Doc App.cp* file. Scroll to the **FindCommandStatus()** routine and change the **cmd_PlayMovie case** section to look like this:

```
case cmd_PlayMovie:
    outEnabled = false;
    break;
```

Again compile, build, and test the program. Now, verify that the Play Movie menu item is disabled.

Moving On

PowerPlant Constructor makes it easy to add menus to a menu bar, add items to those menus, and assign command numbers to each item. This last point is particularly important—the PowerPlant code that handles menu selections does so by way of the unique command number that each menu item has.

The **ObeyCommand()** routine that the application class overrides looks at the command number of the current menu selection to see if it corresponds to a menu item that it knows how to handle. If it doesn't, it passes the command on to PowerPlant code. A similar technique is used in the updating of menu items. **FindCommandStatus()**—another routine that the application class overrides—uses command numbers to enable and disable menu items at the appropriate times.

This chapter ended by applying PowerPlant menu-handling techniques to the *MediaCenter.µ* project. The last of this chapter's three versions of the project results in an application that has six menus—each with enabled menu items. That's the good news. The bad news is that while the newly added application-defined menu items are all enabled, selecting any one of them results in only a playing of the system sound. Getting each menu item to actually do what is expected of it is covered in subsequent chapters, starting with the next chapter. In Chapter 8, "Panes & Views," you'll see how PowerPlant and Constructor make it easy to define the contents of windows. That chapter provides you with the information needed to implement the Open Picture menu item from the Picture menu of MediaCenter.

Panes & Views

In traditional Macintosh programming, the content of a window consists of a single drawing area, or graphics port, that has a single coordinate system. In PowerPlant programming, the content of a window can consist of any number of drawing areas, called *views* or *panes*, that have their own coordinate systems. While panes and views can be nested within one another, each acts as an independent unit that has the ability to draw itself.

Constructor and PowerPlant offer a rich set of pane types that allow you to easily add functioning text edit areas, scrollers, and so forth to any window. In this chapter, you'll see how to use Constructor to lay out the items, or panes—such as buttons and pictures—that are to appear in a window. You'll explore the details of creating a 'PPob' resource to tie all your panes and views together, and then learn how PowerPlant code takes control of these panes and handles their display and response to user input.

For entities unique to your own program, Constructor and PowerPlant allow you to define your own pane type based on the PowerPlant **LPane** class. You'll master the art of making your application-defined pane look and act any way you see fit and enhance the MediaCenter program to use a custom pane to display a picture that can be dragged about a window by the user.

Constructor & 'PPob' Resources

If you've written Macintosh programs without the aid of PowerPlant, you know about the 'DLOG' and 'DITL' resource types. A 'DLOG' defines the characteristics of a dialog box (such as its size and initial screen placement), while a 'DITL' defines the items that appear in a dialog box (such as push buttons, check boxes, and pictures). In PowerPlant programming, the 'PPob' (for PowerPlant object) is loosely analogous to a pairing of a 'DLOG' and 'DITL.' And like a 'DLOG,' a 'PPob' is used as a template from which any number of dialog boxes are based. For a couple of reasons, however, the 'PPob' is far more powerful. First, a 'PPob' isn't just for dialog boxes—it can be used to define either a dialog box or a window. Second, a much greater variety of items can be placed in a 'PPob' resource than can be added to a 'DITL' resource.

You use Constructor to create a 'PPob' resource and add items to it. These items include the same elements added to a 'DITL' resource in non-PowerPlant projects. You'll find that Constructor makes it easy to add buttons, icons, and other items to a 'PPob.' With Constructor, though, you can also easily add icons and pictures that act as buttons, lists, tables, scrollable areas, and more to a dialog box or window.

On the next several pages, we'll look at how Constructor is used to work with 'PPob' resources. Figure 8-1 offers a preview of that material. A Constructor file's 'PPob' resources are listed under the Windows & Views heading. Opening a 'PPob' resource displays its panes in the layout editor. A new pane is added to a 'PPob' by dragging an item from the Catalog window to the layout editor. Characteristics of a pane can be edited in the pane's property inspector. Figure 8-1 shows all of these windows for the one 'PPob' resource found in the *PP Basic Resource.ppob* file—the *.ppob* file CodeWarrior adds to a project created from the Basic PowerPlant project stationery.

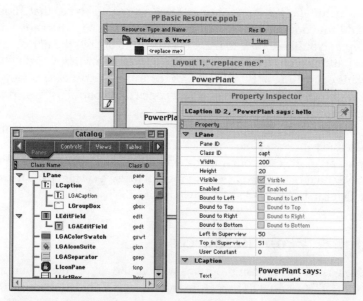

Figure 8-1: Editing a 'PPob' resource in Constructor.

Panes vs. Views

A *pane* is a drawing area that *can't* hold other drawing areas. A *view* is a drawing area that *can* hold other drawing areas, including other views. A *top-level view* has no view above it. That is, while it may have other drawing areas imbedded in it, the top-level view itself isn't "owned by" or embedded within any other view. Typically a top-level view is a window. Within the window are other views (subviews) and panes (subpanes).

To complicate matters a little more, a view is always a pane, but a pane isn't always a view. The **LPane** class is the PowerPlant class from which all panes and views are derived. One of those derived classes is the **LView** class. **LView** inherits the functionality of **LPane**, and then adds a little more. In particular, **LView** adds the ability for **LView** objects to nest other panes and views within it. More information will be available when we discuss PowerPlant pane-related code later in this chapter. For now, be aware that for brevity this book will often use the more generic term *pane* in place of the phrase *pane or view*.

As you have probably already concluded, managing all the views, subviews, and subpanes could become quite complex and confusing. Fortunately, the 'PPob' resource binds these interface elements together in a convenient and powerful way. The 'PPob' resource defines one top-level view and any number of views and panes that are nested within that top-level view.

Example 'PPob' Resources

The *.ppob* file that CodeWarrior supplies as a part of a PowerPlant-based project includes one or more 'PPob' resources. In Chapter 4, "PowerPlant Basics," you saw that the *.ppob* file that is a part of a project resulting from Basic PowerPlant project stationery includes a single 'PPob' resource. That 'PPob' is used as the basis for the "PowerPlant says: hello world" window. Figure 8-2 shows the 'PPob' resource, while Figure 8-3 shows the resulting window.

Figure 8-2: A 'PPob' resource is displayed in Constructor's layout editor.

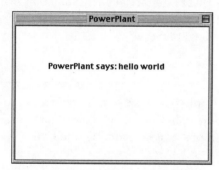

Figure 8-3: The window that results from the 'PPob' resource shown in Figure 8-2.

The *.ppob* file that CodeWarrior includes in a project created from Doc PowerPlant stationery includes two 'PPob' resources. Figure 8-4 shows the 'PPob' resource named Text Window. It holds a single **LTextEdit** view. You're already familiar with the window based on this 'PPob'—it's the text editor window that appears when any version of MediaCenter is launched.

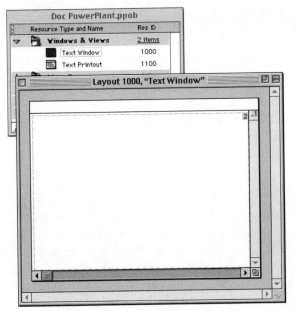

Figure 8-4: The 'PPob' resource used to create a text editing window.

The second 'PPob' in the *Doc PowerPlant.ppob* file (the resource named Text Printout) holds an LPrintout view that *isn't* used as a window. This view is used for managing printing of the active text editor window. The PowerPlant class **LPrintout** has member functions that simplify printing. You'll read more on this topic in Chapter 13, "Printing."

Creating a New PPob Resource

You'll create a new 'PPob' resource for each type of window or dialog box your program will be capable of displaying. To create a new 'PPob,' first click on the Windows & Views heading in Constructor's main window. Then choose New Layout Resource from the Edit menu. The Create New Resource window shown in Figure 8-5 appears. Here you can supply a name and ID for the new resource. The name is for organization purposes only—it gets displayed in the main Constructor window under the Windows & Views heading. The ID is more important—you'll reference this number from within your source code.

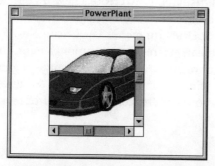

Create New Resource	
Resource Type:	Layout
Kind:	LWindow
Resource Name:	Picture Window
Resource ID:	1500

Cancel Create

Figure 8-5: Creating a new 'PPob' resource.

Editing Panes

Back in Figure 8-2 you saw the 'PPob' resource from the *.ppob* file that's a part of a project created from Basic PowerPlant stationery. Here I'll delete that resource's one pane and replace it with two others. In doing so you'll get an idea of how 'PPob' editing works. As a bonus, you'll also see just how tightly integrated the 'PPob' resource is with PowerPlant code. The program initially generated from the project displays the familiar window with the words "PowerPlant says: hello world" in it. After changing the 'PPob' file—and without touching any of the project's source code—recompiling the project results in an application that now displays a window that holds a scrollable area with a picture in it. Figure 8-3 shows the window that's displayed before the 'PPob' change, while Figure 8-6 shows the window afterward.

The completed project appears in the P01 PaneExample folder in the Chapter 08 folder on this book's Companion CD-ROM. If you want to make the changes yourself, you can edit the Chapter 4 project. To do that, simply open the *FirstPowerPlant.µ* project from the P01 FirstPowerPlant folder in the Chapter 04 folder; then double-click on the *PP Basic Resource.ppob* file name in the project window.

PowerPlant

Figure 8-6: The PaneExample program displays a window that holds a scrollable picture.

Deleting a Pane

To display a 'PPob' resource's views and panes, double-click on the 'PPob' name under the Windows & Views heading in Constructor's main window. Figure 8-7 shows the one pane of the 'PPob' named <replace me> from the *PP Basic Resource.ppob* file. As suggested by the title of the window that appears, 'PPob' resources are edited in Constructor's layout editor.

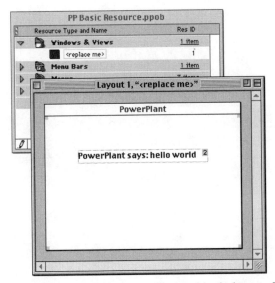

Figure 8-7: A 'PPob' resource displayed in the layout editor.

To delete a pane, first click on it in the layout editor to make it active. Then choose Cut from the Edit menu, or simply press the Delete key. I'll be replacing the text pane with a picture that includes scroll bars, so in preparation I'll delete the text pane now.

Adding a Pane

To add a pane to a 'PPob,' begin by displaying the 'PPob' in the layout editor. Next, choose Catalog from the Window menu. The Catalog window displays all the available types of panes and views recognizable by Constructor. To add an item, click on its name in the Catalog window, then drag and drop it onto the layout editor. In Figure 8-8, I've done this to add an LScroller item to the 'PPob' resource in the *PP Basic Resource.ppob* file.

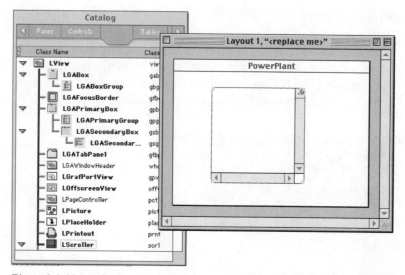

Figure 8-8: Using the Catalog window to add a scrollable area to a 'PPob' resource.

TIP *Click on one of the tabs along the top of the Catalog window to display different categories of items. At this point you won't be familiar with many of the item names. However, since you know that a scroll area has something in it (in this case it will be a picture), you may have properly guessed that an LScroller is a view.*

An added item may not initially have the correct size or be at the desired location in the window to which it's been added. You can change an item's size by clicking on any corner of the item and dragging. You can move an item around a window by clicking anywhere else on the item and dragging. For more precise editing, double-click on the item to reveal its property inspector. Figure 8-9 shows the property inspector for the LScroller.

Whenever you change the value of a property in a property inspector, a black dot appears to the left of the property name. In Figure 8-9, you see that I've edited the value of five properties. Four of these properties are related to the size and placement of the scroller, while the fifth is ID-related.

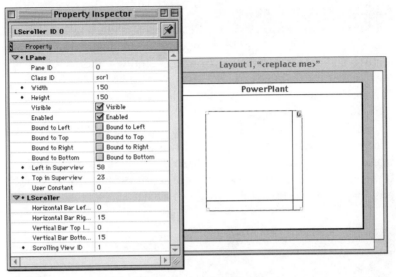

Figure 8-9: The property inspector for an LScroller pane.

I've resized the area the scroller encloses by changing the values of the Width and Height properties. I've also repositioned the scroller in the window by editing the Left in Superview and Top in Superview properties. The window is considered the scroller's *superview* (the view that holds the scroller). The location of the scroller (and any other pane) is determined by the item's top left corner.

Every pane has an ID. By default Constructor gives a new pane an ID of 0. While I've left the Pane ID property of the scroller pane unchanged, pane IDs in general are a topic worthy of note. The particular ID a pane has is usually unimportant. In fact, pane IDs don't have to be unique even within the same 'PPob' resource. For instance, you could create a 'PPob' resource that had numerous panes, each with an ID of, say, 0. The only time that the ID of a pane is important is when the pane is referenced from your project's source code. That won't be the case in this project. However, to provide an example of the referencing of a pane by ID, this chapter's version of MediaCenter uses source code to manipulate a picture pane.

For an LScroller item, an ID does have importance. A scroller needs something to scroll, and that something is defined by another pane. The Scrolling View ID property of an LScroller specifies which pane is to be the recipient of the scrolling. For this example I've specified an ID of 1. Now I need to create a new pane with this ID.

Adding a Second Pane

Additional panes are added to a 'PPob' just as the LScroller was added: drag and drop a pane type from the Catalog window. I want the LScroller to scroll a picture, so I'll drag an LPicture from the Catalog window and drop it within the existing LScroller pane in the layout editor. Referring back to Figure 8-8, you see that the LPicture pane type is listed a little above the LScroller type in the Catalog window.

I want the picture to fit snugly within the boundaries of the scroll area, so I need to reposition and resize the LPicture after dropping it onto the LScroller in the layout window. I also need to set its pane ID to match the Scrolling View ID set for the LScroller. These tasks are accomplished from the picture's property inspector (see Figure 8-10).

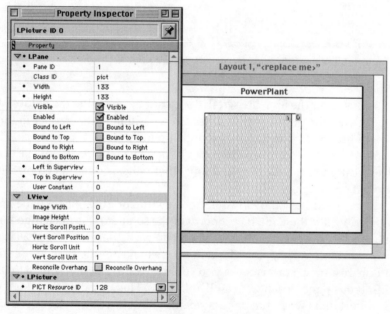

Figure 8-10: The property inspector for a picture pane.

The picture is within the scroller, so the LScroller is the superview of the LPicture. That means that the Left in Superview and Top in Superview properties are set relative to the scroller. I want the top left corner of the picture to be nestled up to the top left corner of the scroller, so I'll set both the Left in Superview and Top in Superview values to 1 (see Figure 8-10).

The size of the LPicture view isn't dependent on the picture that will be displayed—it's dependent on the size the LScroller is set to. Recall that I set the width and height of the scroller to 150 pixels (see Figure 8-9). A Macintosh scroll bar is defined to be 16 pixels wide, so I'll set the Width property of the LPicture to 133 pixels—17 pixels less than the width of the LScroller. Sixteen of those pixels account for the scroll bar—I don't want the picture to overlap it. The one remaining pixel is for the one-pixel offset I specified for the left edge of the picture from the left edge of the scroller (the Left in Superview property of the LPicture). I'll give the Height property of the LPicture the same value of 133.

In the LScroller property inspector, I specified that the item to be scrolled would have an ID of 1. So that's the value I'll use for the Pane ID property of the LPicture.

An LPicture needs to be associated with an actual picture. That picture must be a 'PICT' resource. Use the PICT Resource ID property of the LPicture to specify the resource ID of the 'PICT' to use. In Figure 8-10 you see that the LPicture will be expecting a 'PICT' with an ID of 128 to be available to it. You can store this 'PICT' resource in any resource file that is part of the same project as the *.ppob* file. I chose to add the picture to the *PP Basic Resource.rsrc* file that CodeWarrior added to the project (see Figure 8-11). I could have placed it in any of the project's other resource files. Alternatively, I could have used ResEdit to create a new resource file, added that file to the project, and then added the 'PICT' to that file.

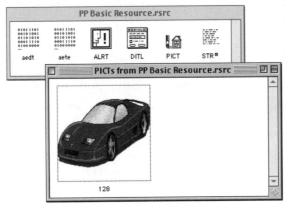

Figure 8-11: Adding a 'PICT' resource that is to be used by an LPicture pane.

Testing the 'PPob' Changes

After using Constructor to make the aforementioned changes to the 'PPob' resource in the *PP Basic Resource.ppob* file, return to the CodeWarrior IDE. With the project open that the *.ppob* file belongs to, choose Run from the Project menu. Because no changes were made to the project's source code, no files will be compiled. Instead, CodeWarrior will simply link the resources to the existing object code. The result will be an application that displays a window with a picture in a scroll area, as shown back in Figure 8-6. When you click on either of the scroll bars, the picture will scroll.

Custom Panes

In the previous section, you saw that a pane corresponds to a PowerPlant class. For instance, Constructor calls a scroller pane an LScroller and a picture pane an LPicture. A *window* is a pane (a top-level view in particular), and it too corresponds to a PowerPlant class—the **LWindow** class. The fact that the pane-naming scheme involves PowerPlant class names is of course no coincidence. Each pane defined in a 'PPob' resource will have a corresponding object when source code creates a window based on that 'PPob.'

The **LWindow** member function **CreateWindow()** is invoked to create a window in source code. This routine's first parameter is the ID of the 'PPob' resource that defines the window and its panes. This next snippet is typical of code that creates a new window:

```
const ResIDT    PPob_PictureWindow= 1500;

LWindow  *theWindow;
theWindow = LWindow::CreateWindow(PPob_PictureWindow, this);
```

The preceding code creates an **LWindow** object. To do that, PowerPlant looks for a 'PPob' resource (one with an ID of 1500 in the preceding example) and uses the data in that resource to build the window. In the code it should be obvious that an **LWindow** object is being created. What isn't so obvious is that other objects are created as well—one object for each pane in the window. If 'PPob' 1500 consists of an LWindow that holds an LScroller pane and an LPicture pane, then the above snippet creates three objects—one each of the **LWindow**, **LScroller**, and **LPicture** classes.

The creation of the pane objects other than the **LWindow** object is implicit—your code allocates memory for the **LWindow** object and PowerPlant takes care of any other allocations. Once created, the pane objects are under the control of PowerPlant code. You saw that to be the case for the **LScroller** and

LPicture objects in this chapter's PaneExample program. That example included no application-defined code to handle scroller actions or picture updating, yet running the program resulted in a window that included functioning scroll bars.

The numerous PowerPlant-supported pane types that can be added to a 'PPob' resource in Constructor will take care of many of your program's interface needs. They won't, however, be enough for every project. Metrowerks couldn't anticipate every possible type of interface element, and every action that every element might be required to perform. For instance, a program may want to display a window holding text that can be clicked on and dragged about the window. Another program may want to include a similar feature that allows a picture to be dragged within a window. For such cases, custom panes must be used.

A *custom pane* is derived from the **LPane** class. The **LPane** class is made up of dozens of member functions, so you aren't completely on your own when you define your own custom pane. PowerPlant code helps in the implementation of a custom pane's features, and your own application-defined code implements the remaining features that are unique to your pane.

The LPane Class

Because a custom pane is derived from the **LPane** class, you should have a good understanding of this important PowerPlant class. The following partial listing of the **LPane** declaration serves as an introduction:

```
class LPane : public virtual LAttachable {
    friend class LView;
public:
    enum { class_ID = 'pane' };

                LPane(LStream *inStream);
    ...
    ...
    virtual LPane*  FindPaneByID(PaneIDT inPaneID);

    void            ResizeFrameTo(Int16 inWidth,
                                  Int16 inHeight,
                                  Boolean inRefresh);
    virtual void    ResizeFrameBy(Int16 inWidthDelta,
                                  Int16 inHeightDelta,
                                  Boolean inRefresh);
```

```
    virtual void      MoveBy(Int32 inHorizDelta, Int32
                              inVertDelta, Boolean inRefresh);
    ...
    ...
    virtual void      ClickSelf( const SMouseDownEvent &inMouseDown);
    Boolean           IsVisible() const;
    virtual void      Show();
    virtual void      Hide();
    virtual void      DrawSelf();
    ...
    ...
}
```

The **LPane** class consists of over six dozen member functions, several of which are shown in the preceding listing. A custom pane inherits all of these functions. A custom pane can define additional member functions, but often it is enough for the pane to simply override a few of the inherited member functions. In particular, a class derived from **LPane** will override **DrawSelf()** and **ClickSelf()**.

The **DrawSelf()** routine specifies what a pane looks like. The body of this routine could be quite simple, such as a call to the Toolbox routine **FrameRect()** to provide an outline of the pane. It could also be much more involved, consisting of several lines of code that draw a complex shape or intricate picture. In any case, PowerPlant code invokes the **DrawSelf()** function to draw the contents of a pane. You'll be responsible for overriding **DrawSelf()** and reimplementing the routine, but PowerPlant will be responsible for invoking the function when appropriate.

The **ClickSelf()** function specifies how a pane should behave when the user clicks the mouse button while the cursor is over the pane. If the pane isn't one that responds to a user's actions, then the function will simply ignore a mouse click. If the pane is an interactive one, then the body of **ClickSelf()** defines what should take place next. For instance, if the pane is draggable, then **ClickSelf()** will track the cursor as the user moves the mouse with the mouse button held down. Like **DrawSelf()**, **ClickSelf()** is invoked by PowerPlant.

Custom Pane Example

In Chapter 7, "Menus," the Picture menu was added to MediaCenter. In that chapter's version of the program, a selection of Open Picture from the Picture menu did nothing more than play the system sound. When properly implemented, this menu item should display the standard Open dialog box to allow the user to choose a 'PICT' file, display that file's picture in a window, and

click and drag the picture about the window. By the end of this chapter, the
Open Picture menu item will do all these things. Here we'll look at how a
custom pane makes it possible to carry out the dragging of a picture—or of
anything else that you'd like to display in a window.

Your knowledge of the **LPicture** class and the type of pane based on this
class might lead you to conclude that this moving-picture pane could perhaps
be created by using Constructor to add an LPicture to a window. That's a good
guess, but it doesn't work for a couple of reasons. First, the PowerPlant
LPicture class is used for the display of a picture that's read from a 'PICT'
resource—it isn't suited for holding picture data from a 'PICT' file. Second, the
LPicture class (and the **LView** class from which it is derived) includes no
provision for dragging a pane. You can see this for yourself by looking at the
LPicture class definition, which is shown here in its entirety:

```
class  LPicture : public LView {

public:
    enum { class_ID = 'pict' };

                    LPicture();
                    LPicture(const LPicture  &inOriginal);
                    LPicture(const SPaneInfo &inPaneInfo,
                        const SViewInfo &inViewInfo,
                        ResIDT          inPICTid);
                    LPicture(LStream *inStream);
                    LPicture(ResIDT inPictureID);

    ResIDT          GetPictureID() const { return mPICTid; }

    void            SetPictureID(ResIDT inPictureID);

    ObsoleteCreatorFunction_(Picture)

protected:
    ResIDT          mPICTid;

    virtual void    DrawSelf();

private:
    void            InitPicture();
};
```

TIP *Because a Constructor pane type corresponds to a PowerPlant class (for instance, an LPicture pane in a 'PPob' resource will become an **LPicture** object), you can look in PowerPlant header files (such as LPicture.h) to get an idea of the functionality of various panes that are listed in Constructor's Catalog window.*

Because **LPicture** lacks the needed functionality, it won't work for the task I'm implementing. In my source code I could define a class derived from **LPicture** and try to add the needed functionality by way of adding or overriding member functions—but that's not a practical solution. **LPicture** is designed to work with a 'PICT' resource, not 'PICT' data from a picture file. Instead, a custom pane is the preferred route to take. On the following pages, I add a custom pane to the MediaCenter project. I don't, however, modify the program such that it opens a 'PICT' file, reads the picture data, and displays the picture in a draggable pane in a new window. Instead, I'll simply alter the project so that choosing Open Picture from the Picture menu opens a new window that displays a draggable rectangle (which just happens to be a custom pane). Figure 8-12 shows how the program looks with a couple of these Picture windows open.

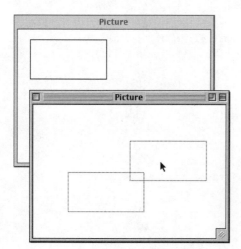

Figure 8-12: Dragging a custom pane in a picture window.

By omitting the MediaCenter-specific picture code, this example will be generic enough that its concepts—and almost all of its code—will be applicable to any custom pane your own program may need. In this chapter's "Panes & the Example Project" section, I'll add a little more code to turn the draggable rectangle into a draggable custom pane that holds a picture.

The completed project appears in the P02 MediaCenter folder in the Chapter 08 folder on this book's Companion CD-ROM. As always, you can follow along and turn the preceding version (found in the P03 MediaCenter folder in the Chapter 07 folder) into this latest incarnation.

Adding a New 'PPob' Resource

In response to an Open Picture selection from the Picture menu, the latest version of MediaCenter will open a new window. This window will be based on a 'PPob' that's not yet in the *Doc PowerPlant.ppob* file. Follow these steps to create the 'PPob:'

1. Click on the Windows & Views heading in Constructor's main window.

2. Choose New Layout Resource from the Edit menu.

3. Enter a name and ID in the Create New Resource window (enter an ID of 1500 if you want your project to match mine).

4. Click the Create button to create the new 'PPob' resource.

The new 'PPob' will now be listed in Constructor's main window (see Figure 8-13). Display the 'PPob' in the layout editor by double-clicking on its name.

Adding a Custom Pane

Your application-defined source code will specify how a custom pane object will look and behave. Like any pane, though, you'll need to include the custom pane in a 'PPob' resource. Because you'll be writing your own class to define the pane (rather than relying on an existing PowerPlant class), there won't be a suitable pane listed in the Catalog window of Constructor. You'll work around this by selecting the generic LPane from the Catalog window and dragging it over to the layout editor displaying the 'PPob.'

To edit the new pane's characteristics, double-click on it to display its property inspector. Figure 8-13 shows this inspector. In this example, the only property of interest is the Class ID.

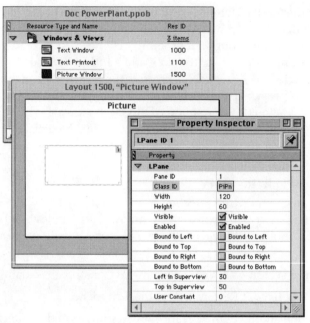

Figure 8-13: The property inspector for an LPane pane.

TIP | *Other custom pane properties that will often be of interest are the ones that determine the pane's placement in a window (Left in Superview and Top in Superview) and the pane's size (Width and Height). If the values of these properties are unknown at the time the pane is created in Constructor (as will be the case for a pane that is to hold a user-supplied picture), these properties can be controlled from source code after the pane object is created—as demonstrated later in this chapter.*

A pane's class ID serves as the link between a pane that is part of a 'PPob' resource and the source code class type used to create the pane object during application runtime. A standard pane type has its class ID listed in the Catalog window of Constructor and in the class declaration in the PowerPlant class header file. Figure 8-14 provides an example: part of the **LScroller** class, as declared in the *LScroller.h* header file. It also shows the class ID of a few panes in Constructor—including the class ID of the LScroller. Note that the definition of the **class_ID** constant in the **LScroller** class definition is the same as the class ID for the LScroller in Constructor.

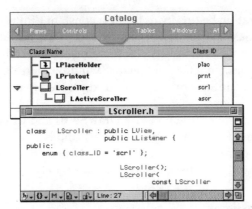

Figure 8-14: A Constructor pane and a PowerPlant class are associated by an identical class ID in each.

For a custom pane, you'll specify a class ID of your own choosing. A class ID must be four characters and must be unique from all PowerPlant-defined class IDs. PowerPlant-defined class IDs are always all lowercase, so including at least one uppercase character in your custom pane's ID ensures that it won't clash with a PowerPlant pane ID. Figure 8-13 shows that I've elected to assign the new pane a class ID of 'PiPn' (to hint that this is a **pi**cture **pa**ne). Later, when I edit the source code in the MediaCenter project, I'll declare an **LPane**-derived class that includes the following line:

```
enum { class_ID = 'PiPn' };
```

That's it for the new pane, and the new 'PPob' resource. Save the *.ppob* file and return to the CodeWarrior IDE.

Declaring the LPane-derived Class

The properties of a custom pane are defined by an **LPane**-derived class in your source code. I'll name my pane class **CPicturePane**. Also typical is to declare the class in its own header file and store the member function definitions in a separate source code file. I've created a *CPicturePane.h* file that holds the following class declaration:

```
class  CPicturePane : public LPane {
public:
   enum { class_ID = 'PiPn' };

                       CPicturePane(LStream *inStream);
protected:
   virtual void        DrawSelf();
   virtual void        ClickSelf(const SMouseDownEvent
                              &inMouseDown);
};
```

The custom class declaration begins by defining a constant ('PiPn') that relates the **CPicturePane** class to the custom pane in the 'PPob' resource. The **CPicturePane** class has a single constructor that PowerPlant code will use to create a **CPicturePane** object when a new picture window is created from the new 'PPob' resource. The **inStream** parameter is discussed in the "Registering the Custom Class" section.

The two **CPicturePane** member functions are **DrawSelf()** and **ClickSelf()**. As discussed, both routines are inherited from **LPane()**, and both routines are invoked by PowerPlant code at the appropriate times. The custom class overrides them so that a **CPicturePane** object behaves appropriately.

Defining the Class Constructor

When a new window opens based on the 'PPob' resource that holds the custom pane, PowerPlant invokes the custom pane class constructor to create a custom pane object. In this example, the opening of a picture window results in PowerPlant invoking the **CPicturePane** constructor. Here's how that constructor is defined:

```
CPicturePane::CPicturePane(
    LStream  *inStream)
        : LPane(inStream)
{
}
```

When PowerPlant invokes the **CPicturePane** constructor, it will pass a pointer to an **LStream** object. This object (which PowerPlant is responsible for creating and keeping track of) holds the 'PPob' data for the window being built. The **CPicturePane** constructor simply passes that pointer on to the constructor of its base class—**LPane**.

PowerPlant organizes 'PPob' data into a stream, the details of which are unimportant. Unless you're curious, you won't have to become familiar with the **LStream** class. If you declare your own custom pane class, simply use the above constructor as a template for the constructor of your own class. Simply replace the two occurrences of **CPicturePane** with the name of your custom pane class.

TIP
*Even if you've never used PowerPlant, you've used streams—you just may not have been aware of it. In C++, **cout** is an object that represents the standard output stream. The code **cout << "Try again.";** writes the words "Try again." to the monitor. A fancier way of saying this is that the data representing text flows along the standard output stream to the monitor.*

Overriding DrawSelf()

A picture pane, as implemented in this current version of MediaCenter, displays nothing more than a frame around the pane—this chapter's next version will give the pane the power to display a picture. When a MediaCenter picture window needs updating, PowerPlant will invoke the custom pane object's **DrawSelf()** member function. Here's the implementation of that routine:

```
void
CPicturePane::DrawSelf()
{
   Rect   theFrame;

   CalcLocalFrameRect(theFrame);
   ::FrameRect(&theFrame);
}
```

   DrawSelf() begins by invoking **CalcLocalFrameRect()**—a routine that the **CPicturePane** class inherited from **LPane**. This function returns the boundary rectangle of the pane. The CalcLocal part of the function name refers to the fact that the returned coordinates are local to the pane's superview (which, for the picture window 'PPob', is the window itself). With the boundaries of the pane known, a framing rectangle can easily be drawn by calling the Toolbox function **FrameRect()**.

TIP
*Note the use of the scope resolution operator (::) preceding the call to **FrameRect()**. The C++ function overloading feature allows one program to contain more than one version of a function. Prefacing a Toolbox function call with the scope resolution operator ensures that it is the Toolbox version of the function that gets called. You can invoke Toolbox functions without using the :: operator, but if you've inadvertently defined an identically named function as a class member function, than the wrong version of the routine will be used.*

   Framing the pane in a rectangle is enough to demonstrate that the pane exists, and that it is the **DrawSelf()** routine that updates it. Hopefully, your custom panes will do much more! If a pane is to display more than a rectangle, the additional display code would appear here in **DrawSelf()**. Use any Toolbox functions to draw text or graphics—whatever is appropriate for the custom pane you want to create.

Overriding ClickSelf()

The dragging of the picture pane is handled by the **ClickSelf()** routine. When a user clicks on a custom pane, PowerPlant code invokes the pane object's **ClickSelf()** function to track the mouse as the user drags it and continually draws a dashed outline of the pane to provide the user feedback. When the user releases the mouse button, the contents of the pane will be redrawn at the new location. Here's a look at **ClickSelf()**:

```
void
CPicturePane::ClickSelf( const SMouseDownEvent &inMouseDown )
{
    Rect      theOldFrame;
    Rect      theNewFrame;
    Point     theOldMouseLoc;
    Point     theNewMouseLoc;
    Int32     theDeltaX;
    Int32     theDeltaY;
    Boolean   theUpdate = true;

    FocusDraw();

    ::PenNormal();
    ::PenPat( &qd.gray );
    ::PenMode( patXor );

    theOldMouseLoc = inMouseDown.whereLocal;
    theNewMouseLoc = theOldMouseLoc;

    CalcLocalFrameRect( theOldFrame );
    theNewFrame = theOldFrame;

    while (::StillDown())
    {
        ::GetMouse(&theNewMouseLoc);

        if (::EqualPt(theNewMouseLoc, theOldMouseLoc) == false)
        {
            ::FrameRect(&theOldFrame);
            theDeltaX = theNewMouseLoc.h - theOldMouseLoc.h;
            theDeltaY = theNewMouseLoc.v - theOldMouseLoc.v;
            ::OffsetRect(&theNewFrame, theDeltaX, theDeltaY);
            ::FrameRect(&theNewFrame);
            theOldMouseLoc = theNewMouseLoc;
            theOldFrame = theNewFrame;
```

```
        }
    }

    theDeltaX = theNewMouseLoc.h - inMouseDown.whereLocal.h;
    theDeltaY = theNewMouseLoc.v - inMouseDown.whereLocal.v;
    MoveBy(theDeltaX, theDeltaY, theUpdate);

    ::PenNormal();
}
```

TIP
> *The user's release of the mouse button results in the pane being redrawn—but it isn't **ClickSelf()** that does it. Instead, PowerPlant code invokes **DrawSelf()**. This means that **ClickSelf()** is pane content–independent—good news for you. If you're satisfied with how **ClickSelf()** works in this example, you can use it—unchanged—as the **ClickSelf()** routine for any of your own custom pane classes. I do that myself later in this chapter when I reuse it in the version of MediaCenter that displays a picture in the custom pane.*

ClickSelf() begins by invoking the **LPane**-inherited **FocusDraw()** routine to prepare for drawing in the pane. Each view has its own local coordinate system, so if a window has several views in it, the window will have several coordinate systems. A pane doesn't have its own coordinate system—it relies on the system of its superview. The call to **FocusDraw()** is necessary so that PowerPlant uses the correct coordinate system when it starts drawing to the pane.

After setting the coordinate system, a few Toolbox routines are called to set up the graphics pen such that it draws a dashed line when drawing takes place. Next, values are assigned to a pair of variables that keep track of the old and new mouse location. Then variables representing the old and new pane boundaries are given initial values. All four of these variables will be updated at each pass through the **while** loop that appears following the assignment to **theNewFrame**.

TIP
> *You didn't have to invoke **FocusDraw()** in **DrawSelf()** because PowerPlant takes care of coordinate transformations when it invokes **DrawSelf()**. PowerPlant doesn't do that when it invokes **ClickSelf()** because a custom pane's implementation of **ClickSelf()** might not result in drawing (the routine may do nothing, or it may drag a pane without providing the user with visual feedback).*

The main purpose of **ClickSelf()** is to track the movement of the mouse for the duration of the user's dragging. A **while** loop with repeated calls to the Toolbox routine **StillDown()** takes care of this. The code within the loop is straightforward. Calls to the Toolbox routines **GetMouse()** and **EqualPt()** get the current location of the mouse (cursor) and determine if a change in position has occurred. If the mouse was moved, a call to **FrameRect()** is made to wipe out the current dashed pane frame, the change in position is calculated, the frame redrawn at the new location, and the old mouse location and old frame coordinates are updated. When the user releases the mouse button, the total change in pane position is calculated and the **LPane**-derived member function **MoveBy()** is called to reposition the pane. To prevent subsequent drawing operations from being performed in a dashed gray pattern, the graphics pen is returned to its normal state before the **ClickSelf()** routine exits.

Registering the Custom Class

The Class ID property of a standard PowerPlant pane in a 'PPob' resource matches the **class_ID** constant defined in a PowerPlant class. This scheme is used in order to properly pair a pane with a class. Before this system can work properly, however, a one-time initialization of all the PowerPlant panes and classes needs to be performed. A PowerPlant-based project typically handles this chore by calling the PowerPlant utility function **RegisterAllPPClasses()** from the application class constructor:

```
CPPDocApp::CPPDocApp()
{
    RegisterAllPPClasses();
    RegisterClass_(CTextView);
}
```

A call to **RegisterAllPPClasses()** takes care of registering the IDs of PowerPlant-defined classes: **LScroller** has an ID of 'scrl,' **LPicture** has an ID of 'pict,' and so forth. **RegisterAllPPClasses()** of course can't know about the class ID of any of your own **LPane**-derived classes—yet they still must be registered. To handle that task, PowerPlant defines the **RegisterClass_()** macro (the underscore clues you into the fact that this is a macro). To make use of this macro, simply pass it one parameter—the name of your **LPane**-derived class. The **RegisterClass_()** macro will expand to invoke the proper PowerPlant code that registers your class.

The preceding snippet shows the **RegisterClass_()** macro being used to register the class ID for the **CTextView** class—a class that is declared in application-defined code that CodeWarrior includes in all PowerPlant-based projects created from Doc PowerPlant project stationery. The application-defined class that I've added to the *MediaCenter.μ* project is named **CPicturePane()**, so the **CPPDocApp** constructor now becomes:

```
CPPDocApp::CPPDocApp()
{
   RegisterAllPPClasses();
   RegisterClass_(CTextView);
   RegisterClass_(CPicturePane);
}
```

Opening a New Window

The custom pane is displayed in a window based on the 'PPob' it resides in—the 'PPob' resource with an ID of 1500. In the *PP Doc App.cp* file define a constant with that value:

```
const ResIDT   PPob_PictureWindow  = 1500;
```

To create a new window, use the constant as a parameter in a call to the **LWindow** member function **CreateWindow()**. In previous versions of MediaCenter, a selection of Open Picture resulted in nothing more than the playing of the system sound. Now it's time to replace the call to **SysBeep()** under the **cmd_OpenPicture case** label in the **CPPDocApp ObeyCommand()** member function with window-opening code:

```
Boolean
CPPDocApp::ObeyCommand(
    CommandT    inCommand,
    void        *ioParam)
{
   Boolean    cmdHandled = true;

   switch (inCommand) {
      ...
      ...
      case cmd_OpenPicture:
         LWindow  *theWindow;
         theWindow = LWindow::CreateWindow( PPob_PictureWindow, this);
         theWindow->Show();
         break;
      ...
      ...
   }
   return cmdHandled;
}
```

Custom Pane Summary

The technique for adding a draggable pane lends itself to the addition of just about any type of custom pane. Here's a summary of the steps you'll perform:

1. Use the Constructor Catalog window to add an **LPane** to the 'PPob' resource that is to be used for the window that displays the pane.

2. Use the new **LPane**'s property inspector to give the pane a four-character class ID.

3. Declare an **LPane**-derived class that includes a **class_ID** constant that matches the pane's four-character class ID, a constructor, and **DrawSelf()** and **ClickSelf()** member functions.

4. Implement the constructor by invoking the **LPane** constructor.

5. Implement **DrawSelf()** such that it draws the content of the pane (invoke whatever Toolbox routines are necessary).

6. Implement **ClickSelf()** so it defines what the pane should do (if anything) in response to a mouse button click on the pane (invoke Toolbox routines and **LPane** member functions as necessary).

7. Register the new pane in the **LDocApplication**-derived application class constructor by calling the **RegisterClass_()** macro.

8. Build a new version of your program and open a window to test out the new custom pane!

Panes & the Example Project

The "Custom Panes" section of this chapter used MediaCenter as the host for a demonstration of how a custom pane is added to a window. While the custom pane did have some of the functionality that the final version of MediaCenter requires, it didn't go far enough. Here I'll take up where the preceding example ended. This chapter's last version of MediaCenter (found in the P03 MediaCenter folder in the Chapter 08 folder) fills in the missing pieces to make the Open Picture menu item do just what's expected of it.

Selecting Open Picture will display the standard Open dialog box. As shown in Figure 8-15, this is where the user selects the 'PICT' file that holds the picture to be displayed in a window.

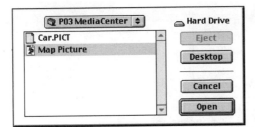

Figure 8-15: The standard Open dialog box, as displayed by MediaCenter.

Once a file is selected, MediaCenter reads the picture data from the file, opens a new window, and displays the picture in it. The picture is displayed in a draggable custom pane. Figure 8-16 shows the Picture window with a picture of a map being dragged.

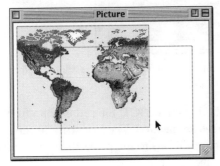

Figure 8-16: A MediaCenter Picture window with a picture being dragged.

Project Resources

Implementing the Picture window requires a 'PPob' resource that will define the look of that window. I've already done the work of adding a 'PPob' to the *Doc PowerPlant.ppob* file in this chapter's custom pane example (P02 MediaCenter)—see the "Adding a New 'PPob' Resource" part of the "Custom Pane Example" section for the details.

The new 'PPob' needs only a single pane—a custom pane that can be used to display a picture. Again, the custom pane example took care of this task (see the "Adding a Custom Pane" part of the "Custom Pane Example" section for the details). Figure 8-17 shows the properties of the custom pane.

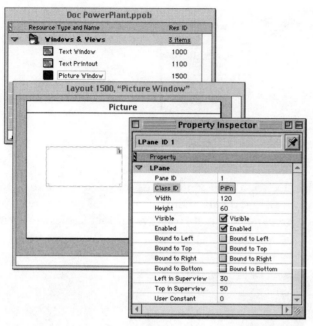

Figure 8-17: The property inspector for the one custom pane used in MediaCenter.

The picture data will be supplied from a 'PICT' file rather than from a 'PICT' resource, so no other new resources are needed. The Constructor file can be closed and our attention turned to additions to the project's source code.

Project Source Code

This chapter's custom pane example defined an **LPane**-derived class named **CPicturePane**. In this version of MediaCenter, I'll expand upon that class. I'll also need to add new member functions to the **LDocApplication**-derived **CPPDocApp**—the application class that CodeWarrior provided.

Adding to the CPicturePane Class Declaration

This chapter's custom pane example introduced you to the application-defined, **LPane**-derived **CPicturePane** class. Even though that example used the custom pane for nothing more than the display of a rectangle, I gave its class the name **CPicturePane** to hint that it could—with a little modification—be used to display and manipulate a picture. Here's how the new version of the **CPicturePane** class looks:

```
class  CPicturePane : public LPane {
public:
   enum { class_ID = 'PiPn' };

                     CPicturePane(LStream *inStream);
   virtual           ~CPicturePane();

   virtual void      SetPicture(PicHandle thePicture);

protected:
   virtual void      DrawSelf();
   virtual void      ClickSelf( const SMouseDownEvent &inMouseDown);

   PicHandle         mPicture;
};
```

New to this version of **CPicturePane** is a data member named **mPicture**, a member function named **SetPicture()**, and a destructor.

The **mPicture** data member will hold a reference to the picture data that defines the picture to be displayed in the custom pane. The **SetPicture()** member function provides a means to set the value of **mPicture**. Macintosh programming conventions dictate that when a **PicHandle** is no longer needed (as when a picture window is closed), the memory that the handle references should be released. That will be the job of the destructor.

Adding to the CPPDocApp Application Class

The code that will be added to respond to a user's choice of Open Picture *could* all go under the **cmd_OpenPicture case** label in the **CPPDocApp** version of **ObeyCommand()**—but it won't. That approach works fine for a few lines of code, but when the handling of a menu item requires several lines of code, it makes sense to add one or more new member functions to the application class. A menu command can then be handled with just a function call or two. No less code is written or executed using this technique, but the size of the **ObeyCommand()** routine is kept to a minimum—which makes it easy for you or others to quickly understand how your program implements menu commands.

I'll add two member functions to **CPPDocApp**. **ShowPictureWindow()** will be called from **ObeyCommand()**. **ShowPictureWindow()** will call **OpenPICTFile()**. Here's how the **CPPDocApp** class declaration is shaping up:

```
class CPPDocApp : public LDocApplication {
public:
                     CPPDocApp();
   virtual           ~CPPDocApp();
```

```
    virtual Boolean         ObeyCommand(
                                    CommandT   inCommand,
                                    void*      ioParam);

    virtual void            FindCommandStatus(
                                    CommandT   inCommand,
                                    Boolean    &outEnabled,
                                    Boolean    &outUsesMark,
                                    Char16     &outMark,
                                    Str255     outName);

    virtual void            ShowPictureWindow();
    PicHandle               OpenPICTFile();

protected:
    virtual void            StartUp();
    virtual void            OpenDocument(
                                    FSSpec *inMacFSSpec);
    virtual LModelObject *  MakeNewDocument();
    virtual void            ChooseDocument();
    virtual void            PrintDocument(
                                    FSSpec *inMacFSSpec);
};
```

Opening a 'PICT' File

The new **ShowPictureWindow()** member function (covered next) is responsible for opening a 'PICT' file, determining the size of the file's picture, opening a window based on the new 'PPob' resource, and adjusting the size of the window's custom pane to match the size of the picture. All but the first task require very little code. Because the opening of a 'PICT' file requires a little extra code, and because it's such a well-defined, single-purpose chore, I've opted to place the file-opening code in its own member function. The details of how **OpenPICTFile()** works have little to do with PowerPlant—so I'll omit a line-by-line explanation of the routine. Following the **OpenPICTFile()** listing, I do, however, summarize how the function works.

```
PicHandle
CPPDocApp::OpenPICTFile()
{
    SFTypeList          theTypeList = {'PICT'};
    StandardFileReply   theReply;
    short               theFileRefNum;
    long                theFileBytes;
    Size                thePICTBytes;
```

```
Handle          theHandle = nil;
PicHandle       thePicture;

UDesktop::Deactivate();
::StandardGetFile(nil, 1, theTypeList, &theReply);
UDesktop::Activate();

if (theReply.sfGood == false)
   return (nil);

::FSpOpenDF(&theReply.sfFile, fsRdPerm, &theFileRefNum);

::GetEOF(theFileRefNum, &theFileBytes);
::SetFPos(theFileRefNum, fsFromStart, 512);

thePICTBytes = theFileBytes - 512;

theHandle = ::NewHandleClear(thePICTBytes);

::HLock(theHandle);
   ::FSRead(theFileRefNum, &thePICTBytes, *theHandle);
::HUnlock(theHandle);

thePicture = (PicHandle)theHandle;

return (thePicture);
}
```

The Toolbox routine **StandardGetFile()** is used to display the standard Open dialog box pictured back in Figure 8-15. Of most importance here is the parameter **theTypeList**, which specifies that files of type 'PICT' be displayed in the Open dialog box. Surrounding the call to **StandardGetFile()** are calls to **Deactivate()** and **Activate()**—member functions that belong to the PowerPlant desktop utility class **UDesktop**. Your windows are under the control of PowerPlant, while Toolbox dialog boxes are under the control of the Toolbox. Deactivating PowerPlant windows while a Toolbox dialog box is displayed resolves any potential conflicts in control. Calls to **Deactivate()** and **Activate()** should encase any Toolbox call that results in the display of a dialog box.

TIP *If you're incorporating existing code into a PowerPlant-based project (perhaps you're an experienced Mac programmer who has written several routines that you use in several projects), then watch for the preceding condition. If your own code includes a call to **StandardGetFile()**, make sure to wrap it in calls to **Deactivate()** and **Activate()**.*

If the user cancels the Open dialog box, **OpenPICTFile()** ends and returns a nil handle to the calling routine (which will be **ShowPictureWindow()** in this example). If the user instead chooses a picture file, **OpenPICTFile()** works with that file.

The Toolbox routines **FSpOpenDF()**, **GetEOF()**, and **SetFPos()** do the following: find the selected file and open its data fork, get the size of the file in bytes, and move the current position marker past the 512-byte header always present in a 'PICT' file. Next, a call to the Toolbox routine **NewHandleClear()** creates a new handle the size of the picture data (less the 512-byte header). The data is then read from the file and stored in the memory referenced by the newly created handle. During the reading of the file, memory is locked to prevent the operating system from compacting memory (which it often does as an efficiency measure).

At this point a generic handle references the picture data in memory. A **PicHandle** is then set to reference this same memory, and the **PicHandle** is returned to the calling routine. You'll see what **ShowPictureWindow()** does with this handle next.

TIP *OpenPICTFile() opens any file of type 'PICT.' If you need this functionality in your own program, use OpenPICTFile() "as is." Since you probably won't be making changes to the code, you should be satisfied with the overview you just read. If for some reason you need a deeper explanation of some or all of the Toolbox functions invoked from OpenPICTFile(), refer to a good Toolbox reference such as the* Files *volume of* Inside Macintosh.

Displaying the Picture Window

In response to an Open Picture menu selection, the **CPPDocApp** member function **ObeyCommand()** invokes another **CPPDocApp** function—**ShowPictureWindow()**:

```
Boolean
CPPDocApp::ObeyCommand(
    CommandT    inCommand,
    void        *ioParam)
{
    Boolean    cmdHandled = true;

    switch (inCommand) {
      ...
      ...
```

```
      case cmd_OpenPicture:
         ShowPictureWindow();
         break;

      ...

      ...
   }
   return cmdHandled;
}
```

Here's how **ShowPictureWindow()** is defined in *PP Doc App.cp*:

```
void
CPPDocApp::ShowPictureWindow()
{
   PicHandle   thePicture;
   Rect        theRect;
   Int16       theWidth;
   Int16       theHeight;
   Boolean     theUpdate = true;

   thePicture = OpenPICTFile();
   if (thePicture == nil)
      return;

   theRect = (**thePicture).picFrame;
   theWidth = theRect.right - theRect.left;
   theHeight = theRect.bottom - theRect.top;

   LWindow  *theWindow;
   theWindow = LWindow::CreateWindow(PPob_PictureWindow, this );

   CPicturePane *thePicturePane;
   thePicturePane = (CPicturePane *)theWindow->FindPaneByID
                                 (paneID_PicturePane);
   thePicturePane->SetPicture(thePicture);
   thePicturePane->ResizeFrameTo(theWidth, theHeight, theUpdate);

   theWindow->Show();
}
```

ShowPictureWindow() begins by invoking the just-described **OpenPICTFile()**. This routine returns a **PicHandle** that references the picture data from a user-selected 'PICT' file. If the user passed on the opportunity to select a file, then **OpenPICTFile()** returns a value of nil and **ShowPictureWindow()** terminates without attempting to open a new window.

If a valid **PicHandle** is returned to **ShowPictureWindow()**, the function first determines the size of the picture. This information will be necessary when it is time to resize the custom pane to match the size of the picture.

Next, a window based on the 'PPob' that holds the custom pane is opened but not shown. Before doing that, **ShowPictureWindow()** establishes a relationship between the picture data in memory and the custom pane in the newly opened window. To do that, a pointer to a **CPicturePane** object is declared:

```
CPicturePane *thePicturePane;
```

This pointer doesn't initially reference the custom pane object. To make that connection, a constant having the value of the pane's ID (as defined in the pane's Pane ID property in Constructor) is declared and then used in a call to the **LWindow** member function **FindPaneByID()**:

```
thePicturePane = (CPicturePane *)theWindow->FindPaneByID(
                                    paneID_PicturePane);
```

Given the ID of a pane, this routine returns a pointer to the pane object that PowerPlant created when it built the window from a 'PPob' resource. **FindPaneByID()** returns a generic **LPane** pointer, so for this situation the returned value must be typecast as a pointer to a **CPicturePane**.

Once the program has a pointer to the custom pane, it can work with that pane. That is, any of the **CPicturePane** member functions can be invoked to act on the pane object. The goal here is to associate the picture in memory with the custom pane object, so the **SetPicture()** function is invoked:

```
thePicturePane->SetPicture(thePicture);
```

SetPicture() does nothing more than take a passed-in **PicHandle** and assign it to **mPicture**—the only data member in the **CPicturePane** class:

```
void
CPicturePane::SetPicture(PicHandle thePicture)
{
    mPicture = thePicture;
}
```

When the custom pane needs updating, PowerPlant will invoke **DrawSelf()** and that routine will use the **PicHandle** stored in **mPicture** to reference the picture data in memory and draw the picture in the custom pane (**DrawSelf()** is covered just ahead).

The pane object now holds a reference to the picture to display, but it needs one more piece of information. When I added the custom pane to the 'PPob' in Constructor, I arbitrarily chose its size. Because the picture to be displayed is user-selected, I had no way of knowing how large a pane the window would need in order to properly display the picture. Now is the time to resize the pane. A call to the **LPane** member function **ResizeFrameTo()** handles that task:

```
thePicturePane->ResizeFrameTo(theWidth, theHeight, theUpdate);
```

The picture's dimensions were calculated earlier in **ShowPictureWindow()**. The last parameter to **ResizeFrameTo()** specifies whether the pane should be updated. Since the window is not yet shown, the value (**true** or **false**) of this parameter is unimportant.

Finally, it's time to show the window. A call to the **LWindow** member function **Show()** does that. The display of a window triggers an update event, and PowerPlant responds by calling the **DrawSelf()** member function for each pane object in the window. The picture window has but a single pane, so only one call to **DrawSelf()** is made.

Drawing the Picture in the Custom Pane

This chapter's custom pane example introduced you to **DrawSelf()**. In that example, **DrawSelf()** was written so that it drew a rectangle along the border of the custom pane. For this version of MediaCenter, I'll use that very same code, and add only a single new line. The Toolbox routine **DrawPicture()** accepts as its two parameters the **PicHandle** of a picture to draw and a pointer to a **Rect** that specifies the location in which to draw the picture. The **mPicture** data member of the **CPicturePane** object provides the **PicHandle**, and the **DrawSelf()** call to the **LPane** member function **CalcLocalFrameRect()** provides the rectangle:

```
void
CPicturePane::DrawSelf()
{
   Rect  theFrame;

   CalcLocalFrameRect(theFrame);
   ::FrameRect(&theFrame);

   ::DrawPicture(mPicture, &theFrame);
}
```

Responding to a Mouse Button Click in the Pane

In discussing this chapter's custom pane example, I stated that the **ClickSelf()** member function was written generically enough that it could be used unaltered by other custom panes. Such is indeed the case. As written, **ClickSelf()** moves a ghost frame in response to the user's dragging of the custom pane.

That technique is sufficient for dragging the picture pane (look back at Figure 8-16 to see the effect), so this version of MediaCenter uses **ClickSelf()** as you saw it listed back in the "Overriding **ClickSelf()**" part of this chapter's "Custom Pane Example" section.

Releasing the Picture-occupied Memory

When picture data is loaded into memory, it's referenced by a **PicHandle**. When a program is through with the data, the memory that the **PicHandle** references should be freed, or released. A picture that was loaded from a 'PICT' resource can be released by making a call to the Toolbox routine **ReleaseResource()**. A picture that was loaded from picture data in a file of type 'PICT' is instead released by making a call to the Toolbox routine **KillPicture()**. That's the routine to use here. The time to release the memory that holds the picture data is when you're absolutely sure the picture is no longer needed. The timing of when to release the memory can be left up to PowerPlant by creating a custom pane destructor that includes the call to **KillPicture()**.

TIP *If you haven't programmed the Mac for a while, here's a quick refresher on Mac memory. The* stack *contains data that is local to routines in the program. Locally declared variables are on the stack during the time the routine is executing. And if the routine calls another function, the parameters passed to the function get stored on the stack. The* heap, *on the other hand, holds an application's executable code. The heap also holds data structures, including objects, created dynamically by the application.*

A custom pane doesn't always need to include a destructor (this chapter's custom pane example didn't). That's because PowerPlant will automatically take care of reallocating the pane object memory. When a window is closed by the user, PowerPlant handles the cleaning up of the memory occupied by the window object and any pane objects related to that window. However, if a pane object allocates additional memory for its own needs, then that pane object is responsible for releasing the additional memory. Here's implementation of the **CPicturePane** destructor:

```
CPicturePane::~CPicturePane( )
{
    ::KillPicture(mPicture);
}
```

Running the Program

With the new resources and code added to the *MediaCenter.μ* project, choose Run from the Project menu to build a new version of MediaCenter. When MediaCenter launches, choose Open Picture from the Picture menu. Choose a 'PICT' file from the Open dialog box that appears. You can open one of the files included in the P03 MediaCenter folder in this chapter's example folder on the Companion CD-ROM or any one of your own picture files. A new window that displays the picture will then appear. Click on the picture and drag it in the window. You can open as many picture windows as you want—you can even open more than one window that displays the same picture.

Moving On

As you've seen, PowerPlant has powerful tools for creating and managing complex interfaces. You learned how to use Constructor to define and lay out the panes of a window, and to create the 'PPob' resource that binds a window and its panes together.

You've also learned how to work with the dozens of predefined pane types available in PowerPlant and Constructor, and also how to customize PowerPlant's **LPane** class to create windows with the specific functionality you want. You've learned how to tie windows in with functions such as opening picture files, and you've significantly upgraded the MediaCenter application.

At this point you know all about menu handling and working with panes. The MediaCenter application is starting to look like a professional piece of work.

Menu and pane handling are only two of a trio of very powerful PowerPlant features, though. The third feature is controls. Controls include check boxes, radio buttons, push buttons, and other interface elements with which the user interacts. A control sends out, or broadcasts, information to an application, and the application responds. MediaCenter makes use of a type of control referred to as picture buttons—as you'll see in the next chapter.

9

Controls

In Chapter 8, "Panes & Views," you saw that a program uses panes to deliver information to the user. In this chapter, you'll learn that panes are also used by the user to submit information to the program. In traditional Macintosh programming, items such as push buttons, check boxes, and radio buttons are used to accomplish this task. The same holds true for PowerPlant-based programming. In PowerPlant, however, such elements are referred to as *controls*, and every control is a type of pane.

PowerPlant simplifies adding controls to a program in the same way it simplifies adding windows and other objects to a program. PowerPlant includes a class for each of the standard types of controls with which Mac users and programmers are familiar, including push buttons, radio buttons, check boxes, and pop-up menus. In addition, PowerPlant also includes classes for other, nonstandard controls such as the disclosure triangle (the small triangle that, when clicked, reveals items in a hierarchical list) and a button whose look is defined by a family of color icons.

When the user clicks on a control, the control broadcasts a message to the program. Objects your program has marked to be listeners listen for and respond to these messages. In this chapter, you'll read all about creating controls, control messages, and how your program should handle them.

Constructor & Controls

You add a control to your program in much the same way you add a pane to it: use Constructor to place the element in a 'PPob' resource; then rely on source code to provide the control's behavior. As you'll see later in this chapter, every control class is derived from the **LControl** class, which itself is derived from the **LPane** class.

Constructor's Catalog window lists each of the control types available to a PowerPlant-based project. Figure 9-1 shows the controls that Constructor allows you to add to a 'PPob' resource.

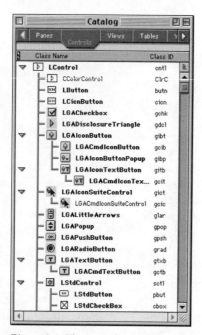

Figure 9-1: The control types Constructor works with.

That Platinum Look

Starting with Mac OS 8, the Macintosh took on what Apple calls a "platinum look"—graphical interface elements in a 3D, grayscale style. Before Mac OS 8, Apple defined a Grayscale Appearance specification. This specification established the rules for programs that wanted to have the platinum look to be present in the not-yet-released Mac OS 8. If your program runs on a computer with Mac OS 8, it will automatically have a platinum look. If it runs on a computer with any version of the Macintosh operating system earlier than Mac OS 8, it won't. With this in mind, Metrowerks defined a number of controls your project can use if you want your program to have the platinum look even when it runs on a Mac running a version of Mac OS 7. Like all controls, a grayscale control begins with an L. To make it readily evident that such a control meets Apple's Grayscale Appearance specification, the L is followed by the letters GA. Figure 9-1 shows that Constructor lists the grayscale controls along with the normal control types.

In most cases, a grayscale control doesn't offer unique features beyond those found in the normal version of the control—the functionality of a grayscale control usually just mimics a normal control. The difference simply lies in the shading given to the drawn control. You'll typically choose one type of control or the other—you won't mix them. For instance, Figure 9-1 shows two types of check boxes listed in Constructor's Catalog window—LStdCheckBox and LGACheckbox. If you use LStdCheckBox in a 'PPob,' the resulting window will display a platinum look check box under Mac OS 8 and an older-style check box under prior versions of the Mac OS. If you use LGACheckbox, the window will always display a platinum look check box.

TIP *In this book's examples, I use standard controls rather than the Grayscale Appearance controls. Users who run example programs (such as the ControlsExample application described ahead) will see controls that match the look they're used to seeing in programs that run under their operating system.*

Adding a Control to a 'PPob'

All the controls that PowerPlant knows about are listed in the Catalog window of Constructor—choose Catalog from the Window menu to reveal that window. Then click on the Controls tab at the top of the Catalog window. The result is shown in Figure 9-2.

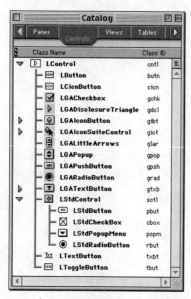

Figure 9-2: The Catalog window displaying control types.

You define a control to be part of a window by using Constructor to add the control to the window's 'PPob' resource. Begin by double-clicking on the 'PPob' resource name in Constructor's main window. Then click on the control type of interest in the Catalog window and drag the control type to the 'PPob' that's displayed in the layout editor. Figure 9-3 shows a layout editor displaying a 'PPob' resource that holds six controls. The controls have ID values of 1 through 6. The item with ID 0 isn't a control—it's an LCaption pane (a pane that holds static text).

TIP *From Figure 9-3, you see that a window isn't limited to holding either controls or panes—it can hold any combination of these items.*

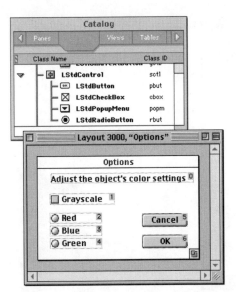

Figure 9-3: A 'PPob' resource that holds a number of controls.

Figure 9-3 shows controls of three standard Macintosh control types: check box, radio button, and push button. The controls correspond to the LStdCheckBox, LStdRadioButton, and LStdButton control types in the Constructor Catalog window, and to PowerPlant classes of the same name.

TIP | *This chapter's* ControlExample.μ *project demonstrates how a project's source code handles a mouse click on a push button. The technique shown in that example is one used by most controls—including a nonstandard control like the picture button (LButton) used in this chapter's versions of MediaCenter.*

Changing a Control's Characteristics _____

Like any pane, you double-click on a control to open a property inspector that reveals characteristics of the control. Figure 9-4 shows the property inspector for a standard check box.

Figure 9-4: Control characteristics are edited in the control's property inspector.

The fields of a control vary depending on the control's type, but because each control is derived from the **LControl** and **LPane** classes, all controls have some fields in common. Of these, the most important is the Pane ID field. This field gives the pane a unique ID in a 'PPob' resource. If you need to find a particular pane from your source code, you'll rely on the **LPane** member function **FindPaneByID()** introduced in the last version of *MediaCenter.µ* in Chapter 8, "Panes & Views." MediaCenter doesn't require the accessing of controls by pane IDs, so an example of this technique is provided in this chapter's *ByIDExample.µ* project.

Another field of interest is the Value Message field—a field common to all types of controls. When a mouse click occurs in a control, PowerPlant automatically returns the control's value message to your program. Your application-defined source code will then use this value message to determine what action to take. For this reason the value message of a control must be unique for each control in any one 'PPob' resource. All the examples in this chapter use control value messages.

As with any newly added pane, a new control probably won't have the correct size or won't be at the desired location in the window where it's been added. You can change a control's size or window placement from the layout editor (by clicking on any corner of the item and dragging or by clicking anywhere else on the item and dragging), or you can enter pixel values in the control's property inspector. From the property inspector, the Width and Height fields affect the control's size, while the Left in Superview and Top in Superview fields affect the control's window location.

Working With Controls

When the user clicks on a control, the control sends a message to your program. However, some object has to be listening for the message for the program to be able to respond to it. In this section, we'll go over designating an object to be a listener for these broadcast messages and determining how the listener responds to a message.

Control Classes

In Chapter 8, "Panes & Views," you saw that PowerPlant defines a class for each type of pane you add to a 'PPob' in Constructor. Controls are a type of pane, so this same one-to-one correspondence is present between PowerPlant classes and controls.

Figure 9-1 shows the controls that Constructor allows you to add to a 'PPob' resource. Figure 9-5 shows the class hierarchy for control-related PowerPlant classes. Note that each control in Figure 9-1 appears as a class in the hierarchy of Figure 9-5.

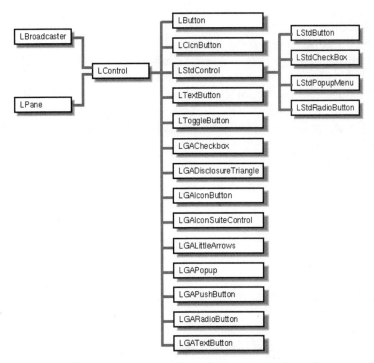

Figure 9-5: The PowerPlant class hierarchy for control-related classes.

TIP *The way scroll bars fit into the control hierarchy is somewhat confusing. In Chapter 8, "Panes & Views," you used the **LScroller** class to add a scroll area to a window. While an individual scroll bar is a control (one can be created from the **LStdControl** class), a scroll area isn't—it's a view (**LScroller** is derived from **LView**). A view can hold other panes, and two of the panes an **LScroller** object can hold are controls—**LStdControl** controls that represent the horizontal and vertical scroll bars that may be present in a scroll area. So while an **LScroller** may hold two controls, the scroll area itself isn't a control.*

Control Base Classes

Each type of control is derived from the **LControl** class, which itself has two base classes: **LBroadcaster** and **LPane**.

All controls have **LBroadcaster** as a base class, so all controls are *broadcasters*. That is, a control can broadcast, or send, messages. A message typically is used to let *listeners* know that a control was just the recipient of a mouse button click. A listener is an object that has the **LListener** class as a base class. A control is a broadcaster, and a window or the application itself is usually the listener. The discussions that accompany each of the examples in this chapter point out the specific relationship of the broadcasters and listeners.

The **LBroadcaster** class is an abstract class—your project won't create any actual **LBroadcaster** objects. Instead, **LBroadcaster** exists to provide the functionality necessary to make objects broadcasters. The following snippet shows the **LBroadcaster** class declaration. Of most interest is the **AddListener()** function. Not all listeners listen for messages from all broadcasters. Instead, a listener object maintains a list of broadcaster objects that it will listen to. To add a broadcaster object to its list, a broadcaster object uses its **AddListener()** member function.

TIP *Read those last couple of sentences carefully. While it may seem like the broadcaster object invokes its **AddListener()** routine to add a listener, this isn't the case. The broadcaster object invokes **AddListener()** to add itself to a listener's list of broadcasters. Note the one **AddListener()** parameter—it's an **LListener** object. This is the listener object that maintains the list to which the broadcaster adds itself. If this seems confusing, just remember that a listening object has a list of broadcaster objects it listens to. Broadcaster objects maintain no such list of objects they broadcast to.*

```
class  LBroadcaster {
public:
                LBroadcaster();
                LBroadcaster(const LBroadcaster
                            &inOriginal);
    virtual     ~LBroadcaster();

    void        AddListener(LListener  *inListener);
    void        RemoveListener(LListener *inListener);

    void        StartBroadcasting();
    void        StopBroadcasting();
    Boolean     IsBroadcasting();

    void        BroadcastMessage(MessageT  inMessage,
                                void      *ioParam = nil);

protected:
    TArray<LListener*>  mListeners;
    Boolean             mIsBroadcasting;
};
```

The second base class to **LControl** is **LPane**. Chapter 8, "Panes & Views," provided you with a sound background in this class, so only a brief mention is necessary here. Anything that's drawn in a window must be a pane, so controls need to be derived from **LPane**. The following snippet shows part of the **LPane** class declaration, with an emphasis on some of the member functions you might have your controls invoke. Notice that your program can call **FindPaneByID()** to gain access to the object that represents a specific control in a 'PPob' resource. You can also use **LPane** member functions to change the size, move, hide, or redisplay a control:

```
class LPane : public virtual LAttachable {
    friend class LView;
public:
    enum { class_ID = 'pane' };

    ...
    ...
    virtual LPane*  FindPaneByID(PaneIDT inPaneID);

    void            ResizeFrameTo(Int16 inWidth,
                                  Int16 inHeight,
                                  Boolean inRefresh);
```

```
virtual void       ResizeFrameBy(Int16 inWidthDelta,
                                  Int16 inHeightDelta,
                                  Boolean inRefresh);

virtual void       MoveBy(Int32 inHorizDelta, Int32
                          inVertDelta, Boolean inRefresh);
...
...
virtual void       Show();
virtual void       Hide();
...
...
};
```

The LControl Class

All controls are derived from the **LControl** class. You've just seen that **LControl** inherits from **LBroadcaster** the functionality to make controls broadcasters and from **LPane** the functionality to make controls behave as any other type of pane. **LControl** goes on to add control-related routines that are common to most types of controls. Here, in part, is the declaration of the **LControl** class:

```
class  LControl : public LPane,
                  public LBroadcaster {
public:
                   LControl();
...
...
MessageT           GetValueMessage();
void               SetValueMessage(MessageT inValueMessage);

virtual Int32      GetValue();
virtual void       SetValue(Int32 inValue);

virtual void       IncrementValue(Int32 inIncrement);

Int32              GetMinValue();
virtual void       SetMinValue(Int32 inMinValue);

Int32              GetMaxValue();
virtual void       SetMaxValue(Int32 inMaxValue);

virtual void       SimulateHotSpotClick(Int16 inHotSpot);
```

```
protected:
    MessageT        mValueMessage;
    Int32           mValue;
    Int32           mMinValue;
    Int32           mMaxValue;
    . . .
    . . .
};
```

All controls have a value message held in the **mValueMessage** data member. When a control is clicked on, PowerPlant passes this value to your program so that your code can handle the mouse button click.

Some controls have a current, minimum, and maximum value associated with them—these values are held in the **mValue**, **mMinValue**, and **mMaxValue** data members. Depending on the type of control, either the current value or a combination of all three indicates the current state of the control. For instance, a check box (an object of type **LStdCheckBox**) only has two states, so only the value in the **mValue** data member is needed to reveal the check box status (0 for off, 1 for on). For a check box, the **mMinValue** and **mMaxValue** data members are unimportant. A scroll bar (an object of type **LStdControl**) has several states (the thumb, or indicator, can be positioned in a wide range along the length of the bar), so it needs to store values in all three data members. The scroll bar's current value, in relation to the minimum and maximum values, indicates where the control's thumb is currently located in the scroll bar.

LControl doesn't supply all the functionality needed by each type of control—classes for the individual control types take care of that.

Broadcasting & Listening

A control is a broadcaster of messages. A message consists of the control's value message (as stored in the **LControl mValueMessage** data member) and a pointer to data. Usually the data is the control's current value (as stored in the **LControl mValue** data member). Armed with this information, the listener that responds to the message (a window or the application) knows what control was clicked on and what state the control is in (such as on or off for a check box control).

Value Messages & Constructor

You use Constructor to create a control and to provide it with a value message. Figure 9-6 shows a 'PPob' resource that includes three controls, all of which are push buttons (controls of type LStdButton). The remaining four items in the 'PPob' resource are panes of type LCaption and LEditField.

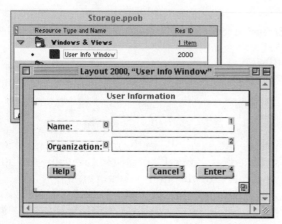

Figure 9-6: A typical 'PPob' resource that holds controls and other pane types.

A control's value message is set by entering a value in the Value Message field of the control's property inspector. If the control is to be either a window's Cancel or OK button, use the pop-up menu to the right of the Value Message to enter one of two PowerPlant-defined constants. These constants are defined in the PowerPlant *PP_Messages.h* header file:

```
const MessageT  msg_OK      = 900;
const MessageT  msg_Cancel  = 901;
```

In the 'PPob' shown in Figure 9-6, the control with a pane ID of 3 is used as the window's Cancel button—see Figure 9-7. This control therefore has a Value Message of **msg_Cancel**, or 901. Looking at the property inspector for the control with a pane ID of 4 (the Enter push button) would reveal that it has a Value Message of **msg_OK**, or 900. Note that while a window's Cancel and OK buttons generally have those names, they don't *have* to.

Chapter 9: Controls ◆ **195**

Figure 9-7: The property inspector for a Cancel push button.

For a control that doesn't represent either the Cancel or OK button, you'll enter a value message of your own choosing. In Figure 9-6, you see that the example 'PPob' has one such control—the Help push button with the pane ID of 5. Figure 9-8 shows the property inspector for this control.

Figure 9-8: The property inspector for a push button other than the Cancel or OK button.

The value you choose for a control's value message doesn't have anything to do with the nature of the control—it simply serves as a way for your program to distinguish with which control the user is interacting. The only requirement is that each broadcaster a listener listens for has a unique value message. For instance, if the window holding the controls is to be the listener (perhaps something will be drawn in the window in response to a click on a control), then every control in the window's 'PPob' resource must have a unique value message. If instead the application itself is to be the listener (perhaps all manner of things can happen as a result of clicking on a control, such as a sound playing or a movie opening), then every control the application listens for must be unique.

If the application is to be the listener and be aware of controls in multiple windows, then it is necessary that controls in multiple 'PPob' resources be unique. If that weren't the case, then the application couldn't distinguish between, say, a click on one window's Play Sound button with a value message of 1001 and a click on another window's Play Movie button with the same value message of 1001. One common scheme programmers use for choosing value messages is to give each control in a 'PPob' a value that is the sum of the 'PPob' resource ID and the control's pane ID. For example, in Figure 9-6, you see that the Help button has a value message of 2005. This number is the 'PPob' resource ID of 2000 and the control's pane ID of 5. Using this scheme ensures that each control in the *.ppob* file will have a unique value message.

TIP *This plan won't work if you assign control pane IDs that are both very large and very small. A control with a pane ID of 1001 in a 'PPob' that has an ID of 1000 results in a value message of 2001. So will a control with a pane ID of 1 in a 'PPob' that has an ID of 2000. This is an unusual scenario, though. Usually programmers give 'PPob' resources ID values of 500, 1000, 1500, and so forth, and give panes ID values of 1, 2, 3, and so on.*

Value Messages & Source Code Constants

In order to respond to mouse button clicks on controls, your application-defined source code needs to be aware of the value messages you've given these controls. This is accomplished by defining a constant for each control which the source code is to be aware of.

A control value message is a 32-bit number, so a constant to represent such a message could be defined to be of the PowerPlant data type **Int32**. For clarity, though, use the PowerPlant data type **MessageT**. Recall from Chapter 4, "PowerPlant Basics," that the **MessageT** type is a synonym for the **Int32** type.

For the 'PPob' shown back in Figure 9-6, only one message constant needs to be defined—a constant for the Help button. Figure 9-8 shows that in Constructor I've given that control a value message of 2005. This snippet shows the constant for the Help button's value message, along with the constant for the resource ID of the 'PPob' that control appears in:

```
const ResIDT    PPob_UserInfo = 2000;
const MessageT  msg_HelpButton = 2005;
```

The Cancel and Enter buttons don't require application-defined constants because their message values come from the PowerPlant-defined **msg_Cancel** and **msg_OK** constants. Those constants are defined in the PowerPlant header file *PP_Messages.h*.

Linking a Broadcaster to a Listener

When a control is clicked on, the control broadcasts a message. In order for an object to act on the message, the object must be a listener and it must include the control in its list of broadcasters to which it listens. The association between broadcasters and listeners is implicit—your code must explicitly add a broadcaster to a listener's list. You do that by invoking the broadcaster's **AddListener()** member function. From the **LBroadcaster** class, here's the **AddListener()** prototype:

```
void AddListener(LListener *inListener);
```

Before invoking **AddListener()** your code needs access to the control object. Because a control is a type of pane, you can use the **FindPaneByID()** function that a control inherits from the **LPane** class. As you saw in Chapter 8, "Panes & Views," the object that **FindPaneByID()** returns is always of type **LPane**, so it needs to be typecast to the particular type of pane class that matches the control. For the Help push button, that means typecasting to an **LStdButton**:

```
LStdButton  *theStdButton;

theStdButton = (LStdButton *)theWindow->
                    FindPaneByID(paneID_HelpButton);
```

The push button control object can now invoke its **AddListener()** function. The parameter to **AddListener()** is the listener object that is to include this control in its list of broadcasters. If the listener is to be the application object, and the code appears in an application-derived class member function, then the call looks like this:

```
theStdButton->AddListener(this);
```

The following version of **ObeyCommand()** ties together the preceding snippets and demonstrates a how a program might link a broadcaster to a listener:

```
const ResIDT      PPob_UserInfo    = 2000;
const PaneIDT     paneID_HelpButton =    5;
...
...
Boolean
CPPStarterApp::ObeyCommand(
    CommandT     inCommand,
    void         *ioParam)
{
    ...
    ...
    switch (inCommand) {

      case cmd_New:
          LWindow  *theWindow;

          theWindow = LWindow::CreateWindow(PPob_UserInfo, this);
          LStdButton  *theStdButton;

          theStdButton = (LStdButton *)theWindow->
                            FindPaneByID(paneID_HelpButton);
          theStdButton->AddListener(this);

          theWindow->Show();
          break;
    ...
    ...
}
```

In the preceding version of **ObeyCommand()** it's assumed that the New command in the File menu results in the display of a window based on the 'PPob' resource shown back in Figure 9-6—a window that, among other items, holds Enter, Cancel, and Help push buttons. The creation of a window that holds controls is the time to link all of the controls to their appropriate listener or listeners—yet the preceding snippet only adds the Help button to the application object's list of broadcasters. Adding all of the controls is covered next.

Linking Several Broadcasters to a Listener

Each control needs to be linked to a listener, which can be done by using the preceding technique repeatedly. That is, invoke **FindPaneByID()** and **AddListener()** for each control in the window. Here's a new version of **ObeyCommand()** that does just that for the Enter, Cancel, and Help buttons in the 'PPob' resource currently being discussed:

```
const ResIDT     PPob_UserInfo      = 2000;
const PaneIDT    paneID_EnterButton =    3;
const PaneIDT    paneID_CancelButton =   4;
const PaneIDT    paneID_HelpButton =     5;
...
...
Boolean
CPPStarterApp::ObeyCommand(
    CommandT     inCommand,
    void         *ioParam)
{
    ...
    ...
    switch (inCommand) {

        case cmd_New:
            LWindow  *theWindow;

            theWindow = LWindow::CreateWindow(PPob_UserInfo, this);
            LStdButton  *theStdButton;

            theStdButton = (LStdButton *)theWindow->
                            FindPaneByID(paneID_EnterButton);
            theStdButton->AddListener(this);

            theStdButton = (LStdButton *)theWindow->
                            FindPaneByID(paneID_CancelButton);
            theStdButton->AddListener(this);

            theStdButton = (LStdButton *)theWindow->
                            FindPaneByID(paneID_HelpButton);
            theStdButton->AddListener(this);

            theWindow->Show();
            break;
    ...
    ...
}
```

Note that for a window that has 10, 20, or more controls, the broadcaster/listener code would be unwieldy. In many situations this can be avoided by using a PowerPlant utility routine named **LinkListenerToControls()**.

As you can see in the previous snippet, such is the case in the current example—all three push buttons have the application object as their listener. This is often the case—all the controls in a window have the same listener. For such situations, the **UReanimator** class member function **LinkListenerToControls()** can be used in place of **AddListener()** calls. Here's the prototype for this useful routine:

```
static void  LinkListenerToControls(
                     LListener *inListener,
                     LView     *inControlContainer,
                     ResIDT     inResListID);
```

The first of the three parameters is the listener object to which one or more controls are to be linked. The second parameter is the **LView** object holding the controls to be linked. The last parameter is the resource ID of a 'RidL' (Resource ID List)—a PowerPlant-defined resource.

The listener object is often the application object. As before, you can use the **this** keyword. The **LView** object that holds the controls will be the **LWindow** object returned by a call to **CreateWindow()**. The 'RidL' ID will be the same ID as the 'PPob' resource that holds the controls. A 'RidL' is an internal resource automatically created by Constructor when you add a control to a 'PPob' resource. Constructor uses this resource as a list of broadcaster pane IDs for the 'PPob.' I've referred to the 'RidL' as internal because Constructor doesn't allow you to view or edit it. Here's what a call to **LinkListenerToControls()** might look like:

```
UReanimator::LinkListenerToControls(this, theWindow, PPob_UserInfo);
```

TIP *Recall that utility class member functions are declared to be static, and as such can be invoked directly—there's no need to first create an object of the class type that defines the member function. Instead, just preface the call with the class name and the scope resolution operator, as shown in the preceding snippet.*

Now let's see what the code under the **cmd_New case** label in the **switch** of **ObeyCommand()** looks like with a single call to **LinkListenerToControls()**, replacing all of the calls to **FindPaneByID()** and **AddListener()**:

```
case cmd_New:
   LWindow  *theWindow;

   theWindow = LWindow::CreateWindow(PPob_UserInfo, this);
   UReanimator::LinkListenerToControls(this, theWindow,
                                 PPob_UserInfo);
   theWindow->Show();
   break;
```

Making an Object a Listener

A control object is automatically a broadcaster. The application object or a window object that will listen to broadcasters is not, however, automatically a listener. To create a listener object, modify the object's class declaration by adding **LListener** as a base class.

As this chapter's examples will show, the application object is often a listener. To this point you've seen the application class declaration written with the **LApplication** class as the base class. To make the application object a listener, include **LListener** as a base class in the application class declaration:

```
class  CPPStarterApp : public LApplication, public LListener {
public:
   ...
   ...
};
```

Like **LBroadcaster**, **LListener** is an abstract class. You'll use **LListener** as I've done in the preceding snippet—as a base class for your derived classes. **LListener** includes only a handful of member functions, and only one of those— **ListenToMessage()**—will see regular use in most of your PowerPlant-based projects. Your listener class declaration should override **ListenToMessage()** as shown here:

```
class  CPPStarterApp : public LApplication, public LListener {
public:
   ...
   ...
   virtual void   ListenToMessage(MessageT inMessage,
                                 void     *ioParam);
   ...
   ...
};
```

ListenToMessage() gets invoked when a control is clicked on. The first **ListenToMessage()** parameter is the value message of the clicked control. The second parameter is a pointer to additional data that may be needed in order to take the action appropriate to handling the mouse click. Typically this data is the control's current value, or state.

Listening for Messages

Any number of objects can be listeners. When a control is clicked on, PowerPlant automatically invokes the proper version or versions of **ListenToMessage()**. Consider this example. The application class is made a listener, as in the previous **CPPStarterApp** class declaration. When a window like the one being discussed (Figure 9-6) is opened, a call to the **Reanimator** utility function **LinkListenerToControls()** links that window's three controls (the Enter, Cancel, and Help buttons) to the application object. If the user clicks on one of the window's buttons, PowerPlant will invoke the application object's version of **ListenToMessage()**. PowerPlant correctly does this because the controls in the window are in the application object's list of broadcasters to listen for.

Each listener implements **ListenToMessage()** such that it handles each of the messages that the listener might receive. Carrying on with the same example, let's see how an application object would respond to a click on a control in the application object's list of broadcasters. First, a constant needs to be defined for each message that the listener listens for. Each constant is a value message of a control, as defined in Constructor in the control's Value Message field. The 'PPob' resource pictured back in Figure 9-6 has three controls, but two of them have value messages defined by the PowerPlant constants **msg_OK** and **msg_Cancel**. Thus only one constant needs to be defined here (refer back to Figure 9-8 to verify the following value):

```
const MessageT    msg_HelpButton    = 2005;
```

The implementation of **ListenToMessage()** uses a switch statement to compare the message sent by the broadcaster (the clicked-on control) to the constants that represent messages that the listener is to respond to. Code under a case label should take the appropriate action to handle a click on the button.

```
void
CPPStarterApp::ListenToMessage(
    MessageT    inMessage,
    void        *ioParam )
{
    #pragma unused( ioParam )
```

```
switch ( inMessage ) {

    case msg_OK:
        // code to support a click on the Enter button
        break;

    case msg_Cancel:
        // code to support a click on the Cancel button
        break;

    case msg_HelpButton:
        // code to support a click on the Help button
        break;
    }
}
```

In the preceding example, a click on the Enter button (msg_OK) might result in saving the user-entered information (refer to Figure 9-6) to a data structure or to an application-defined UserInfo object, and then closing the window. A click on the Cancel button (msg_Cancel) would simply result in the window closing without the user-entered information being saved. A click on the Help button (msg_HelpButton) might open another window—one that displays information about the fields in the first window.

TIP *ListenToMessage() always has the two parameters just shown—yet this version doesn't use the second parameter. The C directive **#pragma unused** is used to prevent the compiler from issuing a warning during compilation. The directive can be removed and the code will successfully compile, but in doing so the CodeWarrior Errors & Warnings window will open and display a "variable is not used in function" warning.*

Control Examples

This chapter's version of MediaCenter includes a control window that holds picture buttons—controls of type **LButton**. A picture button isn't a standard Macintosh control—without PowerPlant and Constructor you'd need to write your own code to turn a picture of any size into a button. While such a control is interesting and useful, your programs will no doubt also make use of standard controls, such as push buttons. The two short projects presented on the following pages demonstrate techniques for working with standard controls.

Push Button Example Project

The *ControlExample.µ* project results in a program that displays the window shown in Figure 9-9. As you've surmised, clicking on the Beep Once button plays the system sound once, while clicking on the Beep Twice button plays the sound twice. With the exception of the Quit item in the File menu, the program's menu items are unimportant.

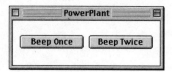

Figure 9-9: The window that results from running the ControlExample program.

The completed project appears in the P01 ControlExample folder in the Chapter 09 folder on this book's Companion CD-ROM.

Adding a Control to the 'PPob' Resource

The *ControlExample.µ* project is created from Basic PowerPlant project stationery. The *PP Basic Resource.ppob* file supplied by CodeWarrior contains a single 'PPob' resource with a name of <replace me> and a resource ID of 1. As you can see in Figure 9-10, I've changed the ID to 1000, deleted the text from within the window (the LCaption item), and resized the window. I've also added what is to be the Beep Once button.

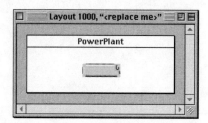

Figure 9-10: Adding a control to the ControlExample.µ project's 'PPob' resource.

To create the Beep Once button, begin by choosing Catalog from the Windows menu. Then click on LStdButton in the Catalog window and drag it to the Layout window displaying the 'PPob' resource. Figure 9-10 shows how the Layout window looks after dropping the new control onto it.

Double-click on the new control to bring up its property inspector. Enter a pane ID in the Pane ID field, a value message in the Value Message field, and a button title, or descriptor, in the Title field. Figure 9-11 shows that I've given the control a pane ID of 1, a value message of 1001 (the sum of the 'PPob' resource ID and the pane ID), and a title of "Beep Once."

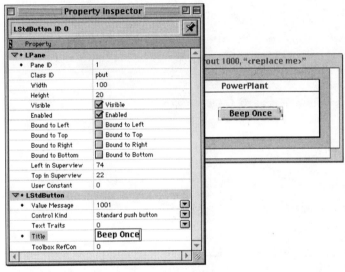

Figure 9-11: Using a control's property inspector to edit the control's pane ID, value message, and title.

It's easiest to properly resize and move the control from the Layout window, so close the property inspector and take care of these tasks.

Adding a Second Control to the 'PPob' Resource

To create the Beep Twice button, repeat the preceding process—starting with the dragging of LStdButton from the Catalog window to the Layout window. Figure 9-12 shows the property inspector for the second control; Figure 9-13 shows the completed 'PPob' resource in a layout window.

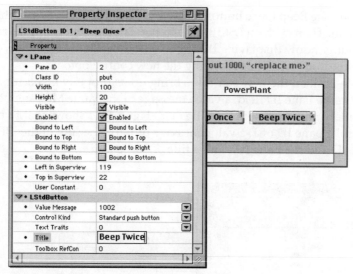

Figure 9-12: Editing the properties of a second control.

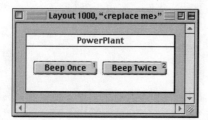

Figure 9-13: The completed 'PPob' resource for the ControlExample.μ *project.*

Making the Application Class a Listener

As is often the case, in *ControlExample.μ* the application object serves as the listener. To make the application object a listener, **LListener** is added as a base class to the **CPPStarterApp** class. The **LListener** member function **ListenToMessage()** is then overridden.

```
class  CPPStarterApp : public LApplication, public LListener {
public:
                     CPPStarterApp();
    virtual         ~CPPStarterApp();

    virtual void    ListenToMessage(MessageT inMessage,
                                    void    *ioParam);
```

```
    virtual Boolean   ObeyCommand(CommandT inCommand,
                                    void    *ioParam);

    virtual void      FindCommandStatus(CommandT inCommand,
                                    Boolean  &outEnabled,
                                    Boolean  &outUsesMark,
                                    Char16   &outMark,
                                    Str255   outName);
protected:

    virtual void      StartUp();
};
```

Linking the Broadcasters to the Listener

The broadcasters—the window's two controls—need to be linked to the listener—the application. That's done with a call to the utility routine **LinkListenerToControls()** after the window holding the controls is opened. While only one line of code needs to be added to the default, the CodeWarrior-supplied version of **ObeyCommand()**, it's an important enough line that it should be shown in the context in which it appears.

The constant **window_Sample** holds the ID of the project's one 'PPob' resource. This constant is used in the creation of the window, then again as the last parameter to **LinkListenerToControls()**. The first parameter is the listener, which is the application object. The call to **LinkListenerToControls()** is invoked by the application object, so the this keyword can be used here. The second parameter is the **LView** that holds the broadcasters to be linked to the listener. The **LWindow** class is derived from **LView**, so the **LWindow** variable **theWindow** can be used here.

```
const ResIDT   window_Sample   = 1000;
...
...
Boolean
CPPStarterApp::ObeyCommand(
    CommandT    inCommand,
    void        *ioParam)
{
    Boolean   cmdHandled = true;

    switch (inCommand) {

        case cmd_New:
            LWindow  *theWindow;
```

```
        theWindow = LWindow::CreateWindow(window_Sample, this);

        UReanimator::LinkListenerToControls( this,
                            theWindow, window_Sample );
        theWindow->Show();
        break;

    default:
        cmdHandled = LApplication::ObeyCommand(inCommand,
                                        ioParam);

        break;
    }

    return cmdHandled;
}
```

Implementing ListenToMessage()

The application object will listen for the two controls in the window—the controls that send out messages of 1001 and 1002 (refer back to Figures 9-11 and 9-12 to see these values in Constructor):

```
const MessageT  msg_OnceButton    = 1001;
const MessageT  msg_TwiceButton   = 1002;
```

The implementation of the **CPPStarterApp** member function **ListenToMessage()** includes a **switch** that compares the value of the message passed in (the value message of the clicked-on control) with the constants just defined.

```
void
CPPStarterApp::ListenToMessage(
    MessageT    inMessage,
    void        *ioParam )
{
    #pragma unused( ioParam )

    switch ( inMessage ) {

        case msg_OnceButton:
            ::SysBeep(1);
            break;
```

```
    case msg_TwiceButton:
        ::SysBeep(1);
        ::SysBeep(1);
        break;
    }
}
```

The *ControlExample.μ* project handles a click on the Beep Once button by invoking the Toolbox function **SysBeep()** to play the system sound a single time. A click on the Beep Twice button is taken care of by invoking **SysBeep()** two times.

Working With Control Objects Example Project

When a window is created, PowerPlant creates an object to represent the window and an object for each pane in the window. A control is a type of pane, so each control exists as an object. The *ControlExample.μ* project code didn't explicitly work with the two control objects that resulted from the creation of the program's one window. Because the broadcasting of a message by a control is done automatically, and because a broadcast message identifies the control it was sent from, there was no need for application-defined code to make use of either control object. This won't always be the case, however. If the code in your own project needs to make use of member functions defined in the control's class or in one of the classes the control is derived from, then your project needs access to the control itself.

The *ByIDExample.μ* project was created from a copy of the *ControlExample.μ* project. The program that results from the *ByIDExample.μ* project opens a single window with two push buttons controls—just as the program built from the *ControlExample.μ* project does. The only difference between the programs is in the wording of the rightmost button's title. In the ControlExample program, the button's title was Beep Twice. Here, in the ByIDExample program, this same button has a title of Beep 2 Times—as shown in Figure 9-14. As you'll soon see, this difference in the two programs is the result of the addition of just a few lines of source code to the *ByIDExample.μ* project.

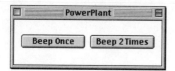

Figure 9-14: The window that results from running the ByIDExample program.

The *ByIDExample.µ* project can be found on the Companion CD-ROM in the P02 ByIDExample folder in the Chapter 09 folder.

Controls & the 'PPob' Resource

The *ByIDExample.µ* project's one 'PPob' resource is identical to the 'PPob' resource that is a part of this chapter's *ControlExample.µ* project. In Figure 9-15 note that the title of the rightmost button doesn't match the final title that this button displays in the ByIDExample program's window (See Figure 9-14). A control class, and the classes it's derived from, include member functions that can be used to change properties of the control. For instance, you can change a button's title, relocate it in its window, hide it, and more. The *ByIDExample.µ* demonstrates how to change a button's title, but the basic technique can be used to perform a variety of tasks on a control.

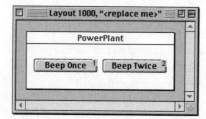

Figure 9-15: The completed 'PPob' resource for the ByIDExample.µ *project.*

Broadcasters & Listener

Most of the code in the *ByIDExample.µ* project is identical to that found in the *ControlExample.µ* project. If you have questions regarding how the *ByIDExample.µ* project sets up the application object to be a listener to the two controls in the program's one window, refer to the walk-through of the *ControlExample.µ* project. Here I'll only summarize what's covered in that section:

- Make the **CPPStarterApp** class a listener by including **LListener** as one of its base classes in the *PP Basic Starter.h* header file.

- Override the **LListener** member function **ListenToMessage()** in the **CPPStarterApp** class declaration in *PP Basic Starter.h*.

■ Link the controls to the application by calling the utility function **LinkListenerToControls()** in the **ObeyCommand()** implementation in the *PP Basics Starter.cp* source code file.

■ Define constants that represent the value messages of the two controls in *PP Basic Starter.cp*.

■ Implement **ListenToMessage()** in *PP Basic Starter.cp*.

Accessing a Control

The *ByIDExample.µ* project uses this chapter's technique of invoking **FindPaneByID()** to obtain an object that represents a control. Once the project has an object, any of the object's member functions can be invoked. Here the **LStdControl** member function **SetDescriptor()** is used to change a button's title, or descriptor.

Begin by defining a constant for the pane ID of the control to be accessed. The *ByIDExample.µ* project only works with the object that represents the Beep Twice button, but for completeness a constant is defined for each of the two controls:

```
const PaneIDT   paneID_OnceButton   =   1;
const PaneIDT   paneID_TwiceButton  =   2;
```

Next, declare a variable to hold the new button title and a variable to hold the control object:

```
Str255         theNewTitle = "\pBeep 2 Times";
LStdButton    *theStdButton;
```

Now the window object should invoke its **FindPaneByID()** function to return the Beep Twice button object to the program. The returned object is a generic **LPane** object, so the code typecasts the object to the control type that matches the button—an **LStdButton**:

```
theStdButton = (LStdButton *) theWindow->
                         FindPaneByID(paneID_TwiceButton);
```

The variable **theStdButton** is an object of type **LStdButton**, so **theStdButton** can invoke any member function of the **LStdButton** class. The **theStdButton** object can also invoke any member function of any class in the chain of classes from which **LStdButton** is derived, including **LStdControl**, **LControl**, and **LPane**. The *ByIDExample.µ* project is interested in changing the title of the Beep Twice button, so **theStdButton** should invoke the **LStdButton** member function **SetDescriptor()**. When a control object invokes this routine, the control's title is changed to whatever string is passed as the sole parameter. Here the Beep Twice button becomes the Beep 2 Times button:

```
theStdButton->SetDescriptor(theNewTitle);
```

The change to the button's title doesn't have to take place immediately upon opening the window that holds the control, but for simplicity that's where I chose to perform this action. You're familiar with the **ObeyCommand()** routine, so this next snippet should look familiar to you. Note the four lines of code that appear after the call to **LinkListenerToControls()**—they're the four lines just described:.

```
const ResIDT   window_Sample   = 1000;
...
...
Boolean
CPPStarterApp::ObeyCommand(
    CommandT   inCommand,
    void       *ioParam)
{
    Boolean   cmdHandled = true;

    switch (inCommand) {

        case cmd_New:
            LWindow  *theWindow;
            theWindow = LWindow::CreateWindow(window_Sample, this);

            UReanimator::LinkListenerToControls(this,
                                theWindow, window_Sample);

            Str255       theNewTitle = "\pBeep 2 Times";
            LStdButton  *theStdButton;

            theStdButton = (LStdButton *) theWindow->
            theStdButton->SetDescriptor(theNewTitle);

            theWindow->Show();
            break;

        default:
            cmdHandled = LApplication::ObeyCommand(inCommand,
                                                ioParam);
            break;
    }

    return cmdHandled;
}
```

Controls & the Example Project

The final version of MediaCenter will have a control window that contains four controls. As shown in Figure 9-16, each of these controls will be a picture button.

Figure 9-16: The Control window from this book's final version of the MediaCenter program.

In this latest version of MediaCenter, I'll add the Control window and one of its buttons to the project. When you build and run this version of MediaCenter, you'll see a Control window that holds the third button from the left—the button that mimics the behavior of the Open Picture menu item in the Picture menu. That is, clicking on the button will result in the display of the standard Open dialog box. Choosing a 'PICT' file from this dialog box then opens a new window that displays the picture held in the selected file. The picture is held in a pane that can be dragged about the window.

You've already seen and walked through all the code that implements the behavior of the Open Picture button—it was presented in Chapter 8, "Panes & Views." Once the Control window with the Open Picture button control has been added, all we need to do is invoke the existing picture-opening code in response to a mouse button click on the button.

After adding the Control window with its one functioning button to the *MediaCenter.μ* project, we'll compile and test the program. With a mastery of controls, it *should* be an easy trick to add a second button to the Control window—and it *is*. I'll need to devote only a few pages to showing how MediaCenter can be modified to include a functioning Play Sound button in the Control window. Clicking on the Play Sound button presents the user with the standard Open dialog box. There the user chooses a sound file, and MediaCenter opens the file and plays the sound it contains.

This latest version of the *MediaCenter.μ* project can be found on the Companion CD-ROM in the P03 MediaCenter folder in the Chapter 09 folder. The version that is discussed later in this chapter—the one that includes two buttons in the Control window—appears in the P04 MediaCenter folder.

Project Resources

MediaCenter is gaining a new type of window—the Control window—so a new 'PPob' resource has to be added to the project's *.ppob* file. The button that will be in this window gets its look from pictures stored as resources, so a couple of 'PICT' resources need to be added to one of the project's resource files.

Creating Button Pictures

When the user clicks on the button in MediaCenter's Control window, the user gets visual feedback to indicate that the button is "down," or depressed. Releasing the mouse button returns the button to its normal state. Figure 9-17 shows the button in both its normal and clicked states. Both button looks are defined by 'PICT' resources added to one of the project's resource files.

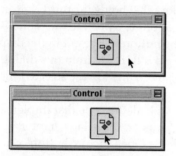

Figure 9-17: A picture button's look changes when it's clicked on.

To create the button's two pictures, first draw them in your favorite paint or drawing program. Figure 9-18 shows the two versions of the Open Picture button, as drawn in a paint program. The second picture will be used by PowerPlant when the user clicks on the button. Thus, this second picture should look similar to the first, but have slightly different shading. Magnification is turned on in the paint program shown in Figure 9-18 to provide you with a look at the differences in the two button pictures.

TIP *Note that the main difference between the two pictures lies in their borders. Each has two dark edges, but which edges have been darkened differs. Also, the content of the rightmost picture (what looks like a document icon with three shapes in it) has been shifted down a pixel and right a pixel. This rightmost picture will provide the button's look when clicked on. If you run the MediaCenter program and click the button, you'll see the effect.*

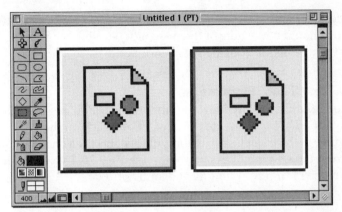

Figure 9-18: Using a paint program to draw the pictures to be used for the display of a picture button.

Adding Button Pictures to a Resource File

After you've drawn the two button pictures, use the graphics program's selection tool to select one of the pictures. Then copy the picture to the clipboard. Now open one of your project's resource files and paste the picture into it. I chose to place the picture in the project's *Doc PowerPlant.rsrc* resource file. Repeat these steps for the second button picture. After pasting both pictures into the *Doc PowerPlant.rsrc* file I had opened using ResEdit, the results looked like those displayed in Figure 9-19.

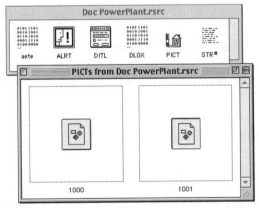

Figure 9-19: Saving two pictures as 'PICT' resources to be used in the display of one picture button.

The particular values you use for IDs for the 'PICT' resources aren't important, but you should make note of them—you'll be using them in the button control that you're about to create in Constructor.

Creating a New 'PPob' Resource

Implementing the Control window requires a new 'PPob' resource that defines the look of that window. To create the new 'PPob,' click on the Windows & Views heading in the main Constructor window and then choose New Layout Resource from the Edit menu. As you see in Figure 9-20, I've given the new resource a name of Control Window and an ID of 2000.

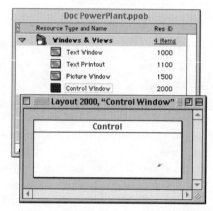

Figure 9-20: Adding a new 'PPob' resource to the MediaCenter's .ppob file.

Double-click on the name of the new 'PPob' to display the resource in the layout editor. You can provide a name for the new window and adjust its size by double-clicking on it to display its property inspector and then editing the values in the Window Title, Width, and Height fields. Figure 9-20 shows the name and size I've selected for the window.

Adding the Button to the New 'PPob'

The new 'PPob' needs a single control—a picture button. Such a button is created from an LButton. If the Catalog window isn't open, choose Catalog from the Windows menu. Then click on the Controls tab to display a hierarchical list of controls. Now click on LButton and drag and drop it anywhere on the new 'PPob' resource displayed in the layout editor. The result will look much like that shown in Figure 9-21.

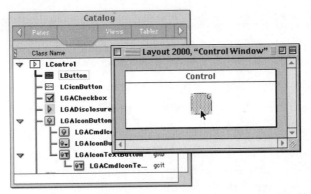

Figure 9-21: Adding a picture button (an LButton) to a 'PPob' resource.

Double-click on the new control to bring up its property inspector. To adjust the size and positioning of the new control, edit the values in the Width, Height, Left in Superview, and Right in Superview. Figure 9-22 shows that I've done that, as well as have provided the control with a pane ID of 1 and a value message of 2001 (the sum of the 'PPob' ID and the control's pane ID).

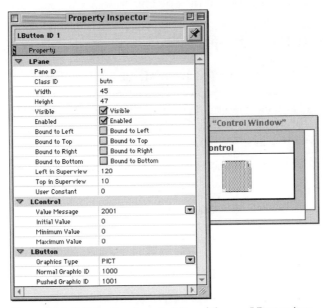

Figure 9-22: Editing the characteristics of the new LButton item.

TIP *You can get the pixel dimensions of any picture by pasting it into the Scrapbook. The size of the picture is listed after the Dimensions label at the bottom of the Scrapbook (with the width listed first and the height second).*

An LButton specifies what type of graphics provides the button's looks. Use the pop-up menu in the Graphics Type field of the property inspector to specify that 'PICT' resources be used. Then enter the resource IDs of the two 'PICT' resources in the Normal Graphic ID and Pushed Graphic ID fields. Notice that the values in these two fields of the property inspector window shown in Figure 9-22 match the IDs of the two 'PICT' resources shown back in Figure 9-19.

With the new 'PPob' created, it's time to add the source code necessary to make the new control functional.

Project Source Code

This latest version of MediaCenter adds two new member functions to the **LDocApplication**-derived **CPPDocApp** class: one function to listen for messages and the other to implement the opening and playing of a sound file.

Adding to the CPPDocApp Application Class

To make the **CPPDocApp** object a listener, add **LListener** as a base class and override the **LListener**-inherited **ListenToMessage()** member function. This is done exactly as shown in this chapter's *ControlExample.μ* and *ByIDExample.μ* projects. The second new member function will be one that holds the code to open the program's Control window, **ShowControlWindow()**. Here's how the **CPPDocApp** class declaration looks now:

```
class CPPDocApp : public LDocApplication, public LListener {
public:
                            CPPDocApp();
        virtual             ~CPPDocApp();

        virtual Boolean     ObeyCommand(
                                CommandT    inCommand,
                                void*       ioParam);

        virtual void        FindCommandStatus(
                                CommandT    inCommand,
                                Boolean     &outEnabled,
                                Boolean     &outUsesMark,
                                Char16      &outMark,
                                Str255      outName);
```

```
   virtual void             ListenToMessage(
                                   MessageT inMessage,
                                   void *ioParam);
   virtual void             ShowControlWindow();

   virtual void             ShowPictureWindow();
   PicHandle                OpenPICTFile();

protected:
   virtual void             StartUp();
   virtual void             OpenDocument( FSSpec *inMacFSSpec);
   virtual LModelObject *   MakeNewDocument();
   virtual void             ChooseDocument();
   virtual void             PrintDocument( FSSpec *inMacFSSpec);
};
```

Listening for Messages

A click on the Control window's one button results in PowerPlant's sending
a message with a value message of 2001 to the listener object's
ListenToMessage() routine (see Figure 9-23). MediaCenter defines a
MessageT constant for each control (there's only one at this point):

```
const MessageT    msg_PictureButton = 2001;
```

    ListenToMessage() is implemented so that it handles this one message.
Later, I'll add other buttons to the Control window. When I do, I'll modify
ListenToMessage() to give it the capability to listen for clicks on the new
buttons:

```
void
CPPDocApp::ListenToMessage(
   MessageT    inMessage,
   void        *ioParam )
{
   #pragma unused( ioParam )

   switch ( inMessage ) {

      case msg_PictureButton:
         ObeyCommand(cmd_OpenPicture, nil);
         break;
   }
}
```

The buttons in the Control window exist as a shortcut for the user—their actions mimic the corresponding menu item. To handle a click on the Open Picture button, all I need to do is invoke the application object's **ObeyCommand()** routine, sending a command of **cmd_OpenPicture()**. As you saw in Chapter 8, "Panes & Views," the result of this command will be the display of the standard Open dialog box from which the user chooses a 'PICT' file to open.

Displaying the Control Window

When a PowerPlant-based application launches, the application object's **StartUp()** member function is automatically invoked. In past versions of MediaCenter, I've used **StartUp()** to open a new, empty text window. In this version of MediaCenter, I do that again—but I also use this routine to open the program's Control window. A call to the new CPPDocApp function **ShowControlWindow()** takes care of this:

```
void
CPPDocApp::StartUp()
{
    ObeyCommand(cmd_New, nil);

    ShowControlWindow();
}
```

TIP *For simplicity I've opted to display the Control window on startup, and leave the window on the screen during the running of the program. Another, more user-friendly way of handling the control window would be to make a Show Control Window/Hide Control Window menu item in a Windows menu.*

Here's how **ShowControlWindow()** is defined in *PP Doc App.cp*:

```
void
CPPDocApp::ShowControlWindow()
{
    LWindow  *theWindow;
    theWindow = LWindow::CreateWindow(PPob_ControlWindow, this);

    UReanimator::LinkListenerToControls(this, theWindow,
                                        PPob_ControlWindow);
    theWindow->Show();
}
```

ShowControlWindow() begins by opening a window based on the 'PPob' that represents the Control window. **LinkListenerToControls()** is then invoked to link, or connect, the window's control to the application. Here this represents the application object, which is the listener; the Window is the **LView** object that holds the control to be linked to the listener, and **PPob_ControlWindow** is the application-defined constant that matches the resource ID of the 'PPob' that holds the control.

Running the Program

With the new resources and code added to the *MediaCenter.μ* project, choose Run from the Project menu to build a new version of MediaCenter. When MediaCenter launches, a new text window will open, as always. Additionally, the Control window will open. Click on the Control window's one button to verify that the standard Open dialog appears. When it does, choose a picture file—a new window will open and the file's picture appears in a draggable pane in the window. Now choose Open Picture from the Picture menu to see that this menu item behaves in the same manner as the Picture button.

Adding a Second Button

Now that you understand how to work with controls, adding a second picture to the Control window in MediaCenter is easy. In this section I'll add a Play Sound button so that the Control window looks like the one pictured in Figure 9-23.

Figure 9-23: The MediaCenter's Control window with a second button added to it.

When the user clicks on the new Play Sound button, the standard Open dialog appears—as shown in Figure 9-24. When it does, MediaCenter filters the files in the selected directory so that only sound files are displayed. Choosing a file causes MediaCenter to play the file's sound.

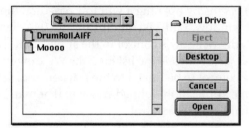

Figure 9-24: The standard Open dialog box that MediaCenter displays to allow the opening of a sound file.

This chapter's second version of the *MediaCenter.µ* project is located on the Companion CD-ROM in the P04 MediaCenter folder in the Chapter 09 folder.

Adding New Button Pictures to a Resource File

The Play Sound control will be another picture button, so two 'PICT' resources need to be added to one of the *MediaCenter.µ* resource files. Figure 9-25 shows all four of the pictures used by the program's two buttons.

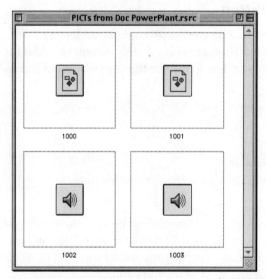

Figure 9-25: The MediaCenter.µ *project's resource file with the picture resources used for the two picture buttons.*

Adding the Button to the 'PPob'

To add a new button to the Control window, begin by opening the *Doc PowerPlant.ppob* file and displaying the Control window 'PPob' in the layout editor. From the Catalog window, drag LButton to the 'PPob' resource.

Edit the new control from its property inspector. Adjust the size of the new control and position it beside the original control—the Open Picture button—by editing the values in the Width, Height, Left in Superview, and Right in Superview fields. Then assign a pane ID and value message to the new control. The original control has a pane ID of 1, so I gave the new control a pane ID of 2. In keeping with my value message numbering scheme (value message equals 'PPob' ID plus the pane ID), I entered 2002 in the Value Message field. Finally, enter the resource IDs of the two 'PICT' resources to be used in the display of the button. I entered 1002 and 1003 to match the resources I added back in Figure 9-25. Figure 9-26 shows the characteristics of the new control.

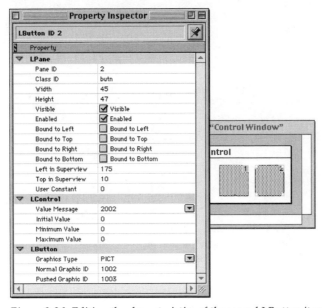

Figure 9-26: Editing the characteristics of the second LButton item.

Adding to the CPPDocApp Application Class

The application object will need to listen for a message sent by the new control. From the previous version of the *MediaCenter.μ* project, the **CPPDocApp** class is already a listener. And by calling **LinkListenerToControls()**, that version of *MediaCenter.μ* also set the application object to listen for messages coming from the window that holds the new control—the program's Control window. The only change I'll make to **CPPDocApp** in the *PP Doc App.h* header file is the addition of the declaration for one new member function:

```
virtual void      PlaySoundFile();
```

Previous versions of *MediaCenter.μ* haven't implemented the Play Sound menu item in the Sound menu, so the ability to play a sound file needs to be added. **PlaySoundFile()** will hold that code and will be invoked in response to either the choosing of the Play Sound menu item or the clicking on the new Play Sound button in the Control Window.

Opening & Playing a Sound File

Playing a sound stored in a sound file requires only a few Toolbox calls. **PlaySoundFile()** makes those calls, and a couple of calls to PowerPlant routines as well. Here's the listing for this new routine:

```
void
CPPDocApp::PlaySoundFile()
{
    SFTypeList          theTypeList = { 'AIFF', 'AIFC'};
    StandardFileReply   theReply;
    short               theFileRefNum;

    UDesktop::Deactivate();
    ::StandardGetFile(nil, 2, theTypeList, &theReply);
    UDesktop::Activate();

    if (theReply.sfGood == true)
    {
        ::FSpOpenDF( &theReply.sfFile, fsRdPerm,
                     &theFileRefNum );
        ::SndStartFilePlay( nil, theFileRefNum, 0, 51200, nil,
                            nil, nil, false );
    }
}
```

You saw a call to the Toolbox routine **StandardGetFile()** in the **OpenPICTFile()** routine that became part of the **CPPDocApp** class back in Chapter 8, "Panes & Views." There it was used to display 'PICT' files in the standard Open dialog box. Here I use it to display a list of sound files—files of type 'AIFF' or 'AIFC.' Surrounding the call to **StandardGetFile()** are calls to the PowerPlant utility routines **Deactivate()** and **Activate()**. Recall that when a Toolbox dialog box is displayed, calls to these routines should be made so that PowerPlant relinquishes, then resumes, control of windows.

If the user selects a file, the **sfGood** field of the structure **theReply** will be **true** and **PlaySoundFile()** will open the file and play its sound. If instead the user cancels the Open dialog box, **PlaySoundFile()** simply terminates.

Opening a sound file involves opening the file's data fork. A call to the Toolbox routine **FSpOpenDF()** takes care of this task. Playing the sound from the data stored in the sound file's data fork is accomplished by invoking the Toolbox function **SndStartFilePlay()**.

TIP *'AIFF' and 'AIFC' are the four-character file types that Apple associates with Audio Interchange File Format (AIFF) and Audio Interchange File Format for Compression (AIFF-C) sound files. These two formats are the common means by which Macintosh sounds are stored. **PlaySoundFile()** opens any file of these two types and plays the sound stored within. Like the picture-opening, application-defined **OpenPICTFile()** routine described in Chapter 8, you should be able to use **PlaySoundFile()** "as is." If, however, you need more information on the Toolbox routines called from **PlaySoundFile()**, refer to a good Toolbox reference such as the Sound volume of Inside Macintosh.*

Responding to a Play Sound Menu Selection

Prior to now, the Play Sound menu item in the Sound menu wasn't fully implemented—choosing this item did nothing more than play the system sound once. To make this menu command fully operational, edit **ObeyCommand()** in *PP Doc App.cp*. In that routine, you'll change the **case cmd_PlaySound** section code from a call to the Toolbox routine **SysBeep()** to a call to the just-added **CPPDocApp** member function **PlaySoundFile()**. Here's how **ObeyCommand()** looks now:

```
Boolean
CPPDocApp::ObeyCommand(
    CommandT    inCommand,
    void        *ioParam)
{
    Boolean   cmdHandled = true;

    switch (inCommand) {

        case cmd_OpenMovie:
            ::SysBeep(1);
            break;
```

```
        case cmd_PlayMovie:
            ::SysBeep(1);
            break;

        case cmd_OpenPicture:
            ShowPictureWindow();
            break;

        case cmd_PlaySound:
            PlaySoundFile();
            break;

        default:
            cmdHandled = LDocApplication::ObeyCommand(
                                        inCommand, ioParam);
            break;
    }

    return cmdHandled;
}
```

Responding to a Click on the New Button

With the adding of a second control comes the need to define a second **MessageT** constant. Here the constant **msg_SoundButton** is set to 2002, the value of the new control's value message as defined in Constructor:

```
const MessageT  msg_PictureButton  = 2001;
const MessageT  msg_SoundButton     = 2002;
```

The previous version of the *MediaCenter.µ* project implemented **ListenToMessage()** so that it listened for a message sent by the Open Picture button. Now I've added a second case section to listen for a message from the new Play Sound button. A call to **ObeyCommand()** mimics the selecting of the Play Sound menu item from the Sound menu:

```
void
CPPDocApp::ListenToMessage(
    MessageT    inMessage,
    void        *ioParam )
{
    #pragma unused( ioParam )
```

```
switch ( inMessage ) {

    case msg_PictureButton:
        ObeyCommand(cmd_OpenPicture, nil);
        break;

    case msg_SoundButton:
        ObeyCommand(cmd_PlaySound, nil);
        break;
    }
}
```

Moving On

Controls can be a helpful part of a program's user interface. Not only can controls such as check boxes, push buttons, and radio buttons make a program easier to use, they can add a professional touch to the program's appearance. In this chapter, I discussed the basics of creating and using controls with PowerPlant: setting up the resource containing the basic information about a control, setting up listener objects to react to a control's message, and determining how the listener object responds to a control's message.

At this point you have a sound understanding of how to implement menus, panes, and controls in your PowerPlant-based projects. You've reached an important milestone, as knowledge of those three topics will take you far in your Macintosh programming endeavors.

Windows and dialog boxes are another important Mac programming topic. In PowerPlant, a dialog box is derived from a window, so both these topics can be covered in a single chapter. You've been exposed to PowerPlant's way of working with windows throughout this book, although they haven't been formally described yet. Each example project has included the creation of one or more windows based on the **LWindow** class. In the next chapter, we'll look at several windows-related characteristics that you haven't encountered yet.

Windows & Dialogs

You're already somewhat familiar with how PowerPlant-based projects work with windows—every example project up to this point has made use of at least one 'PPob' resource to define a window and its contents and the **LWindow** class to create a window object based on the data in the 'PPob' resource. Because the topic of windows isn't new to you, in this chapter we will dispense with much of the introduction and theory and move quickly to techniques for working with windows. This is accomplished in a series of small example projects and one new version of the *MediaCenter.μ* project.

In programming books, the topics of windows and dialogs are often divided into two chapters. With PowerPlant, that's not necessary because dialog boxes differ very little from windows. In Chapter 8, "Panes & Views," you saw that the 'PPob' resource makes it easy to add any type of control to a window. The same is true of a dialog box, also based on a 'PPob' resource. PowerPlant does provide you with a separate dialog box class—**LDialogBox**. However, this class is derived from **LWindow** and provides very little new functionality beyond what that window class offers. Finally, in a PowerPlant-based project, you won't have to rely on the Dialog Manager—the set of Macintosh Toolbox routines that programmers who don't rely on PowerPlant must use. PowerPlant provides a much easier and more powerful way for creating and utilizing dialog boxes.

All this adds up to good news for you. Everything you know about windows applies to dialog boxes, and there are very few dialog-specific things you need to learn.

Windows

As shown in Figure 10-1, the **LWindow** class is a top-level view—a view that can contain any number of panes and views, but isn't itself contained in any other view. As discussed in Chapter 8, "Panes & Views," a window is such a view.

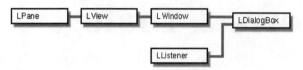

Figure 10-1: Windows and dialogs in the PowerPlant class hierarchy.

TIP *A dialog box is a special case of a window, and is always a listener.*

There are two ways in which you can set a window's attributes: in Constructor and in source code. In this section you'll learn how to use both these methods.

Window Attributes & Constructor

A window begins as a 'PPob' resource. To create a window 'PPob:'

1. Click on the Windows & Views heading and choose New Layout Resource from the Edit menu. The Create New Resource dialog box appears.

2. Optionally enter a resource name.

3. Enter a resource ID.

4. Click the Create button. The new 'PPob' appears under the Windows & Views heading in Constructor's main window.

5. Double-click on the new resource's name to display the resource in a layout window; then double-click on the content area of the window to bring up the property inspector.

Now we're ready to set up the window's peripheral parts and determine its title, position, size, and background color.

Changing the Peripheral Parts of a Window

By default, a new 'PPob' is set to produce a window that has a close box in its title bar, no zoom box in its title bar, and no grow box in its lower right corner. This combination results from the Window Proc field being set to the fourth of the four Document window items in the Window Proc pop-up menu (see Figure 10-2). You can easily change this by selecting a different Document window item from the Window Proc field.

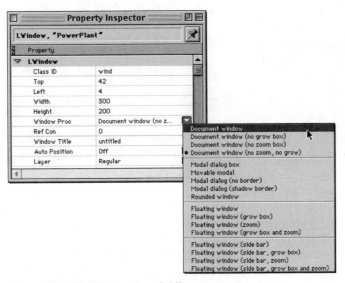

Figure 10-2: The Window Proc field's pop-up menu.

The five menu items beneath the Document window items in the Window Proc pop-up menu are for setting the look of dialog boxes. Some of these items will be covered throughout the chapter.

The remaining items in the Window Proc pop-up menu are for floating windows. A floating window is nothing more than a window that doesn't get hidden by document windows. That is, even when inactive, a floating window will overlap an active document window.

▼ **Floating Windows**

A floating window is used when it's important that a window doesn't become lost on the screen. Typically, a floating window is used to hold a palette of tools. To make a window a floating window, first choose one of the Floating window items from the Window Proc pop-up menu. Then choose the Floating item from the pop-up menu by the Layer field. Figure 10-2 shows the Layer field in the LWindow property inspector. Using Constructor to set a window to be a floating window is all you need to do—you won't have to use any special floating-window class or member functions in your source code. Instead, simply create the floating window as you would a standard document window (see the "Creating a Window" section ahead).

Setting the Title of a Window

The value in the Window Title field of a new 'PPob' resource is the name that appears in the window's title, or drag, bar. The default value is "untitled." Edit this field to provide windows based on the 'PPob' with a title appropriate to the purpose of the window.

TIP *Like any resource, a 'PPob' resource can have a name. This name is used only in the display of the resource in Constructor—it doesn't have anything to do with an object that gets built from the resource. Don't confuse the 'PPob' resource name that appears under the Windows & Views heading in Constructor's main window with the name that appears in the title bar of a window created from the 'PPob.'*

Setting the Positioning of a Window

When a window opens, its placement on the screen is determined by the values used in the Top and Left fields of its 'PPob.' If your program opens more than one window based on the same 'PPob,' each window will open on top of the other. If the user hasn't moved a window from its original position, then the next window that opens will completely hide the original window. This could cause the user to be unaware that more than a single window is open.

To designate that windows open in such a way that they don't completely obscure one another, choose one of the menu items from the Auto Position pop-up menu. Figure 10-3 shows this menu.

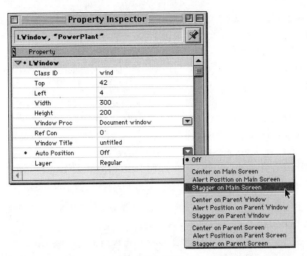

Figure 10-3: The Auto Position field's pop-up menu.

In Figure 10-3, you see that a window can be positioned relative to three things: the main screen, the parent window, and the parent screen. The main screen is always the monitor that holds the menu bar. The parent window is the active window (think of it as the active window spawning a new window). The parent screen is the monitor that holds the parent, or active, window.

Each of the three just-mentioned categories offers the same three positioning options: center, alert position, and stagger. A centered window is just that—it appears in the center of whatever it is positioned relative to (the main screen, the parent window, or the parent screen). The alert position means the window appears centered horizontally and slightly higher than center vertically, in relation to the main screen, parent window, or parent screen. Finally, setting window to stagger means that a new window's position is offset from the currently active window. If staggering is done in relation to the main screen or the parent screen, then windows will open side by side horizontally without any overlap. Once the right edge of the screen is reached, the next window opens beneath the first—this time with an overlap. If staggering is done in relation to the parent window, then each new window is offset several pixels to the right and beneath the parent window. Once the bottom of the screen is reached, a new column of windows starts to the right of the first.

Setting the Window's Size Limits

A new 'PPob' sets a window's minimum size to a width of 0 and a height of 0. While the user won't be able to shrink such a window down to *quite* that small, it is possible to get the window to a size so small as to possibly lose it on a large, cluttered screen. A more realistic minimum size might be 100 pixels in width and height. To reset the window's minimum size, edit the Minimum Width and Minimum Height fields in the LWindow property inspector.

A window's maximum size is determined by the Maximum Width and Maximum Height fields. By default these two fields each have a value of -1. In essence this tells PowerPlant to allow the user to grow the window to the size of the desktop—regardless of how big the monitor (or monitors). Typically you'll leave the values of these two fields as they are. If you're creating a window to be limited in size, you'll probably just eliminate the window's grow box. To do that make sure the Resizable checkbox is unchecked in the property inspector.

Setting the Background Color of a Window

By default, a window has a background color of white. You can easily change that by choosing a different color from the palette of colors presented when you click on the color pop-up menu in the Content Color field. When you set the content color to anything other than white, Constructor adds a 'wctb' resource to the *.ppob* file. The 'wctb' (for window color table) is a standard Macintosh resource type holding color information about a window. The 'wctb' resource isn't displayed in Constructor, but it's there—you can open a *.ppob* file with a resource editor such as ResEdit to see it.

Constructor-Defined Window Attribute Example _____

To test the effect changing 'PPob' LWindow attributes has on the look and behavior of a window, create a new CodeWarrior project based on the Basic PowerPlant stationery. Then double-click on the *PP Basic Resource.ppob* file name in the project window to open the file in Constructor. Double-click on the file's only 'PPob' resource (it's named <replace me>) to display the 'PPob' in a layout editor. Now double-click on the content area of the displayed 'PPob' to bring up the LWindow property inspector. Note that you can double-click anywhere *except* on the "PowerPlant says: hello world" string (clicking on the string will instead open the LCaption property inspector).

To see how a window would be affected by the editing of several of the important window attributes, I made the following changes to the LWindow item. I changed:

- Window Proc to Document so that the window would include a close box and a zoom box.
- Window Title to "Stagger Me."

■ Auto Position to Stagger on Main Screen.

■ Minimum Width and Minimum Height to 100 pixels.

■ Content Color to a very light shade of gray.

Figure 10-4 shows the main monitor after building a program that includes the preceding changes.

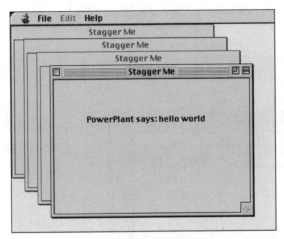

Figure 10-4: Windows based on a 'PPob' that has had some default attributes changed.

The completed project is named *WindowCharacteristics.µ*, and appears in the P01 WindowCharacteristics folder in the Chapter 10 folder on this book's Companion CD-ROM. Feel free to open the *PP Basic Resource.ppob* file in Constructor and make your own changes to the 'PPob' resource. Then return to the *WindowCharacteristics.µ* project and rebuild and run the program to view the effect your changes had on the WindowCharacteristics program.

Creating a Window

Once you have defined a new type of window by creating a new 'PPob' resource in Constructor, you then can use the **LWindow** member function **CreateWindow()** to create any number of windows based on the data in this one 'PPob' resource. Figure 10-5 shows a typical 'PPob' resource displayed in a layout window of Constructor. Figure 10-6 shows how a few windows created from this one 'PPob' would look. The following snippet creates and displays a window built from the data in that 'PPob' resource:

```
const ResIDT   PPob_DrawWindow = 1500;

LWindow  *theWindow;

theWindow = LWindow::CreateWindow(PPob_DrawWindow, this);
theWindow->Show();
```

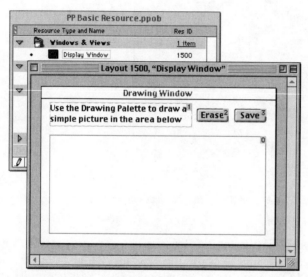

Figure 10-5: A 'PPob' holds the data used to create an LWindow object.

In the preceding snippet, the value of the constant **PPob_DrawWindow** matches that of the 'PPob' resource. The **LWindow** function **CreateWindow()** allocates memory for one window object. Finally, the **LWindow** function **Show()** displays the window.

Any number of windows can be created based on one 'PPob' resource. The New menu item in the File menu of many programs takes advantage of that fact—the same code in the application object's **ObeyCommand()** routine is invoked to open a new window each time that menu item is selected by the user. Multiple windows based on a single 'PPob' resource can also be created from within a loop, as shown in this next snippet. Figure 10-6 shows the result of executing this code:

```
LWindow  *theWindow;
Int16    i;

for (i = 0; i < 3; i++) {
    theWindow = LWindow::CreateWindow(PPob_DrawWindow, this);
    theWindow->Show();
}
```

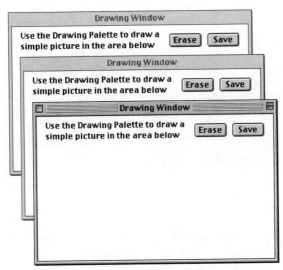

Figure 10-6: Opening multiple windows based on a single 'PPob' resource.

Window Attributes & the LWindow Class

The initial characteristics of a window created in Constructor are not set in stone. The **LWindow** class makes it possible to change window characteristics, such as the window's title or background color, on the fly.

LWindow Attribute Member Functions

The **LWindow** class includes dozens of member functions—many devoted to returning or setting a window's attributes. The emphasis is on these routines in the following edited version of the **LWindow** class declaration:

```
class  LWindow : public LView,
                 public LCommander,
                 public LModelObject {
```

```
public:
    ...
    ...
    void                GetMinMaxSize(Rect  &outRect);

    void                SetMinMaxSize(const Rect  &inRect);

    virtual StringPtr   GetDescriptor(Str255  outDescriptor);
    virtual void        SetDescriptor(ConstStringPtr  inDescriptor);

    virtual void        SetForeAndBackColors(
                              const RGBColor *inForeColor,
                              const RGBColor *inBackColor);

    virtual void        ResizeFrameBy(Int16    inWidthDelta,
                                      Int16    inHeightDelta,
                                      Boolean  inRefresh);

    void                MoveWindowTo(Int16  inHoriz,
                                     Int16  inVert);
    void                MoveWindowBy(Int16  inHorizDelta,
                                     Int16  inVertDelta);

    void                ResizeWindowTo(Int16  inWidth,
                                       Int16  inHeight);
    void                ResizeWindowBy(Int16  inWidthDelta,
                                       Int16  inHeightDelta);
    ...
    ...
}
```

On the following pages, you'll see examples of the use of **SetDescriptor()** to change a window's title and **SetForeAndBackColors()** to set a window's content color. For more information on all of the **LWindow** member functions, refer to the electronic document *PP Core Classes Ref* included on the CD-ROM of any full-featured version of CodeWarrior.

Changing a Window Attribute

Changing an attribute of a window is as easy as invoking the appropriate **LWindow** member function. Consider a window with the new title "Red Window." If the window is accessed via an **LWindow** object named **theWindow**, use this line of code:

```
theWindow->SetDescriptor("\pRed Window");
```

The following version of **ObeyCommand()** shows how a window can have its title and its background color changed at the time the window is created:

```
Boolean
CPPStarterApp::ObeyCommand(
    CommandT    inCommand,
    void        *ioParam)
{
    Boolean    cmdHandled = true;

    switch (inCommand) {

        case cmd_New:
            RGBColor theBackColor = {0xffff,0x0000,0x0000};
            LWindow  *theWindow;
            theWindow = LWindow::CreateWindow(window_Sample, this);

            theWindow->SetDescriptor("\pRed Window");
            theWindow->SetForeAndBackColors(nil, &theBackColor);
            theWindow->Show();
            break;

        default:
            cmdHandled = LApplication::ObeyCommand(inCommand, ioParam);
            break;
    }
    return cmdHandled;
}
```

The **SetDescriptor()** routine requires one parameter—a string that represents the new window title. The **SetForeAndBackColors()** function needs two parameters—the colors to set the window's foreground and background. The foreground color is used for all drawing (including text) in the window, while the background color is used for the content area. If the foreground or background color is to be left unchanged, pass **nil** as that parameter. Colors should be in RGB format. In the preceding example, I've set **theBackColor** to red and then passed this red color to **SetForeAndBackColors()** to be used as thewindow's background color.

The *WindowColor.μ* project, located in the P02 WindowColor folder in the Chapter 10 folder on this book's Companion CD-ROM, includes a *PP Basic Starter.cp* file that has the preceding version of **ObeyCommand()**. Only three lines of code were added to the code supplied as a part of the original CodeWarrior project: the RGBColor variable declaration and the calls to **SetDescriptor()** and **SetForeAndBackColors()**.

The RGB Color Format

RGB stands for red, green, blue. Any other color can be represented by combining various intensities of these three colors. The Macintosh Toolbox defines an **RGBColor** data type that is a structure consisting of three fields. Each field can be assigned an integral value in the range of 0 to 65,535. The larger the number, the more intense (or brighter, or lighter) that color will be. When each of the three values is 65,535, the combined result is white. The smaller the value, the less intense (or darker) that color will be. When each of the three values is 0, the resulting color is black.

When an **RGBColor** variable is declared, it can be assigned its color by assigning values to the three fields. Typically values are given in hexadecimal. The following declaration assigns the **RGBColor** variable **theColor** a value of purple by supplying the red and blue fields with values of **0xffff** (65,535) and the green field a value of **0x0000** (0):

```
RGBColor theColor = {0xffff,0x0000,0xffff};
```

An RGBColor variable can also be supplied with a color by using individual assignment statements to give each field a value. Here **theColor** is set to green:

```
theColor.red   = 0x0000;
theColor.green = 0xffff;
theColor.blue  = 0x0000;
```

Here I've supplied only a brief description of RGB colors—a thorough discussion is beyond the scope of this book. For more information on how color is used in Macintosh programming—including RGB color information—refer to the *QuickDraw* volume of the *Inside Macintosh* series of books.

Finding the Frontmost Window

The *WindowColor.µ* example changed an attribute of a window at the time the window was created. Because the window had just been created, the **LWindow** object was readily available:

```
RGBColor  theBackColor = {0xffff,0x0000,0x0000};
LWindow  *theWindow;

theWindow = LWindow::CreateWindow(window_Sample, this);

theWindow->SetForeAndBackColors(nil, &theBackColor);
```

Such will not always be the case. Often your program will need to alter a window characteristic well after the window has been created. Before the attribute can be changed, the program needs to access the window object. To do this, you'll rely on the **UDesktop** utility function **FetchTopRegular()**.When called, this routine returns an object representing the frontmost, or active, window. With that object, you can then invoke any **LWindow** member function to change characteristics of the frontmost window.

Like the code in the *WindowColor.µ* example, this next snippet uses the **SetForeAndBackColors()** function to set the frontmost window's background color to red. This new code, however, can be used anywhere in a project—not just at the point where the window was created:

```
RGBColor  theBackColor = {0xffff,0x0000,0x0000};
LWindow  *theTopWindow;

theTopWindow = UDesktop::FetchTopRegular();
theTopWindow->SetForeAndBackColors(nil, &theBackColor);

theTopWindow->Refresh();
```

A change to a window's content area doesn't take place until the window requires updating. That typically isn't necessary until the window becomes obscured and then comes back into view. That's too long of a wait—you want the change to be reflected immediately! To make that happen, force an update of the window by calling the **LPane** member function **Refresh()**. Recall that **LWindow** is derived from **LPane**, so a window object can invoke any **LPane** member function as needed.

TIP
*If you look back a few pages, you'll see that **Refresh()** wasn't invoked in the ColorWindow.µ example. That's because the call to **SetForeAndBackColors()** took place on a newly created window and was followed by a call to **ShowWindow()**. **ShowWindow()** causes the necessary update to occur.*

Front Window & Window Attributes Example

Making a change to an existing window is common in programs. Your application may need to change a window's title, alter its background or foreground color, or add new content to it. Because Mac programs don't take actions that catch the user by surprise, it's most likely that such changes will take place in response to a menu item selection. So it behooves us to take a look at a project that generates an application that does just that.

The *FrontWindow.μ* project (located in the P03 FrontWindow folder in the Chapter 10 folder on this book's Companion CD-ROM) adds a new menu to the Apple, File, and Edit menus that CodeWarrior includes in a project based on the Basic PowerPlant project stationery. This Window menu includes a single item: Set Background Color. Choosing this item changes the background color of the frontmost window to red.

As an added bonus, the *FrontWindow.μ* project also demonstrates the enabling and disabling of a menu item based on conditions in the program. That's a common occurrence in a program, so you'll find the inclusion of the code needed to perform this trick beneficial.

TIP *An improvement to the FrontWindow program would be for the Set Background Color menu item to cause a dialog box to appear. This dialog box would allow the user to choose a color to set the window background to, or to cancel the action. We haven't looked at dialog boxes yet, so simply changing the color without getting user input will have to do—for now. Later in this chapter the DialogExample.μ project modifies the FrontWindow.μ project to include this dialog box.*

Resources

The *FrontWindow.μ* project doesn't require any changes to the one 'PPob' resource in the project's *PP Basic Resource.ppob* file, but it does need new menu-related resources. To add a Window menu with a Set Background Color item, follow these steps:

1. Double-click on the one menu bar resource listed under the Menu Bars heading to display the menu bar.

2. Click on the Edit menu in the menu bar editor to highlight it (this sets up Constructor to add a new menu to the right of the Edit menu).

3. Choose New Menu from the Constructor Edit menu to add a new, untitled menu.

4. Type a name for the new menu. As shown in Figure 10-7, I chose to name the new menu Window.

5. Choose New Menu Item from the Constructor Edit menu to add a new untitled item to the menu.

6. Type a name for the new menu item.

7. Double-click on the new menu item name to display the item's property inspector.

8. Enter a command number in the range of 1000 to 65535 in the Command Number field. As shown in Figure 10-7, I chose a value of 1001.

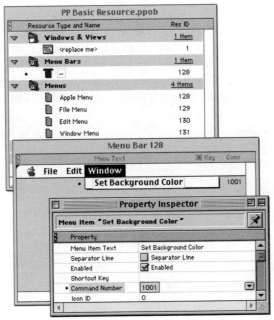

Figure 10-7: Adding a new menu with one item to the PP Basic Resource.ppob file.

With the new menu complete, it's time to work on the project's source code—so return to CodeWarrior and the *FrontWindow.µ* project.

Source Code

Chapter 7, "Menus," described how to add the source code needed to support a menu item. In summary, you follow these steps:

1. Define a constant with a value that matches the Constructor-defined menu item command number.

2. Use the new constant as a label in a new **case** section in the **switch** section of the application's **ObeyCommand()** routine.

3. Under the new **case** label, add the code necessary to support the menu item.

4. Use the new constant as a label in a new **case** section in the **switch** section of the application's **FindCommandStatus()** routine.

5. Under the new **case** label, add the code necessary to support enabling and disabling of the menu item.

Here's the constant that is defined in the *PP Basic Starter.cp* file of the *FrontWindow.µ* project:

```
const  CommandT  cmd_WindowColor   =  1001;
```

You've already seen the code that will be used to change the window's background color. In this chapter's "Finding the Frontmost Window" section, it was presented as a snippet. Here it appears, unchanged, under the **cmd_WindowColor case** label in the implementation of **ObeyCommand()**:

```
Boolean
CPPStarterApp::ObeyCommand(
    CommandT    inCommand,
    void        *ioParam)
{
    Boolean  cmdHandled = true;

    switch (inCommand) {

        case cmd_New:
            LWindow  *theWindow;
            theWindow = LWindow::CreateWindow(window_Sample, this);
            theWindow->Show();
            break;

        case cmd_WindowColor:
            RGBColor  theBackColor = {0xffff,0x0000,0x0000};
            LWindow  *theTopWindow;

            theTopWindow = UDesktop::FetchTopRegular();
            theTopWindow->SetForeAndBackColors(nil, &theBackColor);
            theTopWindow->Refresh();
            break;

        default:
            cmdHandled = LApplication::ObeyCommand(inCommand, ioParam);
            break;
    }
    return cmdHandled;
}
```

With the above version of **ObeyCommand()**, a selection of Set Background Color will turn the background color of the active window red. That accomplishes our primary goal, but there's still one more task to take care of—specifying when the Set Background Color item should be enabled. In past examples, this was handled by simply setting **outEnabled** to **true** in **FindCommandStatus()**. Here, we want to improve upon that code to create a situation where the menu item is disabled when no windows are open. Here's how **FindCommandStatus()** looks:

```
void
PPStarterApp::FindCommandStatus(
    CommandT    inCommand,
    Boolean     &outEnabled,
    Boolean     &outUsesMark,
    Char16      &outMark,
    Str255      outName)
{
    switch (inCommand) {

        case cmd_New:
            outEnabled = true;
            break;

        case cmd_WindowColor:
            LWindow *theTopWindow;
            theTopWindow = UDesktop::FetchTopRegular();
            if (theTopWindow != nil)
                outEnabled = true;
            else
                outEnabled = false;
            break;

        default:
            LApplication::FindCommandStatus(inCommand,
                                    outEnabled, outUsesMark,
                                    outMark, outName);

            break;
    }
}
```

Once again I make use of the **FetchTopRegular()** utility routine. If no windows are open, then this function returns a value of **nil**. I take advantage of that fact by comparing the value returned by a call to **FetchTopRegular()** with **nil**. If the returned value *isn't* **nil**, then a window is open, and **outEnabled** is set to **true** to enable the menu item. If the returned value *is* **nil**, then the Set Background Color menu item isn't applicable, and **outEnabled** is set to **false** to disable the item.

Dialogs

Figure 10-1, which appeared near the start of this chapter, showed the part of the PowerPlant class hierarchy that includes windows and dialog boxes. In that figure, you see that the **LDialogBox** class is derived from the **LWindow** class. That relationship is significant for one very important reason. It means that in PowerPlant, a dialog box is simply a type of window. Because you now know so much about windows, you need very little extra information in order to add dialog box support to your PowerPlant-based projects!

Dialog Boxes & Constructor

You use Constructor to create and lay out the controls and other items that the dialog box requires. Because a dialog box is based on the same type of resource as a window—a 'PPob' resource—you already possess the skills to create a dialog resource in Constructor.

Creating a 'PPob' Resource

You create a 'PPob' to be used for a dialog box as you do for a 'PPob' to be used for a window—with one difference. In the Create New Resource dialog box, you'll change the Kind pop-up menu to display LDialogBox rather than LWindow.

1. Click on the Windows & Views heading and choose New Layout Resource from the Edit menu. The Create New Resource dialog box appears (see Figure 10-8).

2. Click on the Kind pop-up menu and choose LDialogBox.

3. Optionally enter a resource name.

4. Enter a resource ID.

5. Click the Create button. The new 'PPob' appears under the Windows & Views heading in Constructor's main window.

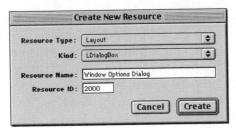

Figure 10-8: Creating a 'PPob' resource to be used for a dialog box rather than for a window.

Editing 'PPob' Resource Attributes

When you bring up the property inspector, the fields will look familiar to you—except for a couple of additions, they're the same as the fields in a window-related 'PPob.' Figure 10-9 shows some of these fields, including the two LDialogBox-specific fields: Default Button ID and Cancel Button ID.

Figure 10-9: A dialog-related 'PPob' includes two fields not found in a window-related 'PPob.'

When you write source code to support a dialog box, you'll find that PowerPlant automatically watches for a mouse button click on the OK or Cancel buttons in your dialog box—provided you specify the pane ID of each of these two buttons in the LDialogBox property inspector. In Figure 10-9, you see that the 'PPob' resource to which the property inspector is describing has an OK button with a pane ID of 1 and a Cancel button with a pane ID of 2. The particular pane ID you give each of these two buttons isn't important—provided that you enter the pane IDs in the LDialogBox Default Button ID and Cancel Button ID fields.

You resize and reposition a dialog box just as you do for a window—by clicking and dragging the dialog in the layout window or by editing the Width, Height, Top, and Left fields in the LDialogBox property inspector. Constructor sets the Window Proc field to Movable modal. That creates a dialog box that can be moved about the screen, but can't be moved behind other windows. You can change this setting from the Window Proc pop-up menu (refer back to Figure 10-2 to see this menu), but Macintosh interface guidelines advise you to make dialog boxes movable modal.

Movable Modal—Huh?

A movable dialog box is one that can be dragged. A modal dialog box is one that "owns" the screen in the sense that the user cannot work with other windows until the modal dialog box is dismissed. While a modal dialog box is open, it controls the screen and the program. In a sense, the open modal dialog box acts as its own mini-program.

Adding Controls to the 'PPob' Resource

A 'PPob' used to hold dialog-related information always contains one or more controls. Minimally the dialog-related 'PPob' will hold a push button (usually labeled "OK") that allows the user to dismiss the dialog box. Additionally there may be a push button (typically labeled "Cancel") that allows the user to back out of whatever changes the dialog box was to make. A dialog-related 'PPob' may also hold any number of other controls, such as radio buttons and check boxes, to allow the user to make changes to some part of the application or to an open document in the application.

You add controls to a dialog-related 'PPob' in the same way that you add controls to a window-related 'PPob'—you drag them from Constructor's Catalog window to the layout window that's displaying the 'PPob.' When you do that for the OK and Cancel buttons, make sure to add the pane IDs of these two items to the Default Button ID and Cancel Button ID fields of the LDialogBox property inspector (see Figure 10-9).

Creating a Dialog Box

PowerPlant makes it extremely easy for your source code to create a dialog box object, display the dialog box, and then watch the user's actions awaiting the time that the OK or Cancel button is clicked.

Dialog Boxes & the StDialogHandler Class

Since movable modal dialogue boxes are so important, it makes sense that Powerplant defines a utility class, **StDialogHandler,** specifically to manage them. **StDialogHandler** is a *stack-based* utility class. In Chapter 4, "PowerPlant Basics," it was mentioned that a stack-based class is one that has a class constructor responsible for setup work and a class destructor responsible for the cleanup work. The **StDialogHandler** class does that, and more.

In a Mac program, memory for an object can be allocated on either the stack or the heap. Memory for an object to be a local variable is always stored on the stack. That's how your program will work with the **StDialogHandler** class— your program will allocate a local **StDialogHandler** variable in the routine to post, or display, a dialog box. This **StDialogHandler** object will be responsible for creating and displaying the dialog box first, then for monitoring the actions that occur in the dialog box, and eventually for removing the dialog box and releasing the memory

Creating a Dialog Box With the StDialogHandler Class

Declaring an **StDialogHandler** variable creates an **StDialogHandler** object. When you declare the variable, you're invoking the **StDialogHandler** constructor. That function requires two parameters. The first is the ID of the 'PPob' resource to be used to build the dialog box object. The second is the dialog box *supercommander*. An object's supercommander is the next-higher-up object in the chain of command. Typically a dialog box object's supercommander is the application object. If the routine creating the dialog box is a member function of the application class, then this supercommander can be referred to using the **this** keyword. Assuming that a dialog box is being created based on a 'PPob' resource whose ID has been defined in the source code by the constant **PPob_MyDialog**, here's how the creation of an **StDialogHandler** object would look:

```
StDialogHandler  theHandler(PPob_MyDialog, this);
```

TIP *In Chapter 7, "Menus," you learned about the chain of command. You read that an object has an object above it in the command hierarchy. If an object can't handle a command, it passes it up the chain of command to the object above it. This higher object is referred to as the lower object's supercommander. With the exception of the application object, which is at the top of the chain of command, every object has a supercommander.*

After the preceding call, an **StDialogHandler** object is created, but a dialog box object isn't. One of the **StDialogHandler** member functions is **GetDialog()**. This routine builds a dialog box based on the 'PPob' resource passed to the **StDialogHandler** constructor. **GetDialog()** returns a dialog box object. Because a dialog box is nothing more than a type of window, the dialog box object is of type **LWindow**:

```
LWindow  *theDialog;

theDialog = theHandler.GetDialog();
```

To display the new dialog box, call the **LWindow** member function **Show()**—just as you would for a window:

```
theDialog->Show();
```

Handling a Dialog Box With the StDialogHandler Class

The previous snippets create a dialog box object and allocate an **StDialogHandler** object to control that dialog box. But nothing has yet been done to have the program monitor the user's actions in the dialog box. A call to the **StDialogHandler** object's **DoDialog()** takes care of that. **DoDialog()** checks if the user performed some dialog-related event, such as clicking on a control. If the user did, **DoDialog()** returns a message that includes information about the clicked-on control. If no dialog-related event has just occurred at the time of the call to **DoDialog()**, then that information will be returned to the program in the form of the **msg_Nothing** constant. Here's how **DoDialog()** is invoked by the **StDialogHandler** object:

```
MessageT  theMessage = theHandler.DoDialog();
```

Calling **DoDialog()** once is sufficient to return only one message—a message that indicates what just happened in the dialog box. To be of real use, **DoDialog()** must be repeatedly called for the duration the dialog box is open. To do this, the call to **DoDialog()** appears in a **while** loop:

```
while (true) {
    MessageT  theMessage = theHandler.DoDialog();

    // If theMessage is the Cancel button, exit

    // If theMessage is instead the OK button, get values
    // of other dialog box controls, take any action based
    // on these values, and exit
}
```

This loop can be thought of as an event-processing loop. Each pass through the body of the loop captures the most recent event and then checks if the event was a click on either the Cancel button or the OK button. A click on the Cancel button will dismiss the dialog box without any other action taking place. A click on the OK button will also dismiss the dialog box—but not until the current values of other controls or text in any edit item is obtained, and action based on those values is taken.

At first glance, it may seem that the above **while** loop is of limited use. Most dialog boxes consist of more controls than simply an OK button and a Cancel button, yet mouse clicks on those two controls are the only events the **while** loop reacts to. The second comment in the above snippet holds the answer. When a user clicks on controls other than the OK or Cancel button, PowerPlant code handles the updating of the control. For instance, a click on a check box results in PowerPlant automatically toggling the state of the check box. PowerPlant code rather than your application-defined code is responsible for checking or unchecking the box. Not until the user clicks on the OK button will your program need to be concerned with the state of other dialog box controls (such as whether the aforementioned check box is checked or unchecked).

Putting It Together: a Dialog Box Routine

Now let's take a look at how an application might go about including a member function that posts a dialog box. First, define a constant with the value of the dialog-related 'PPob' resource ID:

```
const  ResIDT    PPob_MyDialog    = 2000;
```

Next, the declare the dialog box-related routine in the application class declaration:

```
class  CPPStarterApp : public LApplication {
public:
                    CPPStarterApp();
    virtual         ~CPPStarterApp();
    ...
    ...
    virtual void    ShowMyDialog();
    ...
    ...
}
```

Finally, the new member function is implemented following a format similar to this:

```
void
CPPStarterApp::ShowMyDialog()
{
    StDialogHandler  theHandler(PPob_MyDialog, this);
    LWindow         *theDialog;

    theDialog = theHandler.GetDialog();
    theDialog->Show();

    while (true) {
        MessageT  theMessage = theHandler.DoDialog();

        if ( theMessage == msg_Cancel ) {
            break;  // Break out of the while loop
        }
        else if ( theMessage == msg_OK ) {
            // Code to get values from other controls goes here
            // Code to take actions based on values goes here
            break;  // Break out of the while loop
        }
    }
}
```

The **break** that appears in the **if** and **else-if** sections terminates the otherwise perpetual **while** loop. Ending the loop ends the routine. When that happens, the **StDialogHandler** destructor is automatically invoked to clean up by freeing the memory occupied by the **StDialogHandler** object.

One step is omitted in the above function, of course—the comments in the **else-if** section of the **ShowMyDialog() while** loop need to be replaced with code. The code that goes here, however, is dialog-specific. The **ShowColorDialog()** routine in the *DialogExample.µ* project discussed next provides such an example.

Dialog Example

The *DialogExample.µ* project located in the P04 DialogExample folder in the Chapter 10 folder on this book's Companion CD-ROM provides an example of how to implement the display of a movable modal dialog box in response to a menu selection. When executed, the DialogExample program displays the same menu bar as this chapter's FrontWindow example program. Instead of simply changing the front window's background color to red, however, selecting the program's Set Background Color item from the Window menu displays the dialog box shown in Figure 10-10.

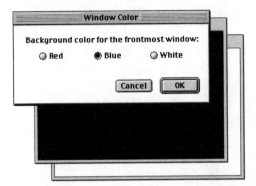

Figure 10-10: The result of running the DialogExample program.

The three radio buttons in the dialog box act as a one group—clicking on one turns the previously on button off and turns the clicked button on. Clicking the OK button changes the active window's background to the selected color. Clicking the Cancel button leaves the active window's background unchanged.

Creating the 'PPob' Resource

Creating the project's dialog-related 'PPob' resource is easy. Begin by clicking on the Windows & Views heading in the *PP Basic Resource.ppob* file and then choosing New Layout Resource from the Edit menu. Set the items in the Create New Resource dialog box to match those shown in Figure 10-11. Then click the Create button.

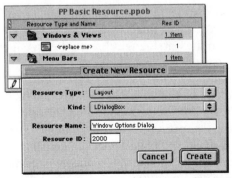

Figure 10-11: Creating the DialogExample.µ *project's one dialog-related 'PPob.'*

Display the new 'PPob' resource in the layout editor and open the dialog box property inspector. Most of the fields can be left as is. You will, however, want to edit the last two fields—Default Button ID and Cancel Button ID. Set these two fields to the pane ID values you'll be giving the OK and Cancel buttons. In Figure 10-12 you see that I'm anticipating giving the dialog box an OK button with a pane ID of 1 and a Cancel button with a pane ID of 2.

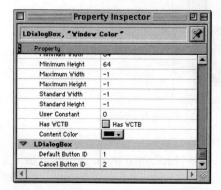

Figure 10-12: Editing the fields of the dialog-related 'PPob' resource.

TIP

The DialogExample.μ *project adds one menu to those supplied by CodeWarrior—a Window menu with a Set Background Color item in it. To support this menu, the project's* PP Basic Resource.ppob *file uses the same menu resources described in this chapter's* FrontWindow.μ *project—refer to that project's description if you have questions about the project's menu-related resources.*

Adding Controls to the 'PPob' Resource

Add the dialog box controls by dragging push buttons (LStdButton) and radio buttons (LStdRadioButton) from the Catalog window to the layout editor. Also drag a text item (LCaption) to the window.

You need to provide a title and pane ID for the two push buttons. Double-click on one of the push button items to display its property inspector; then fill in the Title and Pane ID fields. Repeat for the second push button item. The text and pane IDs I used for the two push buttons are shown in Figure 10-13. In a similar fashion, provide the title and pane ID for each of the three radio buttons. The property inspector for a radio button is shown in Figure 10-14. Constructor will have given each radio button item an initial value of Off. You'll want one of the three radio buttons to be On when the dialog box opens in the DialogExample program. For any one of the three buttons, choose On from the Initial Value pop-up menu. Finally, double-click on the LCaption item and enter text in its Text field. Now position the controls as shown in Figure 10-13, or in any way you see fit.

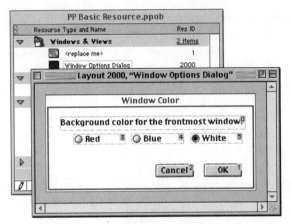

Figure 10-13: The completed dialog-related 'PPob' resource.

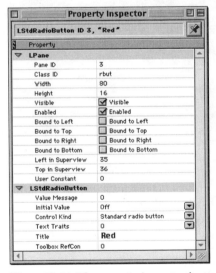

Figure 10-14: The property inspector for an LStdRadioButton item.

Grouping the Radio Buttons Together in the 'PPob' Resource

Adding radio buttons to a dialog box doesn't automatically group them together. You use an LRadioGroup item to tell PowerPlant that a number of radio buttons are related. When you do that, PowerPlant code becomes responsible for coordinating turning off one button and turning on another in response to a click on one button in the group.

To group a number of buttons together, select them in the layout window and then choose Make Radio Group from the Arrange menu. An LRadioGroup isn't a pane, so no addition will be made to the dialog box. Because Constructor won't give you any visual feedback, you may want to verify that the grouping was made by choosing Show Object Hierarchy from the Layout menu. The Hierarchy window that appears provides an overview of the items in the 'PPob' resource. Double-click on the LRadioGroup item to see its property inspector. In Figure 10-15 you see that the three radio buttons have become a part of the LRadioGroup.

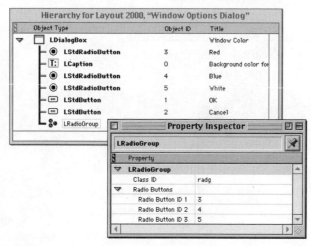

Figure 10-15: The property inspector for an LRadioGroup.

With the addition of the LRadioGroup item, the project's resources are complete—now, on to the source code.

Dialog-Related Source Code Constants

When it comes time to create an **StDialogHandler** to display the dialog box, you will need the dialog's 'PPob' resource ID. And once the dialog box OK button is clicked, the radio button pane IDs will need to be accessed. The *PP Basic Starter.cp* file defines constants for these four values:

```
const  ResIDT    PPob_ColorDialog   = 2000;
const  PaneIDT   paneID_RedRadio    =    3;
const  PaneIDT   paneID_BlueRadio   =    4;
const  PaneIDT   paneID_WhiteRadio  =    5;
```

Adding to the CPPStarterApp Class Declaration

When the user chooses Set Background Color from the program's Window menu, an application-defined routine holding the dialog-related code will execute. This **ShowColorDialog()** function will be the newest member function in the **CPPStarterApp** class:

```
class  CPPStarterApp : public LApplication {
public:
                    CPPStarterApp();
    virtual         ~CPPStarterApp();

    virtual Boolean  ObeyCommand(CommandT inCommand,
                                 void*    ioParam);

    virtual void     FindCommandStatus(CommandT inCommand,
                                       Boolean  &outEnabled,
                                       Boolean  &outUsesMark,
                                       Char16   &outMark,
                                       Str255   outName);

    virtual void     ShowColorDialog();

protected:

    virtual void     StartUp();
}
```

Displaying the Dialog Box

ShowColorDialog() gets called in response to the user's choosing Set Background Color from the Window menu. This chapter's *FrontWindow.μ* project added a new case label to the switch in **ObeyCommand()**. In that example, a command of **cmd_WindowColor** was handled by determining the front window and then setting that window's background color to red. Here that same constant is again added to **ObeyCommand()**. In this project, however, a command of **cmd_WindowColor** is handled by invoking **ShowColorDialog()**:

```
Boolean
CPPStarterApp::ObeyCommand(
    CommandT   inCommand,
    void       *ioParam)
{
    Boolean   cmdHandled = true;

    switch (inCommand) {
```

```
   ...
   ...
   case cmd_WindowColor:
      ShowColorDialog();
      break;
   ...
   ...
   }
   return cmdHandled;
}
```

Implementing ShowColorDialog()

The implementation of **ShowColorDialog()** closely follows the dialog-related function format established earlier in this chapter. Here you get to see how a click on an OK button is handled:

```
void
CPPStarterApp::ShowColorDialog()
{
   StDialogHandler  theHandler(PPob_ColorDialog, this);
   LWindow          *theDialog;

   theDialog = theHandler.GetDialog();
   theDialog->Show();

   while (true) {
      MessageT  theMessage = theHandler.DoDialog();

      if ( theMessage == msg_Cancel ) {
         break;
      }
      else if ( theMessage == msg_OK ) {
         Boolean          theButtonOn = false;
         Int32            thePaneID = paneID_RedRadio;
         Int32            i;
         LStdRadioButton  *theRadioButton;

         for (i=0; i<3;i++) {
            theRadioButton = (LStdRadioButton *)
                        theDialog->FindPaneByID(thePaneID);
            theButtonOn = theRadioButton->GetValue();
            if (theButtonOn)
               continue;
            else
               thePaneID++;
         }
```

```
RGBColor theBackColor;

switch (thePaneID) {

    case paneID_RedRadio:
        theBackColor.red    = 0xffff;
        theBackColor.green  = 0x0000;
        theBackColor.blue   = 0x0000;
        break;

    case paneID_BlueRadio:
        theBackColor.red    = 0x0000;
        theBackColor.green  = 0x0000;
        theBackColor.blue   = 0xffff;
        break;

    case paneID_WhiteRadio:
        theBackColor.red    = 0xffff;
        theBackColor.green  = 0xffff;
        theBackColor.blue   = 0xffff;
        break;
    }

    LWindow *theTopWindow;
    theTopWindow = UDesktop::FetchTopRegular();
    theTopWindow->SetForeAndBackColors(nil, &theBackColor);
    theTopWindow->Refresh();

    break;
    }
  }
}
```

ShowColorDialog() first responds to a click on the OK button by determining which of the three radio buttons was on at the time of the mouse button click. To do that, we walk through the three radio buttons, checking each one to see if it's on. At each pass through the loop, the **LPane** member function **FindPaneByID()** is invoked to get a radio button object, and then that object's **LPane GetValue()** function is called. Because a radio button's two possible values (0 for off and 1 for on) correspond with PowerPlant's definition of a **Boolean** variable's values (0 for **false** and 1 for **true**), we can assign the returned value to the **Boolean** variable **theButtonOn**. If **theButtonOn** is true, then the one button that's on has been found and the **for** loop can be exited.

Next, a **switch** is used to compare the pane ID of the radio button that's on to the pane IDs of the three radio buttons. Each radio button is handled in a similar way—by assigning values to the three fields of the **RGBColor** variable **theBackColor**. With **theBackColor** set to the user's color choice, the front window is determined and its background color set.

Simple Dialogs

Creating an **StDialogHandler** object to take care of posting and handling a dialog box is relatively simple. For the case of a dialog box that consists of just a few items, though, PowerPlant offers an even easier way to do things.

A dialog box is usually used to solicit input from the user. Often the dialog box only asks the user to enter either a single number or a single string. Figure 10-16 shows such a dialog box requesting a single number. For these two particular cases, PowerPlant offers the **AskForOneNumber()** and **AskForOneString()** functions as a part of the **UModalDialogs** utility class. Calling one of these functions displays a dialog box based on a 'PPob' resource and then takes control of the program to handle actions that take place in the dialog.

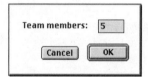

Figure 10-16: A dialog box used to obtain a single user-entered number.

Obtaining a Single User-Entered Number

Making use of PowerPlant's **UModalDialogs** class is as easy as defining a simple 'PPob' resource in Constructor and then making a single function call.

Constructor & the Simple Dialog

To define a simple dialog box that accepts a single number as input, create a dialog-related 'PPob' resource—as described in this chapter's "Dialog Boxes and Constructor" section. Then use the Catalog window to add two LStdButton items to serve as OK and Cancel buttons. Open the property inspector of each and assign the Value Message field of one the constant **msg_OK**, and the Value Message field of the other a value message of **msg_Cancel**. When the dialog is displayed in your program, PowerPlant will look for these two types of value messages—so make sure to use these constants. Next, add a single LEditField item to be used to accept the user-entered number. Finally, add LCaption items as necessary in order to include descriptive text in the dialog box. Figure 10-17 shows how the 'PPob' would look for the dialog box pictured back in Figure 10-16.

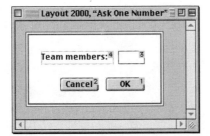

Figure 10-17: The 'PPob' resource on which the Figure 10-16 dialog box is based.

AskForOneNumber() & the Simple Dialog

Using the **UModalDialogs** utility routine **AskForOneNumber()** is as easy as invoking it from anywhere in your application-defined code. Here's the prototype for the routine:

```
Boolean AskForOneNumber(LCommander  *inSuper,
                        ResIDT      inDialogID,
                        PaneIDT     inEditFieldID,
                        Int32       &ioNumber);
```

The first **AskForOneNumber()** parameter is the dialog box supercommander. That's usually the application object, so the **this** keyword suffices. (Refer to the "Creating a Dialog Box With the StDialogHandler Class" section in this chapter for information on the supercommander and the use of the **this** keyword.) The second parameter is the resource ID of the 'PPob' that holds the data from which to build the simple dialog box. The third parameter is the pane ID of the one edit item in the dialog box. Going into the function, the final parameter holds a number to be placed in the edit box upon the opening of the dialog box. Coming back from this routine, the **ioNumber** parameter holds the user-entered value.

The **AskForOneNumber()** routine and the other **UModalDialogs** utility functions that **AskForOneNumber()** calls do all the work necessary to support a modal dialog box used to obtain a single number. Other than the line that actually invokes **AskForOneNumber()**, there's no need to write any application-defined supporting code. When the user dismisses the dialog box by clicking the OK button, **AskForOneNumber()** returns the user-entered value from the one edit box in the dialog box. This value is returned in the fourth parameter of **AskForOneNumber()**. If the user dismisses the dialog box by clicking the Cancel button instead, this last parameter holds the original value that was passed to **AskForOneNumber()**—a user-typed number in the edit box is ignored. Once the user dismisses the dialog box, your program can then act on this returned value.

The following snippet provides a look at how **AskForOneNumber()** can be used:

```
const ResIDT     PPob_AskNum      = 2000;
const PaneIDT    paneID_AskEdit   =    3;


Int32    theNumber = 5;
Boolean  result;

result = UModalDialogs::AskForOneNumber(this, PPob_AskNum,
                                        paneID_AskEdit,
                                        theNumber);
if (result)
{
   // Code to do something with theNumber
}
```

If the user clicked the OK button, **result** will be **true** and the program should use the returned edit box number as appropriate. If the Cancel button dismissed the dialog box, **result** will be **false** and no action should be taken.

Obtaining a Single User-Entered String

Once you know how to use **AskForOneNumber()**, you also know how to use the **UModalDialogs** utility routine **AskForOneString()**. The following discussion assumes you read the preceding "Obtaining a Single User-Entered Number" section, so if you skipped it, page back and read it before continuing.

Constructor & the Simple Dialog

You use Constructor to define a simple dialog box that accepts a single string as input just as you did when including a single number input dialog box in a project. Make sure to include an OK push button with a Value Message field value of **msg_OK**, a Cancel push button with a Value Message field value of **msg_Cancel**, and an text edit box. Other text or picture items are optional.

AskForOneString() & the Simple Dialog

You use the **UModalDialogs** utility routine **AskForOneString()** in the same way you use **AskForOneNumber()**. The first three parameters to **AskForOneString()** are identical to those in **AskForOneNumber()**. The fourth parameter differs—it holds a string rather than a number. Going into the function, the **ioString** holds a string to be placed in the edit box upon the opening of the dialog box. Coming back from this routine, the parameter holds the user-entered string. Here's the prototype for the routine:

```
Boolean AskForOneString(LCommander   *inSuper,
                        ResIDT       inDialogID,
                        PaneIDT      inEditFieldID,
                        Str255       &ioString);
```

To post the dialog box and monitor the user's actions, invoke **AskForOneString()**. When the dialog box is dismissed, check the value of **result**. If **result** is **true**, use the returned string in subsequent code. If **result** is **false**, no additional action should be taken by your code. This next snippet provides a look at how **AskForOneString()** is used:

```
const ResIDT    PPob_AskStr     = 4000;
const PaneIDT   paneID_AskEdit  =    3;

Str255    theString = "\pName";
Boolean   result;

result = UModalDialogs::AskForOneString(this, PPob_AskNum,
                                        paneID_AskEdit,
                                        theString);
if (result)
{
    // Code to do something with theString
}
```

Simple Dialog Boxes Example _____

The *SimpleDialogs.μ* project located in the P05 SimpleDialogs folder in the Chapter 10 folder on this book's Companion CD-ROM uses the **UModalDialog** class to display both a number and string dialog box. When the SimpleDialog program runs, the dialog box shown in Figure 10-18 is displayed. Clicking the Cancel button dismisses the dialog box, and nothing further occurs. Clicking the OK button dismisses the dialog box and displays another dialog box—the one shown in Figure 10-19. Clicking either the Cancel or OK button in this second dialog box dismisses it.

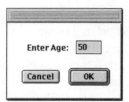

Figure 10-18: The first dialog box displayed by the SimpleDialogs program.

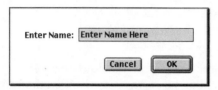

Figure 10-19: The second dialog box displayed by the SimpleDialogs program.

Resources

SimpleDialogs.µ is a project created from the Basic PowerPlant project statio-nery. The project's *PP Basic Resources.ppob* file needs two dialog-related 'PPob' resources added to it. To create the first 'PPob,' click on the Windows & Views heading and choose New Layout Resource from the Edit menu. The project's source code will be using the 'PPob' resource ID, so make sure the Create New Resource dialog box looks like the one shown in Figure 10-20 before clicking the Create button.

Figure 10-20: Creating the first of two dialog-related 'PPob' resources for the SimpleDialog.µ *project.*

A dialog box under the control of a **UModalDialogs** routine can be either a modal dialog or a movable modal. The *SimpleDialogs.µ* project uses both types. To make this first 'PPob' a movable modal dialog, begin by displaying the 'PPob' in the layout editor. Then open the LDialogBox property inspector. Finally, choose Movable modal from the Window Proc pop-up menu.

Use the Catalog window to add two LStdButton controls, one LEditField pane, and one LCaption pane to the 'PPob.' Item titles and placement aren't important, but the pane ID numbers should match those pictured in Figure 10-21.

Figure 10-21: The completed 'PPob' resource for the first of two dialog boxes.

Create the second 'PPob' as you created the first. In the Create New Layout dialog box give the 'PPob' an ID of 3500. Open the 'PPob' in the layout editor and add the same four pane and controls as were added to the first 'PPob.' Figure 10-22 shows how this 'PPob' should look. Again, only the pane IDs are of significance.

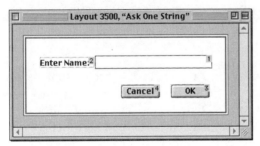

Figure 10-22: The completed 'PPob' resource for the second of two dialog boxes.

Source Code

The **AskForOneNumber()** and **AskForOneString()** routines each require a 'PPob' resource ID as a parameter. These functions also require the pane ID of the dialog box text edit item. Define a constant for each of these four values (refer to Figures 10-21 and 10-25 to see these values in Constructor):

```
const ResIDT    PPob_AskForNumber      = 3000;
const PaneIDT   paneID_AskNumberEdit   =    1;
const ResIDT    PPob_AskForString      = 3500;
const PaneIDT   paneID_AskStringEdit   =    1;
```

The number dialog box is displayed when the program launches, so the application class **StartUp()** member function is the place to add the call to **AskForOneNumber()**. When **AskForOneNumber()** terminates, the local variable result will specify whether the OK button was clicked. If it was, the program will post the string dialog box. A call to **AskForOneString()** takes care of that chore. The following version of **StartUp()** is the only *PP Starter App.cp* code altered from the default code CodeWarrior places in the project:

```
void
CPPStarterApp::StartUp()
{
    ObeyCommand(cmd_New, nil);

    Int32    theNumber = 50;
    Str255   theString = "\pEnter Name Here";
    Boolean  result;

    result = UModalDialogs::AskForOneNumber(this,
                                PPob_AskForNumber,
                                paneID_AskNumberEdit,
                                theNumber);
    if (result) {
        result = UModalDialogs::AskForOneString(this,
                                PPob_AskForString,
                                paneID_AskStringEdit,
                                theString);
    }
}
```

The *SimpleDialog.µ* example is somewhat contrived: nothing is done with either the returned number or the returned string. You can quickly test your knowledge of using the **UModalDialogs** class by adding a little of your own code. For instance, instead of calling **AskForOneString()** when the user clicks the OK button of the **AskForOneNumber()** dialog box, check the user-entered number returned by **AskForOneNumber()** first. Then display the **AskForOneString()** dialog box only if the value of **theNumber** is within a certain range.

Windows & the Example Project

This chapter's version of the *MediaCenter.µ* project (which can be found on the Companion CD-ROM in the P06 MediaCenter folder in the Chapter 10 folder) moves the MediaCenter closer to completion by implementing one of the two menu items in the Movie menu and by adding the third of four Control window buttons. After building MediaCenter from this section's project, you'll have an application that looks like that shown in Figure 10-23.

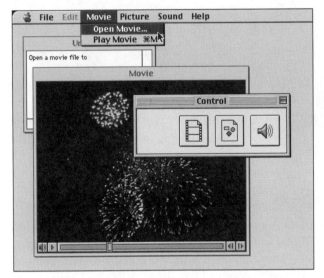

Figure 10-23: This chapter's version of the MediaCenter program.

The Control window has one other change besides the addition to the new Open Movie button—the window now has a light gray background to match the platinum look introduced in Mac OS 8.

You'll be able to test the opening of a QuickTime movie by either clicking the Open Movie button in the Control window or by selecting Open Movie from the Movie menu. When you do that, you'll see the standard Open file dialog box. Selecting a movie from this dialog box has the effect of loading the movie file data to memory and displaying the movie in a window. Running along the bottom of the movie window is a standard QuickTime movie controller—as shown in Figure 10-23. Play the movie by clicking on the controller's Play button. The Play Movie menu item in the Movie menu is implemented in Chapter 11, "Debugging & Testing the Application," giving you a second means of playing an open movie.

Like other types of MediaCenter windows, the window holding the movie will be based on a 'PPob' resource. Here, however, there will be a new twist. Because the size of the movie won't be known until the user selects it, the window's size will need to be adjusted from source code rather than from Constructor.

QuickTime—Cross Platform Star

Throughout Apple's ups and downs, QuickTime has been its shining star. QuickTime is now a cross-platform technology—the Windows 95/NT version is a feature-for-feature match to the Mac OS version. QuickTime will also be a part of Apple's new Rhapsody operating system. If you're going to pick one Mac technology to support, QuickTime isn't a bad choice! That's why I'll spend a little time here and in Chapter 11, "Debugging & Testing the Application," describing how to work with QuickTime. For a more complete source of information, refer to the *QuickTime* and *QuickTime Components* volumes of *Inside Macintosh*.

Project Resources

The Control window is gaining a new button—so ResEdit or Resorcerer needs to be run to add a pair of new picture resources to the project. Constructor will see a little use too—a new 'PPob' resource needs to be added for use in the display of a QuickTime movie, and the already-present Control window 'PPob' needs to be edited to set the Control window's background color.

Creating & Adding Button Pictures

In Chapter 9, "Controls," you saw that a picture button (an LButton item) requires that two 'PICT' resources be present in a project resource file. This version of the *MediaCenter.µ* project adds one new picture button, so two new pictures need to be created, copied, and pasted into the project's *Doc PowerPlant.rsrc* file to join the four 'PICT' resources already in that file. Figure 10-24 shows the two pictures I'm using.

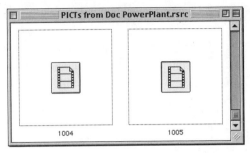

Figure 10-24: Saving two pictures as 'PICT' resources to be used in the display of the one new picture button.

Adding the Button to the New 'PPob'

The Control window 'PPob' needs one new LButton control added to it. You can do that by opening the 'PPob' resource in a layout editor and then either dragging LButton from the Catalog window to the layout editor or copying one of the existing two LButton items in the 'PPob' and pasting the copied item back in to the layout editor. In either case, you want to edit the new LButton item's characteristics. Double-click on the LButton to display its property inspector.

From the property inspector, you can adjust the item so it is positioned alongside the two original buttons, as shown in Figure 10-25. Then give this LButton a pane ID of 3 and a value message of 2003. Now scroll down to the bottom of the property inspector and use the pop-up menu beside the Graphics Type field to assign that field a value of 'PICT.' Assign the proper 'PICT' resource ID values to the Normal Graphic ID and Pushed Graphic ID fields (these numbers must match the resource IDs of the new 'PICT' resources, as shown back in Figure 10-24).

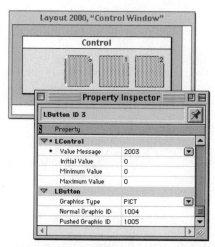

Figure 10-25: Editing the characteristics of the new LButton item.

Creating a New Movie Window 'PPob' Resource

Implementing the display of QuickTime movies means that a new window needs to be opened each time the user opens a movie:

1. Click on Windows & Views in the main Constructor window.

2. Choose New Layout Resource from the Edit menu.

3. Give the new resource an ID of 2500.

4. Optionally provide a name for the resource.

5. Click the Create button.

Unlike other 'PPob' resources, I won't be editing this new one. The window's size (just big enough to hold whatever movie the user chooses, along with a movie controller along the bottom of the window) and contents (the user-selected movie) will both be set from source code.

Changing the Control Window Background Color

In keeping with the platinum look of Mac OS 8 and beyond, the Control window is to have a light gray background. Open the Control window 'PPob' and double-click on the content area of the window displayed in the layout editor to display the LWindow property inspector. Use the Content Color pop-up menu to change the Control window's background color to a light gray (see Figure 10-26). That's it the last you'll read about the background color of this window—there's no source code needed to implement the new color setting.

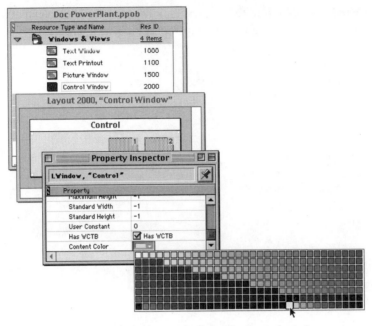

Figure 10-26: Setting the background color of the Control window.

Project Source Code

This newest version of the *MediaCenter.µ* project adds one new member function to the **LDocApplication**-derived **CPPDocApp** class—a function that opens a QuickTime movie file and displays the movie in a window.

Adding to the CPPDocApp Application Class

The code to display the standard Open file dialog box, open a QuickTime movie file, and display the movie data in a new window is in one new **CPPDocApp** member function: **ShowMovieWindow()**. The only addition to the **CPPDocApp** class declaration in the *PP Doc App.h* header file looks like this (refer to the "Controls and the Example Project" section of Chapter 9, "Controls," to see the complete listing for the **CPPDocApp** class):

```
virtual void     ShowMovieWindow();
```

Responding to an Open Movie Menu Selection

To create a support the Open Movie item in the Movie menu, invoke the new **CPPDocApp** member function **ShowMovieWindow()** from the application's **ObeyCommand()** function. In previous versions of *PP Doc App.cp*, a selection of

Open Movie resulted in nothing more than the playing of the system sound. Here I've replaced the call to **SysBeep()** under the **cmd_OpenMovie case** label:

```
Boolean
CPPDocApp::ObeyCommand(
    CommandT    inCommand,
    void        *ioParam)
{
    Boolean    cmdHandled = true;

    switch (inCommand) {
        case cmd_OpenMovie:
            ShowMovieWindow();
            break;
        ...
        ...
    }
    return cmdHandled;
}
```

Listening for Messages

A click on the Control window's new Open Movie button results in PowerPlant sending a message with a value message of 2003 (see Figure 10-25) to the application object's **ListenToMessage()** routine. The *PP Doc App.cp* file defines a **MessageT** constant for each button control, of which there are now three:

```
const MessageT   msg_PictureButton   = 2001;
const MessageT   msg_SoundButton     = 2002;
const MessageT   msg_MovieButton     = 2003;
```

ListenToMessage() was implemented in Chapter 9, "Controls," to handle clicks on the Open Picture and Play Sound buttons. Here I add a **msg_MovieButton case** section to the routine's **switch**. A call to **ObeyCommand()** mimics the selection of the Open Movie item from the Movie menu:

```
void
CPPDocApp::ListenToMessage(
    MessageT    inMessage,
    void        *ioParam )
{
    #pragma unused( ioParam )

    switch ( inMessage ) {
```

```
        case msg_PictureButton:
            ObeyCommand(cmd_OpenPicture, nil);
            break;

        case msg_SoundButton:
            ObeyCommand( cmd_PlaySound, nil );
            break;

        case msg_MovieButton:
            ObeyCommand( cmd_OpenMovie, nil );
            break;
    }
}
```

QuickTime & PowerPlant

The routines that make up the Macintosh Toolbox are logically divided into managers. The **main()** routine of each example has called the **UQDGlobals** utility class member function **InitializeToolbox()** to initialize these managers. **InitializeToolbox()** doesn't initialize QuickTime routines, though. Apple has organized these routines into what it calls the Movie Toolbox. It takes a separate call to **Initialize()** from the **UQuickTime** utility class to initialize QuickTime. I'll place this function call in the **CPPDocApp** constructor so QuickTime gets initialized right when the program starts:

```
CPPDocApp::CPPDocApp()
{
    RegisterAllPPClasses();

    RegisterClass_(CTextView);

    RegisterClass_(CPicturePane);

    UQuickTime::Initialize();
}
```

Toolbox managers don't need any kind of explicit clean-up on your part—quitting an application automatically takes care of this. The Movie Toolbox is a little different. In a PowerPlant-based project, you'll call the **UQuickTime** class utility function **Finalize()** when finished working with QuickTime. The **CPPDocApp** destructor is a good place to add this call:

```
CPPDocApp::~CPPDocApp()
{
    UQuickTime::Finalize();
}
```

TIP *If you've worked with QuickTime in projects that weren't PowerPlant-based, you called the Toolbox routines **EnterMovies()** and **ExitMovies()** near the start and finish of a program. You don't need to make these calls in a PowerPlant-based project—the **UQuickTime** class makes the calls for you.*

Defining Movie Window Constants

A QuickTime movie is displayed in a window. In Constructor, I created a new 'PPob' with a resource ID of 2500 for this purpose. The 'PPob' didn't have any panes in it—but it will. The **ShowMovieWindow()** function will create a pane on the fly. That pane will have a pane ID of 1. *PP Doc App.cp* defines two constants that hold these values:

```
const ResIDT   PPob_MovieWindow  = 2500;
const PaneIDT  paneID_MoviePane  =    1;
```

ShowMovieWindow() may be the lengthiest routine in the *MediaCenter.µ* project. Rather than cover it all in one shot, I'll break it up into a few more manageable chunks.

ShowMovieWindow(): Opening a Movie File & Movie Window

A click on the Open Movie button in the Control window or a selection of Open Movie from the Movie menu results in a call to the **CPPDocApp** member function **ShowMovieWindow()**. That routine starts by declaring a variable of type **Movie**. A call to the **UQuickTime** utility routine **GetMovieFromFile()** presents the user with the standard Open file dialog box. Choosing a QuickTime movie from this dialog box results in the movie's data being loaded into memory. This function returns a pointer to this movie data. The pointer is held in the **Movie** variable **theMovie**. A check of this variable will reveal whether the loading of the movie data was successful—a **theMovie** value of **nil** means the loading failed and the **ShowMovieWindow()** function terminates:

```
Movie  theMovie;
theMovie = UQuickTime::GetMovieFromFile();
if (theMovie == nil)
    return;
```

The movie data is now in memory, but nothing is displayed on the screen. Now it's time to create a new, empty window that will hold the movie:

```
LWindow  *theWindow;
theWindow = LWindow::CreateWindow(PPob_MovieWindow, this );
```

There's no way to anticipate the exact screen size of the movie the user selects, so the newly created window needs to be resized to match the dimensions of the movie. A few calls to Macintosh Toolbox routines helps here. When passed a **Movie** variable, the **GetMovieBox()** function fills in a **Rect** variable with the dimensions of the movie:

```
Rect  theMovieBox;
```

```
::GetMovieBox(theMovie, &theMovieBox );
```

While variable **theMovieBox** does hold the coordinates of the movie, the left and top values are not guaranteed to each be 0. In a bit, I'll be "laying" the movie in a pane in the window, so I'll want the upper left corner of the movie to be at a coordinate of (0, 0) so that it fits snugly into this pane. A call to the Toolbox routine **OffsetRect()** repositions the rectangle **theMovieBox** to have left and top values of 0—without affecting the size of the movie:

```
::OffsetRect(&theMovieBox, -theMovieBox.left,
            -theMovieBox.top);
```

Finally, a call to the Toolbox routine **SetMovieBox()** informs the **Movie** variable **theMovie** that the coordinates of the movie's bounding rectangle have been changed:

```
::SetMovieBox(theMovie, &theMovieBox);
```

ShowMovieWindow(): Creating a Pane to Display the Movie

The movie will be displayed in a pane in the window—but the 'PPob' the window is based on doesn't include a pane! I could have included one when I created the 'PPob' in Constructor, but if I had, the attributes I assigned to the pane would be useless now. Fortunately, that's not a problem. Just as you can change an **LWindow** object's attributes from source code, you can change a pane's attributes from code, too. You can even create a new pane from source code. To create a pane on the fly, declare an **SPaneInfo** variable:

```
SPaneInfo  thePaneInfo;
```

SPaneInfo is a structure that specifies the attributes of a new pane. Here are the attributes I chose:

```
thePaneInfo.paneID = 1;
thePaneInfo.width = theMovieBox.right;
thePaneInfo.height = theMovieBox.bottom;
thePaneInfo.left = 0;
thePaneInfo.top = 0;
thePaneInfo.visible = true;
thePaneInfo.enabled = true;
```

```
thePaneInfo.bindings.left = false;
thePaneInfo.bindings.right = false;
thePaneInfo.bindings.top = false;
thePaneInfo.bindings.bottom = false;
thePaneInfo.userCon = 0;
thePaneInfo.superView = theWindow;
```

Most of the attributes should be familiar to you. The **paneID** is, of course, the ID of the pane. The width and height specify the dimensions of the pane. The pane is to hold the movie, so I want those values to match the size of the movie. The left and top fields specify where the pane will be situated in the window. I want the upper left corner of the pane in the upper left corner of the window. Note that this doesn't have to be the case—a QuickTime movie can appear anywhere in a window and doesn't have to be the exact size of the window.

I want the pane to be visible, of course—so the visible field is set to **true**. I've also set it to be enabled, which means it's capable of responding to mouse button clicks. That feature won't be used here, so this setting choice was arbitrary. A pane's binding refers to whether it will move about in a window as the window is resized. Each of the four binding fields are set to **false**, meaning the pane will sit tight in the window. Setting a value to true means that the pane will move as a window grows (the edge of the pane is bound to the moving edge of the window). The **userCon** field of a pane is a 32-bit value that can be used for any purpose. Here, as often is the case, this field is set to 0 to designate that it is unused. (Note that in Chapter 11, "Debugging & Testing the Application," you'll see an example of a rather interesting use for this field.) The superview field specifies the pane's superview, which is the window itself.

ShowMovieWindow(): Adding a Controller to the Movie

The pane information is all filled in, so it's time to make use of the pane. An open QuickTime movie will be displayed in a window with a standard movie controller running along the bottom of the window. The PowerPlant **LMovieController** class is used to create a movie controller object and associate that object with a pane and a movie. The first parameter to the **LMovieController** constructor is the pane to hold the movie. The second parameter is the Movie variable that points to the movie data. When invoked, the **LMovieController** constructor first creates a new movie controller. It then attaches the controller to the window to hold the movie (it determines which window to use from the value in the **SPaneInfo** parameter's superview field). Finally, it associates the movie with the pane:

```
LMovieController  *theController;
theController = new LMovieController(thePaneInfo, theMovie);
```

ShowMovieWindow(): Resizing & Displaying the Movie Window

A controller is attached to a movie—it runs along the bottom of the movie. Both the movie and the controller fit inside the window displaying the movie. Now it's time to set the window's size so that it matches the dimensions of the rectangle defined by the movie and the attached controller. I already have a rectangle that holds the dimensions of the movie—the variable **theMovieBox** was set to that size earlier. A standard movie controller is always 16 pixels in height, so all I need to do is add 16 to the bottom field of the rectangle **theMovieBox** to obtain the correctly sized rectangle:

```
theMovieBox.bottom += 16;
```

Now a call to the **LWindow** function **DoSetBounds()** changes the size of the window to match the size of the movie plus the controller:

```
theWindow->DoSetBounds(theMovieBox);
```

At this point we're *almost* all set to show the window! The previous step properly sized the window, but it placed the window in the very upper-left corner of the screen (recall that the left and top values of **theMovieBox** were each 0). I'll move the window out onto the screen a little by defining a variable of type **Point**, assigning its two fields appropriate pixel coordinate values, and then invoking the **LWindow** function **DoSetPosition()** to reposition the window:

```
Point  thePoint;
thePoint.h = 30;
thePoint.v = 60;
theWindow->DoSetPosition(thePoint);
```

Now that the window holds the movie and controller and has been resized; it's finally time to let the user see the window:

```
theWindow->Show();
```

ShowMovieWindow() Source Code Listing

You've seen the code for **ShowMovieWindow()** in bits and pieces—now it's time to take a look at it in its entirety:

```
void
CPPDocApp::ShowMovieWindow()
{
   Movie  theMovie;
   theMovie = UQuickTime::GetMovieFromFile();
   if (theMovie == nil)
      return;
```

```
LWindow  *theWindow;
theWindow = LWindow::CreateWindow(PPob_MovieWindow, this );

Rect  theMovieBox;

::GetMovieBox(theMovie, &theMovieBox );
::OffsetRect(&theMovieBox, -theMovieBox.left,
            -theMovieBox.top);
::SetMovieBox(theMovie, &theMovieBox);

SPaneInfo  thePaneInfo;
thePaneInfo.paneID = 1;
thePaneInfo.width = theMovieBox.right;
thePaneInfo.height = theMovieBox.bottom;
thePaneInfo.left = 0;
thePaneInfo.top = 0;
thePaneInfo.visible = true;
thePaneInfo.enabled = true;
thePaneInfo.bindings.left = false;
thePaneInfo.bindings.right = false;
thePaneInfo.bindings.top = false;
thePaneInfo.bindings.bottom = false;
thePaneInfo.userCon = 0;
thePaneInfo.superView = theWindow;

LMovieController  *theController;
theController = new LMovieController( thePaneInfo, theMovie);
Point  thePoint;
thePoint.h = 30;
thePoint.v = 60;

theMovieBox.bottom += 16;
theWindow->DoSetBounds(theMovieBox);
theWindow->DoSetPosition(thePoint);

theWindow->Show( );
}
```

Running the Program

With the new resources and code added to the *MediaCenter.μ* project, choose Run from the Project menu to build this latest version of MediaCenter. After MediaCenter launches, click on the Control window's Open Movie button to verify that the standard Open file dialog appears. When it does, choose a movie file—there are a couple included in the Sample Movie Files folder on the Companion CD-ROM. A new window will open, and the movie appears in it. Test out the movie's controller to make sure that everything works. Now choose Open Movie from the Movie menu to see that this menu item behaves in the same manner as the Open Movie button.

Moving On

In a PowerPlant-based project, you create a window by defining a 'PPob' resource in Constructor and then calling the **LWindow** member function **CreateWindow()** to use that resource's data to build a new window object. In the 'PPob' resource you set the attributes (such as size, location, color, and so forth) that the window will initially have. Once a window object is created, you can use **LWindow** member functions to alter any of these 'PPob'-defined characteristics.

PowerPlant defines a dialog box to be little more than a special type of window. The primary differences between a dialog box and a window is that a dialog box is automatically a listener, and a dialog box can automatically respond to clicks on its OK and Cancel buttons. Typically you'll rely on the **StDialogHandler** class to take care of much of the work of displaying and then monitoring the action in a dialog box.

At this point, the bulk of the MediaCenter example project is complete. The primary parts left to add are printing and file support. Using traditional Macintosh programming techniques, these two program features can be somewhat awkward to implement. As you'll see in the next two chapters, programming with PowerPlant removes much of the mystery and effort in taking care of these behind-the-scenes features.

Debugging & Testing the Application

T he previous pages have demonstrated how to include all the main interface components in your own Macintosh programs. You can now add menus,
controls, windows, and dialog boxes to any of your applications. And by this
point in the book, you have developed a solid understanding of working with
Constructor, PowerPlant classes, and the CodeWarrior IDE. That makes this as
good a time as any to congratulate yourself and take a short break from programming. While this chapter doesn't let you off the hook completely (you
will be writing *some* code!), the emphasis is on examining existing code.

In this chapter, you'll learn about the Metrowerks source-level debugger
MWDebug. Even though you've been programming with CodeWarrior for a
while now, you may not have heard of MWDebug. That's because this
debugger is seamlessly integrated into the CodeWarrior IDE—it's used by
simply making a couple of menu selections. Here you'll see how to use this
debugger to track down programming errors and investigate how the Mac
and PowerPlant work with memory.

Metrowerks provides two additional utilities to help you improve your
application's performance. MW Profiler makes it easy to profile your code.
Profiling involves the timing of routines to see which ones bog down application performance. ZoneRanger monitors a program's use of memory. You run
both ZoneRanger and your application at the same time, and ZoneRanger
displays how objects are allocated and released by your program.

CodeWarrior Projects & Targets

A CodeWarrior project can *target* different platforms. That is, a project can be used to build an application that runs on computers with different processors. As a Mac programmer, you will be interested in targeting older, 68K-based Macintoshes, new PowerPC-based computers, or both. In most instances, you'll want to create a fat binary application—that type of program targets both the 68K and PowerPC platforms. If a user has a 68K-based Mac, launching the fat application only runs a 68K version of the program. If a user instead has a PowerPC-based computer, then launching the same fat application loads a different version of your program into memory—a version that consists of PowerPC-native instructions that run faster than their 68K-native versions.

The disadvantage to creating a fat binary version of your program is program size. Because a fat binary holds two sets of program code, it's roughly twice as large as a version that targets only one or the other of the two Macintosh processor families. If for some reason you're intentionally constraining the platform your program can run on (that is, only on 68K-based Macs or only on PowerPC-based Macs), then you'll want to choose a 68K or PPC project stationery rather than a FAT stationery in order to save the user some disk space.

If you're targeting both 68K-based and PowerPC-based computers, then you'll want to test both versions of your application. This chapter deals with nothing but application testing, so now is a good time to dig deeper into a topic that hitherto has only been touched upon—working with different targets from one CodeWarrior project.

Choosing the Project Target

A single CodeWarrior project can have multiple targets. For instance, a project created from a FAT project stationery, such as the *MediaCenter.μ* project, can be used to generate a 68K application, a PowerPC-native application, and a fat binary application. To see the available targets for a project, click on the Targets tab near the top of the project window. Figure 11-1 shows how the project window looks when the Targets tab is selected for this chapter's version of *MediaCenter.μ*.

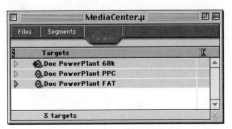

Figure 11-1: The Targets tab reveals the platforms to which an application can be targeted.

While a project can have multiple targets, it can only build one application at a time. You select the target that an application is to be built for by selecting the Targets tab in the project window and then clicking on the target. The arrow pointing to Doc PowerPlant 68k back in Figure 11-1 shows that a 68K version of MediaCenter will be generated when Run or Make is next selected from the Project menu.

TIP *Throughout this book, we've been using FAT project stationery. Doing so makes it easy to build a 68K, PowerPC, or fat binary version of an application. While the final version will most likely be a fat binary (to please users of any type of Mac), having the option to target one type of processor is helpful during the testing phase of application development.*

Adjusting Project Settings

The second from last item in the Edit menu is used to adjust the settings for the active project as they apply to the current target. This menu item's name is initially the name of the target followed by the word "Settings." Figure 11-2 provides an example. That figure shows the *MediaCenter.μ* project, which was created from the Doc PowerPlant FAT project stationery. The project window shows that the project is set to generate a 68K application, so the Edit menu displays the project settings menu item as "Doc PowerPlant 68k Settings."

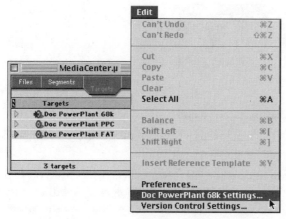

Figure 11-2: The name of the project settings menu varies depending on which target is selected in the project window.

Choosing the project settings menu item (regardless of its exact name) for a project currently targeting the 68K-based Mac displays a settings dialog box like the one shown in Figure 11-3. The PowerPC version of this settings dialog box is very similar, though of course, Target Settings Panel list items such as 68K Target (under the Target heading) appear as PPC Target, and so forth.

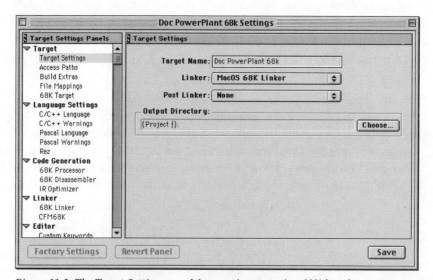

Figure 11-3: The Target Settings panel for a project targeting 68K-based computers.

This project settings dialog box provides a wealth of project options. The settings displayed in the dialog box vary with the item selected from the scrollable Target Settings Panels list. Clicking on Target Settings under the Target heading reveals a *panel* holding a number of settings pertaining to the currently selected target. In Figure 11-3 you see that the Target Name edit box allows you to enter a new target name. If you do that, dismissing the dialog results in the new target name appearing in the project window, as shown in Figure 11-4. Figure 11-4 also shows that changing the target name changes the name of the second to last menu item in the Edit menu.

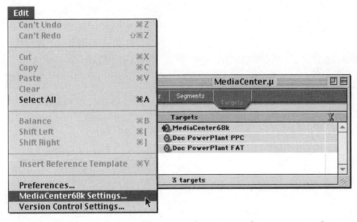

Figure 11-4: The project settings menu item name changes to match a target name change.

Adjusting Application Settings

The target name serves as a reference in the project window—it doesn't have anything to do with the name to be given to the application generated from a project. To change the name of the application, use the Edit menu to again bring up the project settings dialog box. As shown in Figure 11-4, the second to last menu item now has the new target name. Select the item and display the panel that holds the File Name edit box. Which panel this setting appears in depends on the current target type. For a 68K project, click on 68K Target under the Target heading in the Target Settings Panels list. For a PowerPC project, click on PPC Target under the Target heading. For a fat application, click on MacOS Merge under the Linker heading. In all cases, enter a name in the File Name edit box to assign a new name to the application that results from subsequent builds. Figure 11-5 shows that the File Name edit box is highlighted in anticipation of entering a new name for an application targeting the Macintosh 68K platform.

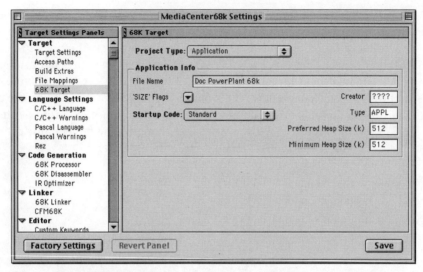

Figure 11-5: The 68K Target panel for a project targeting 68K-based computers.

TIP

If running your application results in low memory conditions, raise the heap size that gets dedicated to your program. Do this by increasing the values in the Preferred Heap Size and Minimum Heap Size edit boxes in the 68K Target and PPC Target panels. Figure 11-5 shows this panel for a 68K target. That figure shows that the RAM requirements for this version of the MediaCenter program will be half a megabyte (512K).

Metrowerks' Debugger

The Metrowerks CodeWarrior IDE includes an integrated high-level debugger—MWDebug. Because it's a high-level debugger, debugging takes place in a source code environment. That is, you don't have to know assembly language to make use of the debugger. With the debugger enabled, you can halt the execution of your program at any time and see exactly at what point in the code the program is executing. You can view the source code just executed, the source code about to be run, and the values of variables at of the time the program. Being able to examine just what is happening at any point in the running of your program at the source-code level makes it easy to debug your program if it doesn't behave as expected. And as your program grows in complexity, you can be assured that somewhere down the line it *won't* behave as planned!

Starting the Debugger

You'll find the MWDebug application in the Helper Apps folder in the Metrowerks CodeWarrior folder. While MWDebug is an application and can be launched like any program, you'll more often than not run this debugger indirectly from within the CodeWarrior IDE. When you want to debug a program, first launch the CodeWarrior IDE and open the program's CodeWarrior project. Then choose Enable Debugger from the Project menu. That won't start the debugger, but it will ready the project for debugging. Looking in the Project menu, you'll notice that the Enable Debugger item is now named Disable Debugger to allow you to toggle debugging back off. The Run menu item has also changed. To let you know that the running of your program from within the CodeWarrior IDE will now take place with the debugger on, the Run item is now named Debug.

After choosing Enable Debugger from the Project menu to turn debugging on, choose Debug to start debugging. When you do this, your program won't immediately start up. Instead, the debugger will take control and the three debugger windows shown in Figure 11-6 appear. Use these windows to control the execution of your program and to examine the effect different lines of code have on your program.

TIP
After choosing Debug, you may notice that some source code files get recompiled before the debugger starts. That's a normal course of affairs, so don't be alarmed.

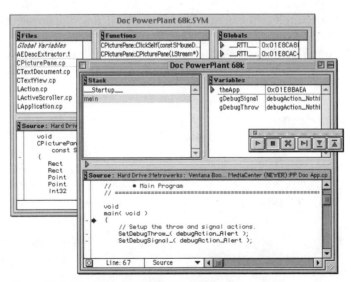

Figure 11-6: The windows of the Metrowerks debugger.

Debugger Windows

The smallest window is the *control window* and is used to step through the instructions of your program. Doing that enables you to see the state of your program at any given time. The window whose title bears the program's name is the *program window*. When you stop the execution of the program, this window displays the source code just executed. Finally, the *browser window* is used to view source code in project files. Unlike the program window, which only shows code being executed, the browser window lets you browse through code in any project window.

The Program Window

The program window is where you monitor source code that has just been executed or is about to be executed. This window consists of three areas, or panes:

- **Stack Pane**. The stack pane lists the order of the functions as they appear on the stack. As one function calls another, the function addresses are saved on the stack so the program can find its way back to the original calling routine. This list of functions is referred to as the *call chain*. When a C++ program is launched, execution always begins at **main()**. So when debugging starts, **main()** will be listed in the stack pane.

- **Variables Pane**. The variables pane lists variables local to the currently executing routine and global variables affected by the this same routine. To the right of each variable is the value that variable had at the time execution was halted. When a program launches, variables local to **main()** are listed in this pane. Typically, this will be the application object variable **theApp**. If **main()** calls the PowerPlant routines **SetDebugSignal()** and **SetDebugThrow()**, then PowerPlant global variables **gDebugSignal** and **gDebugThrow** will also be listed.

TIP | *The debugging functions **SetDebugSignal()** and **SetDebugThrow()** were introduced in Chapter 4, "PowerPlantBasics." Invoking these two routines allows your source code to include calls to other PowerPlant debugging routines. For more information on PowerPlant debugging, refer to* The PowerPlant Book, *an electronic document that appears as an Acrobat file named* PowerPlant Book.pdf *on one of the CD-ROMs in the CodeWarrior Professional package.*

- **Source Pane**. This pane consists of the source code for the file containing the currently executing code. When a program is launched and debugging is enabled, program execution is poised to begin at the start of **main()**—but the program doesn't start to run. Instead, action is paused to allow you to set *breakpoints*. A breakpoint is a marker set by a line of code. You set a breakpoint at a line by clicking just to the left of that line. Doing that places a small breakpoint marker to the left of the line. Once program execution begins, the program will run until a breakpoint is encountered. At that time, you can look at the variables pane to see if the variables listed there hold the values you expect them to have. You can remove an existing breakpoint by clicking on its marker.

After setting one or more breakpoints, you're ready to start your program running. To do that, choose Run from the debugger Control menu. Your program will start up just as if it had been launched from the desktop. The program will run as always, with one major exception. When execution reaches a line of code that holds a breakpoint, execution will halt and the source code from the file that holds the breakpoint displays in the source pane of the debugger program window.

The Browser Window

When a program is built, CodeWarrior generates a file with an extension of *.SYM*. This file holds symbols such as routine names and variable names. When you run the project's program with debugging enabled, the debugger looks to this one *SYM* file to get information about code and variables in all of the files that make up the project. Armed with this information, the debugger is capable of displaying the source code, along with places where breakpoints can be set, for any file in a project. Because the debugger program window shows only the source code from the file currently executing, you'll use the browser window to set breakpoints in other source code files. The browser window is comprised of four panes:

- **File Pane**. This area lists all the source code files, including PowerPlant files, that are part of the project being debugged. Clicking on a file name in this pane displays a list of that file's functions in the functions pane of the browser window. All of the source code of that file is displayed in the browser source pane that makes up the bottom of the browser window.

- **Function Pane**. This area lists all of the functions that make up whatever source code file is currently selected in the file pane. Clicking on a function name reveals the global variables the function affects. The source code in the browser source pane automatically scrolls to display the code for the selected function.

■ **Globals Pane**. When Global Variables is selected in the file pane, this area displays the global variables that play a part in the currently selected function in the functions pane.

■ **Browser Source Pane**. In this area, you'll always find the source code that makes up whatever file is currently selected in the file pane. Set a breakpoint in this pane by clicking to the left of a line of code to break on. Remove a breakpoint by again clicking to the left of the line.

You'll use the browser window to look at source code and set breakpoints in files other than the one currently displayed in the program window. Consider the situation shown in Figure 11-6. The program window is displaying **main()**, a routine in the *MediaCenter.μ* project's *PP Doc App.cp* file. If I want to set the debugger to break when the MediaCenter program updates or redraws the picture in an open picture window, I won't be able to do that from the program window. That's because the source code for redrawing a picture isn't in the file currently displayed in the program window—it's a part of the *CPicturePane.cp* file. To set the breakpoint, I would:

1. Click on the browser window to activate it.

2. Click on the *CPicturePane.cp* file name in the file pane to display its code in the browser source pane at bottom of the browser window.

3. Scroll to the appropriate section of code in the browser source pane.

4. Click to the left of the line to be marked as a breakpoint.

The Control Window

When your program is running and it reaches a breakpoint, execution halts immediately. At that time, you can check out your program's state by looking at variable values in the variables pane of the debugger program window or by looking at the source code displayed in the source pane of the debugger program window. Here you can verify that the code you *expect* to be executing *is* in fact executing. Then, it's time to restart the program. You use the six buttons in the control window (the smallest window shown back in Figure 11-6) to start, stop, and restart your program. Here's the purpose of the first three buttons:

■ **Run**. Use the left-most button to initially start program execution and restart program execution after a breakpoint has been reached.

■ **Stop**. Click the button second from the left in the control window to stop program execution at any time—regardless of whether any breakpoints are set.

■ **Kill**. To terminate the running of your program, click the button third from the left. To start execution again, click the Run button—but execution begins from **main()** as if the program were being launched.

If you don't go with one of these options and you haven't set any breakpoints in the Source pane, your program runs as it normally would. If you've set a breakpoint, and the program reaches the line of code marked with that breakpoint, your program stops executing and the *current statement arrow*—the small arrow that appears to the left of one line of code in the source pane of the debugger window—moves to the line containing the breakpoint.

Once your program has halted, you can use the Run button to restart execution. If you want to slow things down and execute only a single line of code, use the three remaining control window buttons. These buttons all perform the same when an application-defined function *isn't* the next line of code to execute. In such a case, only the line of code that the *current statement arrow*—the small arrow that appears to the left of one line of code in the source pane of the debugger window—is pointing to executes. If the line of code to execute is a function call, then the buttons perform as follows:

- **Step Over**. The fourth control button from the left executes the function call and then moves the current statement arrow down to the next line.

- **Step Into**. The fifth button from the left executes only the first line of code in the function being invoked. The current statement arrow then moves to the next line in this function. Unlike the Step Over button, which executes the entire called function in one shot, this button allows you to step line-by-line through the routine.

- **Step Out**. The rightmost control button allows you to execute the remaining lines in a function, you've stepped into (by using the Step Into button, of course). Once inside a function, you can exit by clicking this button. That executes the remaining lines in the function and then returns the current statement arrow to the line of code that follows the call to the just-executed routine.

TIP *The function of each of the Control window buttons is paralleled by a menu item in the debugger's Control menu. Whether you use the Control window buttons, the Control menu items, or the menu item Command key equivalents to control debugging is simply a matter of personal preference.*

Profiler & Code Profiling

Keeping execution time down is always important, but for some applications more so than others. If your program's intent is to rapidly display graphics (games can be *very* time-critical), then you'll want to shave off all time-wasting code—no matter how slight a difference it might make. If your program has some routines that take very long to execute (some image filtering tasks may take *hours* to run), then rewriting some sections of code may save the user a wait of several minutes—even if the execution time is reduced by only a small percentage. As you run your program and observe its behavior, you may feel that you have a pretty good inkling as to which routines are bogging down the program's execution time. Or, you may not. A project might be very large, and determining where delays take place can be difficult. Another project may perform an operation divided among several routines, and it may not be obvious which routine is hindering overall performance. For situations such as these, you want to profile your source code—you want to study the timing of its functions. Metrowerks Profiler allows you to do this.

To use the Metrowerks Profiler, include a Profiler library in your project and use the PowerPlant **StProfileSection** class. This class lets you specify which routines should be timed and writes the timing information to a file. After you've put your program through its paces and terminated it, run the MW Profiler program to open and examine the file that the **StProfileSection** class generated. By looking at the information in the file, you'll be able to determine where your program is spending most of its time. Armed with this knowledge, you'll know which functions are worthy of your optimization efforts.

Setting Up a Project for Profiling

Profiling isn't included by default in PowerPlant projects, so you'll need to do a little setup work before making use of the **StProfileSection** class. In short, you'll add one or two Profiler libraries and a PowerPlant source code file to your project and apply a project setting or two. How you set up your project for profiling depends on whether your project targets a 68K Macintosh or a PowerPC-based Mac. Here I'll cover both bases by assuming that your project is based on a FAT project stationery. If it's not, you'll use only the information that pertains to your project's target.

Adding the Profiler Libraries

Profiling code is held in a library that you add to your project. For a 68K target, you add one library; for a PPC target, you add a different library. For a fat target, you add them both.

Assuming you're working with a project based on FAT project stationery, add the two libraries one at a time. Follow these steps to first add the 68K Profiler library:

1. Click on the Targets tab in the project window; then click on the 68K target.

2. Click on the Files tab in the project window; then click on the Libraries group heading.

3. Choose Add Files from the Project menu.

4. Use the Add dialog box pop-up menu to navigate to the Profiler 68K folder (path is Metrowerks: Metrowerks CodeWarrior: MacOS Support: Libraries: Profiler 68K).

5. Double-click on the *Profiler68k(Large).Lib* Profiler library.

6. Click the Done button.

7. Check only the 68K target in the Add Files dialog box that appears (see Figure 11-7).

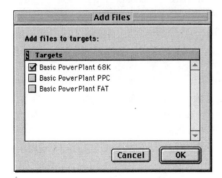

Figure 11-7: Adding a Profiler library to a single target.

With the 68K Profiler library added to the project, turn your attention to the PowerPC version of the library. The steps for adding that library are similar to the ones you just followed:

1. Click on the Targets tab in the project window; then click on the PPC target.

2. Click on the Files tab in the project window; then click on the Libraries group heading.

3. Choose Add Files from the Project menu.

4. Use the Add dialog box pop-up menu to navigate to the Profiler PPC folder (path is Metrowerks: Metrowerks CodeWarrior: MacOS Support: Libraries: Profiler PPC).

5. Double-click on the *ProfilerPPC.Lib* Profiler library.

6. Click the Done button.

7. Check only the PPC target in the Add Files dialog box that appears.

After adding the two libraries, your project will look similar to the one shown in Figure 11-8. Displaying the contents of the folders in the Libraries group shows that both Profiler libraries are now part of the project. Note that only one of the two libraries will have a checkmark to the left of its name. A checked file is one that is *touched*—it's a file that is either new to the project or has been edited since the last compilation of the project. While both Profiler libraries are newly added, CodeWarrior knows that only one of the files is to be included in the next compilation. In Figure 11-8, only the PPC library is checked because at this time the project has the PowerPC target selected.

TIP *When viewing a project window, you might not be able to tell which target is selected. You can tell in one of two ways. As you've just read, you can click on the Targets tab in the project window. Alternately, you can choose the Show Window Toolbar item from the Toolbar submenu in the Window menu. Choosing that item displays a toolbar under the tabs in the project window. That toolbar includes a pop-up menu that displays the current target (as well as letting you choose a different target).*

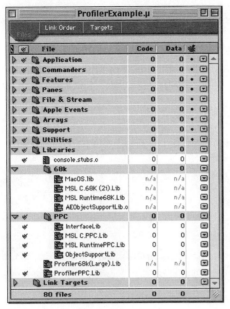

File	Code	Data	🔻
▷ ✔ 🗀 Application	0	0	• 🔻
▷ ✔ 🗀 Commanders	0	0	• 🔻
▷ ✔ 🗀 Features	0	0	• 🔻
▷ ✔ 🗀 Panes	0	0	• 🔻
▷ ✔ 🗀 File & Stream	0	0	• 🔻
▷ ✔ 🗀 Apple Events	0	0	• 🔻
▷ ✔ 🗀 Arrays	0	0	• 🔻
▷ ✔ 🗀 Support	0	0	• 🔻
▷ ✔ 🗀 Utilities	0	0	• 🔻
▽ ✔ 🗀 Libraries	0	0	🔻
✔ 📄 console.stubs.o	0	0	🔻
▽ 🗀 68k	0	0	🔻
📚 MacOS.lib	n/a	n/a	🔻
📚 MSL C.68K (2i).Lib	n/a	n/a	🔻
📚 MSL Runtime68K.Lib	n/a	n/a	🔻
📚 AEObjectSupportLib.o	n/a	n/a	🔻
▽ ✔ 🗀 PPC	0	0	🔻
✔ 📚 InterfaceLib	0	0	🔻
✔ 📚 MSL C.PPC.Lib	0	0	🔻
✔ 📚 MSL RuntimePPC.Lib	0	0	🔻
✔ 📚 ObjectSupportLib	0	0	🔻
📚 Profiler68k(Large).Lib	n/a	n/a	🔻
✔ 📚 ProfilerPPC.Lib	0	0	🔻
▷ 🗀 Link Targets	0	0	🔻
80 files	0	0	

Figure 11-8: A project set up to include profiling in both the 68K and PowerPC targets.

Turning On the Generation of Profiler Information

Profiling your application is something you do before building the final version of the program. When you're ready to make the final build, you'll want to omit profiling so your application no longer generates timing data output files. The CodeWarrior IDE makes it easy to toggle profiling on and off.

Adding a Profiler library to a project isn't sufficient to start profiling. To do that, you need to adjust a setting in the Settings dialog box. Profiling can be turned on or off independently for either the 68K or PowerPC target. For the 68K target, choose the project settings menu item in the Edit menu. Then click on 68K Processor under the Code Generation heading in the Target Settings Panels list to display the 68K Processor panel. To turn profiling on, check Generate Profiler Information (see Figure 11-9).

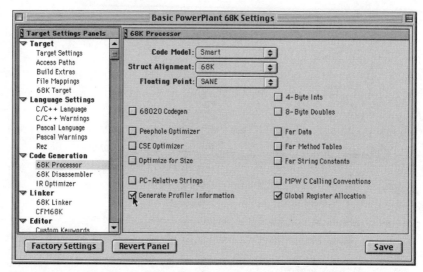

Figure 11-9: Turning on profiling for a project currently targeting 68K computers.

If your project is currently set to target the PowerPC platform, again choose the project settings menu item in the Edit menu. Here you click on PPC Processor under the Code Generation heading in the Target Settings Panels list to display the PPC Processor panel. Turn profiling on by checking Generate Profiler Information.

Adding the Profiler Source Code File to the Project

In order for a project to make use of a PowerPlant class, the header file and source code file that declare and implement that class must be a part of the project. A CodeWarrior project based on PowerPlant stationery automatically includes all the files that support commonly used PowerPlant classes. Profiling is an optional feature, so the *UProfiler.h* and *UProfiler.cp* files aren't automatically included in PowerPlant-based projects. You'll add the header file to the project by adding an **#include** directive in your application-defined source code (covered ahead). You'll add the source code file to a project window by first clicking on the name of the group to add the file to, and then choosing Add Files from the Project menu. For organization purposes, it makes sense to click on the Utilities group to designate that the *UProfiler.cp* file be listed with other PowerPlant utility files.

After choosing Add Files from the Project menu, use the pop-up menu in the Add Files dialog box to locate the *UProfiler.cp* file—Figure 11-10 shows the long path you'll take to get to the Utility Classes folder that holds this file. Once the file is displayed in the Add Files dialog box list, click the Add button, and then the Done button.

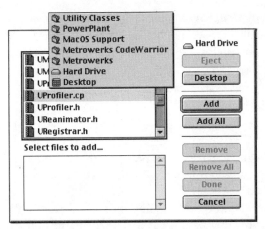

Figure 11-10: Adding the UProfiler.cp *source code file to a project.*

Including the Profiler Header File

The *UProfiler.h* header file declares the **StProfileSection** class. To make this class known to the compiler, you need to include this header in your project's source code—right along with other PowerPlant header files. Open the project's source code file that includes **main()** (such as *PP Basic Starter.cp* or *PP Doc App.cp*) and add the following **#include** directive near the start of the file:

```
#include "UProfiler.h"
```

Using the StProfileSection Class

The **StProfileSection** class consists of nothing more than a constructor and a destructor. You use the class by simply declaring a local **StProfileSection** variable. The declaration of that variable tells the Profiler to start profiling whatever code follows. Profiling ends when the routine that declares the local **StProfileSection** variable ends. As the routine terminates, the local variable is destroyed, and its destructor is automatically invoked by PowerPlant.

TIP   *Recall from Chapter 4, "PowerPlant Basics," that a PowerPlant class with a name beginning with an S is stack-based. As a local variable, an **StProfileSection** object is stored on the stack. As you see here, one of the advantages of a stack-based class is that when an object is destroyed, cleanup is automatic.*

The StProfileSection Constructor

Creating an **StProfileSection** variable involves invoking the **StProfileSection** constructor. Here's the constructor's prototype:

```
StProfileSection(Str255  inDumpFileName,
                 Int16   inNumFunctions,
                 Int16   inStackDepth);
```

The first of the three constructor parameters is the name to be assigned to the profiling output file created as a result of profiling code. This name is in the form of a Pascal string. When you execute a program that includes profiling, an output file will be generated each time an **StProfileSection** object is created. Thus if the object is created in a routine that gets invoked three times, after quitting the program, you'll find three profiling files in the program's folder. The name you provide as the first parameter will be the name of the first file. Subsequent files will have a number appended to the file name. For instance, a parameter of "\pProfilerOut" will result in profiling files with the names *ProfilerOut*, *ProfilerOut1*, *ProfilerOut2*, and so forth.

An **StProfileSection** object allocates extra memory for its own use. The second and third parameters determine the amount of memory the object should reserve. The second parameter is the number of functions to be profiled. If you create the **StProfileSection** object in a routine that calls only a few functions, you need to keep in mind that these called functions themselves invoke other routines. In a PowerPlant-based project, the number of application-defined routines provides little insight into the actual number of routines invoked. That's because the call to one PowerPlant routine may result in numerous other PowerPlant routines. For this reason, you'll set the second parameter to the **StProfileSection** constructor much higher than your own code might indicate. A value of 300 or more is usually justified.

The final parameter to the **StProfileSection** constructor should be the size of the *call chain*—the greatest number of functions that may be on the stack during the existence of the **StProfileSection** object. As one function invokes another, the call chain grows in size as the program keeps track of where it is to return after each routine terminates. Like the second **StProfileSection** constructor parameter, the value of this third parameter may be larger than you suspect. In a PowerPlant-based project the call chain can be 20 or greater.

To create the **StProfileSection** object you declare an object. A typical declaration might look like this:

```
StProfileSection  theProfile("\pProfilerData", 300, 20);
```

If you've selected second or third parameter values that are too small, you'll hear about it. When you build and run your program, an alert like the one pictured in Figure 11-11 appears if profiling fails. If you encounter this alert, increase the size of the second or third parameters (most likely the second) and then rebuild and run the program again.

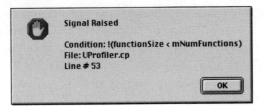

Figure 11-11: The alert that appears when StProfileSection parameter values are too small.

Profiling a Routine

Once you've set up a project to make use of the Profiler, profiling a routine is easy—just choose a routine to profile and then declare an **StProfileSection** object near the start of that routine. You can test this out by creating a PowerPlant-based project and adding an **StProfileSection** declaration to an existing routine. Here I've done that by editing the *PP Starter App.cp* file from a project created from Basic PowerPlant FAT project stationery. The only change I've made to the **ObeyCommand()** routine is the addition of the **StProfileSection** declaration:

```
Boolean
CPPStarterApp::ObeyCommand(
    CommandT    inCommand,
    void        *ioParam)
{
    StProfileSection  theProfile("\pObeyCommand", 300, 20);

    Boolean  cmdHandled = true;

    switch (inCommand) {

        case cmd_New:

            LWindow  *theWindow;
            theWindow = LWindow::CreateWindow(window_Sample, this);
            theWindow->Show();
            break;

        default:
            cmdHandled = LApplication::ObeyCommand(inCommand, ioParam);
            break;
    }
    return cmdHandled;
}
```

When the program executes the **ObeyCommand()** routine, an **StProfileSection** object is created. The object begins recording profiling information and continues doing so until the routine ends. When that happens, the object destroys itself—but not before it dumps the saved data to a file named *ObeyCommand*.

You'll find a profiling example project named *ProfilerExample.µ* in the P01 ProfilerExample folder in the Chapter 11 folder on this book's Companion CD-ROM. That project includes the preceding version of **ObeyCommand()**.

Profiler Output File

You examine the results of a profiling session by examining the profiling output file that's been saved to the same folder that holds the profiled application. You can view this file by double-clicking its icon or by launching the MW Profiler application and then opening the file by choosing Open from the File menu. The file will look similar to the one shown in Figure 11-12.

			ProfileObeyCommand						

Method: Detailed Timebase: PowerPC Saved at: 8:01:03 PM 8/15/97 Overhead: 0.491

Function Name	Count	Only	%	+Children	%	Average	Maximum	Minimum	Stack Spac
▽ LApplication::ObeyCommand(long,void*)	1	0.003	0.0	6.757	100.0	0.003	0.003	0.003	1674
▽ LApplication::SendAEQuit()	1	0.046	0.7	6.754	100.0	0.046	0.046	0.046	2026
▷ LApplication::DoQuit(long)	1	0.000	0.0	0.178	2.6	0.000	0.000	0.000	2090
UAppleEventsMgr::MakeAppleEvent...	1	1.460	21.6	1.460	21.6	1.460	1.460	1.460	2090
UAppleEventsMgr::SendAppleEvent...	1	5.064	75.0	5.064	75.0	5.064	5.064	5.064	2090
LCommander::IsSyntheticCommand(lo...	1	0.000	0.0	0.000	0.0	0.000	0.000	0.000	2026

Figure 11-12: An example of a Profiler output file, as viewed in MW Profiler.

At first glance, the amount of data in the file may seem overwhelming—but in fact it's well organized and easy to interpret once you know what type of data each of the columns holds. In the following discussions of the file columns, I'll provide specific references to the first row—the row listing information for the **ObeyCommand()** routine—shown in Figure 11-12:

■ **Function Name**. The first column lists each function profiled. When the file is opened, only the first-level routines (the ones invoked directly by the profiled function) appear. Clicking on an arrow icon by a function name reveals the second level of invoked functions. Because **ObeyCommand()** was the profiled routine in the file shown in Figure 11-12, all other profiled functions are subordinate to this routine.

- **Count**. Following the function name is the number of times the function was invoked during the profiling session. **ObeyCommand()** was invoked one time.

- **Only**. This column indicates how much time, in milliseconds, was spent in the function. Here "only" indicates that the value listed is the time spent only in this one function—it doesn't include time spent in *children functions*. A child routine is one invoked by the profiled routine. For **ObeyCommand()**, all other listed routines are children. They are all invoked either directly by **ObeyCommand()** or indirectly by routines **ObeyCommand()** invokes. The time spent in **ObeyCommand()** was only three thousandths of one millisecond, hinting that most of the profiled time was spent in **ObeyCommand()** children routines.

- **%**. This column holds the same information as the Only column, but the data is expressed as a percentage of time spent in this one routine. The 0.003 milliseconds spent running **ObeyCommand()** code represents 0.0 percent of the time spent in that routine. Obviously, *some* time was spent executing the few instructions that make up **ObeyCommand()**. The time was so slight that rounding reduced the indicated time to 0. The fact that this time is listed as 0.0 percent of the routine's execution time implies that almost all the processing time spent executing **ObeyCommand()** is actually devoted to the execution of its children routines.

- **+Children**. This column indicates how much time was spent in both the listed function and all its children. From the point **ObeyCommand()** begin executing to the point the routine terminated took 6.757 milliseconds.

- **%**. Here the +Children value is expressed as a percentage. Because **ObeyCommand()** was the profiled function, 100.0 percent of the profiled time was spent here in **ObeyCommand()** and its children.

- **Average**. This column is useful for gaining information about routines that execute more than once. For routines whose time may vary from execution to execution (perhaps the function is an application-defined routine that opens a picture or manipulates data), the execution time may vary considerably. If a routine executes only a single time, this column and the next two columns (Maximum and Minimum) will all have the same value. **ObeyCommand()** ran only once, so all three columns list their execution time as 0.003 milliseconds.

- **Maximum**. If a routine executes more than once, the maximum execution time may be of value to you.

- ■ **Minimum**. For a routine that executes more than once, the minimum value may be of importance in determining just how fast the routine is capable of executing.

- ■ **Stack Space**. This column lists the largest size the stack grows to during the execution of the profiled function. During the execution of **ObeyCommand()**, the stack reached a maximum size of 1674 bytes.

ZoneRanger

When a program is launched, the operating system reserves a block of memory dedicated to holding that program's code and data. As your program runs, it dynamically creates and deletes objects. These objects, which can be the data representing windows, pictures, sounds, structures that hold strings and numbers, and so forth, are placed in this reserved memory. If your program manages memory properly, then the process of adding and removing objects in memory should go smoothly. If your program *doesn't* adequately manage memory, then the program can behave in unexpected ways—including crashing.

A debugger can help you catch some memory-related problems, but that tool doesn't provide you with the big picture. The Metrowerks ZoneRanger utility does.

Working With ZoneRanger

ZoneRanger is an application, so to make use of it, you launch it like any other program. ZoneRanger watches all running programs and provides you with feedback on any or all of them. This feedback takes on several forms, including a graphical representation of the contents of the block of memory in which your application is running. ZoneRanger helps you understand how Macintosh memory is organized, and how efficiently it's being used by your application.

Launching ZoneRanger results in the display of the Heap Zones window shown in Figure 11-13. If you have any applications running when you start up ZoneRanger, you'll notice that their names appear in the list in the Heap Zones window. Also named in this list are ZoneRanger, System, Process Manager, and Finder. ZoneRanger is of course running, so it's listed here. The other three names are system-related programs always running on a Macintosh.

Figure 11-13: The Heap Zones window displays the names of all running applications.

To the operating system, each executing application is a *process*. Each process has its own application partition. This partition includes an area referred to as the application *heap*. The heap has a zone header that holds information (such as the number of bytes that make up the heap) needed by the operating system. Marking the end of the heap is a zone trailer. Together the zone header, the heap, and the zone trailer are called the *heap zone*. The name of the window in Figure 11-13 clues you into the fact that ZoneRanger monitors the heap zone of each process.

To use ZoneRanger, simply launch the program whose heap zone you want to monitor. When you run the program, its name appears in the list of processes in the ZoneRanger Heap Zones window. You can view the program's memory in any of the four ways listed at the bottom of the Heap Zones window pictured in Figure 11-13. To select a view option, check its check box in the Heap Zones window. Then double-click on the program's name in the list. When you do that, a window will open for each checked viewing option.

I launched ZoneRanger and then arbitrarily chose Apple's SimpleText text editor as a program to monitor. Each of the four display options is summarized shortly. The figures all are from monitoring SimpleText, but the general concepts of what information is conveyed in each figure applies to any application.

The 1D Graphical Display

To open a 1D Graphical window for a process, check the Open 1D Graphical Display check box in the Heap Zones window and then double-click on the name of the program of interest. A window like the one shown in Figure 11-14 appears.

Figure 11-14: The ZoneRanger 1D Graphical Display window.

The 1D Graphical window displays an application's heap zone in one row. Different types of memory are displayed in different colors. Click on the rightmost of the three small icons present in the lower left of the 1D window to see the colors ZoneRanger assigns to free blocks (unused) or are referenced by a pointer or handle. Figure 11-15 shows this menu, along with the icon used to display the menu.

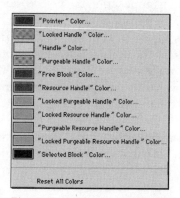

Figure 11-15: The memory block color key pop-up menu.

To view the contents of a block of memory, click on the block. Doing that displays the following information about the block in the bottom of the window: its type (such as pointer), starting address, and size in bytes. To get more information on that same block, press the Option key and click on the middle of the three small icons in the lower left of the window. Figure 11-16 shows the pop-up list that appears.

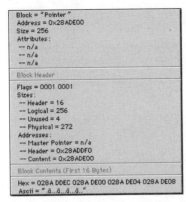

Figure 11-16: Getting information about a particular block of memory.

The 2D Graphical Display

The 2D Graphical Display shows memory in a graphical manner similar to the way the 1D Graphical Display shows it. Here, however, the memory doesn't go straight across a window that scrolls horizontally. Instead, the display wraps around to a new row when it reaches the right edge of the display window. Compare Figure 11-17 with Figure 11-14 to see the difference in the display of memory for the SimpleText process. As with the ID display, you can get more information about a block by option-clicking on the middle of the three icons in lower left part of the window.

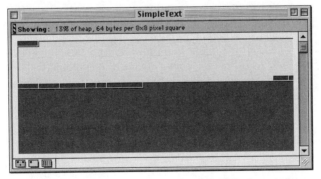

Figure 11-17: The ZoneRanger 2D Graphical Display window.

The Summary Display

The 1D Graphical Display, the 2D Graphical Display, and the yet-to-be-discussed Histogram Display show memory in a graphical format. The Summary Display provides a means of looking at memory numerically. Figure 11-18 shows the Summary Display window for the SimpleText process.

Blocks:	Used	Free	Pointers	Handles...	🔒	🗑	📄
138	121	17	9	112	3	17	28
510816	131792	379024	2048	129744	48928	25616	53712

Figure 11-18: The ZoneRanger Summary Display window.

The top row of the Summary Display window lists the number of blocks of different types. From left to right, these types are total blocks, used blocks, free blocks, pointers, handles, locked, purgeable, and resource data. Each figure in the second row of the window lists the total bytes occupied by the blocks in the columns.

The Histogram Display

The Histogram Display option displays process memory in the form of a histogram. Figure 11-19 shows the histogram for the SimpleText process. The criteria for placing a block in one vertical bar or another is size. Each vertical bar represents a different range of block sizes, with each range increasing from left to right. For instance, the selected bar in Figure 11-19 (the solid dark bar that has its outline extended to the top of the window) represents blocks that are at least 8 bytes but less than 16 bytes in size. Along the bottom of the window, you see that for the SimpleText process 16 blocks fall into this size range.

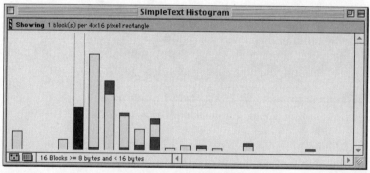

Figure 11-19: The ZoneRanger Histogram Display window.

ZoneRanger Example Project

The *ZoneRangerExample.μ* project (located in the P02 ZoneRangerExample folder in the Chapter 11 folder on this book's Companion CD-ROM) demonstrates how ZoneRanger can be used to gain insight into a program's use of memory. This project is based on the Basic PowerPlant FAT project stationery, so both 68K and PowerPC versions of the application can be built. In either case, when you run the program, a window displaying a picture appears. In Figure 11-20 you see that I launched ZoneRanger and then launched the 68K version of the ZoneRangerExample program.

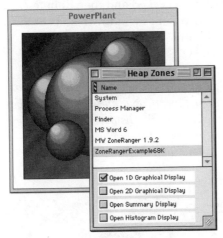

Figure 11-20: The example application window and the ZoneRanger Heap Zones window.

To examine how this program uses memory, I'll open the 1D Graphical Display and monitor any changes in this window as the program runs.

Project Resources

The *ZoneRangerExample.μ* project uses the default source code CodeWarrior adds to a project based on Basic PowerPlant FAT stationery. The only changes I've made to the project involve resources.

Instead of the program's window including a "PowerPlant says: hello world" string, the ZoneRangerExample program's window includes a picture. To replace the text with a picture, I deleted the LCaption item in the *PP Basic Resource.ppob* file's only 'PPob' resource and added an LPicture item. I used the LPicture property inspector to set the item's size and 'PICT' resource ID to match those of a picture I drew. I then opened the *PP Basic Resource.rsrc* file and pasted the picture into that file.

Following the application-naming technique described in this chapter's "CodeWarrior Projects and Targets" section, I then built two versions of the program—ZoneRangerExample68K and ZoneRangerExamplePPC. Building two versions allows me to check both to see if their memory requirements vary. In this discussion, I'll only be looking at the 68K version.

Monitoring the Example Program

Launching ZoneRanger and then the 68K version of the example program results in the display of the ZoneRanger Heap Zones window and then the example program's window—as shown back in Figure 11-20. Leaving only the Open 1D Graphical Display checkbox checked and then double-clicking on the example program's name in the Heap Zones window results in the opening of a 1D window like that shown in Figure 11-21.

TIP *By using a combination of the Increase Resolution, Decrease Resolution, Zoom In, and Zoom Out items in the Configure menu, you can vary the displayed size of the blocks of memory in the 1D window. While the displayed size of the blocks will change—allowing you to see more or less of the total memory picture—the displayed sizes remain proportional to one another.*

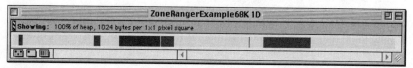

Figure 11-21: Using the 1D Graphical Display window to monitor the ZoneRangerExample68K program.

You can explore what's in the ZoneRangerExample68K program's memory partition by clicking on blocks of memory in the 1D Graphical Display window. When you click on a block, the block's type, starting address, and size are displayed along the bottom of the 1D Graphical Display window.

Looking for Particular Data in Memory

To make use of graphics stored in a 'PICT' resource, a program makes a copy of the picture data in the resource and loads that data into memory. A 'PICT' resource can be small or quite large—depending on the complexity of the picture. Here I'll see if ZoneRanger allows me to find the picture data for the one picture present in the example program's window.

For the test project, I intentionally made the resulting program small and the size of the picture displayed in the program's window large—it's about 113K in size. That makes the picture easy to find in memory. If the picture were small, you could still find it—it would just take a little more investigating.

Since a resource is referenced by a handle, I will search for the picture data that way. Clicking on the rightmost of the three icons in the lower left of the 1D Graphical Display window brings up the ZoneRanger color key which reveals that a block of memory referenced by a handle appears as a yellow block. I then click on yellow blocks to find one with a size close to that of the 'PICT' resource—113K. In Figure 11-22 I've found that block. Clicking on the first large block in memory (it's the darkest block in Figure 11-22) reveals that it's 113,276 bytes in size. That makes it a pretty safe guess that this block represents the picture data for the picture displayed in the example program's one window. Double-clicking on the block opens a window that displays the contents of the block. Figure 11-24 shows that the block contents include the word "PICT."

TIP   *You can verify the 'PICT' resource's size by opening the* PP Basic Resource.rsrc *file in ResEdit, displaying the 'PICT' resource, and typing Command+I. That provides you with information about the 'PICT' resource—including its size in bytes.*

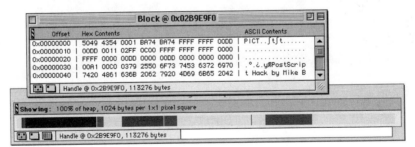

Figure 11-22: Viewing block information in the 1D Graphical Display window.

TIP *Depending how much you already know about Macintosh memory, ZoneRanger can narrow your search for a particular block of memory. The ZoneRanger Configure menu holds a few menu items that change block colors to highlight some specific types of blocks. For instance, handle blocks are normally all shown in yellow. Checking the Show Resource Handles item in the Configure menu leaves handle blocks yellow—except for the ones that hold resource data. These blocks turn pink. That makes looking for resource-related blocks of memory much easier.*

The hexadecimal representation of 'PICT' data may not be of much use to you, so ZoneRanger provides another way to get information about this block of memory. After clicking on the block, Option-click on the middle of the three small icons in the lower left of the 1D Graphical Display window to reveal a list of block information. In Figure 11-23 you see that this list reveals not only that the block holds 'PICT' data, but that it also holds data from a 'PICT' resource with an ID of 128.

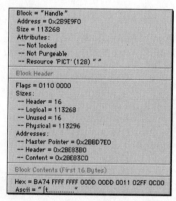

Figure 11-23: Getting information about the block that holds the 'PICT' data.

Observing a Block in Memory as a Program Executes

In a well-behaved application, closing a window that displays a picture should result in the program releasing the picture data when the operating system performs its periodic cleanup. As a program executes, the Memory Manager frees up unused blocks so the manager can reuse that memory to hold other data. Because pictures can occupy a significant amount of memory, I want to ensure that my example program is properly releasing picture data.

To perform the test, I simply close the program's one open window. With no windows open, there's no picture to display, and the system should consider the picture data block releasable. Looking at the 1D Graphical Display window, however, I notice that the block is still yellow (representing a handle block) rather than green (representing a free block). The operating system doesn't always *purge* memory—release now-unused blocks—at predictable times, so perhaps the purging just hasn't taken place yet. ZoneRanger provides a Purge item in the Special menu that forces a purge. Choosing that item should do the trick—but it doesn't! To my chagrin, the picture data block remains in memory as a handle. Let's see why.

Solving the Unreleased Block Dilemma

PowerPlant code takes care of many of the cleanup tasks in a program. Because a picture is added to a window by placing an LPicture item in a 'PPob' and then forgetting about it (you don't write any application-defined supporting code), I'm making the assumption that PowerPlant includes the code that releases the 'PICT' when a window is finished with it. Taking another look at the picture data block's information in ZoneRanger reveals that one of the block's attributes is *Not Purgeable* (see Figure 11-23). That sounds like a situation that would prevent PowerPlant from doing its job. Neither PowerPlant nor Constructor created the 'PICT' resource—I did. So perhaps in some way *I* was responsible for making sure the 'PICT' was marked as a purgeable resource when I added it to the project's *PP Basic Resource.rsrc* file. I can take a look at the original resource by using ResEdit to open the *PP Basic Resource.rsrc* file. Double-clicking on the 'PICT' icon and then typing Command+I brings up the Info window for the 'PICT.' This window lists the resource's attributes. Sure enough, the Purgeable attribute isn't checked. In Figure 11-24 I've checked this attribute.

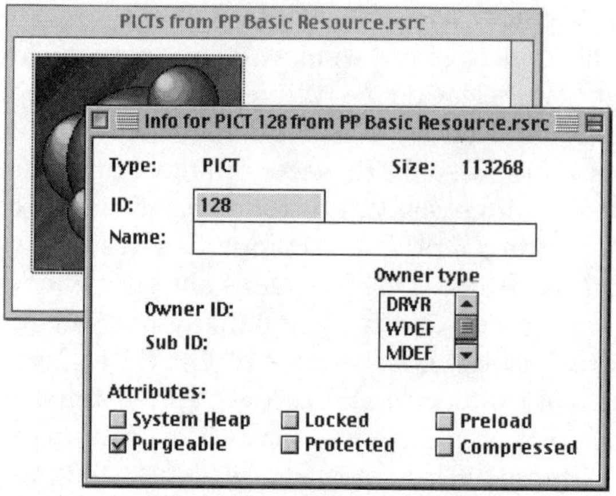

PICTs from PP Basic Resource.rsrc

Info for PICT 128 from PP Basic Resource.rsrc

Type: PICT   Size: 113268

ID: 128

Name:

Owner type

Owner ID: DRVR
              WDEF
Sub ID: MDEF

Attributes:
☐ System Heap   ☐ Locked   ☐ Preload
☑ Purgeable   ☐ Protected   ☐ Compressed

Figure 11-24: Using ResEdit to get 'PICT' information.

To get the example program to use the altered resource, I need to open the *ZoneRangerExample.μ* project and rebuild the ZoneRangerExample68K program. Choosing Make from the Project menu will do that by simply linking the touched resource file to the project's existing object code. Running ZoneRanger and the new version of the program will demonstrate that the picture data block now gets released when the program's window is closed and Purge is selected from ZoneRanger's Special menu.

Debugging & Testing the Example Project

This chapter's version of the *MediaCenter.μ* project (found in the P03 MediaCenter folder in the Chapter 11 folder on this book's Companion CD-ROM) adds support for the Play Movie menu item in the Movie menu. While the user will most likely choose to play an open movie by clicking on the Play button in the movie's controller, I've opted to add a menu item to give the user a second means of performing this act. More importantly, I've also added this menu item for the purpose of demonstrating a few programming techniques. By adding support for the Play Movie menu item, you'll learn how to:

- Attach information of your choosing to a particular window.

- Retrieve attached window information at any point in your program.

- Enable and disable a menu item depending on whether a particular type of window is open.

- Play a QuickTime movie without the need for a movie controller.

While you could perform all of these operations without the use of the debugger, I'll make use of it to demonstrate that the debugger is more than just a tool for finding bugs—it's also useful for gaining insight into your program's memory use and testing programming techniques you devise.

Playing a QuickTime Movie

For playing a movie, PowerPlant relies on the **LMovieController** class. If you want your program to be able to play a movie without the aid of a controller, you'll use Macintosh Movie Toolbox calls rather than PowerPlant code. First, make sure the movie is set to its start by calling **GoToBeginningOfMovie()**:

```
Movie  theMovie;

GoToBeginningOfMovie(theMovie);
```

Now ready the movie for playing by calling **StartMovie()** to ensure that the movie is active and set to its proper playback rate. While the **StartMovie()** function's name implies the movie will now be playing, it isn't—**StartMovie()** only prepares for the start of playing:

```
StartMovie(theMovie);
```

To carry out playing of the entire movie, call **MoviesTask()**. This function handles loading movie data from the movie file, displaying the movie frames, and playing the movie's soundtrack (if present). The first parameter to **MoviesTask()** is the movie to work with. A second parameter value of 0 tells the Movie Toolbox to allocate whatever time is necessary to perform these tasks. If more than one movie is open, a call to **MoviesTask()** will play only a part of one movie and then jump to the other movie to service it. Thus **MoviesTask()** needs to be called within a loop in order to play an entire movie. To determine when to stop calling **MoviesTask()**, use **IsMovieDone()** as the loop termination test. Recall that while not required, it's good practice to preface Toolbox calls with the :: operator to make it clear that the function calls are Toolbox calls rather than calls to PowerPlant class member functions. Here's the complete movie-playing snippet:

```
Movie  theMovie;

::GoToBeginningOfMovie(theMovie);
::StartMovie(theMovie);
do {
    ::MoviesTask(theMovie, 0);
} while (::IsMovieDone(theMovie) == false);
```

The preceding snippet will be placed under the **cmd_PlayMovie** command in the **ObeyCommand()** routine:

```
case cmd_PlayMovie:
   Movie    theMovie;

   // Need to get the movie to play here

   ::GoToBeginningOfMovie(theMovie);
   ::StartMovie(theMovie);
   do {
      ::MoviesTask(theMovie, 0);
   } while (::IsMovieDone(theMovie) == false);
   break;
```

As you can see in the preceding snippet, I've omitted one critical step—the local Movie variable needs to be assigned a value. When the user chooses Play Movie from the Movie menu, it's assumed a movie has already been opened and is displayed in a window (that task is taken care of by a selection of Open Movie from the Movie menu). Before the **cmd_PlayMovie** code can play a movie, it has to be determined which movie to play. How that problem can be solved is described next.

Attaching Information to a Window

In Chapter 10, "Windows & Dialogs," you saw how to add a movie controller to a window holding a QuickTime movie. After opening a movie, opening a new window, and creating a pane to hold the movie, a new **LMovieController** object is created and associated with the pane and the movie:

```
LMovieController  *theController;
theController = new LMovieController(thePaneInfo, theMovie);
```

Recall that in creating the pane, the pane was associated with the window to hold the movie (the pane's superView field was set to the **LWindow** object). That's why the **LMovieController** constructor doesn't need the **LWindow** object as a parameter—the **LPane** parameter lets the **LMovieController** object indirectly know with which window it is to be associated.

When a QuickTime movie window is clicked on and made active, the window's controller is also made active. And a click on the controller's Play button plays the correct movie in the window. Obviously, PowerPlant knows how to keep track of a window that holds a movie and a controller. But how does your application bundle this information together so it can relate a controller and a movie to a window? In the previous section, you saw that if the program needs to do something with a QuickTime movie window, such as play the window's movie, the program needs a Movie variable as a parameter to the various Toolbox calls that will be made. In MediaCenter, the opening of a movie window occurs in the **ShowMovieWindow()** routine. The window, movie controller, and movie are all kept track of as **LWindow**, **LMovieController**, and Movie variables local to **ShowMovieWindow()**. The code that implements the playing of a movie in response to a Play Movie menu item selection, however, isn't in **ShowMovieWindow()**. Obviously some technique is needed to obtain the front window and determine what movie is associated with that window.

The LWindow mUserCon Field

An **LWindow** object gets its attribute information from the LWindow item in the 'PPob' resource from which the object is based. As shown in Figure 11-25, one of the fields of the **LWindow** is User Constant. An **LWindow** object has an **mUserCon** field that gets assigned whatever value is in the Constructor-defined User Constant field at the time the window object is built. While other **LWindow** data members are used to store window attribute information, the **mUserCon** member is available for whatever use you want. That is, it's four bytes of memory you can use to associate any data you want with any window you want.

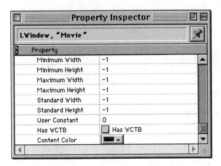

Figure 11-25: The User Constant field allows you to set a window's mUserCon data member.

As shown in Figure 11-25, the User Constant field in Constructor is initially set to 0. If your program will make use of this field, it's up to your application-defined code to set it to some other value. The **LWindow** class conveniently includes a member function named **SetUserCon()** (which it inherits from the **LPane** class) that does just that. The **mUserCon** data member is four bytes in size, so **SetUserCon()** has a single parameter of type **Int32** (the PowerPlant-defined data type equivalent to the C/C++ **long** data type). This next snippet creates a window object and then assigns the object's **mUserCon** data member to a value of 99:

```
LWindow  *theWindow;
Int32     theUserCon = 99;

theWindow = LWindow::CreateWindow(PPob_MyWindow, this);

theWindow->SetUserCon(theUserCon);
```

At any time, your program can get the current value of a window's **mUserCon** data member by calling another **LWindow** member function—**GetUserCon()**:

```
Int32    theUserCon;
theUserCon = theWindow->GetUserCon();
```

Uses for the **mUserCon** data member may not be immediately be apparent—but they soon will be.

Attaching a Movie to a Window

Now that we have a general technique for storing information in an **LWindow** object, it's time to use the scheme for our particular needs—storing a movie with a window.

Associating a Movie With a Window

When a movie is opened in MediaCenter, it would be beneficial to establish a long-term association between the movie and the window in which it appears. Then, after **ShowMovieWindow()** terminates, the program could still easily access the movie. If the window the movie was affiliated with was the front window, a call to the **UDesktop** utility routine **FetchTopRegular()** would return the **LWindow** object. Once the program had an **LWindow** object, it could access the window's movie.

A **Movie** variable is a pointer to a movie. On a Macintosh, a pointer is always four bytes in size, which just happens to be the size of an **LWindow** object's **mUserCon** data member. In theory, then, a **Movie** variable could be used as a parameter to **SetUserCon()** to set an **LWindow** object's **mUserCon** data member to the value of the **Movie** variable. That's what's being done in this snippet, where a **Movie** variable named **theMovie** is being typecast to the match the **SetUserCon()** parameter type of **Int32**:

```
theWindow->SetUserCon((Int32)theMovie);
```

Using this scheme, the **LWindow** object's **mUserCon** data member holds a pointer to the movie data in memory. Any time the program needs to access the window's movie, the program should call **FetchTopRegular()** to get the **LWindow** object and then call **GetUserCon()** to retrieve the movie pointer:

```
LWindow *theWindow;
Movie    theMovie;

theWindow = UDesktop::FetchTopRegular();
theMovie = (Movie)theWindow->GetUserCon();
```

That's the theory, anyway. To see if it holds up, I'll type in the code and then run the debugger. While I should be able to get the code to work without using MWDebug, this concept is new and I'll want to prove to myself that things work for the reasons I *think* they work. A user may end up with five, ten, or more movies open at one time, and I want to make sure things will go smoothly in those cases.

Setting the mUserCon Data Member Value

The **ShowMovieWindow()** routine opens a movie and a window to display that movie. After those two tasks are performed, I can add a call to **SetUserCon()** to store the address of the movie data in the window object's **mUserCon** data member. I've put a comment in place of the somewhat lengthy section of code that ends the **ShowMovieWindow()** routine—refer to Chapter 10, "Windows & Dialogs," if you need a refresher on this function:

```
void
CPPDocApp::ShowMovieWindow()
{
   Movie  theMovie;
   theMovie = UQuickTime::GetMovieFromFile();
   if (theMovie == nil)
      return;

   LWindow  *theWindow;
   theWindow = LWindow::CreateWindow(PPob_MovieWindow, this );

   theWindow->SetUserCon((Int32)theMovie);

   // Finish up: create a pane to hold the movie, create
   // a new movie controller, show the window
}
```

Testing the Setting of mUserCon

I still need to add code to **ObeyCommand()** to implement playing a movie, but until then I can run a quick check to see if my scheme is working. I'll compile the new version of *PP Doc App.cp* and run MediaCenter under control of the debugger. After choosing Enable Debugger and then Debug from the Project menu, the debugger windows appear. **ShowMovieWindow()** is defined in the same file as **main()**, so I can just scroll through the debugger program window's source pane until I reach the **ShowMovieWindow()** code. I'll set a breakpoint at a line following the setting of **mUserCon** to a value of **theMovie**, and then click the Run button in the control window or type Command-R to start the program running. MediaCenter will run as expected.

I need to open a movie to test my new code. I can choose Open Movie from the Movie menu or click on the Open Movie button in the MediaCenter Control window. After choosing a movie file from the standard Open dialog box, execution will reach the breakpoint and the program will pause. Figure 11-26 shows the current statement arrow at the breakpoint.

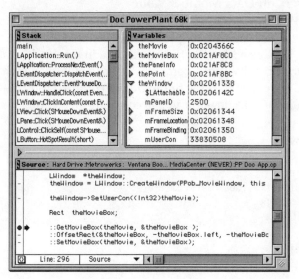

Figure 11-26: Examining the value of mUserCon and theMovie.

The call to **SetUserCon()** has just executed, so the **mUserCon** data member of the window object **theWindow** should have a value that matches the value of **theMovie**. Looking at the variables pane in the debugger program window in Figure 11-26 doesn't readily provide this information. That's because the value just assigned to **mUserCon** (33830508) is listed in decimal format, while the value of the pointer variable **theMovie** (0x0204366C) is shown in hexadecimal. Metrowerks debugger is a powerful tool, so you can imagine there is a simple solution to this—and there is. You can change the format of any variable value by clicking on the variable name in the variables pane and then choosing a different format from the Data menu shown in Figure 11-27.

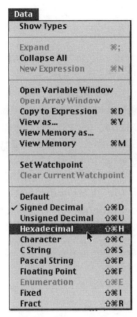

Figure 11-27: The debugger Data menu lets you set the format in which a value is displayed.

You see that you have a multitude of formats from which to choose. I click on **mUserCon** in the variables pane and choose the Hexadecimal item. After doing that, the variables pane reveals that the value of **mUserCon** matches the value of **theMovie**. So far, my plan is working—this one **LWindow** object now has an **mUserCon** value that points to the data of the movie to be associated with the **LWindow** object. After **ShowMovieWindow()** executes, the object will retain this reference to the movie.

Getting the mUserCon Data Member

When the user chooses Play Movie from the Movie menu, PowerPlant issues a **cmd_PlayMovie** command and passes it to **ObeyCommand()**. To date, the implementation of this command has consisted of nothing more than a call to **SysBeep()**. I'll initiate the changes to the handling of this command by replacing the call to **SysBeep()** with the following code:

```
case cmd_PlayMovie:
   LWindow  *theWindow;
   Movie     theMovie;

   theWindow = UDesktop::FetchTopRegular();
   theMovie = (Movie)theWindow->GetUserCon();
```

The preceding snippet calls the **UDesktop** utility routine **FetchTopRegular()** to obtain the front window object. Then this **LWindow** object invokes its **GetUserCon()** member function to return the object's **mUserCon** value to the program. This value is returned as an **Int32** type, so it needs to be typecast to the **Movie** type before assigning it to the variable **theMovie**.

At this point, **ObeyCommand()** can play the QuickTime movie by using the **Movie** variable. Or can it? To make sure this local **theMovie** variable has the value the original **ShowMovieWindow() theMovie** variable had, I'll again make use of the debugger.

Testing the Getting of mUserCon

Test the newly added code by performing the following steps:

1. Run the *MediaCenter.µ* project with debugging enabled.

2. Scroll through the debugger's program window source pane to **ObeyCommand()**.

3. Set a breakpoint at a line following the call to **GetUserCon()**—as shown in Figure 11-28.

Figure 11-28: Checking the value of a window object's mUserCon data member.

4. Run the program and again open a movie file. If you've left the original **ShowMovieWindow()** breakpoint in place, execution will pause in that routine. Make note of the value of **theMovie**. In a moment, you'll be comparing this value of **theMovie** to the value of **mUserCon** returned to the program in the **ObeyCommand()** function.

5. Continue program execution by clicking the control window Run button or by typing Command+R. **ShowMovieWindow()** will continue executing, and the movie will appear in a window.

6. Choose Play Movie from the Movie menu. The **ObeyCommand()** breakpoint will be reached, and again the program will pause.

7. Compare the value of **theMovie** to the value recorded from the **ShowMovieWindow()** function—they should match.

TIP *Write down the value of **theMovie** on a scrap of paper. Yes, programmers do still occasionally have to make use of that old-fashioned medium! Also note that when you run MediaCenter, the value of **theMovie** won't match mine. The value is a memory address, and **theMovie** will end up in a different area of memory when you run the program.*

You now know the movie-playing plan is on track—MediaCenter can have any number of windows open, including any number of movie windows—and the program will be able to pair the proper movie with the proper window at any time. To make full use of this new technique, though, the code for playing a movie needs to be added to the **cmd_PlayMovie** section in **ObeyCommand()**.

Playing the Movie

In this chapter's "Playing a QuickTime Movie" section, you saw the complete code for playing a movie. All you need to do now is add that code in the appropriate place. A menu choice of Play Movie initiates a **cmd_PlayMovie** command sent to **ObeyCommand()**, so that's where the code fits. Here's how the **cmd_PlayMovie** case section now looks:

```
case cmd_PlayMovie:
   LWindow *theWindow;
   Movie    theMovie;

   theWindow = UDesktop::FetchTopRegular();
   theMovie = (Movie)theWindow->GetUserCon();

   GoToBeginningOfMovie(theMovie);
   StartMovie(theMovie);
   do {
      MoviesTask(theMovie, 0);
   } while (IsMovieDone(theMovie) == false);
   break;
```

Adjusting a Menu Item

At this point, the Play Movie menu item works as expected—when a movie is open. If Play Movie is selected when a movie hasn't yet been opened, however, the situation won't be quite so satisfactory. A **cmd_PlayMovie** command will still be issued, and **ObeyCommand()** will still execute the code under the **cmd_PlayMovie** case label. When that happens, **theMovie** will end up with a value of **nil**. That's because the call to **FetchTopRegular()** won't return a valid pointer to a movie. Instead it will return a value of **nil** if no windows are open, or a value of 0 if the front-most window isn't a movie window (the window object's **mUserCon** data member will be 0—as set in Constructor). The movie-playing code will still attempt to execute, but **theMovie** variable used as a parameter to the Toolbox calls won't yield pleasing results. Most likely the program will get caught in an infinite loop as the **do-while** loop attempts to play a nonexistent movie to completion.

TIP   *As MediaCenter is now written, at least one window will always be open. The Control window doesn't have a close box, so it is always present. I don't want to rely on this always being the case, however. In a subsequent version of MediaCenter, I could use Constructor to supply the Control window with a close box, or I could add a menu item that allows the user to close and reopen this window. If I write my menu-adjusting code making the assumption that there will always be a window open, my code will work—now. But it could break in the future if I make one of the above Control window changes.*

To avoid the preceding pitfall, the Play Movie menu item should be enabled only when appropriate—only when the front-most window is a movie window. In Chapter 7, "Menus," you saw that the **FindCommandStatus()** routine sets **outEnabled** to **true** to enable a menu item and **false** to disable that item. To this point, MediaCenter has set **outEnabled** to **true** for each application-defined menu item. Here we have an exception to this "always enabled" code.

There are two situations when Play Movie should be disabled: when no windows are open, and when windows are open but the active window isn't a movie window. We'll check for these situations. If either is the case, we'll disable Play Movie. Otherwise we can enable the menu item to let the user play the movie in the active window.

Begin by assuming the worst, and set **outEnabled** to **false**. We'll only toggle **outEnabled** to **true** if it turns out a movie window is indeed open and active:

```
outEnabled = false;
```

Now obtain the front window object. A call to **FetchTopRegular()** takes care of that task:

```
theWindow = UDesktop::FetchTopRegular();
```

If no windows are open, **FetchTopRegular()** returns **nil**. In that case, we can stop any further investigation and leave **outEnabled false**. If a window is open, **theWindow** will have a non-**nil** value, and we'll proceed by getting the window object's **mUserCon** value:

```
if (theWindow != nil) {
   theUserCon = theWindow->GetUserCon();
```

A window without a movie has an **mUserCon** value of 0, as assigned by default in Constructor. A window with a movie has an **mUserCon** value that represents a valid address, which is always nonzero. So a comparison of this user constant to the value 0 reveals if the window holds a movie. If it's non-zero, toggle **outEnabled** to **true**. Otherwise, leave **outEnabled** at its initialized value of **false**:

```
if (theUserCon != 0)
   outEnabled = true;
```

Here's how the completed code looks when placed under the **cmd_PlayMovie** case section in **FindCommandStatus()**:

```
case cmd_PlayMovie:
   Int32   theUserCon;
   LWindow *theWindow;

   outEnabled = false;

   theWindow = UDesktop::FetchTopRegular();

   if (theWindow != nil) {
      theUserCon = theWindow->GetUserCon();
      if (theUserCon != 0)
         outEnabled = true;
   }
   break;
```

Running the Program

After making all the described changes, build a new version of MediaCenter. Run the program and put it through its paces. As you open and close windows, check the Movie menu. MediaCenter now can display four different types of windows at the same time: text, picture, movie, and control. Regardless of what combination of these windows is open, the Play Movie menu item should only be enabled when a movie window is open *and* active. When that's the case, choosing Play Movie should play the movie in the active window from start to finish.

Moving On

Metrowerks supplies you with an arsenal of powerful tools for ensuring your program is in full working order.

■ MWDebug is a source-level debugger that can be turned on from the CodeWarrior IDE, and then used to track down bugs or investigate and test programming techniques you may want to implement.

■ MW Profiler consists of a code library you add to a project and a to viewer application. You profile your code to determine which routines are demanding too much processor time.

■ ZoneRanger is an application used to monitor a program's use of memory. After building a version of your program, run ZoneRanger and your application to verify that your program releases memory at appropriate times.

With the inclusion of fully-functional menus, controls, windows, and dialog boxes in your application, the bulk of your programming chores are complete. That's why I brought up application testing now, instead of at the very end of the book. Software product development is an ongoing affair, though, so we should press on and investigate a couple of final touches that can be added to any program: file input and output, and printing. Programmers often get tripped up by these behind-the-scenes features, so you'll be pleased to find out PowerPlant handles most of the work in implementing both. Proof of this is in the short length of the last two chapters!

Enhancing the Application

Files & Input/Output

Opening a file, displaying its contents in a window, and then doing a variety of tasks with the displayed data—including saving it and printing it—involves quite a bit of code that a programmer typically finds cumbersome to implement. Fortunately, PowerPlant hides much of these low-level programming details from you. In this chapter, you'll see how your project can define its own document class based on some existing PowerPlant classes. This class inherits much of the functionality needed to work with windows that serve as documents.

Document & File Classes

A program user tends to think of a window as a document, while the operating system considers a file on disk a document. In PowerPlant, a document falls between these two definitions—a document object serves to relate a window with a file.

In creating documents you'll rely on four PowerPlant classes—one of which you're already familiar with:

- **LDocApplication** is the class your project's application class will be derived from. **LDocApplication** is derived from **LApplication**. This class is responsible for creating and opening documents. All versions of the *MediaCenter.µ* project have been based on the **LDocApplication** class.

- **LDocument** is the class that defines the routines for working with a document once it is opened. The closing, saving, and printing of a document are all handled via **LDocument** member functions.

- **LSingleDoc** is derived from **LDocument**. **LDocument** is an abstract class, so your own document class will be derived from **LSingleDoc**. This class serves to bind one window with one file on disk.

- **LFile** serves as a reference to a file on disk. A document (an object of a class derived from **LSingleDoc**) exists in memory, not on disk. A single document object is connected to a single **LFile** object to allow access (reading and writing) to a file.

Documents & the Doc PowerPlant-Based Project

Throughout this book, we've based projects on Doc PowerPlant project stationery. Doing so created a project that included a few files support a document-centric application. Because the classes and routines in these files implement standard document actions for a text file (such as opening, creating, saving, and printing), throughout the following discussions I'll be interjecting comments regarding this type of project. That allows you to see a specific example of each topic as it's covered. The following classes are defined in files that are a part of any Doc PowerPlant project stationery–based project and will be mentioned in the next sections.

CPPDocApp. This class is derived from **LDocApplication**, which itself is derived from **LApplication**. Because this class appears in projects based on a Doc PowerPlant project stationery, it includes member functions that support working with documents. Examples of such member functions include **OpenDocument()** and **PrintDocument()**.

TIP | *CPPDocApp is a Metrowerks-supplied class, but it isn't a PowerPlant-defined class. Every PowerPlant-based project must define one **LApplication**- or **LDocApplication**-derived class. Metrowerks provides **CPPDocApp** to give you a starting point from which you can build. You could just as easily remove the CPPDocApp.cp file from a project and add a new file that defines a completely different application-derived class.*

CTextDocument. This class is derived from **LSingleDoc**, which is derived from **LDocument**. **CTextDocument** defines the actions associated with a document that supports text editing. Examples of its member functions include **IsModified()** and **DoRevert()**.

TIP *CTextDocument is another Metrowerks-supplied class that isn't a part of the PowerPlant framework. Document-centric projects make use of the CTextDocument class, but not all PowerPlant-based projects do. A PowerPlant-based project that originates from different project stationery (such as the Basic PowerPlant stationery) doesn't include the CTextDocument.cp file.*

LDocApplication

The basic tasks of creating a new document and opening an existing one are typically initiated by the user from the application's File menu. So it is the application's responsibility, rather than a document's, to handle these tasks. The application takes care of these chores from it's application class—the class derived from **LDocApplication**.

LDocApplication is derived from **LApplication**. The additional features that **LDocApplication** adds to those provided by its base class are, unsurprisingly, document-related. **LDocApplication** is a commander—you know that because it includes **ObeyCommand()** and **FindCommandStatus()** member functions. Using PowerPlant-defined command constants for standard File menu items such as New and Open means that PowerPlant automatically responds when a user selects one of these items. Your application will thus be notified of such an event and will be able to react accordingly.

TIP *Recall from Chapter 7, "Menus," that the Doc PowerPlant.ppob file CodeWarrior includes in a document-centric project has a File menu resource that defines all the standard File menu items such as New, Open, and so forth. By default these items have the command number values that PowerPlant recognizes. Use the Command Number pop-up menu in a menu item's property inspector to see a list of command number constants.*

The CPPDocApp Application Class

CodeWarrior supplies a new project based on Doc PowerPlant stationery with an application class named **CPPDocApp**. You're familiar with the **CPPDocApp** class because it is the heart of all of the versions of the *MediaCenter.μ* project. During the course of the book, we've added a number of member functions to this application class, though, so you may not recall how the original, Metrowerks-supplied version of this class looks:

```
class CPPDocApp : public LDocApplication {
public:
                        CPPDocApp();
    virtual             ~CPPDocApp();

protected:
    virtual void        StartUp();
    virtual void        OpenDocument( FSSpec *inMacFSSpec);
    virtual LModelObject * MakeNewDocument();
    virtual void        ChooseDocument();
    virtual void        PrintDocument( FSSpec *inMacFSSpec);
};
```

Most of the functions defined in **CPPDocApp** are inherited from **LDocApplication** and overridden. You'll read about these routines later in this chapter.

Responding to LDocApplication Menu Item Selections

Choosing New or Open from the File menu typically tells PowerPlant to issue a **cmd_New** or **cmd_Open** command and direct that command to a target object. The commands work up the command chain to the application object, at which point they are handled.

Because the **CPPDocApp** class derived from the **LDocApplication** class doesn't override this inherited routine, the **LDocApplication** version of **ObeyCommand()** gets invoked by PowerPlant in response to a menu selection. Here you see that among the commands that the **LDocApplication** version of **ObeyCommand()** handles are **cmd_New** and **cmd_Open**:

```
Boolean
LDocApplication::ObeyCommand(
    CommandT   inCommand,
    void       *ioParam)
{
    Boolean  cmdHandled = true;

    switch (inCommand) {
```

```
      case cmd_New:
         SendAECreateDocument();
         break;

      case cmd_Open:
         ChooseDocument();
         break;

      case cmd_PageSetup:
         SetupPage();
         break;

      default:
         cmdHandled = LApplication::ObeyCommand(inCommand, ioParam);
         break;
   }
   return cmdHandled;
}
```

Creating a New Document

In response to a New menu selection, PowerPlant issues a **cmd_New** command that is received by the **LDocApplication** version of **ObeyCommand()**. This routine calls the **LDocApplication** member function **SendAECreateDocument()** to issue an Apple Event so AppleScript can record the act of creating a new document. **SendAECreateDocument()** then calls another **LDocApplication** member function—**MakeNewDocument()**. The **LDocApplication** function **MakeNewDocument()** does nothing more than return a **nil** pointer:

```
LModelObject*
LDocApplication::MakeNewDocument()
{
   return nil;
}
```

Your project's **LDocApplication**-derived class should override **MakeNewDocument()** in order to create a new document of the document class type your project defines. Here's how the **CPPDocApp** version of **MakeNewDocument()** creates a new, empty **CTextDocument** object:

```
LModelObject *
CPPDocApp::MakeNewDocument()
{
   return new CTextDocument( this, nil );
}
```

To create a new document of a type your program supports, your project's application class need only override **MakeNewDocument()**—as done previously.

Opening a Document

The **LDocApplication** version of **ObeyCommand()** invokes its **ChooseDocument()** member function in response to a **cmd_Open** command. Expecting an application that supports the opening of documents to override this routine, **LDocApplication** defines it to be empty:

```
void
LDocApplication::ChooseDocument( )
{
}
```

The **CPPDocApp** does indeed override the inherited **ChooseDocument()**, as follows:

```
void
CPPDocApp::ChooseDocument( )
{
    // Deactivate the desktop.
    ::UDesktop::Deactivate();

    // Browse for a document.
    SFTypeList   theTypeList = {'TEXT'};
    StandardFileReply    theReply;
    ::StandardGetFile( nil, 1, theTypeList, &theReply );

    // Activate the desktop.
    ::UDesktop::Activate();

    // Send an apple event to open the file.
    if ( theReply.sfGood ) SendAEOpenDoc( theReply.sfFile );
}
```

The **CPPDocApp** version of this routine is typical of how an application implements the choosing of a document: displaying the standard Open file dialog box and then issuing an Apple Event stating that a document has been opened. This last task is handled by the **LDocApplication** member function **SendAEOpenDoc()**. Neither **ChooseDocument()** nor **SendAEOpenDoc()** actually opens the selected file. After issuing the Apple Event, **SendAEOpenDoc()** invokes another **LDocApplication** function to do that—

OpenDocument(). What follows next in the opening of a file is a similar scenario to the creation of a new document—**LDocApplication** defines **OpenDocument()** to be empty, expecting that a program's application class will override the routine to implement the opening of a document as it sees fit:

```
void
LDocApplication::OpenDocument(
    FSSpec* /* inMacFSSpec */)
{
}
```

CPPDocApp does in fact override **OpenDocument()**, and chooses to implement this routine by creating a new object from a class type not yet described—the **CTextDocument** class. The **FSSpec** parameter to **OpenDocument()** represents the path to the file on disk to be associated with the new document. This parameter comes from the just-described **ChooseDocument()** routine. In creating a new document object, the **FSSpec** parameter is assigned to the **mFile** data member in the **CTextDocument** object—thus making a connection between the new document object and a file on disk. **CTextDocument** class and its **mFile** data member are described ahead:

```
void
CPPDocApp::OpenDocument(
    FSSpec    *inMacFSSpec )
{
    // Create a new document using the file spec.
    new CTextDocument( this, inMacFSSpec );
}
```

LDocument & LSingleDoc

Once a document is opened (whether newly created or opened from a file on disk), the document becomes responsible for itself. That is, tasks such as the saving, closing, and printing the document should be handled by the document rather than by the application.

The **LDocument** class is an abstract class that is a type of commander—it can respond to menu commands. Another very important commander with which you've had experience is the **LDocApplication** class. Being a commander means **LDocument** has its own version of **ObeyCommand()**. **LDocument** includes a number of member functions PowerPlant automatically invokes in response to menu item selections. Many of these routines are empty, and serve only to be overridden by a class derived from **LDocument**.

This scheme allows an application-defined class to include member functions that are automatically called at the appropriate times by PowerPlant, and redefine these member functions such that they serve the possibly unique needs of the derived class objects.

When a user refers to a document, he or she is most likely referring to the window displaying the contents of a file on disk. Between the window that serves as a user interface and the data stored in the file is a document object that references the file data that gets loaded into memory. The **LSingleDoc** class bonds a window to a document object, as well as to a file on disk. **LSingleDoc** is derived from **LDocument** and is the base class from which you will derive your own document class.

The CTextDocument Document Class

The **CTextDocument** class provides a good example of how a project should set up an application-defined document class. Being derived from **LSingleDoc** (and thus **LDocument**) means that a **CTextDocument** object (which we think of as a document) inherits the ability to automatically respond to menu items the document is to handle directly (such as Close and Save).

```
class CTextDocument : public LSingleDoc {
public:
                 CTextDocument(LCommander *inSuper,
                               FSSpec     *inFileSpec);

    virtual Boolean  IsModified();

    virtual void     DoAESave(FSSpec &inFileSpec,
                             OSType inFileType);
    virtual void     DoSave();
    virtual void     DoRevert();
    virtual void     DoPrint();

protected:
    CTextView *      mTextView;

    void             NameNewDoc();
    void             OpenFile(FSSpec &inFileSpec);
    void             SetPrintFrameSize(void);
};
```

The **LSingleDoc** class from which **CTextDocument** is derived defines two data members: **mFile** and **mWindow**. These members supply the link between the **CTextDocument** object and a window and a file.

Because this Metrowerks-supplied class does exactly what I want—creates and handles text files—it has remained untouched in all of this book's examples.

Responding to LDocument Menu Item Selections

Choosing Close, Save, Save As, Revert, Print, or Print One from the File menu causes PowerPlant to issue a PowerPlant-defined command constant and direct that command to a target object. This target will be the active document, which is responsible for handling the command.

The **CTextDocument** class that is derived from the **LDocument** class doesn't override this inherited routine, so it is the **LDocument** version of **ObeyCommand()** called by PowerPlant in response to one of the just-mentioned menu selections:

```
Boolean
LDocument::ObeyCommand(
   CommandT  inCommand,
   void      *ioParam)
{
   Boolean  cmdHandled = true;

   switch (inCommand) {

      case cmd_Close:
         AttemptClose(true);
         break;

      case cmd_Save:
         if (mIsSpecified) {
            SendSelfAE(kAECoreSuite, kAESave, false);
            DoSave();
            break;
         }

      case cmd_SaveAs:
         FSSpec  fileSpec;
         AskSaveAs(fileSpec, true);
         break;

      case cmd_Revert:
         // Invoke DoRevert() here
         break;
```

```
    case cmd_Print:
        // Invoke DoPrint() here
        break;

    case cmd_PrintOne:
        // Set up to print one copy of the active document
        // Invoke DoPrint() here
        break;

    default:
        cmdHandled = LCommander::ObeyCommand(inCommand, ioParam);
        break;
    }
    return cmdHandled;
}
```

Closing a Document

In response to a selection of Close from the File menu, PowerPlant issues a **cmd_Close** command. The **LDocument** member function **AttemptClose()** and the **LDocument** member function it invokes—**DoAEClose()**—take care of the work of closing an open document window. Your own **LDocument**-derived class won't need to override either of these routines.

Saving a Document

A choice of Save from the File menu results in the **LDocument** member function **DoSave()** being called. **DoSave()** is an empty routine that your **LSingleDoc**-derived class will override. The **CTextDocument** class does this as follows:

```
void
CTextDocument::DoSave()
{
    // Open the data fork.
    mFile->OpenDataFork( fsRdWrPerm );

    // Get the text from the text view.
    Handle  theTextH = mTextView->GetTextHandle();

    // Lock the text handle.
    StHandleLocker  theLock(theTextH);

    // Write the text to the file.
    mFile->WriteDataFork(*theTextH, ::GetHandleSize(theTextH));
```

```
// Close the data fork.
mFile->CloseDataFork();

// Saving makes doc un-dirty.
mTextView->SetDirty(false);
}
```

When a file was opened, a reference to the file on disk was placed in the **CTextDocument** data member mFile. Here in **DoSave()**, the data fork of that file is opened so the fork can be written to. The contents of a **CTextDocument** document is text that exists in a single view. The **CTextDocument** saves the document's data by obtaining a handle to this view, locking it (so that the memory the handle references can't get shifted by routine Mac OS memory compaction), and writing the data referenced by the handle to the open data fork. The fork is then closed.

Once the **DoSave()** routine is written, responding to a Save As menu selection is easy. The **LDocument AskSaveAs()** member function is complete—your document class won't need to override it. **AskSaveAs()** displays the standard Save dialog box. To actually save the data to the file, **AskSaveAs()** calls the **DoSave()** routine your document class has just implemented.

Printing a Document

A document is responsible for printing itself, so a selection of Print from the File menu isn't taken care of in either the **CPPDocApp** or **LDocApplication ObeyCommand()** function. Instead, the **cmd_Print** command issued by PowerPlant is handled by the **ObeyCommand()** function in the PowerPlant **LDocument** class. There, the **LDocument** member function **DoPrint()** is invoked. **DoPrint()** is another empty function—it exists to be overridden by your project. The **CTextDocument** class derived from **LDocument** does this. Printing is described in Chapter 13, so refer to that chapter to see how the **CTextDocument** member function **DoPrint()** handles printing.

LFile

A file on disk is represented by an object of the **LFile** class. This class supplies the connection to a document and to the data in a file on disk. When a file is opened, an object of type **LFile** is returned to and stored in the **mFile** data member of the document object. When a document needs to read from or write to a file, the document object accesses its **mFile** data member.

Files & the Example Project

Thanks to Metrowerks' creating and adding the **CTextDocument** class to projects created from Doc PowerPlant stationery, the MediaCenter program has supported file input and output from its first version back in Chapter 6, "Setting up the Project." So instead of focusing on the **CTextDocument** class, which has already been described in this chapter, this chapter's version of the *MediaCenter.μ* project (which can be found on the Companion CD-ROM in the P01 MediaCenter folder in the Chapter 12 folder) will be an exercise in adding a picture button to a window and then supporting that button in application-defined code. There's still a connection to files, though—the new button is responsible for opening an existing text file.

In this section you'll add the last button—the Open Text button shown in Figure 12-1—to the Control window. The addition of a single constant and a few lines of code to the **CPPDocApp** member function **ListenToMessage()** is then enough to support a mouse button click on the new button.

Figure 12-1: The look of the final version of the MediaCenter Control window.

Resources

Adding a new picture button to a window should be second nature to you by now—so this section cruises though the process.

Creating & Adding Button Pictures

A picture button requires that two 'PICT' resources be present in a project resource file. Figure 12-2 shows the two pictures I created in a paint program and then pasted into the *MediaCenter.μ* project's *Doc PowerPlant.rsrc* resource file.

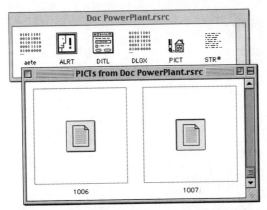

Figure 12-2: The two 'PICT' resources used by the new picture button.

Adding the Button to the New 'PPob'

The Control window 'PPob' requires the addition of one new LButton control. Do that by opening the 'PPob' resource and then copying an existing LButton item so some of the control attributes (such as Height and Width) will be already correctly set. Figure 12-3 shows the 'PPob' with all four LButton items in it.

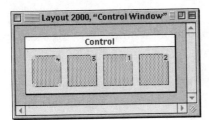

Figure 12-3: The completed 'PPob' used for the Control window.

Double-click on the LButton to display its property inspector. Here you need to set the following fields: Pane ID, Left in SuperView, Top in SuperView, Value Message, Normal Graphic ID, and Pushed Graphic ID. Figure 12-4 shows the values I used.

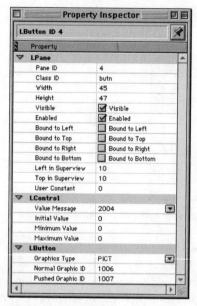

Figure 12-4: The Property Inspector settings for the new LButton control.

Source Code

Adding support for the new button doesn't require the addition of any new member functions. Instead, only the existing **CPPDocApp** function **ListenToMessage()** needs to be updated.

First, define a constant that holds the message value of the new button control. Recall from Figure 12-4 that the new control has a message value of 2004:

```
const MessageT  msg_TextButton   = 2004;
```

Next, incorporate the new constant into the application class **ListenToMessage()** routine by adding a new **case** section. The purpose of the button is to open an existing text file. That's exactly what a choice of Open from the File menu does, so the code under the new **case** label consists of nothing more than a call to the application class version of **ObeyCommand()**, with a parameter of **cmd_Open** being passed:

```
void
CPPDocApp::ListenToMessage(
    MessageT    inMessage,
    void        *ioParam )
{
    #pragma unused( ioParam )
```

```
switch ( inMessage ) {

    case msg_TextButton:
        ObeyCommand( cmd_Open, nil );
        break;
    ...
    ...
    }
}
```

Moving On

If your application will open windows that represent documents, consider defining a class derived from the **LSingleDoc** class. In doing so, an object of your application-defined class inherits the power of both the **LSingleDoc** class and its **LDocument** base class. If you leave the command numbers of the standard menu items in the File menu set to their default values, then PowerPlant will automatically invoke the proper **LDocApplication** or **LDocument** member function in response to a user's selection of a File menu item such as New, Open, Save, and so forth. A few of these routines are fully implemented by the **LDocApplication** and **LDocument** classes—but most aren't. Instead, your **LSingleDoc**-derived class will override the existing functions and implement its own version of each.

MediaCenter has turned into an application chock full of features. But one important feature is only partially implemented—printing. Thanks to the Metrowerks-supplied **CTextDocument** class, MediaCenter supports the printing of text documents. But the user might find it valuable if he or she is given the opportunity to print the picture displayed in an open Picture window. In the last chapter, you'll see how the **CTextDocument** class implements the printing of a text window, and how the final version of the *MediaCenter.μ* project can make use of the same technique to implement printing a different type of window.

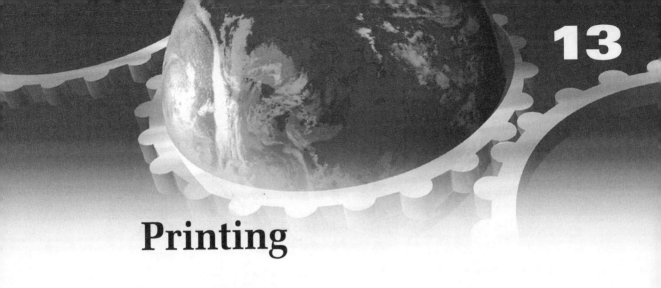

Printing

There's a good chance a user may want the option of having a hard-copy version of whatever your program displays. Sending the contents of a window to the printer can be a tricky task to implement in a project—but not if the project is PowerPlant-based. In this chapter, you'll learn how to use the **LPrintout** and **LPlaceHolder** classes to round out your application by providing printing support.

Constructor is an interface-building tool, and printing typically has nothing to do with a program's interface. But surprisingly, Constructor plays a big role in setting up your project for the support of printing. In this chapter, you'll see how a 'PPob' resource can be used not only to create a window, but also to serve as a template for the layout of a printed page. The two PowerPlant classes are then introduced to show you how to get a window's content to appear on a printed page, using the look established by the new 'PPob' resource.

Constructor & Printing

Constructor is a tool for designing and defining interface elements—components of your program the user can see, such as windows, menus, and controls. As our discussion turns to printing—a topic involving the behind-the-scenes act of software communicating with hardware—your first thought may very well be that Constructor plays little or no role in a project that supports printing. Constructor does, however, play a large role in bringing print capabilities to your application.

Although the end product of printing—the printed page—may be a visual element, the act of printing itself isn't. As a program prints a page or pages, the user notices no changes on the screen. Constructor's involvement in printing arises from the interesting way that PowerPlant handles printing—the details of which unfold as this chapter progresses. For now, simply think of printing in terms of views. PowerPlant places the focus of printing on views, and as you're well aware, Constructor is your tool for creating views.

'PPob' Resources & Printing

A window whose content may be printed also has a second 'PPob' resource associated with it. This second 'PPob' resource, however, *won't* result in a new window being created.

In Chapter 8, "Panes & Views," you read that while a 'PPob' is *usually* created to serve as a holder of window attributes and content, it doesn't *have* to be used for this purpose. A 'PPob' can be used as the basis for different types of view objects, of which an **LWindow** object is only one. (Recall from Figure 10-1 in Chapter 10, "Windows & Dialogs," that the **LWindow** class is derived from the **LView** class.) In the case of printing, this second 'PPob' is used by an **LPrintout** view object.

The 'PPob' used by the **LPrintout** object serves as a temporary placeholder of a window's content. In fact, an **LPrintout** 'PPob' is a top-level view that includes one or more views of a type named **LPlaceHolder**. When printing is to take place, the contents of an **LWindow** object are temporarily moved to the **LPlaceHolder** or **LPlaceHolders** in an **LPrintout** object. After printing, the **LPrintout** object contents are restored in the **LWindow** object.

This seemingly roundabout way of doing things is necessitated by the fact that view classes (such as **LView** or its derived **LWindow** class) don't have printing functionality built into them. Instead, the **LPrintout** and **LPlaceHolder** classes handle the details of printing any type of view.

CTextDocument Class & 'PPob' Resources

Chapter 12, "Files & Input/Output," covered the application-defined **CTextDocument** class that CodeWarrior includes in a PowerPlant-based project created from Doc PowerPlant project stationery. Because you're familiar with the **CTextDocument** class and because the class includes routines for printing, it makes sense to continue to use this class in this chapter's examples.

The **CTextDocument** class is used to create window objects that each hold a single text-editing area. Figure 13-1 shows 'PPob' 1000—the 'PPob' resource that the **CTextDocument** class uses when creating a new **CTextDocument** window object. Note that the 'PPob' includes an LTextEdit item that occupies the entire window content area.

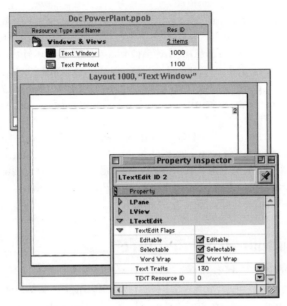

Figure 13-1: The one view in the LWindow 'PPob' used by the CTextDocument class.

Because the **CTextDocument** class supports the printing of the contents of a **CTextDocument** window, an **LPrintout** 'PPob' must be defined in addition to the **LWindow** 'PPob.' The **LPrintout** 'PPob' needs to include a single **LPlaceHolder** item that, like the **LWindow** 'PPob' LTextEdit item, occupies the entire content of the 'PPob.' Figure 13-2 shows this **LPrintout** 'PPob.'

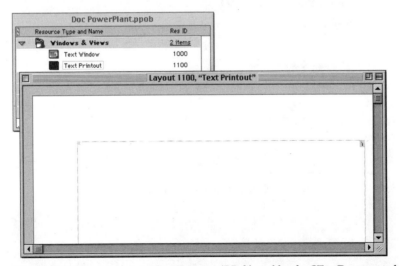

Figure 13-2: The one view in the LPrintout 'PPob' used by the CTextDocument class.

In general, the **LPrintout** 'PPob' can be thought of as a single printed page. The **LPlaceHolder** or **LPlaceHolders** in the 'PPob' define where printing will take place on the page. For a **CTextDocument** object, it's assumed that the object's text should be printed on paper that has margins. That's why the **LPlaceHolder** item in Figure 13-2 doesn't fill the entire **LPrintout** 'PPob'— page margins were taken into account when the **LPlaceHolder** item was sized to fit in the **LPrintout** 'PPob.'

A **CTextDocument** window consists of only one view that needs to be printed. Your windows may have more views. For instance, if a window displays a company logo near the top and text in the remainder of the window, then the corresponding **LPrintout** 'PPob' would include two **LPlaceHolder** items—one for the logo and one for the text.

Creating an LPrintout 'PPob' Resource

You create an **LPrintout** 'PPob' much as you create an **LWindow** 'PPob.' The following steps show that the difference lies in specifying the kind of 'PPob' resource you're creating. Here are the steps:

1. Open the *.ppob* file that holds the **LWindow** 'PPob' that requires a companion **LPrintout** 'PPob.'

2. Click on Windows & Views in the main Constructor window.

3. Choose New Layout Resource from the Edit menu. The Create New Resource dialog box shown in Figure 13-3 appears.

4. Select **LPrintout** from the Kind pop-up menu.

5. Enter a 'PPob' resource ID.

6. Optionally enter a 'PPob' resource name.

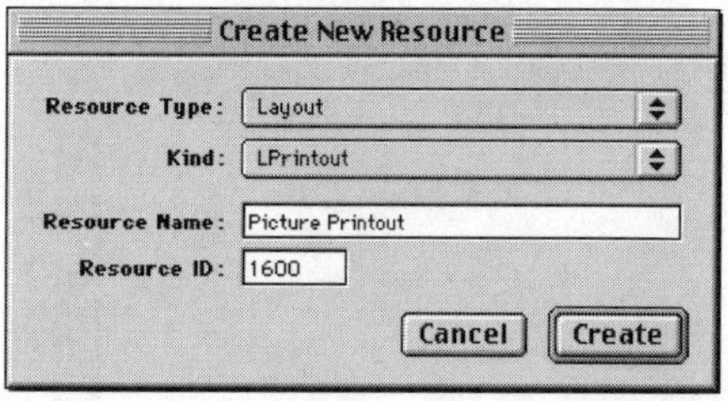

Figure 13-3: Creating a 'PPob' to be used for printing.

Adding an LPlaceHolder to the 'PPob' Resource _____

An **LPrintout** 'PPob' is edited just like an **LWindow** 'PPob.' Display the 'PPob' in the layout window and drag an **LPlaceHolder** item from the Catalog window to the layout window. Figure 13-4 shows that this item is found under the Views tab in the Catalog window. Items you add to the **LPrintout** 'PPob' will always be **LPlaceHolder** items. Because the **LPrintout** 'PPob' will only be used during printing and won't ever display its views on screen, adding other types of panes and views is pointless.

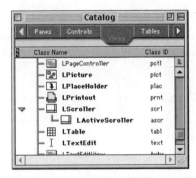

Figure 13-4: The LPlaceHolder item is found under the Views tab in the Catalog window.

Typically, the only changes you'll need to make to an **LPlaceHolder** affect the view's pane ID and location in the 'PPob.' These characteristics are controlled from the Pane ID, Width, Height, Left in Superview, and Top in Superview fields under the **LPane** heading in the **LPlaceHolder** item's property inspector. While you'll always want to allow for a page margin when positioning the view, you won't always make the view the size of an entire window. Instead, the **LPlaceHolder** should be the size of the companion **LWindow** 'PPob' view to be printed. If the **LWindow** 'PPob' view size is variable (as is the case for the MediaCenter custom pane that holds a user-supplied picture), the initial size of the **LPlaceHolder** view is unimportant. You'll adjust the size of such an **LPlaceHolder** view from your source code, just before printing. This chapter's version of MediaCenter provides a specific example of that technique.

Source Code & Printing

To implement the printing of a window, a program creates an **LPrintout** object based on an **LPrintout** 'PPob.' This **LPrintout** object then orchestrates the:

- Moving of views from an **LWindow** object to **LPlaceHolders** in the **LPrintout** object.
- Sending of the contents of **LPlaceHolder** views to the printer.
- Returning of each **LPlaceHolder** view content to the **LWindow** object from which it came.

Once again, I'll rely on the familiar as I discuss how the preceding steps are implemented. The Metrowerks-defined **CTextDocument** class supports printing, so on the following pages I'll use snippets from that class definition.

Creating an LPrintout Object

Printing a window's contents begins with the creation of an **LPrintout** object. This object is based on the **LPrintout** 'PPob,' a companion to the window's **LWindow** 'PPob.' The **LPrintout** constructor has just one parameter—the ID of the **LPrintout** 'PPob' resource. Here's how the **CTextDocument** member function **DoPrint()** creates an **LPrintout** object. Refer back to Figure 13-2 to see the 'PPob' resource on which this object is based:

```
const ResIDT   rPPob_TextPrintout  = 1100;

LPrintout  *thePrintout = LPrintout::CreatePrintout( rPPob_TextPrintout);
```

After creating the **LPrintout** object, it's time to gain access to the placeholder or placeholders in the **LPrintout** object. The **LPrintout** object is a view, so its **FindPaneByID()** member function can be invoked to obtain an **LPlaceHolder** object. Here's a specific example from the **DoPrint()** member function of the **CTextDocument** class:

```
const PaneIDT  kTextPlaceholder  = 1;

LPlaceHolder  *thePlaceholder;
thePlaceholder = (LPlaceHolder *)thePrintout->
                        FindPaneByID(kTextPlaceholder);
```

Here an **LPlaceHolder** object is declared and then created. The variable **thePrintout** is the **LPrintout** object shown in the snippet prior to the preceding code.

At this point the program has access to the placeholder, but it has yet to move a window view to the placeholder view: that's accomplished by invoking the **LPlaceHolder** member function **InstallOccupant()**. This routine has two parameters. The first is the view to be moved to the placeholder. The second parameter is optional; if used, it should be a constant that specifies how the first-parameter view should be positioned within the placeholder. Typically the **LPlaceHolder** and the view to be installed are the same size, and no formatting is used—the view is simply placed snug within the placeholder. The **CTextDocument** member function **DoPrint()** includes the following code to install the **CTextDocument** window's one view (which the window object keeps track of in its **mTextView** data member) into the **LPrintout** object's one **LPlaceHolder**:

```
thePlaceholder->InstallOccupant(mTextView, atNone);
```

A **CTextDocument** window object holds only a single view, so the corresponding **LPrintout** object only holds one **LPlaceHolder**. For a window that holds more than one view, the preceding steps of invoking **FindPaneByID()** to obtain a **LPlaceHolder** object and calling **InstallOccupant()** to move the contents of a window view to the placeholder view would need to be repeated for each view.

Printing With the LPrintout Object

With a window's view installed in an **LPlaceHolder**, it's time to print. The **LPrintout** member function **DoPrintJob()** manages the details of sending the occupant of the placeholder view to the user's printer. Here's how the **CTextDocument** member function **DoPrint()** takes care of printing:

```
thePrintout->DoPrintJob();
```

The **DoPrintJob()** function needs no parameters. All the details of printing, such as paper size and page breaks, are handled by the **LPrintout** object. The **LPrintout** member function **DoPrintJob()** takes care of the printing of whatever views are currently installed in the **LPrintout** object's placeholders at the time **DoPrintJob()** is invoked.

After initiating printing, delete the **LPrintout** object. This act returns the moved view to its original location in the window it came from:

```
delete thePrintout;
```

Printing & the Example Project

Printing a MediaCenter text window has already been taken care of—the Metrowerks-defined **CTextDocument** class has handled text document printing from the very first version of MediaCenter. MediaCenter doesn't, however, support the printing of a picture window—so we'll add that feature here. You'll find the final version of the *MediaCenter.μ* project in the P01 MediaCenter folder in the Chapter 13 folder on this book's Companion CD-ROM.

When you run this last version of MediaCenter, choose Open Picture from the Picture menu. After selecting a picture file, a window displaying the picture appears. Now select Print from the Picture menu to print the picture. Figure 13-5 shows how your Mac's screen might look if you open one of the example 'PICT' files included on the Companion CD-ROM.

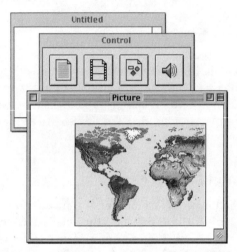

Figure 13-5: A typical picture as displayed in the MediaCenter Picture window.

Resources

This final version of MediaCenter includes new resources to support a Print item in the Picture menu and an **LPrintout** 'PPob' for use in printing Picture windows.

Adding a New Menu

You're experienced in adding a menu item to an existing menu, so I won't linger on the new menu-related resource. Instead, refer to Figure 13-6 to see that the new item is added after the Open Picture item and given a command ID of 5002.

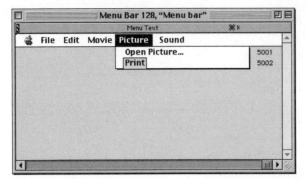

Figure 13-6: The new Print menu item added to the existing Picture menu.

Creating an LPrintout 'PPob' Resource

Create a new **LPrintout** 'PPob' as described in this chapter's "Creating an **LPrintout** 'PPob' Resource" section. Figure 13-7 shows the Create New Resource dialog box just before the dialog box Create button is clicked.

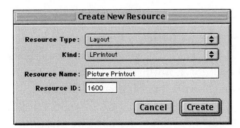

Figure 13-7: Creating a 'PPob' to be used in the printing of a MediaCenter Picture window.

Adding an LPlaceHolder to the 'PPob' Resource

The **LWindow** 'PPob' used to define MediaCenter picture windows holds a single item—the **LP**ANE that the program uses as a custom pane. That means that the new **LPrintout** 'PPob' needs only one placeholder. In Figure 13-8 you see that I've already dragged an **LPlaceHolder** from the Catalog window to the **LPrintout** 'PPob.'

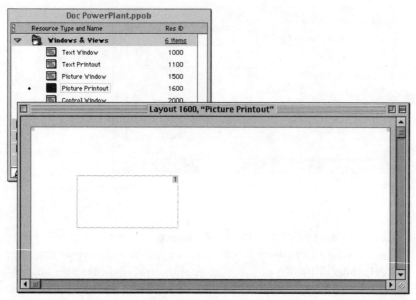

Figure 13-8: The LPrintout 'PPob' requires a single LPlaceHolder item.

The size of a picture displayed in a MediaCenter varies, so the size of the **LPlaceHolder** in the **LPrintout** 'PPob' will have to vary as well. Because the size of the placeholder won't be known until runtime, the size I select now won't matter. I will, however, set the placeholder's top left corner in the top left corner of the 'PPob'—after allowing for a margin of an inch on the left and top of the page. There are 72 pixels to an inch, so that's the number I use for both the Left in Superview and Top in Superview fields of the **LPlaceHolder** property inspector—as shown in Figure 13-9. This same figure also shows that I gave the placeholder a pane ID of 1. The particular value I choose for this ID isn't critical, but it is important that I make note of the value for later use in the defining of a source-code constant.

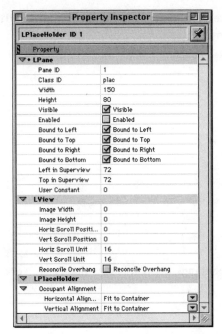

Figure 13-9: The attributes of the LPlaceHolder item.

With the new 'PPob' complete, it's time to implement picture printing in the *PP Doc App.cp* source code file.

Source Code

In this chapter, you've seen how knowledge of just three new functions—**CreatePrintout()**, **InstallOccupant()**, and **DoPrintJob()**—are all that's necessary to get started with printing. The *MediaCenter.μ* project makes use of these routines from within a single new member function added to the **CPPDocApp** class.

Printing & the Print Menu Item

A selection of Print from the Picture menu causes PowerPlant to generate a command with a value of 5002 (see Figure 13-6). MediaCenter defines a new constant to match this command value:

```
const CommandT  cmd_PrintPicture  =  5002;
```

A new **case cmd_PrintPicture** section appears in **ObeyCommand()** to handle an occurrence of this command:

```
CPPDocApp::ObeyCommand(
    CommandT  inCommand,
    void      *ioParam)
{
    Boolean  cmdHandled = true;

    switch (inCommand) {

        case cmd_PrintPicture:
            PrintPictureWindow();
            break;
        ...
        ...
        default:
            cmdHandled = LDocApplication::ObeyCommand( inCommand, ioParam);
            break;
    }
    return cmdHandled;
}
```

Choosing Print from the Picture menu results in a new **CPPDocApp** member function being invoked—**PrintPictureWindow()**. We'll look at this routine just ahead.

FindCommandStatus() gets called by PowerPlant repeatedly during the execution of MediaCenter. To tell PowerPlant to enable the newly added menu item, include a new **case cmd_PrintPicture** section in that **FindCommandStatus()**:

```
void
CPPDocApp::FindCommandStatus(
    CommandT  inCommand,
    Boolean   &outEnabled,
    Boolean   &outUsesMark,
    Char16    &outMark,
    Str255    outName)
{
    switch (inCommand) {
```

```
        case cmd_PrintPicture:
            outEnabled = true;
            break;
        ...
        ...
        default:
            LDocApplication::FindCommandStatus(inCommand,
                                    outEnabled, outUsesMark,
                                    outMark, outName);
            break;
    }
}
```

Implementing Printing

This chapter's "Source Code & Printing" section covered printing as it applies to the **CTextDocument** class. Included in that section was the code for:

- Creating an **LPrintout** object.
- Accessing that object's placeholders.
- Moving a window view into a placeholder.
- Printing the placeholder's content.

Here, you'll see that the printing code I've added to the **CPPDocApp** class is very similar—starting with the creation of the **LPrintout** object (see Figure 13-7 to see the 'PPob' resource ID being set to 1600):

```
const ResIDT   PPob_PicturePrintout  =  1600;

LPrintout  *thePrintout;
thePrintout = LPrintout:: CreatePrintout( PPob_PicturePrintout);
```

Next, access to the **LPrintout** object's one placeholder is gained by invoking that object's **FindPaneByID()** member function (refer to Figure 13-9 to see where the **LPlaceHolder** item is given a pane ID of 1):

```
const PaneIDT   paneID_PictPrintPane  =  1;

LPlaceHolder *thePlaceHolder;
thePlaceHolder = (LPlaceHolder *)thePrintout->
                    FindPaneByID(paneID_PictPrintPane);
```

To get a reference to the view to be printed, access to the window holding the picture is needed. This window object's one pane holds the picture to print. **FetchTopRegular()** returns the window object; then **FindPaneByID()** returns the custom pane object. That object is typecast to an **LView** object:

```
const PaneIDT  paneID_PicturePane  = 1;

LWindow  *theWindow;
LView    *theView;
theWindow = UDesktop::FetchTopRegular();
theView = (LView *)theWindow->
                    FindPaneByID(paneID_PicturePane);
```

Before placing the picture into the placeholder, the placeholder needs to be resized to match the dimensions of the picture. The size of the picture is obtained by invoking the picture view's **GetFrameSize()** member function. This function sets the **width** and **height** fields of the passed-in parameter **theFrameSize**, which is of the PowerPlant-defined type **SDimension16**.

```
SDimension16  theFrameSize;
theView->GetFrameSize(theFrameSize);
```

This picture's size is then applied to the placeholder by invoking the placeholder's **ResizeFrameTo()** member function:

```
thePlaceHolder->ResizeFrameTo(theFrameSize.width,
                            theFrameSize.height, true);
```

Resizing the placeholder view in this way leaves the specification of where the view's top left corner is to start on the printed page—in and down an inch from the top left of the paper. **ResizeFrameTo()** doesn't move the view; it just extends the view's width and height to the values in its first two parameters. The last parameter is a **Boolean** value indicating whether the newly sized view should be updated.

TIP

*Here you see how to easily shrink or enlarge a printout in relation to the original. Just pass **ResizeFrameTo()** values that are smaller or larger than the window view dimensions. Make sure to keep the printed view proportional to the original view by multiplying or dividing the width and height by the same value.*

Finally, it's time to install the Picture window's one view into the **LPrintout** object's one placeholder and send the resulting placeholder content to the printer via the **LPrintout** object. The mechanism for moving the window view into the placeholder view is the **LPlaceHolder** member function **InstallOccupant()**. Printing is achieved by invoking the **LPrintout** member function **DoPrintJob()**:

```
thePlaceHolder->InstallOccupant(theView, atNone);

thePrintout->DoPrintJob();
```

When incorporating the new **PrintPictureWindow()** function in the *CPPDocApp.cp* file, make sure to also include its declaration in the **CPPDocApp** class declaration in the *CPPDocApp.h* header file. Here's the routine in its entirety:

```
void
CPPDocApp::PrintPictureWindow()
{
    LPrintout *thePrintout;
    thePrintout = LPrintout::
                    CreatePrintout(PPob_PicturePrintout);

    LPlaceHolder *thePlaceHolder;
    thePlaceHolder = (LPlaceHolder *)thePrintout->
                    FindPaneByID(paneID_PictPrintPane);

    LWindow  *theWindow;
    LView    *theView;
    theWindow = UDesktop::FetchTopRegular();
    theView = (LView *)theWindow->
                    FindPaneByID(paneID_PicturePane);

    SDimension16  theFrameSize;
    theView->GetFrameSize(theFrameSize);

    thePlaceHolder->ResizeFrameTo(theFrameSize.width,
                                theFrameSize.height, true);
    thePlaceHolder->InstallOccupant(theView, atNone);

    thePrintout->DoPrintJob();

    delete thePrintout;
}
```

Conclusion _____

Printing details are handled by the PowerPlant class **LPrintout**. Like an **LWindow** object, an **LPrintout** object is based on information from a 'PPob' resource. Unlike an **LWindow** object, an **LPrintout** object doesn't appear on screen. Instead, it uses **LPlaceHolder** items to serve as a template that specifies how a window's views should be laid out on a printed page. In your source code, you create an **LPrintout** object based on the **LPrintout** 'PPob' and then move a window's views to the placeholder views that populate the **LPrintout** object. A call to the **LPrintout** member function **DoPrintJob()** sends the contents of the **LPrintout** views to the printer.

Before this chapter, no mention of a Print menu item in the Picture menu appeared. That's because while the Print item will indeed print the contents of a Picture window, code needs to be added to make this menu item completely usable. In particular, **FindCommandStatus()** needs to be modified so that the Print item is only enabled when a Picture window is open and active. Chapter 11, "Debugging & Testing the Application," provides one example of how this can be done. Consider this new menu item an incomplete enhancement to MediaCenter.

After completing the Print menu item implementation, keep on programming! Take the last version of the *MediaCenter.µ* project and turn it into a project that generates the next great, full-featured, media-rich Mac application! Delete code, add code, and add new classes and new member functions. Pore through the PowerPlant-related books that Metrowerks includes as electronic documentation on the pair of CD-ROMs that make up the CodeWarrior Professional package. You'll be especially interested in the tutorials in *The PowerPlant Book* and the extensive list of PowerPlant classes and their member functions in the *PowerPlant Core Classes Reference* (Acrobat file names *PowerPlant Book.pdf* and *PP Core Classes Ref.pdf*, respectively). Metrowerks gives you permission to distribute programs that result from PowerPlant-based projects, and Ventana and I give you permission to use any of the MediaCenter code. Whether you base your own application on MediaCenter code or start from scratch, take full advantage of the work Metrowerks has put into PowerPlant!

Finally, you might want to port your world-class application to Apple's newest operating system, Rhapsody. Or, perhaps, to Windows 95/NT. For tips and suggestions on how Metrowerks CodeWarrior can help with your porting endeavors, read Appendices D and E.

section IV

Reference Information

appendix A

About the Companion CD-ROM

The CD-ROM included with your copy of *The Metrowerks CodeWarrior Professional Book* contains a limited version of CodeWarrior for 68K Macintosh, including C/C++ compilers, Mac toolbox, and PowerPlant. It also includes ANSI libraries on 68K Macintosh and example files written by the author of the book.

Navigating the CD-ROM

To find out more about the CD-ROM and its contents, please open the "README.HTM" file in your favorite browser. You will see a small menu offering several links, including a link to install the software, and another link to access the author example files.

Software

The software provided on the Companion CD-ROM is described below.

- ■ **Author Files**. The author files can be found in the *Resources* folder.

- ■ **Metrowerks CodeWarrior Lite**. Metrowerks CodeWarrior, the world's most powerful Integrated Development Environment (IDE), is the complete solution for serious, industrial-strength programming. Now you can explore the factory and check out the tools with CodeWarrior Lite. You get an editor, source-level debugger, class browser, and compilers for C and C++ for 68K Macintosh, along with sample projects to give you some hands-on experience. CodeWarrior Lite gives you the opportunity to explore our award-winning, intuitive IDE for yourself. When you are ready to step up to the big leagues, the commercial version of CodeWarrior Professional also supports Java and Pascal, and allows you to develop for Power Macintosh, Macintosh, Windows 95, and Windows NT. Check out CodeWarrior Lite today and find out why CodeWarrior is the industry standard in Mac-hosted development tools!

  CodeWarrior Lite is a downloadable demonstration version of the CodeWarrior IDE. CodeWarrior Lite will not allow you to create new projects.

Notes Regarding Metrowerks Technical Support

Metrowerks is proud to offer free world-class technical support on all its commercial products. Metrowerks will not provide technical support for CodeWarrior Lite; however, you can access the benefits of Metrowerks' technical support by upgrading to a commercial product for as little as US$79. For more information, contact Metrowerks at 1-800-377-5416, or via e-mail at sales@metrowerks.com.

Copyright © Metrowerks Inc. and its Licensors. All rights reserved.

Installing the Example Projects

The installer doesn't copy the example projects to your hard drive. To do that, you'll drag one of the two Book Examples folders that are present in the *Resources* directory of the Companion CD-ROM to your hard drive. Typically, programmers keep projects somewhere in the main CodeWarrior folder, so you'll want to do the same by dropping this folder onto the main CodeWarrior folder on your drive.

CodeWarrior Lite Users

If you're installing and using CodeWarrior Lite, you'll copy only the Book Examples Lite folder to your hard drive. For copyright purposes, CodeWarrior Lite doesn't come with all of the PowerPlant source code files. Instead, it comes with the PowerPlant header files and a single library (PowerPlantLib68K) that holds all of the PowerPlant code in an already-compiled format. Each example project in the Book Examples Lite folder includes the PowerPlantLib68K library rather than the PowerPlant source code files. Each of these example projects can thus be compiled with CodeWarrior Lite.

CodeWarrior Professional Users

If you own a full-featured version of CodeWarrior (that is, if you've bought CodeWarrior Professional), then you'll copy only the Book Examples Full folder to your hard drive. Each example project in this folder includes the PowerPlant source code files. You'll be able to open any of these files and view the source code that makes up the PowerPlant application framework. Again, note that if you are using CodeWarrior Lite you must use the example projects from the Book Examples Lite folder—you won't be able to compile the example projects from this Book Examples Full folder.

Technical Support

Technical support is available for installation-related problems only. The technical support office is open from 8:00 A.M. to 6:00 P.M. Monday through Friday and can be reached via the following methods:

- Phone: (919) 544-9404 extension 81
- Faxback Answer System: (919) 544-9404 extension 85
- E-mail: help@vmedia.com
- FAX: (919) 544-9472
- World Wide Web: **http://www.vmedia.com/support**
- America Online: keyword *Ventana*

Limits of Liability & Disclaimer of Warranty

The author and publisher of this book have used their best efforts in preparing the CD-ROM and the programs contained in it. These efforts include the development, research, and testing of the theories and programs to determine their effectiveness. The author and publisher make no warranty of any kind expressed or implied, with regard to these programs or the documentation contained in this book.

The author and publisher shall not be liable in the event of incidental or consequential damages in connection with, or arising out of, the furnishing, performance, or use of the programs, associated instructions, and/or claims of productivity gains.

Some of the software on this CD-ROM is shareware; there may be additional charges (owed to the software authors/makers) incurred for their registration and continued use. See individual program's README or VREADME.TXT files for more information.

appendix B

Moving From
C to C++

The source code that makes up the PowerPlant application framework is written in C++. If you're like many Macintosh programmers, you're familiar with C rather than C++. That means a little background material is in order. This chapter describes the C++ language, with an emphasis on using it in programming the Mac. This chapter doesn't attempt to teach you *everything* there is to know about C++. Instead, we'll cover only the basics, and a few select object-oriented topics. Using PowerPlant means just that—using it. You won't rewrite any of the PowerPlant code, and you won't have to understand all of it. What you will do is combine existing PowerPlant code with your own source code to create a project consisting of more code than you'd ever want to, or be able to, write on your own.

The Very Basics of C++

The most interesting aspects of C++ are the elements that make it an object-oriented language. In particular, classes, and objects created from these classes, differentiate C++ from C. The C++ class and objects are topics that dominate this appendix. First, however, we need to address a few trivial—but necessary—C++ topics. We've also included in this section two very simple C++ example projects; the first uses standard C++, and the second uses standard and Macintosh-specific C++.

C++ is C *Plus* More

C++ is a superset of C. That is, C++ is C, and more. If you're a C programmer that's good news—it means that your time spent learning C wasn't wasted. In C++, you'll use the same operators (such as +, -, *, /, and +=) and the same decision and control statements (such as **if**, **if-else**, **for**, and **while**). In fact, you can turn a project that includes C code into one that instead uses C++ code by simply changing the extension of the source code files from *.c* to *.cp*. When you do that, CodeWarrior will compile the project's code using its C++ compiler rather than its C compiler. While this approach technically does produce a C++ program, it doesn't produce an object-oriented one. Here you'll see a few of the enhancements to the C language. A little later in this chapter, you'll see the more important differences that make C++ a more powerful programming language than C.

C++ Comments

C++ uses the same comment marker as C, but also adds a new marker. To include a comment that spans multiple lines, use the C comment marker to begin the comment (/*) and to end the comment (*/). This snippet provides an example:

```
/* The following loop will execute n number
   of times, where n is a user-supplied value */
   for ( index = 0; index < n; index++) {
      x *= 2;
   }
```

The pairing of the /* and */ markers can also be used to write one-line comments—but C++ introduces a slightly more elegant means of producing such comments. Any source code line that begins with two slashes (//) is viewed as a comment by the C++ compiler. In C++, the preceding snippet could be rewritten as follows:

```
// The following loop will execute n number
// of times, where n is a user-supplied value
   for ( index = 0; index < n; index++) {
      x *= 2;
   }
```

Input & Output

C++ defines an iostream facility that allows a program to send a sequence of any number of variables, constants, and characters to an output stream. This facility also defines an input stream that allows for the easy conversion of incoming data to variables. In C++, these streams are referred to as **cout** and **cin**. The C language defines similar streams: the **printf()** and **scanf()** streams.

To output data, the **cout** stream is used in conjunction with the insertion operator (<<). To send input data to a program, the **cin** stream is used in conjunction with the extraction operator (>>). The insertion operator can be referred to as the "put to" operator, while the extraction operator can be referred to as the "get from" operator. Here's an example of each:

```
float  number;

cout << "Enter a number and I'll double it:";

cin >> number;
number *= 2;

cout << number;
```

The **cout** stream can be used with more than one insertion operator. For instance, if the value of a variable named **numDays** is 30, then the following line of code will generate an output of "There are 30 days in this month."

```
cout << "There are " << numDays << " days in this month.";
```

Header Files

C++ source code listings make use of header files, or include files, just as C listings do. To bring the source code from a header file into a source code file, use the **#include** preprocessor directive as you would in C.

C++ programs that make use of the **cin** and **cout** streams just discussed need to include the *iostream.h* header file—it holds the declarations needed by the **cout** and **cin** identifiers and the << and >> operators. Here's how this **#include** directive looks:

```
#include <iostream.h>   // so compiler recognizes cin, cout
```

Function Prototypes

A function prototype lets the compiler get an early look at how an application-defined function call should be made. A function prototype lists a function's return type, function name, and a list of parameter types. Function prototypes are helpful in C, but *required* in C++. As an example, consider the following function:

```
long  Square( short num )
{
   return ( num * num );
}
```

The function prototype for the **Square()** function appears near the top of the source code listing that holds the function definition (or in a header file included in this source code file). Here's how the prototype would look:

```
long  Square( short num );
```

The compiler is only interested in the prototype to see if subsequent calls to the function follow the correct format—so the names of a function's parameters aren't important. For that reason, an alternate way of writing a function prototype is to omit the name of each parameter. The following prototype would work equally as well as the previous one:

```
long  Square( short );
```

Standard C++ Example Project

This first example project results in an a simple application that squares a predefined number and displays it to the output device. Because the source code for the aptly named SimpleStandardC++ program doesn't use any Mac-specific C++, you could compile and run it on a computer other than a Macintosh. Here's the complete listing:

```
#include <iostream.h>

long  Square( short num );

void  main()
{
    short  worth = 8;
    long   result;

    result = Square( worth );
    cout << result;
}


long  Square( short num )
{
    return ( num * num );
}
```

The SimpleStandardC++ project appears in this appendix's folder in the book examples folder on the Companion CD-ROM.

Source Code Walkthrough

SimpleStandardC++.cp begins with an **#include** directive that makes the compiler aware of the routines in the standard C++ library *iostream.h*. Next comes a function prototype for the program's one routine (other than **main()**). This line also demonstrates that a C++ one-line comment can appear on a line that also holds source code.

With the preliminaries out of the way, it's on to the starting point of the program—**main()**. Here you'll find the declaration of two variables. The first declaration is also an initialization—it assigns the variable of type **short** a value of 8. The second declaration creates a variable of type **long**. Recall that these two data types—the **short** and the **long**—are also available in C.

Next comes a call to the application-defined function **Square()**. Here you see that a C++ program can define a function, and make a call to that function, just as it would in a C program.

The **main()** function ends by displaying the value returned by **Square()**. Where does the number 64 get displayed? To the output device. On a DOS machine, the output device is typically the computer's screen. Macintosh programs, however, don't ever write directly to the screen—they instead write to a window. From the listing of SimpleStandardC++, you can see there's no code that displays a window. If there were, the program wouldn't be standard C++. Just ahead, you'll see how the CodeWarrior IDE handles this dilemma.

CodeWarrior Project

When you write the code that's to become a Macintosh application, you won't use only standard C++, because the C++ language includes no provisions for creating menus, windows, and dialog boxes—the interface elements found in Mac programs. Still, there may be times when you'd like to enter, compile, and run some standard C++ code. For instance, your further studies of the C++ language might bring you to the classic C++ text, *The C++ Programming Language*, by Bjarne Stroustrup. This book has much to offer all programmers—even though it covers standard C++ rather than Mac-specific C++. To allow you to view the output of a standard C++ program, the CodeWarrior IDE provides you with *SIOUX*—Simple Input/Output User eXchange.

When you include the SIOUX library in your CodeWarrior project, your resulting application will be able to receive input and display output in a SIOUX *console window*. Such a window allows you to use standard C and C++ input and output code such as **scanf()** and **cout** without making use of Macintosh dialog boxes or windows to accept input and display output.

The SimpleStandardC++ project uses SIOUX. To create such a project, you simply use one of the ANSI C++ Console project stationeries—I used the ANSI C++ Console 68K stationery. As mentioned previously, and is the case with all of the examples discussed in this book, you'll find a copy of the project on the Companion CD-ROM. If you learn best from recreating examples from scratch, follow the steps listed in Chapter 2, "Using the CodeWarrior IDE," for creating a new project. If you do that, use the ANSI Console 68K project stationery (you find this stationery under the C/C++ heading under the MacOS heading in the project stationery dialog box—other versions of CodeWarrior may differ).

To compile and test the code, choose Run from the Project menu. A SIOUX console window will open; it serves as the output device, so it displays any text or numbers directed to it by **cout** statements. In the case of the SimpleStandardC++ program, the value of variable **result** appears in the console window. Figure B-1 shows the console window, with the window holding the source code listing in the background.

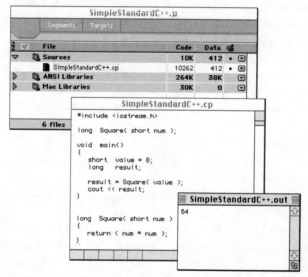

Figure B-1: The SimpleStandardC++ project, source code, and console windows.

Modifying SimpleStandardC++
You can easily modify SimpleStandardC++ to accept input as well as display output. The following version of **main()** prompts the user to enter a number, accepts the user's typed value, squares it, and then displays the result:

```
void main()
{
    short   value;
    long    result;
```

```
      cout << "Enter a value to square: ";
      cin >> value;

      result = Square( value );
      cout << "The square of " << value << " is " << result;
}
```

This modified version of the SimpleStandardC++ project appears in the P02 SimpleStandardC++ (cin) folder in the Appendix B folder on the Companion CD-ROM.

Macintosh C++ Example Project

The Metrowerks CodeWarrior IDE supports all standard C++ data types, operators, keywords, and so forth. It also supports the Macintosh Toolbox and data types particular to Macintosh programming. The SimpleStandardC++ example demonstrated a few of the features of C++. But because it uses a console window rather than a "real" Mac window, that program wasn't very Mac-like. This next example modifies SimpleStandardC++ such that the program sends its output to a Macintosh window. The result is a program I've named SimpleMacC++. Here's the complete listing from the *SimpleMacC++.cp* file:

```
long  Square( short num ); // function prototype

void  main()
{
   short     worth = 8;
   long      result;
   WindowPtr window;
   Str255    string;

   InitGraf( &qd.thePort );
   InitFonts();
   InitWindows();
   InitMenus();
   TEInit();
   InitDialogs( OL );
   FlushEvents( everyEvent, OL );
   InitCursor();

   result = Square( worth );
   NumToString( result, string );
```

```
    window = GetNewWindow( 128, nil, (WindowPtr)-1L );
    SetPort( window );
    MoveTo( 10, 20);
    DrawString( string );

    while ( !Button() )
        ;
}


long  Square( short num )
{
    return ( num * num );
}
```

The SimpleMacC++ project appears in this appendix's folder in the book examples folder on the Companion CD-ROM.

Source Code Walkthrough

Unlike the SimpleStandardC++ program, the SimpleMacC++ program displays its output in a Macintosh window rather than to the computer's output device (or console window in the case of SimpleStandardC++ running on a Mac). So the SimpleMacC++ source code doesn't need the *iostream.h* header file.

SimpleMacC++ adds variables of two Mac-specific types to the **short** and **long** variables found in SimpleStandardC++. The first is a **WindowPtr** used to reference the program's window, while the second is a **Str255** variable used in the drawing of the program's result to the window. You'll recognize the **WindowPtr** and **Str255** data types from your days of programming the Macintosh using the C language. After the variable declarations, it's on to the initialization of the Macintosh Toolbox. Again, you'll recognize some or all of the eight calls used to accomplish this task—they're the same routines used in C projects.

Next comes a call to the application-defined **Square()** function. The value returned by this function is of type **long**. To be useful for output, this value needs to be converted to a string. That's exactly what the Toolbox routine **NumToString()** does.

The next line of code calls the Toolbox function **GetNewWindow()** to load a copy of a 'WIND' resource with an ID of 128 into memory. The resource file that is part of the SimpleMacC++ project defines a single resource—the 'WIND' resource shown in Figure B-2.

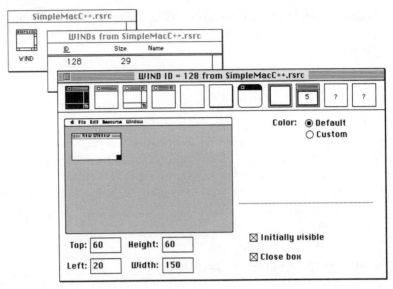

Figure B-2: The SimpleMacC++ 'WIND' resource.

To display the value returned by **Square()**, SimpleMacC++ calls three Toolbox functions. The first, **SetPort()**, ensures that drawing takes place in the newly opened window. The second, **MoveTo()**, moves the invisible graphics pen 10 pixels in from the window's left edge and 20 pixels down from the bottom of the window's title bar. The third, Toolbox call, **DrawString()**, performs the actual drawing of the string.

When the program reaches the closing brace of **main()**, it terminates. To prevent that from happening immediately after the call to **DrawString()**, SimpleMacC++ enters a **while** loop. Each call to the Toolbox routine **Button()** returns a **Boolean** value that tells whether the user has pressed the mouse button. As long as that's *not* the case (as indicated by the use of the logical NOT operator, "!"), the program remains in a "do nothing" loop.

CodeWarrior Project

If you'll be recreating the SimpleMacC++ project to facilitate your learning, follow the Chapter 2 process for creating a new project (use the Basic Toolbox 68K stationery as shown in that chapter). You should already be familiar with the use of the resource editor ResEdit. If you're not, refer to Chapter 2, "Using the CodeWarrior IDE," to see how to create the resource file and 'WIND' resource that is part of that file.

To compile and test the code, choose Run from the Project menu. A window will open, in which the number 64 will display—the result of squaring the number 8.

Classes: Structures Enhanced

In C, the structure is used to store related data. In C++, the class is used for the same purpose. As you'll see in this section, the *class* has some characteristics in common with the structure; it also has differences from the structure that make it a much more powerful programming tool. To understand C++ (and PowerPlant), you need a solid understanding of the C++ class. So it will be worthwhile to review the predecessor of the C++ language class, the C language structure.

Reviewing the C struct Data Type

When you want to store data about several similar items, you keep the information in records. One example would be the organization of a coin collection. For each coin, you might note the type (such as United States penny), the year (such as 1941), and the worth (such as $2.50). Because you'll keep track of the same information for each coin, the format of each record is the same. When programming in C, you set up such records using the **struct** keyword.

Defining a C struct

A structure "bundles together" any number of *members*. Each member is a variable, which can be of any C data type, such as **short**, **long**, or **float**. Members can also be of C data types specific to Mac programming, such as **Str255**, **Rect**, or **PicHandle**. By grouping several variables together into a single package, you create a simple means of keeping related data together. The following is an example of a structure that could be used to hold information about a single coin in a collection:

```
struct  Coin {
   Str255  type;
   short  year;
   float  worth;
};
```

A structure *template*, or structure *specifier*, describes the format of a structure. A structure template starts with the C keyword **struct**. Next, on the same line comes the structure specifier's *name*, or *tag*. In the preceding example, the structure's name is **Coin**. Following the name are the structure members, enclosed between opening and closing braces. The **Coin** structure has three members: a **Str255**, a **short**, and a **float**. The structure specifier ends with a semicolon.

Declaring a C struct Variable

A structure specifier defines what a particular structure looks like—but it doesn't create any structures usable by your program. Just as, say, **long** defines a data type that can be used to hold a number in four bytes of memory, a structure defines a data type that can be used to hold a number of values. And just as you make use of the **long** data type by declaring variables to be of type **long**, you make use of a structure specifier by declaring variables to be of that structure type. The following snippet declares three structure variables of type **Coin**:

```
Coin   thePenny;
Coin   theDime;
Coin   anotherPenny;
```

The preceding three declarations all use the same structure as their data type. That means that each of the three structure variables will consist of a **type**, **year**, and **worth** member. The **Coin** structure specifier has been used to "stamp out" the three structure variables.

Assigning a Value to a C struct Data Member

A structure variable consists of more than one value—each member of a structure has its own value. Assign any one member a value by first naming the structure and the member, and place a structure member operator (a period) between them. Then assign the selected member a value. The following snippet provides an example that assigns a value of 1941 to the **year** member of a **Coin** structure variable named **thePenny**:

```
Coin   thePenny;

thePenny.year = 1941;
```

Using Functions to Access C struct Members

If your program will be working with more than one structure variable of the same type, or if throughout the program's execution it will be assigning and reassigning values to the members of a single structure variable, you should write a function that handles the assignments:

```
void EnterInfo( Coin *theStruct, Str255 theType,
                short theYear, float theWorth )
{
```

```
    // make assignments to the type, year, and
    // worth members of the passed-in structure
}
```

The **EnterInfo()** routine accepts four parameters. The first is a pointer to the **Coin** structure variable to work with. Pass a pointer to the structure rather than the structure itself so that any changes made to the structure by the function remain in effect after the execution of the function finishes. The remaining three parameters are the three values to be assigned to the members of the structure being worked with. Now, after declaring a **Coin** structure variable, assign all the members of that variable values in one line of code:

```
Coin  thePenny;
EnterInfo( &thePenny, "\pUS penny", 1941, 2.50 );
```

The C++ Class

Because C++ is a superset of C, you can use C data types in a C++ program. Knowing this, it should make sense that in C or C++ projects you *can* use structures to group related data. But instead of working with structures, your C++ projects are much more likely to group data using classes—something available in C++ but not in C.

Advantages of the C++ Class

Earlier you saw that it's often advantageous for you to define functions that operate on the members of a structure. You write such a function to avoid having to repeat the same block of code throughout your source code—as is always the case with a function. The purpose of the C++ class is to take the usefulness of this member-function relationship one step further. Where a structure consists of only members, a class consists of members *and* functions.

In the C structures discussion, I defined a **Coin** structure specifier that consisted of three members. This structure then relied on the application-defined function **EnterInfo()** to assign values to its members. To achieve the same results using a class rather than a structure, a C++ program would define a class specifier that consists of both *data members* and *member functions*. Figure B-3 illustrates this with a class named **CCoin**. I've elected to preface my class name with an uppercase 'C' for "class" to help you quickly recognize this name as a class when it appears in source code listings. However, this is not a requirement in naming a class.

TIP   *The terms* data member *and* member function *are specific to C++. When discussing object-oriented programming without regard for a specific language, we can refer to the data of a class as instance variables and the functions of a class as methods. Think of* instance variable *and* method *as generic OOP terms and* data member *and* member function *terms specific to C++.*

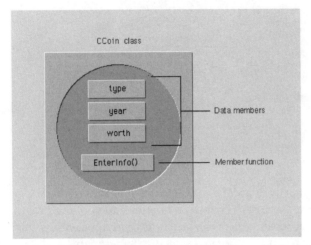

Figure B-3: The specifier for the CCoin C++ class.

I'll have more to say about data members, member functions, and the exact syntax of a class specifier later on. Here I'll discuss why it is be beneficial to bind functions and data into one entity. Using Figure B-4 as the starting point, you see that the primary difference between a class and a structure is that in the class, the functions "belong" to the class. In the structure, there is no direct correlation between the structure and the function(s) the structure uses.

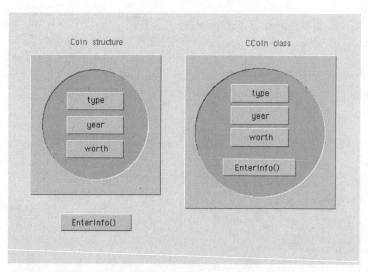

Figure B-4: The C Coin structure and the C++ CCoin class.

One of the primary advantages of the class over the structure is *security*. In this case, the word "security" is used in reference to you, the programmer—not to end-users or to someone who attempts to tamper with your program. While any function can operate on a structure's members, only the member functions of a class—the functions listed as a part of the class—can operate on the data members of a class. When you plan a class to be used in a program, you decide what functions will be needed in order to adequately work with the data members of that class. Any other functions you write for the program will *not* be able to affect the data members of this class. Object-oriented languages often refer to this *data hiding* by the more technical term *encapsulation*. The purpose of creating an object is to *encapsulate* a set of attributes and behaviors into a single entity. In doing so, the object's attributes—its data—get hidden from "the rest of the world." Keeping an object's data private is good—it keeps the object self-contained and prevents accidental modification of the data by other code in the application.

Why is such security important in a program? In the smallest of programs, it's not. But in real-world, large-scale applications written by several programmers, it is. If the coin collection program were written in C using a structure, more than one programmer could, without the knowledge of the other programmers, write a function that intentionally or unintentionally altered the values of the structure's members. In the C project, there's no quick and easy way to determine which of the possibly hundreds of functions defined by the programmers are capable of manipulating a structure's members. This isn't the case for a C++ project, because the only functions that can alter class data members are the member functions defined to be a part of the class. Using classes and C++, determining which functions affect certain data members is simple—the member functions are listed right along with the data members in each class specifier.

Defining a Class

Like a structure, a class groups together any number of data items. In a structure, one data item is referred to as simply a *member* of the structure. In a class, a data item is referred to as a *data member*. Again, like the structure, an individual data item in a class is treated as a variable—each data member variable can be of any C data type. Unlike the structure, however, a class holds both data and functions. In C++, the functions are referred to as member functions. The following class specifier is an example of a class that could be used to hold the same coin information used in this chapter's structure examples:

```
class  CCoin {
   public:
      void  EnterInfo( Str255 theType,
                       short theYear,
                       float theWorth );
   private:
      Str255  type;
      short   year;
      float   worth;
};
```

Besides the inclusion of functions, the preceding example illustrates a couple of other differences between the **CCoin** class template, or specifier, and the **Coin** structure specifier. One is that a class specifier uses the **class** keyword in place of the **struct** keyword. Another is that a class includes a specification of an access level for the class functions and for the class data. In the **CCoin** class, the **public** keyword is used to signify that the one function can be accessed from anywhere in a program, and the **private** keyword is used to signify that the three data members can only be accessed via member functions. The **public** and **private** keywords are discussed in more detail ahead.

Objects

In C++, a variable of a class type is referred to as an *instance* of that class, or an *object* of that class (the terms are interchangeable).

Creating an Object

Like a structure specifier, a class specifier defines the format of a data type but doesn't create any variables. To create a variable, use the class specifier as you would any other data type. The following snippet declares a pointer to a **CCoin**:

```
CCoin  *thePenny;
```

Declaring a pointer creates a variable, but it doesn't allocate any memory. Instead, memory needs to be allocated dynamically—as the program executes. To complete the act of creating an object, use the **new** operator:

```
thePenny = new CCoin;
```

Just as a data type defined by the C or C++ language (such as **int**, **short**, or **long**) is used to create any number of variables of that type, so is a single class used to create any number of objects of that type. Here three **CCoin** objects are created:

```
CCoin  *thePenny;
CCoin  *theDime;
CCoin  *anotherPenny;

thePenny = new CCoin;
theDime = new CCoin;
anotherPenny = new CCoin;
```

Each of the three objects in the preceding snippet is of type **CCoin**, so each consists of a **type**, **year**, and **worth** data member, as well as an **EnterInfo()** function. Figure B-5 shows three **CCoin** objects that were all declared using the **CCoin** class specifier.

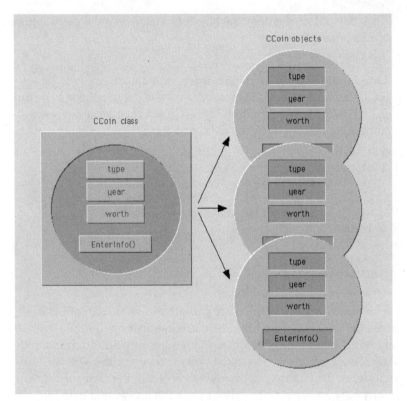

Figure B-5: Any number of CCoin objects are created from the one CCoin class.

Assigning Values to Object Data Members

For a structure variable, you saw that the assignment of a structure member was performed using the member access operator (.), as in this example:

```
Coin  thePenny;
```

```
thePenny.year = 1941;
```

In certain circumstances, C++ also allows the structure member operator to be used to make assignments. First an object is declared and created:

```
CCoin  *thePenny;
```

```
thePenny = new CCoin;
```

To access a data member, the object (which is really a pointer to an object) needs to be dereferenced:

```
(*thePenny).year = 1941;
```

One condition must be met in order for a data member to be accessed in the preceding manner: the data member must be declared using the **public** keyword. Looking at the definition of the **CCoin** class, you can see that the data members are instead declared to be **private**:

```
class  CCoin {
   public:
      void  EnterInfo( Str255 theType,
                       short theYear,
                       float theWorth );
   private:
      Str255  type;
      short   year;
      float   worth;
};
```

Having data members that are **private** means that an object can't directly access the members using the structure member operator. Instead, the data can only be accessed indirectly through member functions defined within the same class. Limiting access to data members coincides with the idea of encapsulation, or data hiding, as discussed earlier. In the next section you'll see exactly how an object with **private** data can access that data.

Member Functions

A C++ class member function is similar to a C function. The primary difference is that a C function acts upon any program data, while a C++ member function acts on only data that is part of the same class that defines the member function.

Implementing a Member Function

A class definition includes a list of the member functions to be part of that class. You've seen that the **CCoin** class has a single member function named **EnterInfo()**:

```
class  CCoin {
   public:
      void  EnterInfo( Str255 theType,
                       short theYear,
                       float theWorth );
```

```
    private:
        Str255  type;
        short   year;
        float   worth;
};
```

The listing of a member function in a class definition serves as a prototype for the function—it lets the compiler know the name of the function, its return type, and the number and types of its parameters. The listing of the member function doesn't define that function. That's done outside the class definition.

Define, or implement, a function that is to be a member function for a class as you would a C function—with one addition. Between the function return type and the function name, list the name of the class the function is to be part of, along with the scope resolution operator (created by typing two colons, ::). The following shows how the **CCoin** class **EnterInfo()** member function could be implemented. Note that the return type and the parameter types match the information as given in the function prototype in the **CCoin** class definition:

```
void  CCoin::EnterInfo( Str255 theType, short theYear, float theWorth )
{
    long  numBytes;

    numBytes = theType[0] + 1;
    BlockMoveData( theType, type, numBytes );

    year = theYear;

    worth = theWorth;
}
```

The **EnterInfo()** function takes the three values passed to it and assigns each to one of the three data members in the **CCoin** class. In the **EnterInfo()** member function, you can see that the three assignments are made with no mention of the object to be acted upon. No object is passed to the member function, and no object name or structure member operator is used in conjunction with the data member names. This member function definition, part of the **CCoin** class, refers to **CCoin** class data members—but doesn't refer to any particular **CCoin** object. Recall that a class definition itself is not an object—it is analogous to a data type. From a data type, any number of objects are created. Each object is allocated storage for its own set of data members. And each object will be able to invoke the **EnterInfo()** member function to act on its own set of data members.

TIP | *The use of the Macintosh Toolbox function **BlockMoveData()** is necessary to copy the **theType** string to the type data member. In Mac programming, a string can't be copied directly to a string variable except upon initialization of the variable. After that, the use of a memory-copying function such as **BlockMoveData()** is required.*

Invoking a Member Function

A member function is invoked by an object. To invoke the function, the object must be of the same class type as the member function. For instance, only an object of the **CCoin** class can invoke the **CCoin** member function **EnterInfo()**. If the program also defined another class (perhaps a **CStamp** class if the program kept track of both stamp and coin collections), objects of the second class type couldn't invoke **EnterInfo()**.

For an object to call a member function, use the pointer operator (which is created by typing a hyphen followed by the greater than character, **->**). To the left of the **->** is the object's name, and to the right is the name of the member function to invoke. The member function name is followed by parentheses, between which are any arguments the function requires. The following line of code invokes the **EnterInfo()** member function for a **CCoin** object named **thePenny**. Assume that, prior to this line of code, a **CCoin** variable was declared and an object created:

```
thePenny->EnterInfo("\pSteel Penny, 1943, 1.50 );
```

The result of executing the preceding code is that the type data member of the **thePenny** object has a value of Steel Penny, the year data member has a value of 1943, and the worth data member has a value of 1.50 (for one dollar and fifty cents).

Earlier you saw the keyword that precedes the list of data members specifies the level of access for the data members. Declaring data members private means they can only be accessed by member functions of the same class. From your observations of the **CCoin** class, you should have noticed that there is also a keyword precedes the list of member functions. This keyword specifies the degree of access a program has to the member functions of a class. Declaring the member functions of a class **public** means the functions can be invoked by an object of this class type from anywhere in the program.

TIP | *Making member functions accessible from any point in the program doesn't violate the principle of data hiding. It's the data of an object you want shielded from easy access, so data is usually declared to be **private**. You'll want your program's objects to be able to use their own member functions at any time, so member functions are usually declared to be **public**.*

Accessor Member Functions

The **EnterInfo()** member function gives a **CCoin** object a means of supplying values to each of its data members. If the **CCoin** class was to be of real use, it would also need a member function that returned the current values of the data members to the program. A more elegant feature would be for the **CCoin** class to define a number of member functions, each of which either sets or returns the value of a single data member. Here's how such a pair of routines would look for setting and returning the year data member:

```
void  CCoin::SetYear( short theYear )
{
   year = theYear;
}
```

```
short  CCoin::GetYear( void )
{
   return year;
}
```

Most object-oriented programs call such routines *accessor member functions*—their sole purpose is to *access* a data member. Here's how the **CCoin** class would look if defined using accessor member functions:

```
class  CCoin {
   public:
      void    SetType( Str255 theType);
      Str255  GetType(void);
      void    SetYear(short theYear);
      short   GetYear(void);
      void    SetWorth(float theWorth);
      float   GetWorth(void);

   private:
      Str255  type;
      short   year;
      float   worth;
};
```

TIP *Because a member function can also be called a method, you may see accessor member functions referred to as accessor methods.*

If you're an astute reader, you may conclude that it would be more succinct to define only two member functions in place of the six listed in the preceding version of the **CCoin** class: one member function to set the values of all of the data members and another to return all the values of the data members. While such a technique would work, it would actually be less useful than the preceding approach. There will be many times a program will need to access only one data member—so for each data member there should be a pair of member functions that allow for that possibility. Consider the following snippet. In it, the year data member of a **CCoin** object is set to a value of 1943. At a later point in the program, the value of the year data member is returned and saved to the **short** variable **theShort**. Since the program has no need to change the values of the other data members, or to return the current values of the other data members to the program, there is no need to define and invoke all-encompassing functions that work with all data members.

```
short    theShort;
CCoin   *thePenny;

thePenny = new CCoin;

thePenny->SetYear( 1943 );

// other code here

theShort = thePenny->GetYear();
```

The use of accessor functions is demonstrated in the Accessor project that appears in this appendix's folder in the book examples folder on the Companion CD-ROM.

Constructors & Destructors

Every class has at least one constructor function—a function invoked upon creation of an object of the class type. The purpose of a constructor is to handle any initialization tasks warranted for new objects of a particular class type.

Default Constructor
The **new** operator creates a new object and allocates memory for that object. The **new** operator then invokes the object's constructor. If a class doesn't define a constructor, an empty default constructor is implicitly created for that class and that function gets invoked. Even though it performs no action, this default constructor is necessary. The **new** operator always invokes a constructor, so one

must exist for each class. The **CCoin** class doesn't define a constructor, so the default constructor is invoked in the following snippet:

```
CCoin  *thePenny;

thePenny = new CCoin;  // create new object, call constructor
```

Class-Defined Constructors

To define a constructor for a class, create a function that has the same name as the class. The function cannot have a return type and can have any number of parameters that make sense. Here's another version of the **CCoin** class, followed by the implementation of the **CCoin** constructor:

```
class  CCoin {
   public:
            CCoin( void );

      void   SetType( Str255 theType);
            // other member functions here

   private:
      Str255  type;
      short   year;
      float   worth;
};

CCoin::CCoin( void )
{
   Str255  emptyStr = "\p";
   long    numBytes;

   numBytes = emptyStr[0] + 1;
   BlockMoveData( emptyStr, type, numBytes );

   year = 0;
   worth = 0.0;
}
```

The **CCoin** constructor initializes the type data member to an empty string and then goes on to initialize both the year and worth data members to zero. The call to this constructor looks like this:

```
CCoin  *thePenny;

thePenny = new CCoin();
```

A class can define more than one constructor. When an object of the class type is created, the number of parameters passed will determine which version of the constructor gets invoked. The following is still another version of the **CCoin** class. Here, two constructors are listed in the class definition. The implementation of the first has already been shown—the snippet shows only the newer constructor—the one that assigns to the data members of an object the values passed during the object's creation:

```
class  CCoin {
   public:
            CCoin( void );
            CCoin( Str255 initType,
                 short  initYear,
                 float  initWorth );

       void    SetType( Str255 theType);
               // other member functions here

   private:
      Str255  type;
      short   year;
      float   worth;
};


CCoin::CCoin( Str255 initType,
            short initYear,
            float initWorth )
{
   long  numBytes;

   numBytes = initType[0] + 1;
   BlockMoveData( initType, type, numBytes );

   year = initYear;
   worth = initWorth;
}
```

The following line shows how the preceding version of the **CCoin** constructor gets executed:

```
CCoin  *theNickel;

theNickel = new CCoin( "\pBuffalo", 1918, 3.50 );
```

The use of constructors is demonstrated in the Constructor project that appears in this appendix's folder in the book examples folder on the Companion CD-ROM.

Destructor

Just as the **new** operator triggers the execution of a constructor function, the **delete** operator triggers the execution of a destructor function. Just as a class isn't required to define a constructor, a class isn't required to define a destructor. If it doesn't define a destructor, then an empty (a "do-nothing") destructor will be defined for the class, and this function will automatically be executed upon the deletion of an object.

Like a constructor, a destructor has the same name as the class that defines it, and has no return type. To distinguish it from the constructor, the destructor precedes its name with the tilde character (˜).Unlike a constructor (which may have no parameters, or optionally, may have any number of parameters), a destructor *never* has parameters. If the **CCoin** class defined a destructor, the class definition would look like this:

```
class  CCoin {
   public:
                CCoin( void );
                CCoin( Str255 initType,
                      short   initYear,
                      float   initWorth );
                ˜CCoin( void );

        void    SetType( Str255 theType);
                // other member functions here

   private:
        Str255  type;
        short   year;
        float   worth;
};
```

While a constructor is a useful tool for initializing object data members, a destructor is less useful—and is often unnecessary. It may be helpful to initialize data upon object creation, but there is no analogous need to "deinitialize" this same data just before the object is deleted. For the sake of a concrete example, though, I supply the following simple destructor. This implementation of a destructor simply draws a line of text to a window when a **CCoin** object is deleted:

```
CCoin::˜CCoin( void )
{
   MoveTo( 20, 20 );
   DrawString( "\pCoin record deleted." );
}
```

This next snippet declares a **CCoin** coin object and then uses the **new** operator to allocate memory for the object and to invoke a **CCoin** constructor to assign values to the object data members. After that, it's assumed that a window is opened and other events take place. Next the **delete** operator is used to destroy the **CCoin** object. It is this act that triggers the invocation of the **CCoin** destructor:

```
CCoin       *thePenny;

// open a window

thePenny = new CCoin("\pPenny", 1968, 0.20);
// other code
delete thePenny;
```

The use of a destructor is demonstrated in the Destructor project that appears in this appendix's folder in the book examples folder on the Companion CD-ROM.

When a class defines a destructor, its purpose typically is to release any memory an object may have allocated in its constructor function. For instance, an object may have a pointer or handle as one of its data members—a **PicHandle** used to keep track of a picture is one example. Upon creation, such an object may use its constructor to allocate the memory to be used to hold the data this pointer or handle references—a call to the Toolbox function **GetPicture()** to load 'PICT' resource data into memory and return a handle to that data would work for a data member of type **PicHandle**. In such a case, the object's destructor should release the memory allocated in the constructor—a call to the Toolbox function **ReleaseResource()** would work for the picture data referenced by a data member of type **PicHandle**.

Inheritance

Your C++ application won't be constrained to a single class—you can write as many classes as make sense for your application. Some of these classes will be completely unrelated. Others—ones that are meant to model similar things—will be related. Here you'll see how C++ makes it easy to write a new class based on an existing one, and how such a new class inherits the data members and member functions of the class upon which it is based.

Derived Classes

If your application is to model something that can be described by more than one category of related things, you should use derived classes. C++ allows you to write a new class that takes advantage of the code defining an existing class.

Base Classes, Derived Classes & Inheritance

In C++, you can write a single *base class*—a class that holds code common to any number of other classes. Each of these additional other classes is a *derived class*; each *inherits* the contents of the base class and then goes on to add its own additional content.

TIP | *A base class can be called a superclass, and a derived class can be called a subclass. In Metrowerks documentation, you're most likely to see the terms base class and subclass.*

Consider a class that consists of a single data member named **variable1** and a single member function named **function1()**. You can see such a class in the upper left of Figure B-6. This class serves as a base class from which another class will be derived. Beneath the class in this same figure is a single object of this class type. In the upper right of the figure is a class derived from the base class. Like its base class, this derived class (or subclass) happens to define a single data member (named **variable2**) and a single member function (named **function2()**). But if you look at an object created from this derived class—the object pictured at the bottom right of the figure—you can see that it consists of the combined contents of both the base class and the derived class.

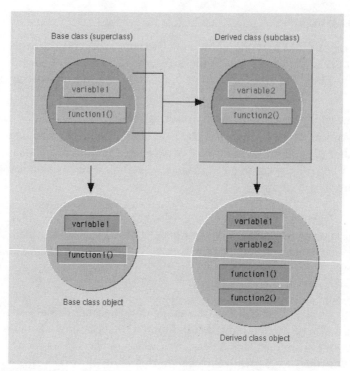

Figure B-6: A subclass inherits the data members and member functions from its superclass.

Creating a Derived Class

Any class can serve as a base class—a class from which other classes are to be derived. To create a class that is derived from another class, begin the class definition as always: use the **class** keyword followed by the name of the new class. Instead of following the class name with an opening brace, though, add a colon, an access specifier, and the name of the class to serve as the base class. Here's how a class named **CGoldCoin** would look if it were derived from the **CCoin** class:

```
class CGoldCoin : public CCoin {

    public:
        // member functions

    private:
        // data members
};
```

A derived class should be created when an existing class comes close to, but falls short of, supplying the needs of an object. The **type**, **year**, and **worth** data members of the **CCoin** class might be all the information needed to adequately keep track of most coins. But for gold coins, perhaps it would make sense to keep track of the gold content. To accommodate objects that represent gold coins, I *could* simply add a **percentGold** data member and "set" and "get" accessor member functions to the existing **CCoin** class—but such a data member and member functions wouldn't apply to the majority of coin objects (which don't happen to represent gold coins). So instead I'll use the existing **CCoin** class as a base class and derive a new class from it. This new derived class need only include data and functions that pertain to a gold coin. The data and functions common to all coins (including gold coins) will be inherited from the **CCoin** base class. Here I've filled in the **CGoldCoin** class definition:

```
class CGoldCoin : public CCoin {

public:
            CGoldCoin( void );
            CGoldCoin( Str255 initType,
                       short  initYear,
                       float  initWorth,
                       float  initPercentGold );

    void    SetPercentGold( float thePercentGold);
    float   GetPercentGold( void );

  private:
    float   percentGold;
};
```

The preceding definition includes only one data member, but each **CGoldCoin** object will consist of four data members: **percentGold**, **type**, **year**, and **worth** (the last three being inherited from the **CCoin** class). Also inherited by the **CGoldCoin** class are the member functions of the **CCoin** class. If **CCoin** class defines "set" and "get" accessor functions for each of its three data members, then those functions will be inherited by the **CGoldCoin** class and will be available to any **CGoldCoin** objects. Taking advantage of an existing class (**CCoin**) to quickly and easily create a new class (**CGoldCoin**) demonstrates that power of inheritance. In this next snippet a **CGoldCoin** object is created.

After that the **SetPercentGold()** function defined by the **CGoldCoin** class is invoked and then the **SetWorth()** member function inherited from the **CCoin** class is called:

```
CGoldCoin  *theGoldCoin;

theGoldCoin = new CGoldCoin();
theGoldCoin->SetPercentGold(99.2);
theGoldCoin->SetWorth(430.00);
```

While the **CGoldCoin** class inherits the **CCoin** class constructors, you'll note that it still defines its own constructor functions as well. The topic of derived class objects and constructor invocation is a bit tricky, so I'll give that topic its own section.

Constructors & Derived Class Objects

When an object of a derived class is created, its own constructor is called. Before that constructor is executed, however, the default constructor (the constructor that has no parameters) of the object's base class is first called. Consider this snippet:

```
CGoldCoin  *theGoldCoin;

theGoldCoin = new CGoldCoin();
```

The effect of this use of the **new** operator would be to:

1. Create a **CGoldCoin** object.

2. Execute the **CCoin()** constructor.

3. Execute the **CGoldCoin()** constructor.

Earlier I implemented the **CCoin** constructor such that it initialized the **CCoin** data members (**type**, **year**, and **worth**) to null values (such as an empty string or the value zero). Here's a reminder of what that **CCoin** constructor looks like:

```
CCoin::CCoin( void )
{
   Str255  emptyStr = "\p";
   long    numBytes;

   numBytes = emptyStr[0] + 1;
   BlockMoveData( emptyStr, type, numBytes );

   year = 0;
   worth = 0.0;
}
```

If creating a new **CGoldCoin** object invokes the preceding **CCoin** constructor, then the initialization of the data members inherited from the **CCoin** class is taken care of. The one new data member defined by the **CGoldCoin** class, however, isn't initialized by the **CCoin** constructor. That needs to be handled by the **CGoldCoin** constructor:

```
CGoldCoin::CGoldCoin( void )
{
    percentGold = 0.0;
}
```

The creation of an object of a derived class results in the automatic invocation of both the base class constructor and the derived class constructor. Regardless of how many constructors the base class defines, the parameterless version gets invoked—unless the derived class constructor specifies otherwise. Consider the second of the two constructors that the derived **CGoldCoin** class defines. Here's the prototype for that function:

```
CGoldCoin( Str255 initType,
           short  initYear,
           float  initWorth,
           float  initPercentGold );
```

The purpose of this constructor is to supply initial values to each of the four data members of a new **CGoldCoin** object. A call to this constructor would look like this:

```
CGoldCoin  *theGoldCoin;

theGoldCoin = new CGoldCoin( "\pGold", 1995, 430.00, 99.2 );
```

Recall that the second of the two **CCoin** base class constructors takes care of the task of supplying the three **CCoin** data members with values:

```
CCoin::CCoin( Str255 initType,
              short initYear,
              float initWorth )
{
    long  numBytes;

    numBytes = initType[0] + 1;
    BlockMoveData( initType, type, numBytes );

    year = initYear;
    worth = initWorth;
}
```

If the creation of a new **CGoldCoin** object could invoke the preceding **CCoin** constructor rather than the parameterless version called by default, then the **CGoldCoin** constructor would only have to supply a value to the **percentGold** data member. C++ makes this possible, as shown here:

```
CGoldCoin::CGoldCoin( Str255 initType,
                      short initYear,
                      float initWorth,
                      float initPercentGold ) :
CCoin( initType, initYear, initWorth )
{
    percentGold = initPercentGold;
}
```

Note the title line of the **CGoldCoin** constructor. Following the list of **CGoldCoin** parameters comes a colon and then a call to the **CCoin** base class constructor to execute. Recall that the **CCoin** constructor has three parameters, so those parameters must be supplied in this call. In the preceding code, you see that the first three parameters to the **CGoldCoin** constructor (**initType**, **initYear**, and **initWorth**) are passed along to the **CCoin** constructor.

Figures B-7 through B-10 illustrate what takes place when a new **CGoldCoin** object is created using the four-parameter **CGoldCoin** constructor. In Figure B-7 you see that the **new** operator is responsible for allocating memory for the new **CGoldCoin** object.

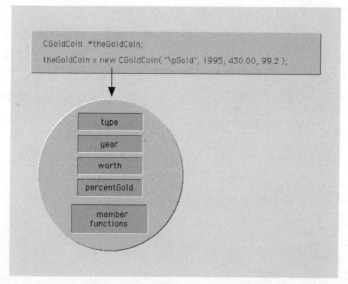

Figure B-7: The new operator allocates memory for a new object of the class type named after the operator.

Next, the **CGoldCoin** constructor is invoked—but its body isn't executed. Instead, the **CCoin** constructor is called. Figure B-8 shows that the call to the **CCoin** constructor passes along the first three of the four arguments passed to the **CGoldCoin** constructor.

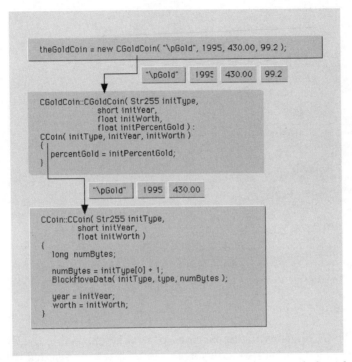

Figure B-8: The creation of a new derived class object causes the base class constructor to execute.

The **CGoldCoin** constructor now executes, assigning values to the **type**, **year**, and **worth** data members of the **CGoldCoin** object. This is illustrated in Figure B-9.

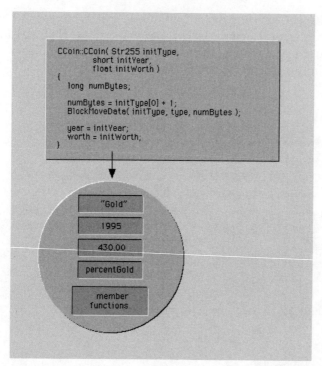

Figure B-9: The base class constructor may initialize object data members, as in the case of the CCoin class.

After the **CCoin** constructor executes, control is returned to the **CGoldCoin** constructor. That function executes its one line of code to assign a value to the **percentGold** data member of the **CGoldCoin** object—as shown in Figure B-10.

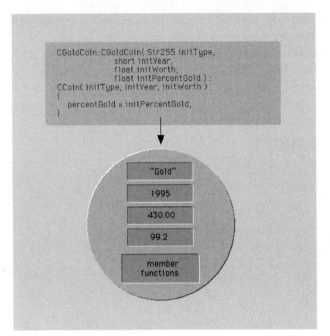

Figure B-10: The derived class constructor executes after the base class constructor has completed its execution.

An example of a derived class and the chain of constructor calls is presented in the Derived project that appears in this appendix's folder in the book examples folder on the Companion CD-ROM.

Overriding Member Functions

A derived class inherits all the member functions defined in its base class. As you've witnessed, this means that an object of a derived class type can invoke any of these inherited member functions as if they were defined directly in the derived class. Gaining the use of these prewritten member functions is one of the biggest advantages of implementing a derived class. There will be times, however, when the functionality of an inherited member function doesn't quite meet the needs of a particular derived class. In such cases, the derived class can redefine the unsatisfactory inherited member function and use this new version in its place. In effect, the derived class *overrides* the inherited member function.

In order for a derived class to override an inherited base member function, define the base class version of the function using the **virtual** keyword; it precedes the return type of the member function in the definition of the base class.

Consider a base class function that's to write a one-line message to an open window. The function has no return value and no parameters. If it's desirable to include the option to allow the function to be overridden by derived classes, then the function prototype would look like this:

```
virtual void  WriteMessage( void );
```

The following snippet modifies the **CCoin** class to include just such a member function:

```
class  CCoin {
   public:
                  CCoin( void );
                  CCoin( Str255 initType,
                         short  initYear,
                         float  initWorth );

           void  SetType( Str255 theType);
                 // other member functions here

      virtual void  WriteMessage( void );

   private:
      Str255  type;
      short   year;
      float   worth;
};
```

Here's how the **CCoin** class could implement the **WriteMessage()** member function. This example assumes that the purpose of this routine is to simply display a line of text to provide confirmation that a new coin record has been created:

```
void  CCoin::WriteMessage( void )
{
   MoveTo( 20, 20 );
   DrawString( "\pNew coin record created." );
}
```

TIP *The **WriteMessage()** routine is provided as a simple demonstration of how a member function can be overridden. Knowing what you do about constructors, it should be evident that a constructor would be a more suitable place to display a "record created" string.*

Because the **CCoin** class defines the **WriteMessage()** function as **virtual**, a class derived from **CCoin** can, if desired, override **WriteMessage()**. For example, if the **CGoldCoin** class wanted to have a **WriteMessage()** function that was more specific—such as one that stated a gold coin record was just created—it could override **WriteMessage()** and implement a new version that wrote a different message. Here's a new version of the **CGoldCoin** class. The only difference between this version and the prior incarnation of this class is the addition of the **WriteMessage()** function:

```
class CGoldCoin : public CCoin {

    public:
                CGoldCoin( void );
                CGoldCoin( Str255 initType,
                        short   initYear,
                        float   initWorth,
                        float   initPercentGold );

        void    SetPercentGold( float thePercentGold);
        float   GetPercentGold( void );

        void    WriteMessage( void );

    private:
        float   percentGold;
};
```

As you look over the class definition, note that the **WriteMessage()** function isn't declared **virtual**. While the **virtual** keyword is mandatory in the base class (so the function is available for overriding by derived classes), it isn't required in the derived class definition. If the **CGoldCoin** class won't serve as a base class for other classes, then there's no need to declare **WriteMessage()** as **virtual** in **CGoldCoin**. If, on the other hand, the **CGoldCoin** class might itself serve as a base class for other derived classes, then **CGoldCoin** should declare the **WriteMessage()** function **virtual** so these derived classes also have the option of overriding this function.

TIP *The preceding discussion implies that a derived class can serve as a base class. It can. Consider classes **A**, **B**, and **C**. Class **A** can serve as a base class for class **B**. If class **C** uses class **B** as its base class, it is directly derived from class **B** and indirectly derived from class **A**. That is, class **C** will inherit all of the data members of classes **A** and **B** (because class **B** inherits all class **A** data members and then defines its own data members) and will have access to all of the member functions of classes **A** and **B** (because class **B** inherits class **A** member functions and defines its own member functions).*

Now that the **CGoldCoin** class has opted to override the **WriteMessage()** function, it must implement its own version of this routine. Here's one way it could do that:

```
void  CGoldCoin::WriteMessage( void )
{
   MoveTo( 20, 40 );
   DrawString( "\pNew gold coin record created." );
}
```

When a derived class overrides a base class member function, it is that overridden function that a derived object executes. Consider this next snippet:

```
CCoin       *theCoin;
CGoldCoin  *theGoldCoin;

// open a window

theCoin = new CCoin();
theGoldCoin = new CGoldCoin();

theCoin->WriteMessage();
theGoldCoin->WriteMessage();
```

The preceding snippet begins by declaring and then creating a **CCoin** object and a **CGoldCoin** object. Next, each object invokes the **WriteMessage()** member function. When the **CCoin** class object **theCoin** invokes this function, the **CCoin** version of the function executes to draw the first line of text shown in the window in Figure B-11. When the **CGoldCoin** class object **theGoldCoin** invokes this function, the **CGoldCoin** version executes to draw the second line of text in the same window.

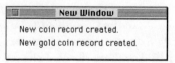

Figure B-11: The calling of a function by a base class object and a derived class object can have different outcomes.

An example of a derived class that overrides a base class member function is presented in the Override project that appears in this appendix's folder in the book examples folder on the Companion CD-ROM.

Moving On

The C++ language is a superset of the C language—everything you know about C applies to C++. In particular, your knowledge of the C structure provides you with a good lead-in to how data is organized in C++. The C++ class is analogous to the C struct in that both consist of members that hold data. The C++ class betters the C struct, however, because it also defines any number of functions that belong to the class and exist to operate on the data within the class. This binding of data and functions is referred to as encapsulation, a concept that makes it easier for programmers to better understand the relationships between a program's data and routines.

The code that makes up the PowerPlant application framework is written in C++, so an understanding of C++ is important to understanding PowerPlant. Of course, understanding application frameworks is important to understanding PowerPlant as well! If you don't have experience working with an application framework, make sure to read Appendices D and E. It covers application framework basics, along with some PowerPlant-specific information that will introduce you to working with Metrowerks' powerful Macintosh application framework.

appendix C

Glossary

680x0 The family of microprocessors used in all Macintosh computers before the arrival of the PowerPC family of chips. *See also 68K and PPC*.

68K Short for "680x0." Computers driven by a microprocessor that is a part of the Motorola family. These CPUs are no longer used in new Macs, having been replaced by the PowerPC family of microprocessors. A new CodeWarrior project based on project stationery including "68K" in its name means the project will generate an executable that runs on both 68K-based and PPC-based computers. Running on a PPC-based computer, however, means that the executable will not take advantage of the faster PowerPC instruction set.

application-defined class A class you define, as opposed to one that is a part of the PowerPlant application framework. Your own application-defined class may or may not be derived from a PowerPlant class.

broadcaster An object that issues a message intended for a listener object's response. Typically a control (such as a button) is a broadcaster, and a window or the application is the listener. *See also listener*.

chain of command A menu item selection results in a command being issued. The command always targets the active object. If the command wasn't intended for that object, it gets passed up to the next higher object next in the object hierarchy. A typical chain of command from bottom to top can be an item in a window (such as a text box) up to the window that holds the item up to the application itself.

command   In PowerPlant, a menu item is known as a command. The user's selection of a menu item issues a command that PowerPlant automatically receives and passes to your application from processing.

command number   A constant used to associate one menu item in a resource with source code written to respond to a selection of that menu item.

commander   An object capable of handling a command. Commander objects are all derived from the PowerPlant **LCommander** class.

Constructor   Metrowerks' own resource editor, designed to create and edit PowerPlant-specific resources such as the 'PPob.' A Constructor file name typically has an extension of .ppob. *See also **'PPob' resource**.*

Copland   The Macintosh operating system that *was* to replace System 7. Apple scrapped this effort after numerous delays. The 1997 release of the Mac OS 8 operating system included some of the planned features of Copland, and subsequent versions of the Mac OS will include more.

fat binary application   (Or fat application or fat binary.) An executable that includes two complete sets of program code. When a fat application is launched on a 68K-based computer, the code consisting of 680x0 instructions is loaded to memory. When the same application is launched on a PPC-based computer, the code consisting of PowerPC instructions is instead loaded to memory. A new CodeWarrior project based on project stationery including "FAT" in its name means the project will be one that can generate a fat binary application, a 68K application, or a PPC application. Which executable is generated is set from the Target tab in the project window. *See also **68K** and **PPC**.*

IDE   Integrated Development Environment. A single application used to integrate and control a number of programming tools, including a source code editor, compilers, linkers, and a debugger.

listener   An object that listens for a message issued by a broadcaster object. A listener then responds appropriately to the message. Typically a window or an application is the listener, and listens for messages sent by a control (such as a button). *See also **broadcaster**.*

'Mcmd' resource   Metrowerks has developed the 'Mcmd' (menu command) resource as PowerPlant's means of keeping track of menu items. A single 'Mcmd' resource specifies all of the items in one menu. Constructor keeps 'Mcmd' information under the Menu heading.

MW Profiler   A code library you add to a project, as well as a viewer application. You profile your code to determine which routines are demanding too much processor time.

MWDebug   A source-level debugger that can be turned on from the CodeWarrior IDE, and then used to track down bugs or to investigate and test programming techniques you may want to implement.

pane   An independent drawing area that exists in a window. A pane has its own coordinate system. A pane is created and added to a window resource (a 'PPob' resource) in Constructor. To make use of the pane from source code, a project uses the PowerPlant LPane class or one of several classes derived from LPane. *See also* **View**.

PowerPC   The family of microprocessors that has replaced the Motorola 680x0 family as the processor that drives a Macintosh or Mac-clone computer. *See also* **PPC** *and* **68K**.

PowerPlant   Metrowerks application framework that exists to simplify the development of full-scale Mac OS programs. An application framework is a body of source code that handles the tasks basic to most programs running on a specific platform. To use PowerPlant, you add to a project some or all of the many C++ source code files that make up the PowerPlant application framework. You then add some of your own source code to the project. Your own source code will use many C++ classes that the PowerPlant code defines.

PPC   Short for "PowerPC." Computers driven by a PowerPC microprocessor are often referred to as PPC-based or PowerPC-based. A new CodeWarrior project based on project stationery that includes "PPC" in its name means the project will generate an executable only runs on PPC-based computers.

'PPob' resource   Metrowerks defines a 'PPob' (PowerPlant object) resource as one that holds information about one type of window. This resource holds window attributes (such as the window's initial size and screen placement) as well as some or all of the contents of a window (such as pictures, text, and buttons).

project   CodeWarrior uses the concept of a project to organize all of the files to be compiled and linked into a single executable. The project itself is a single file opened from the CodeWarrior IDE. Once opened, the contents of the project are displayed in a project window.

project stationery   A template that tells CodeWarrior which files to initially include in a new project.

stack-based class   A PowerPlant class used to create an object that exists on the stack. Typically such a class is used to create an object local to a routine. When the object is created, the object's constructor is responsible for all the setup work. When the routine ends, PowerPlant is responsible for deleting the object and calling its class destructor to take care of all the cleanup work.

subpane   A pane within a view is said to be that view's subpane. *See also pane, view, and **superview**.*

supercommander   The object immediately above another object in the chain of command. *See also **chain of command**.*

superview   Every pane or view, with the exception of the top-level view (which is typically a window), is contained in another view. A view that contains another pane or view is said to be the superview of that pane or view. *See also **pane, view**, and **subpane**.*

target   A command is always aimed at a single object. This object is said to be the target of the command. *See also **command**.*

'Txtr' resource   Metrowerks has devised a powerful way for a PowerPlant-based project to easily assign a multitude of text traits to any text in your program. The 'Txtr' (text traits) resource lets you specify and package together a variety of text characteristics. You can then use this 'Txtr' resource in conjunction with any text in order for all of the traits to be applied to that text.

universal header files   (Or universal interface files.) This is the set of Apple-supplied header files that include function prototypes for the Macintosh Toolbox functions. CodeWarrior projects automatically include the most commonly required of these universal header files.

utility class   A PowerPlant class that doesn't have a dependency on any other class. A utility class can be used on its own, without the need of an object. To invoke a utility class, list the class name, followed by the scope resolution operator (::), followed by the name of one of the class member functions.

value message   The message is issued by a broadcaster. A listener is able to identify the broadcaster by this message and respond appropriately. A clicked-on control is an example of the issuing of a value message.

view   A type of pane. A view is more powerful than an "ordinary" pane because it can have other panes and views nested within it. A window is a top-level view that typically contains other panes and views.

ZoneRanger   An application used to monitor a program's use of memory. After building a version of your program, run ZoneRanger and your application to verify that your program releases memory at appropriate times.

appendix D

Moving to Rhapsody

CodeWarrior Latitude is a porting tool designed to help programmers quickly port their existing Mac OS application to a UNIX application. If your CodeWarrior project currently targets the Mac OS, CodeWarrior Latitude will make it easy to retarget the project for a UNIX platform such as Sun Solaris. How does such a tool help a programmer who is interested in porting a Mac OS application to a Rhapsody application? Because underneath its dazzling GUI, Rhapsody is a UNIX OS.

About CodeWarrior Latitude

CodeWarrior Latitude is a set of shared libraries that mimic the functions of the Macintosh Toolbox. In short, you use Latitude by recompiling the source code of a completed Mac OS-targeted project, and linking the resulting object code with these Latitude libraries. The result is an executable that runs native on a UNIX machine.

As Apple improves and finalizes Rhapsody for its release to the general public, Metrowerks will update CodeWarrior Latitude as well, to provide maximum performance.

What You Need _____

Besides a Macintosh or Mac-compatible computer on which you develop your Mac OS-targeted application, you need a UNIX-based system to which you'll transfer your original project files, make some (possibly trivial) source code changes, and compile and build the new UNIX-targeted application.

What You Do _____

Once you've performed the one-time installation of CodeWarrior Latitude and walked through an example port, you'll see that using this development tool isn't difficult. Performing the install and then using the product for the first time, however, requires that you read the *Latitude_Guide.pdf* Acrobat file included on the CodeWarrior Latitude CD-ROM. That document provides an extremely thorough look at each step you need to take, so here I'll simply provide a brief overview in order for you to see what's in store. To use CodeWarrior Latitude, do the following:

1. Copy a completed Mac OS-targeted project to UNIX.

2. Perform any necessary source code conversions.

3. Build a UNIX-targeted executable.

Copy a Project to UNIX _____

You need to move a Mac OS-targeted project to a UNIX environment where it can be ported and built into a UNIX executable. This involves mounting a UNIX directory on your Macintosh, creating a new directory to serve as an application folder, and placing a Macintosh executable and all original source code files in this directory.

Perform Source Code Conversions _____

The amount of work necessary to convert an application varies from project to project. For each project, though, you'll begin by running the prepare_sources command. This command runs the prepare_sources script to automatically convert many common non-ANSI constructs to ANSI ones. The prepare_sources script takes care of many of the edits necessary in porting your source code. There may, however, be other changes that need to be made manually. The *Latitude_Guide.pdf* document lists these possible changes in detail.

Build an Executable

You build a UNIX-targeted executable by entering the make command. The resulting application can be run on your UNIX system.

The Ported Application & Rhapsody

Your new application will run in what Apple refers to as the Yellow Box. Your ported application will retain the same feature set it had originally, but will now be native to the Yellow Box. That means your ported program benefits from Rhapsody technologies such as running in protected mode.

After porting a Mac OS to Rhapsody, you can use the Yellow Box API to begin to incorporate Yellow Box features into the new version of your program. Porting an application means generating a new set of source code, and into this new code can be added any calls that are native to the Yellow Box. That is, you can enhance an application by adding calls to the Yellow Box functions that support multithreading—a feature not found on the Mac OS.

appendix E

CodeWarrior & Windows Programming

This book is about Mac programming, for Mac programmers. So it's assumed your platform of choice is the Macintosh. Getting to know one operating system and all the ins and outs of programming it is comfortable—like settling into a favorite overstuffed chair. Unfortunately, economic realities of the software business dictate that eventually you'll need to get up out of that chair and program for a second, or even a third, operating system. In particular, Macintosh programmers are often called upon to work on Windows 95 or Windows NT projects. While Metrowerks can't quickly teach you how to write Windows-targeted applications, they can help out a bit by letting you develop such programs from the familiarity of your Macintosh and the CodeWarrior IDE.

CodeWarrior & Windows 95/NT

As of this writing three operating systems host the CodeWarrior IDE: Mac OS, Windows 95/NT, and BeOS. That's beneficial to a programmer who has to, say, write Windows-targeted applications at work and is also working on a Macintosh-targeted program at home. For each project this person could use the CodeWarrior IDE—thus saving the time to learn the intricacies of two software development packages. The confusion of working on two different machines (such as a Power Mac and a Wintel computer), perhaps on a daily basis, can be minimized if programming for each takes place within the same environment.

TIP

> *The Mac OS and Windows versions of CodeWarrior appear on separate CD-ROMs within the one CodeWarrior Professional package. If you bought CodeWarrior Professional, you own two separate, complete versions of the CodeWarrior IDE. The BeOS version of the CodeWarrior IDE is called BeIDE, and is available from Metrowerks as a separate package.*

Providing an easy way to switch programming efforts from one machine to another is one benefit of going with the CodeWarrior IDE. There's a second— and this one is pretty nice for programmers who spend most or all of their time on a Macintosh. The Macintosh version of the CodeWarrior IDE lets a programmer target the Windows 95/NT platforms. You'll still need to know about programming for Windows, but you'll be able to do all your Windows programming from a Macintosh.

To create a Windows-targeted application you launch the CodeWarrior IDE on your Mac—just as you always do. When you create a new project, though, you'll use a Win32 project stationery (Win32 stands for 32-bit versions of Windows, which is what Windows 95 and Windows NT are, and what Windows 3.1 and prior aren't). From this project you'll enter your source code and eventually build a Windows-targeted program. To test the resulting program you'll need either a Windows machine, a PC card in your Macintosh, or Windows emulation software on your Macintosh (SoftWindows by Insignia Solutions and VirtualPC by Connectix being two worthy candidates in this last category).

CodeWarrior Windows Tools

The following sections list the tools that Metrowerks supplies you with in order to write a Windows application from your Macintosh.

TIP

> *While the Mac OS-hosted Windows tools are included in the CodeWarrior Professional package, they may not have made it on to your hard drive during your installation of CodeWarrior for Macintosh. One way to see if they did is to verify that a folder named Win32/x86 Support is present in your Metrowerks CodeWarrior folder. If it's not, rerun the CodeWarrior installer, check the check boxes that pertain to Windows, and perform an install (items you've previously installed will not be affected by this action).*

Compilers & Linkers

For a CodeWarrior project that targets the Mac OS, you choose New from the File menu of the CodeWarrior IDE to create a new, empty window in which to type your code. After entering your code, you build an application by compiling and linking it to other compiled source code, resources, and libraries. You do the same for a CodeWarrior project that targets the Windows OS.

The behind-the-scenes actions of compiling and linking are taken care of by the Metrowerks C/C++ compiler—the same compiler that compiles your Mac-targeted source code. Metrowerks can use the same compiler because this is a *front-end compiler*—it converts source code into a representation that is independent of the target. After the front-end compiler generates its code, however, a second compiler goes to work. Metrowerks has an x86 *back-end compiler* that coverts the front-end-generated code into object code recognized by the x86 family of microprocessors.

After all your Windows source code is compiled, the CodeWarrior Win32/x86 linker takes over to build a stand-alone Windows application. This linker works just as the Mac linker does: it links any number of object code files and libraries to form a single program.

Resource Compiler

As of this writing the CodeWarrior IDE requires that you provide Windows resource information in the form of standard Win32 resource scripts, then compile these scripts to turn them into resources. These resources are linked by the Win32/x86 linker during the building of the application.

Win32 Support

Windows source code consists of calls to any number of functions defined in the Win32 application programming interface (API). Metrowerks provides you with a full set of Win32 header files and libraries to allow CodeWarrior projects to invoke these functions from your C, C++, or Pascal code. Additionally, Metrowerks includes the full source code for the Microsoft Foundation Classes (MFC)—the Microsoft object-oriented application framework that takes care of many of the basic tasks of a Windows application.

Windows & CodeWarrior Projects

You can use the Macintosh version of the CodeWarrior IDE to create a CodeWarrior project that targets the Windows platform. All the steps in application development—with the exception of running the final program—can be performed from the CodeWarrior IDE. To generate a Windows 95/NT stand-alone application, follow these steps:

1. Choose New Project from the File menu.

2. Use the New Project dialog box to choose a new Win32/x86 project stationery. Figure E-1 shows some of the Win32/x86 C/C++ stationeries. Click on a stationery name, then click on the OK button.

Figure E-1: Choosing a Win32/x86 project stationery.

3. In the Name New Project dialog box, use the pop-up menu to move to the folder that is to house the new project folder, supply a name for the new project, and then click the OK button.

4. A new project window that holds all the necessary files to support a Windows-targeted application appears. Look over the file names (as shown in Figure E-2) to become familiar with them.

5. Replace the code in the Metrowerks-supplied *main.c* file (shown in Figure E-3) with your own Windows source code.

WindowsEx.prj
Files
Link Order
Targets
File
Code
Data
Source 0 0
main.c 0 0
MSL ANSI Libraries 0 0
ANSICX86.LIB 0 0
MWCRTL.LIB 0 0
Win32 SDK Libraries 0 0
COMDLG32.LIB 0 0
GDI32.LIB 0 0
KERNEL32.LIB 0 0
USER32.LIB 0 0
7 files 0 0

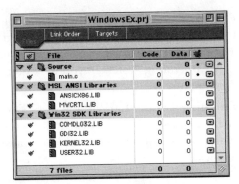

Figure E-2: A project window for a project that targets the Windows OS.

TIP *Readers new to Windows programming will benefit from the brief walkthrough of the source code that appears in Figure E-3. That overview appears in the following section.*

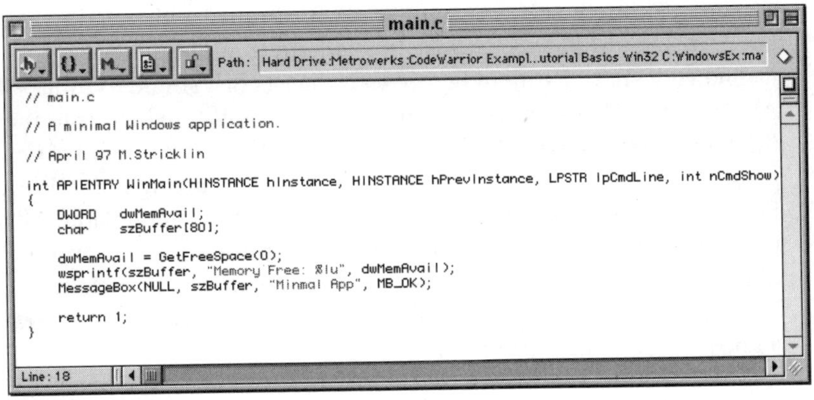

main.c
Path: Hard Drive:Metrowerks:CodeWarrior Exampl...utorial Basics Win32 C:WindowsEx:ma
// main.c
// A minimal Windows application.
// April 97 M.Stricklin
int APIENTRY WinMain(HINSTANCE hInstance, HINSTANCE hPrevInstance, LPSTR lpCmdLine, int nCmdShow)
{
DWORD dwMemAvail;
char szBuffer[80];
dwMemAvail = GetFreeSpace(0);
wsprintf(szBuffer, "Memory Free: %lu", dwMemAvail);
MessageBox(NULL, szBuffer, "Minmal App", MB_OK);
return 1;
}
Line: 18

Figure E-3: The example Windows source code provided by Metrowerks.

6. Choose Make from the Project menu to build a stand-alone program. Because the Mac-hosted CodeWarrior IDE isn't capable of running a Windows-targeted application (such a program can only run under the Windows 95 or Windows NT operating systems), you won't be able to choose Run from the Project menu.

7. Test your application by running it under the Windows OS. Do that by copying the resulting *.exe* file to a PC-formatted disk and then transferring it to a Windows machine, or by running Windows-emulation software on your Macintosh.

Windows Programming

If you've never programmed for the Windows operating system, you've some mind-set adjustments to make. Don't be too alarmed, though. As someone familiar with programming for a graphical user interface, you have a leg up on someone who has never programmed for the Mac or Windows.

I won't attempt to tackle the involved topic of Windows programming techniques here, but I will offer just a quick couple of points about the code shown in Figure E-3. If you aren't already familiar with Windows programming, this might put you at ease (or perhaps it might not!).

The very short listing in Figure E-3 consists of a single routine—**WinMain()**. All Windows C projects define such a routine—it's analogous to the **main()** function found in non-Windows C projects. When the Windows OS launches a program, this routine serves as the application's starting point. Within the Figure E-3 version of **WinMain()**, three function calls are made. All are routines defined for you as part of the Win32 application programming interface (API). Just as writing a Macintosh program requires a knowledge of the Macintosh API (the Macintosh Toolbox), writing a Windows program requires a knowledge of the Windows API.

The first function call is to the Win32 routine **GetFreeSpace()**. This function returns the amount of free memory that's available to the application.

The next function invoked from **WinMain()** is **wsprintf()**—the Windows version of the standard C function **sprintf()**. Like **sprintf()**, **wsprintf()** works just as **sprintf()** does—it formats a passed-in string and stores it to a character array buffer. Here it's used to merge the string "Memory Free:" with the value returned by **GetFreeSpace()**, and to store the new string in the character buffer **szBuffer**. Windows defines its own version of most of the standard ANSI C routines—you can distinguish one from other Win32 API functions (such as the just-mentioned **GetFreeSpace()**) by the leading lowercase w in its name.

The final call is to the Win32 API function **MessageBox()**. In Windows, a message box is analogous to a Macintosh alert. The **MessageBox()** routine displays and handles a message box until the user dismisses it. The example message box displays the string that was previously stored in the character array **szBuffer**. Clicking the message box OK button dismisses the message box and ends the simple program.

For more information on Windows programming, check out the Mac to Windows.pdf document that's included in the CodeWarrior Professional package. This Acrobat file is an electronic version of the book *From Mac to Windows* by Stephen Chernicoff. For a Windows application programming interface reference, refer to the MS Win32 Ref document that's also a part of that same package. This QuickView file lets you look up or browse through any of the routines that make up the Windows API. (QuickView is a document display application that's included with all versions of CodeWarrior).

appendix F

Web Sites of Interest

For more information on Macintosh programming, investigate the following World Wide Web sites.

Metrowerks Home Page
\<http://www.metrowerks.com\>
Metrowerks' home page supplies late-breaking CodeWarrior news and product information. Use this page to branch to other Metrowerks pages that hold information about CodeWarrior products, documentation, technical support, and more.

Metrowerks Tools Page
\<http://www.metrowerks.com/tools\>
This page, accessible from the Metrowerks home page, holds free CodeWarrior IDE software and PowerPlant updates and patches. From here you can move to another page that holds a number of downloadable contributed PowerPlant classes—new PowerPlant classes that fellow programmers have created and uploaded to Metrowerks. This page is also the place to go to reach Metrowerks technical support staff by e-mail.

Apple Developer World
<http://www.devworld.apple.com>
Download all sorts of Macintosh programming documentation—direct from
Apple. Once here, be sure to check out the page's two pop-up menus. Choose
a topic from the Cool Areas pop-up menu (such as Sample Code or Technotes);
then click the Go button to move to the Web page that holds information about
the selected topic. Or, choose a topic from the Hot Technologies pop-up menu
(such as QuickTime or Rhapsody), and then click the Go button.

Macintosh Programming Frequently Asked Questions
<http://www.best.com/~ckt/faq>
The Web page title says it all. Visit this page to find answers to many of the
most commonly asked questions about programming for the Macintosh.

Author's Home Page
<http://members.aol.com/DanSydow>
Here's my home page. Stop by and visit, and drop me a line.

Index